COMMON WORDPERFECT FEATURES

Toolbar Button	Shortcut	Function	
	CTRL-N	Create new blank document	
	CTRL-O	Open existing document	File | Open
	CTRL-S	Save document with current name	File | Save
	F3	Save document with different name or format	File | Save As
	CTRL-P	Print document	File | Print
	CTRL-X	Cut selected text or graphic to Clipboard	Edit | Cut
	CTRL-C	Copy selected text or graphic to Clipboard	Edit | Copy
	CTRL-V	Paste Clipboard contents	Edit | Paste
	CTRL-Z	Undo last formatting action	Edit | Undo
	CTRL-SHIFT-R	Redo previous Undo action	Edit | Redo
		Copy formatting from one location to another	Format | QuickFormat
		Insert Clipart image	Insert | Graphics | Clipart
		Insert text box	Insert | Text Box
		Begin outline or paragraph numbering	Insert | Outline/Bullets & Numbering
		Create bullet list	Insert | Outline/Bullets & Numbering

Toolbar Button	Shortcut	Function	Menu Command
		Change the magnification of the document display	View | Zoom
		Switch between Web view and document view	File | Internet Publisher
		Display the PerfectExpert panel	Help | PerfectExpert
\<None\>	F8	Format document with styles	Format | Styles
abc	ALT-CTRL-P	Find the Previous occurrence of current word or selection	
abc	ALT-CTRL-N	Find the Next occurrence of current word or selection	
		Select most recently used fonts	
	CTRL-W	Insert symbol or special character	Insert | Symbol
infer		Display suggestions for misspelled words, synonyms, or grammar suggestions	Tools | Proofread | Prompt-As-You-Go

HANDY SHORTCUT KEYSTROKES

Keystroke	Function
SHIFT-F1	Help What Is
CTRL-K	Switch case of selected text
CTRL-SHIFT-L	Move to new line without starting new paragraph
CTRL-SHIFT-V	Paste without formatting
CTRL-HYPHEN	Insert soft hyphen
CTRL-SPACEBAR	Insert hard space
CTRL-W	Insert symbol
F7	Indent paragraph
CTRL-SHIFT-Q	Set QuickMark
CTRL-Q	Find QuickMark
CTRL-BACKSPACE	Delete current word
CTRL-DELETE	Delete to end of line
F9	Display Font dialog box

WordPerfect 8

Answers!
Certified Tech Support

About the Author . . .

Bob Bringhurst is a renowned WordPerfect
expert. He was contracted by Corel to create
the reference manuals and online help systems
for both Corel WordPerfect Suites (7 and 8), and
is a regular columnist for *WordPerfect for
Windows Magazine*.

WordPerfect 8

Answers!
Certified Tech Support

Bob Bringhurst

Osborne McGraw-Hill
Berkeley • New York • St. Louis • San Francisco
Auckland • Bogotá • Hamburg • London
Madrid • Mexico City • Milan • Montreal
New Delhi • Panama City • Paris • São Paulo
Singapore • Sydney • Tokyo • Toronto

Osborne/**McGraw-Hill**
2600 Tenth Street
Berkeley, California 94710
U.S.A.

For information on translations or book distributors outside the U.S.A., or to arrange bulk purchase discounts for sales promotions, premiums, or fund-raisers, please contact Osborne/**McGraw-Hill** at the above address.

WordPerfect 8 Answers!
Certified Tech Support

1234567890 AGM AGM 901987654321098

ISBN 0-07-882449-4

Publisher	**Copy Editor**
Brandon A. Nordin	Judy Ziajka
Editor-in-Chief	**Proofreader**
Scott Rogers	Jeffrey Barash
Acquisitions Editor	**Indexer**
Joanne Cuthbertson	Richard Shrout
Project Editor	**Computer Designer**
Claire Splan	Roberta Steele
Editorial Assistant	**Illustrator**
Gordon Hurd	Lance Ravella
Technical Editor	**Series Design**
Dana Stohlton	Peter Hancik

Contents @ a Glance

Contents

Acknowledgements

When I watch the Academy Awards, I don't want to hear the winners thank everyone who played even a remote part in their accomplishment. Instead, I want them to hold up the Oscar, say "Thank you," and then sit down and shut up so that the ceremony can continue. But after getting so much help while working on this book, I understand why people feel obligated to thank anyone they ever met. So here goes my list.

The people at Osborne/McGraw-Hill did a great job in helping me write this book. Claire Splan and Judy Ziajka gave me great editing advice, and I couldn't have written the book without Joanne Cuthbertson's help. And thank you too, Gordon Hurd.

This book wouldn't be as comprehensive and accurate as it is without Dana Stohlton's help. Dana battled through injuries and pain medication to tech edit this book.

I want to thank my parents, Fred and June, for bringing me into this world and caring for me all these years.

I want to give special thanks to my biking buddies—Elden, Doug, Rick, Brad, Stuart, Scott, Jeremy, and Gary—who understood that I had a book to write and convinced me to ride anyway. Bouncing along the trails in Grove Canyon, Tibble Fork, and Benny Creek brought things back into perspective for me.

Introduction

"A worker may be the hammer's master, but the hammer still prevails. A tool knows exactly how it is meant to be handled, while the user of the tool can only have an approximate idea."

-Milan Kundera

In this book, you may not find answers to common questions like "How do I create a bulleted list?" or "How do I copy and paste text?" I looked long and hard for true-to-life questions that may cause people to spend valuable time making long-distance calls to get answers. Here are some examples:

When I place an image in a table, it becomes compressed and distorted. What's wrong?

How do I create styles for a Question/Answer format?

What happened to the Web Page Expert?

When I edited a table, I got an IPF error message. Why did this happen?

To find these true-to-life questions, I relied heavily on Stream International's expertise. Stream's technical support staff was kind enough to provide me with an extensive list of questions that cause people to pick up the phone. I also pored over issues of *WordPerfect for Windows* magazines and other newsletters, browsed through my e-mail to find all the WordPerfect questions I've answered over the years, and tracked the Corel User groups to see what WordPerfect 8 issues are giving people fits. Unfortunately, I wasn't able to include every question in this book—but I hope I came up with enough questions (and answers) so that when you get stumped while working in WordPerfect, your first thought will be, "Let's see what the *Answers* book has to say about this." That's my hope, anyway.

If you have a question that you think should have made it into this book, please send me an e-mail message at the following address: *bbringhurst@compuserve.com*. I'll do my best to answer your question.

Top Ten FAQs

Answer Topics!

Top Ten FAQs @ a Glance

The technical support staff at Stream International was kind enough to generate this list of the ten most frequently asked questions. This chapter includes questions that deal with topics such as uninstalling WordPerfect 7 after you have installed WordPerfect 8, speeding up WordPerfect, and salvaging corrupt documents. Even if you haven't yet experienced any of these problems, read through this chapter—you may find something that will help you in the future.

 1. I installed WordPerfect 8, but it didn't replace WordPerfect 7 during the installation. I then removed WordPerfect 7, but now error messages appear when I run WordPerfect 8. What should I do?

Some files and directories are shared between the two applications. You can remove WordPerfect 7 after you install WordPerfect 8, but some of the WordPerfect 8 program files will be affected. Try uninstalling and reinstalling WordPerfect 8.

If the error messages still appear when you try to start or run WordPerfect, the Windows 95 registry may contain incorrect settings, causing problems in WordPerfect 8. Try the following to get WordPerfect 8 running properly again:

1. If you have not yet removed WordPerfect 7, click Start on the Windows taskbar and then choose Settings | Control Panel. Double-click Add/Remove Programs, select Corel WordPerfect Suite 7, and choose Add/Remove. Follow the prompts to remove WordPerfect 7.

2. To remove WordPerfect 8, first make sure the Corel WordPerfect 8 CD is in the CD-ROM drive. Then click Start on the Windows taskbar and choose WordPerfect Suite 8 | Setup & Notes | Corel Remove Program.

3. Look through the menu items until you see a list of installed applications. Select WordPerfect 8 and then follow the steps to remove WordPerfect 8 from your computer.

4. Once the program files have been removed, you may need to remove the WordPerfect 7 entries from the Windows 95 registry. To do this, you can download CLEANREG.EXE from the Internet from the following Web site:

ftp://ftp.corel.com/pub/suites/coreloffice/

Note: CLEANREG.EXE should be used only on systems running Windows 95. Do not use this program if you are using a Windows NT system. Running CLEANREG.EXE expands the file into CLEANWP7.EXE and CLEANWP7.CFG. CLEANWP7.EXE is the file that you should double-click to clean the WordPerfect 7 entries from the Windows 95 registry.

5. Restart the computer and then reinstall WordPerfect 8.

If the error messages still appear when you try to run WordPerfect 8, uninstall WordPerfect, delete the Suite8 folder and all subfolders manually, and then use a third-party uninstaller program or Microsoft's RegClean 4.1 program (RegCln41.exe) to clean the registry.

Note: Microsoft's RegClean program is supposed to search for and delete any key in the registry that refers to a program file that has been deleted. Use your favorite Internet search utility to search for the RegClean utility. After you clean up the registry, you should be able to install WordPerfect 8 properly and avoid these error messages.

If WordPerfect still doesn't run properly, you'll need to take more drastic measures—but only if you're sure you know what you're doing. Uninstall WordPerfect 8 again and run the Registry Editor (regedit.exe) to manually remove references to WordPerfect in the Windows 95 registry. *Remember: Unless you know exactly what you're doing, don't edit the registry—and if you do know how to edit the registry, be sure to first make a backup copy of your registry settings* (choose Registry | Export Registry in the Registry Editor). Instead of editing the registry on your own, you may want to play it safe and call Corel Technical Support to have a technician walk you through the process. Otherwise, you may damage your registry and make unwanted changes to your Windows system.

2. I chose Format | Labels, but no labels are listed in the dialog box. How do I display the label definitions?

The labels file in WordPerfect 8 is called WP_WP_EN.LAB. In a typical installation, this file is in the Corel\Suite8\Programs folder. Either this file has been moved to a different folder or deleted or the Files Settings dialog box is pointing to the wrong place.

First, find out where the labels file is located on your computer. To do so, click Start on the Windows taskbar and then choose Find | Files or Folders. Select the drive where the Corel WordPerfect Suite is installed, type **wp_wp_en.lab** in the Named text box, and click Find Now. If you can't find this file, reinstall WordPerfect 8.

If you do find the labels file, choose Tools | Settings in WordPerfect and then double-click Files. Click the Labels tab and then specify the location of the labels file as shown in Figure 1-1. You can either change the location specified in the Default Label File text box, or you can move the labels file to this location.

3. WordPerfect prints blank pages. What's wrong?

If your printer feeds blank pages during a print job, you may have discovered a bug that wasn't fixed when WordPerfect was shipped. You can use the Corel WordPerfect Suite 8 Service Pack #1 to fix this problem. Download Service Pack #1 (wp8sp1.exe) from the following Web address:

ftp://ftp.corel.com/pub/WordPerfect/wpwin/8.

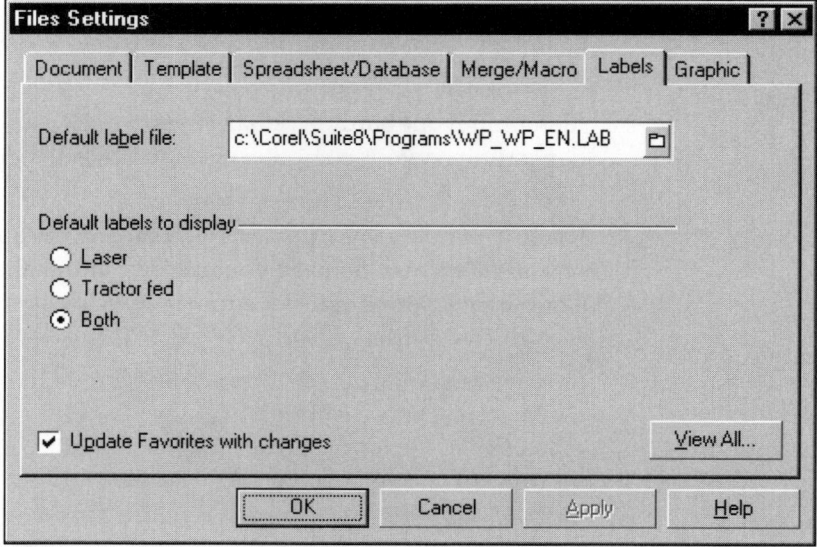

Figure 1-1.   Specify the location of the labels file

 **Warning:**   *This Service Pack works only in English versions of Corel WordPerfect Suite 8.*

❓ 4. How can I speed up WordPerfect?

Here are some suggestions for making WordPerfect run faster:

⇨ Free up memory by not running as many applications at startup. To do this, right-click the Start button on the taskbar and then choose Open. Double-click the Programs folder and then the StartUp folder. Move any shortcuts in this folder to another folder for backup. Make sure you know the purpose of the files you're moving. When you're done, restart your computer and make sure everything works okay. If you experience errors, you may want to copy the items back to the StartUp folder.

⇨ Run WordPerfect in Draft view (choose View | Draft). Draft view is faster than Page or Two Page view. You cannot see headers, footers, and footnotes in your document, but when it's time to work on layout issues, you can easily switch back to Page view by choosing View and then Page.

⇨ Turn off the Preview option in the File Open dialog box. Choose File | Open and then click the Preview button in the dialog box to turn off this option.

⇨ Close any other applications you don't need while you're working in WordPerfect.

⇨ Make sure your hard drive has enough free space (at least 25 MB, depending on your computer) for Windows to perform file swapping.

⇨ Run the Windows 95 Disk Defragmenter and Scan Disk utilities on a regular basis. To use these utilities, click Start on the taskbar. Choose Programs | Accessories | System Tools and then select the utility you want to run.

⇨ Remove any fonts you don't need. To remove fonts, click Start on the taskbar. Choose Settings | Control Panel and double-click Fonts. Select the fonts you don't need (hold down CTRL to select multiple items) and choose File | Delete.

Warning: *Do not remove any of the system fonts that Windows uses for the desktop. Don't delete any fonts that begin with "MS," such as MS Sans Serif, MS Serif, or MS Dialog, or common fonts such as Times New Roman, Arial, Helvetica, and Courier.*

⇨   Beef up your system. If you have less than 16 MB of RAM, you should strongly consider adding more memory. You may also want to add a faster hard drive and video card. However, if you plan on purchasing a new computer in the near future, you may not want to sink any more money into your current computer.

5. I'm having a problem in one document, but I can't duplicate it in another document. What's wrong with the document?

Sometimes problems arise in a document that can't be duplicated in other files or in a blank window. These types of problems are rarely bugs in the software. Usually, the problem is a damaged portion of the file that will need to be removed. Document damage or corruption can occur in a variety of ways. The most common reasons for document damage are hardware problems, such as lost clusters and cross-linked files.

If you believe a document is corrupt, here are some troubleshooting options you can try:

⇨   First check to make sure that the problem isn't caused by a code. Place the insertion point in the problem area and then choose View | Reveal Codes. If you can't find a code that's causing the problem, your file may be corrupt. If you see garbage characters (!@#$%^) or unknown codes in Reveal Codes, the file is likely corrupt. In this case, try deleting the problem area, saving the file under a new name, and then re-creating the area that was lost. If you receive an error message while doing this, try selecting everything but the corrupted area and save the selection as a file.

⇨   Try copying and pasting the contents of the file to a new blank document. To do this, choose Edit | Select | All. Press CTRL-C to copy the file and then click the New Blank Document button on the toolbar. Press CTRL-V and then see if the problem still exists.

⇨   If the problem is in a table, try copying the entire table and pasting it into a new document. In some instances, you may need to create a table grid with the same number of columns and rows as the problem table in a blank document window. Copy the problem table to the clipboard and paste it into the existing table grid. Any table structure editing that you applied to the original table will be copied to the new table. Sometimes damage may be in a particular row. Try deleting that entire row, inserting a new row, and re-creating the lost information.

⇨ To salvage your text, save the file as an ASCII file. When you save in ASCII format, you will lose all formatting codes and special features; all that will remain is the text of the file. In most cases, this is the part you would most prefer not to have to re-create. Choose File | Save As, select ASCII DOS Text from the File Type drop-down list, and then choose Save. Open the document and save it as a WordPerfect document.

⇨ If you cannot open the file, try to insert the file (choose Insert | File) into a blank document. If that doesn't work, use the Preview button in the Open File dialog box to salvage the text. You can use the mouse to select and copy text, and then you can paste the text into a blank document. You will salvage the text, but you will lose any special formatting codes.

⇨ If your computer has a virus, it may appear that one or more of your documents is corrupt. You should take measures for protecting your computer against viruses. In addition to backing up your system regularly, you should obtain an anti-virus program and make a habit of using it regularly to protect your files against infection, especially if you download files from the Internet or copy program files from disks.

? **6. When I choose File | New, I don't see any templates or experts. How do I include WordPerfect 6.1 templates in WordPerfect 8?**

The templates and experts used in previous versions of WordPerfect have been replaced by *projects*. When you select a project, a PerfectExpert panel appears on the left side of the screen, as shown in Figure 1-2. You can use the suggestions in this panel to work on your document.

To use any templates you created in WordPerfect 6.1 and 7, you can copy the template files to the Custom WP Templates folder. This folder is usually located in C:\Corel\Suite8\Template.

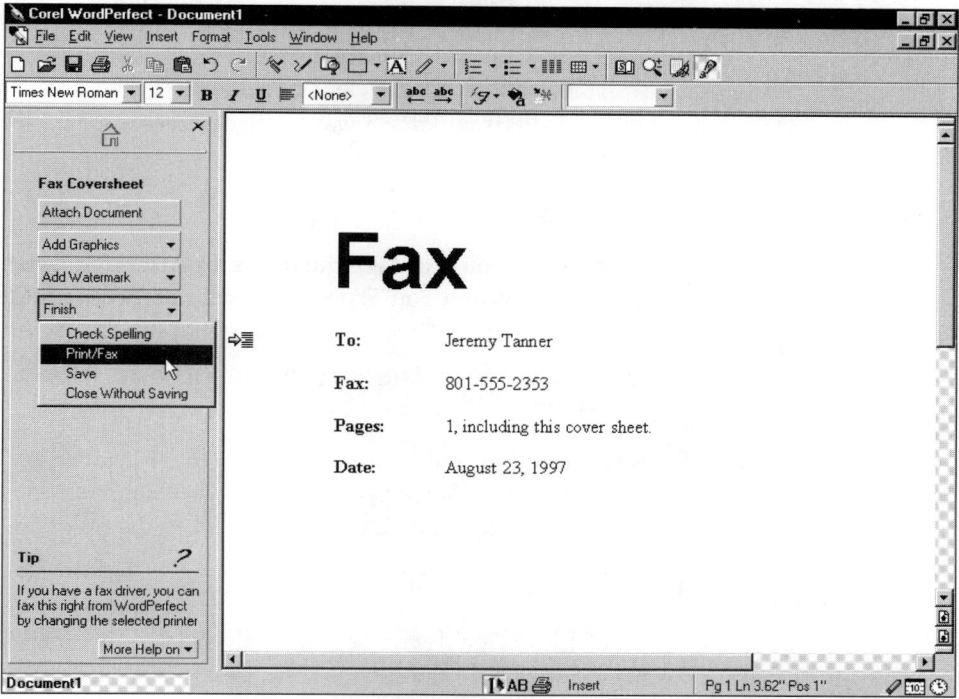

Figure 1-2.   You can use a project, for example, to create and print or send a fax cover sheet

   *Note:*   *Template files in WordPerfect 7 are usually located in C:\Corel\Office7\Template. Template files in WordPerfect 6.1 are usually located in C:\Office\Wpwin\Template.*

After you copy the files to the Custom WP Templates folder, you can create documents based on these templates. Choose File | New and then select Custom WP Templates from the drop-down list. Your copied templates should appear in the list box.

7. Why does WordPerfect format the text as a hyperlink when I type a Web address?

If you type Internet addresses such as **http://www.corel.com** in your document, WordPerfect will automatically format these items as hyperlinks. The QuickLinks feature creates a hyperlink after you type a hyperlink or e-mail address in your document followed by a space, tab, or indent. You can then click these items to jump to that Web site directly from your WordPerfect document. Like other QuickCorrect options such as SmartQuotes and QuickBullets, QuickLinks can be turned on or off. If you don't want Web addresses formatted as hyperlinks, here's how to turn off this option:

1. Choose Tools | QuickCorrect.

2. Click the QuickLinks tab and deselect the Format Words as Hyperlinks When You Type Them option. Then click OK.

? 8. How can I convert a table to a merge data file in WordPerfect 8?

If you have all your names and addresses in a WordPerfect table, you don't need to retype the entries in a new data file. Instead, you can convert the table to a merge data file by doing the following:

1. Choose View | Reveal Codes.

2. Move the insertion point before the Tbl Def code at the beginning of the table and then press DEL.

3. Select the Convert Contents to Merge Data File (Use Text in First Row as Field Names) option in the Delete Table dialog box. Then click OK.

? 9. What WordPerfect 8 system files should I back up so that if I ever have to reinstall WordPerfect, I don't have to go back and reinvent the wheel?

You may want to save your Address Book. To save the information in the Corel WordPerfect 8 Address Book, you need to export it. Choose Tools | Address Book. In the Address Book dialog box, choose Book | Export. When prompted, select Entire Address Book. In the Folders list box, switch to the folder where you want to save your backup copy, such as C:\MyFiles\Backup, and then type a filename, such as **Addrs.abx**. Click OK and then Close. To later restore your Address Book settings, choose Tools | Address Book. Then choose Book | Import. Select your ABX file and click OK.

Settings (Preferences) are stored in the Windows 95 registry. These registry files (USER.DAT and SYSTEM.DAT) are hidden files in your Windows directory. Windows 95 automatically makes a backup copy of these files each time you start your computer, so you don't need to back them up.

 *Note:*   *If you need to restore your registry settings, click the Start button on the taskbar and choose Run. Type* **regedit** *and click OK. In the Registry Editor, choose Help | Help Topics, select Restoring the Registry, and click Display.*

⇨ Toolbars, keyboard setup, and so on are stored in the default template, WP8US.WPT. This file is saved in C:\Corel\Suite8\Template\Custom WP Templates. You may want to copy this file to a backup folder.

⇨ Speller, QuickCorrect, and Grammatik word lists are stored in WT80US.UWL. This file is saved in your Windows directory. You may want to copy this file to a backup folder.

⇨ Macros you record are stored in the C:\Corel\Suite8\Macros\WPWin folder. Copy any macros you have created to a backup folder.

10. I want the footer to indicate both the current page number and the total pages in my document. How do I create this effect?

The Page Numbering feature has a "Page x of y" format that you can quickly select. This effect takes a little more work to accomplish in a header or footer, but here's what you do:

1. Place the insertion point in the header or footer where you want the numbering to appear.

2. Type **Page**, press the spacebar, click the Page Numbering button on the property bar, and select Page Number.

3. Press the spacebar, type **of**, and then press the spacebar again.

4. Click the Page Numbering button on the property bar and select Total Pages.

Setup, Speed, and Performance

Answer Topics!

Setup, Speed, and Performance @ a Glance

⇨ As you prepare to install Corel WordPerfect Suite 8, you may have some questions regarding where to install the program, which components to add, and what to do with previous versions of WordPerfect. Also, in most cases, you will have no trouble installing WordPerfect, but in those few instances in which things go wrong, the problem is not always easy to fix, especially if you upgraded from Windows 3.1 to Windows 95; old managers and other utilities can gum up the works. This chapter provides answers to both common and arcane questions related to installation of Corel WordPerfect 8.

⇨ If you're upgrading from a previous version of WordPerfect, you'll want to know whether your existing documents, macros, templates, Address Book entries, and styles are compatible with Corel WordPerfect 8. This chapter answers your questions.

⇨ As software become more powerful, the size of programs increases, so software companies such as Corel determine which components are installed by default and which components are left on the CD, where they can be added later, as required. If this configuration is not suitable for your particular needs, you can use the Custom install option to add suite components to your hard drive. You can also remove components, and you can even remove the whole suite. This chapter answers questions about adding and removing suite components.

⇨ Once you install WordPerfect, you want it to run without error, and you also want it to run as fast as possible on your computer. This chapter answers questions about improving speed and performance and changing startup options and tells you where to go to get more information about WordPerfect.

INSTALLING COREL WORDPERFECT

? ## My computer has only 8MB of RAM. Can I run Corel WordPerfect for Windows?

To run the applications in the Corel WordPerfect Suite 8 for Windows, your computer must meet the following *minimum* requirements:

Operating system	Windows 95, Windows NT 4.0, or higher
Processor	486/66 or higher
Recommended RAM	8MB or higher
Disk space for compact setup	50MB
Disk space for typical setup	120MB
Disk space for full custom installation	350MB

Remember that these are the *minimum* requirements. If you have only 8MB of RAM, you may find yourself wandering off for a snack while WordPerfect tries to work. If you want to run WordPerfect, you should look into beefing up your RAM to at least 16MB. Also, make sure you don't fill up your hard drive; if you do, your system will bog down, and you'll find yourself watching error messages instead of accomplishing your work.

? ## I already have WordPerfect 7 for Windows. Do I need to remove it before I install WordPerfect 8?

No, you do not need to remove Corel WordPerfect 7 for Windows, nor do you have to remove any previous version of WordPerfect for Windows, such as 5.1, 5.2, 6.0a, or 6.1, though you can if you want. If you do want to remove a previous version of WordPerfect, *you should do so before installing Corel WordPerfect 8*. When you install Corel WordPerfect 8, most of the files are placed in different folders automatically. However, a few files are shared between versions 7 and 8. Therefore, removing WordPerfect 7 after installing WordPerfect 8 has been known to cause problems—especially if you don't have much disk space available. For information on removing WordPerfect, see "Adding and Removing Suite Components" later in this chapter.

Here are some advantages and disadvantages of leaving previous versions of WordPerfect on your computer:

Advantages of Leaving the Corel WordPerfect 7 Suite on Your Computer

⇨ The Corel WordPerfect 7 Suite includes several features and applications that you may want to use. Envoy, Sidekick, CorelFLOW, Dashboard, QuickTasks, and some WordPerfect templates and experts didn't make it into the Corel WordPerfect 8 Suite, and you may want to keep these around.

⇨ You may want to have the choice of using WordPerfect 7 or WordPerfect 8.

Disadvantages of Leaving the Corel WordPerfect 7 Suite on Your Computer

⇨ You may run out of disk space, which will cause all sorts of problems when you try to run Windows applications.

⇨ If you leave WordPerfect 7 on your computer when you install WordPerfect 8 and then try to uninstall WordPerfect 7, you can cause problems. Sometimes these problems can be fixed by simply uninstalling and reinstalling the Corel WordPerfect 8 Suite, while other times the problems require you to spend hours trying to clean out the registry.

 *Note:*   *If you remove WordPerfect 7 after installing WordPerfect 8 and you experience problems, remove and reinstall WordPerfect 8.*

❓ Will Corel WordPerfect Suite 8 work with Windows NT 3.51 workstations?

No. Corel WordPerfect Suite 8 will not work on Windows NT 3.51 workstations. It should be installed on systems running Windows NT 4.0 or Windows 95.

❓ How do I install Corel WordPerfect Suite 8?

It's easy to install Corel WordPerfect for Windows. All you have to do is insert the Corel WordPerfect Suite 8 CD into the CD-ROM drive, wait a moment for AutoRun to display a setup window containing various options, and then click Corel WordPerfect Suite Setup. Then follow the instructions on your screen.

If the AutoRun feature of Windows 95 isn't enabled on your system, click the Start button on the taskbar and choose Run. In the Run dialog box, type **d:\autorun.exe**, where **d** represents the drive letter of your CD-ROM drive. Then click OK and follow the instructions on your screen.

During setup, you can select which programs and components you want installed. You do this from the Installation Type screen, shown in Figure 2-1. If you have any questions while you install the software, refer to the remainder of this chapter.

What Is Installed

When you install Corel WordPerfect Suite 8, you can include the following:

⇨ WordPerfect 8

⇨ Quattro Pro 8

⇨ Presentations 8

⇨ Desktop Application Director 8 (icons located on the right side of the Windows 95 taskbar)

⇨ Photo House, Envoy Viewer 7, Bitstream Font Navigator 2.0, and Netscape Navigator 3.0

⇨ More than 12,000 clipart images

⇨ More than 1,000 TrueType fonts

⇨ More than 200 photos

Note: *The programmers didn't finish the CorelCENTRAL product on time for it to be shipped with the suite. However, you can order it by calling Corel at 1-800-772-6735.*

❓ Should I select Typical, Compact, or Custom installation?

In a Compact installation, only the minimum program files are installed, so you should avoid this type of installation unless you don't have much real estate left on your hard drive. In a Typical installation, you can select which applications you want to install and where you want

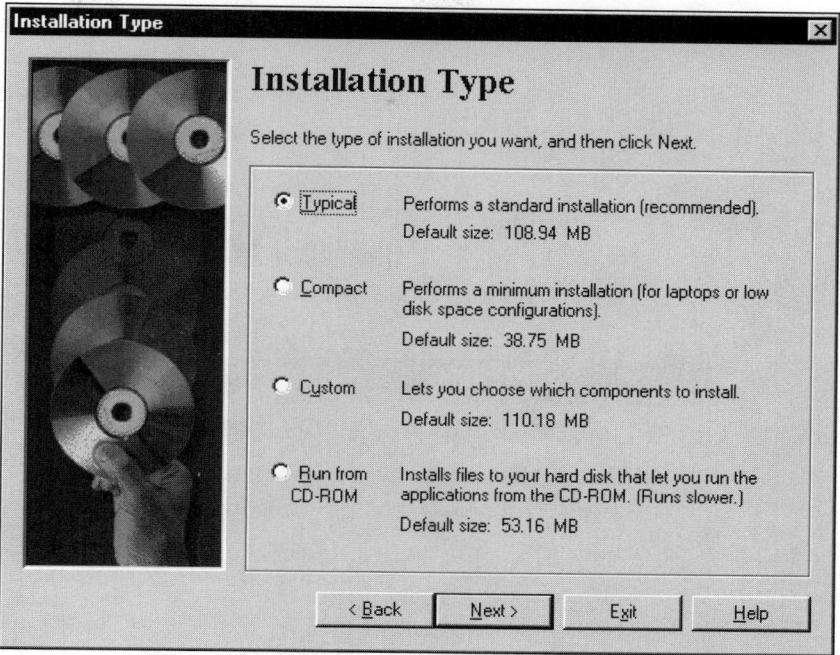

Figure 2-1.   Select the type of Corel WordPerfect Suite 8 installation you want to use

to install them. However, a Typical installation does not install every item that is available for each application. A Custom installation lets you select which components are installed for each application.

In previous versions of WordPerfect, the best choice was almost always the Typical installation. However, with WordPerfect 8, you may want to consider selecting the Custom installation so you can add some useful components that aren't otherwise installed. For example, only the most common macros and *projects* (formerly called *templates* and *experts*) are installed by default in the Typical installation, but the Custom installation allows you to select additional macros and projects. If you write programmable macros or Java scripts, you can use the Custom installation to include WordPerfect Macro Help or Java Applet Support.

Tip: *After you install Corel WordPerfect 8, you can always use the Custom installation later to add or remove components. See "Adding and Removing Suite Components" later in this chapter.*

? How do I install only WordPerfect?

If you don't need Quattro Pro, Presentations, or any of the other applications included in the Corel WordPerfect Suite, you don't have to install them. Regardless of whether you choose the Custom or Typical installation option, you can select the programs that are installed on your hard drive. When the Select Components screen appears, deselect all the options except WordPerfect 8. Then continue with the installation.

? I am a network administrator at a company that just purchased Corel WordPerfect Suite 8. How can I get more information on network administration?

Read the Release Notes on your Corel WordPerfect 8 CD. Click the Release Notes button at the Welcome Screen after choosing setup or follow these steps:

1. Insert the Corel WordPerfect Suite 8 CD and then select the Release Notes option.

2. Click the Contents tab, then double-click the Corel WordPerfect Suite 8 Network Release Notes book icon.

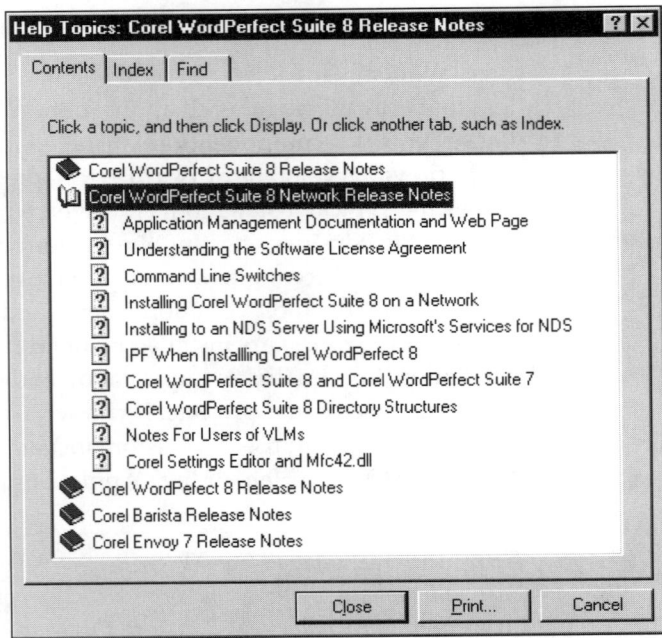

3. Double-click any of the topics you want to learn more about.

 **Note:**   *A network administrator's manual is available from the Corel BBS at (801) 221-5197. Contact Corel for additional information.*

I installed WordPerfect 8, but when I select the shortcut to start it, the computer locks up. How can I fix this problem?

One possible problem is an outdated command in your CONFIG.SYS file, such as device=c:\qemm\qemm386.sys ram.

You can use the System Configuration Editor to open the CONFIG.SYS file, as shown in Figure 2-2.

1. Click the Start button on the taskbar and choose Run. Then type **sysedit** and press ENTER.

2. On the System Configuration Editor screen, click the CONFIG.SYS window to select it and look for the line

```
device=c:\qemm\qemm386.sys ram
```

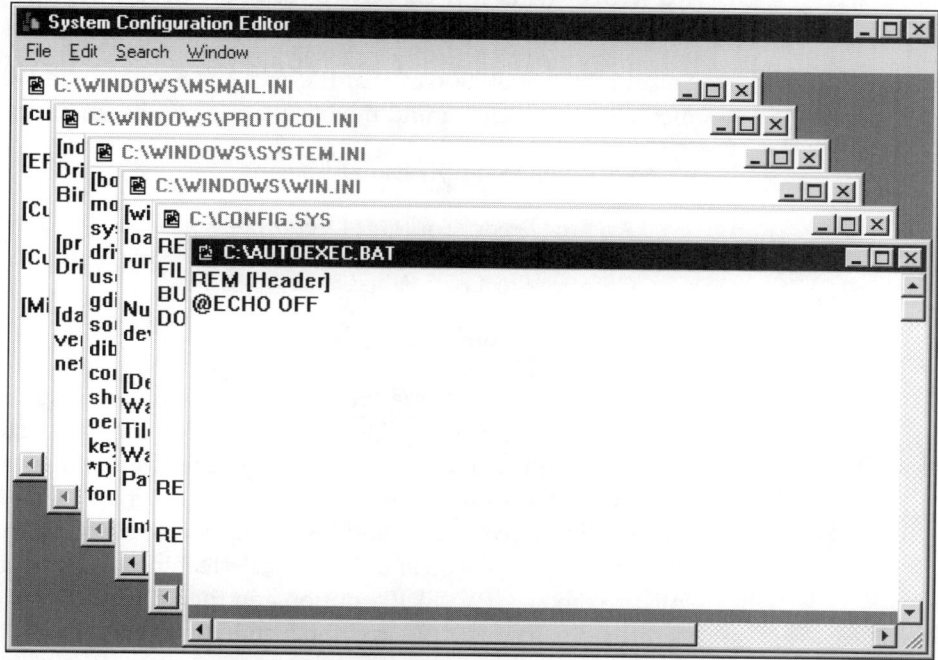

Figure 2-2.   Use the System Configuration Editor to edit system files

Before this line type **rem** followed by a space, so the line looks like this:

```
rem device=c:\qemm\qemm386.sys ram
```

3. Save the file and restart your computer.

WordPerfect for Windows should start. If the program still does not start properly, try reinstalling WordPerfect.

❓ I installed WordPerfect 8. Now Microsoft Exchange no longer functions. How can I get Exchange to work?

This problem occurs if you're running an older version of Windows 95 or Microsoft Exchange. There is a conflict among Corel WordPerfect Suite 8, Microsoft Exchange, and the Windows 95 operating system. To eliminate problems, you need to install the Microsoft Exchange Update for Windows 9. The name of this file is EXUPDUSA.EXE (the filename may be different for localized versions of Windows 95).

To obtain the Exchange update file, visit Microsoft's Web site for upgrades and support at **http://www.microsoft.com/exchangesupport**.

❓ During installation, a decompression error message appeared. What does this mean and what should I do?

During the installation of WordPerfect 7 or 8, one of the following messages may appear and the installation process may stop:

"Archive Decompression *filename*"

"Archive Error: Couldn't Decompress *filename*"

"Compressor Load Failed"

"Cannot Decompress *filename*"

Any of these messages may appear when files are not copied from the CD properly or when files being copied to the hard drive are damaged in the copy process. These messages sometimes also appear even when there are no errors or problems during installation. Try restarting your computer and installing WordPerfect again. If the same message appears and the WordPerfect installation continues to fail, use the /COPYVERIFY option and then the other procedures described in this section until the installation succeeds.

Run Setup Using the /COPYVERIFY Startup Option

The install program that ships with WordPerfect 8 (and most versions of WordPerfect 7) includes a startup switch called /COPYVERIFY. This switch performs a byte-by-byte comparison between each file copied to the hard drive and the source file on the CD. If any differences are noted, an entry is written in the WPI8.LOG file (COI7.LOG for the Corel Office Professional 7 version and WPI7.LOG for Corel WordPerfect Suite 7). You can find these files in your TMP directory or within the Corel directory. Here's how to run the startup option:

1. Click the Start button on the taskbar and choose Run. Then type **d:\setup.exe /copyverify**, where *d* identifies your CD-ROM drive.

2. Open the WPI8.LOG file in Notepad or any text editor.

3. If any file in the log is designated as corrupt, rename it or delete it and then replace it manually by copying the corresponding file from the CD to the proper location on the hard drive.

4. Rename the WPI8.LOG file and repeat steps 1 through 3 until you can verify that all the files have been copied correctly.

If installation continues to fail even after you've verified it using the /COPYVERIFY switch, try the following procedures. You may need to use them in conjunction with /COPYVERIFY to solve the problem.

Close All Applications and Release System Resources

Make sure that all other applications are closed and system resources are as free as possible. You may need to remove items from the StartUp folder temporarily. To do this, right-click the Start button on the taskbar and then choose Open. Double-click the Programs folder and then the StartUp folder. Move any shortcuts in this group to another folder. When you finish the installation process, you can move these items back to the StartUp folder.

Reregister Shared Components

If you complete the installation but problems still occur with shared components, try using PFREG.EXE to register the shared components again. To run PFREG, use Windows Explorer to locate PFREG.EXE, usually found in C:\Corel\Suite8\Programs (C:\Corel\Office7\ Shared in Corel WordPerfect 7). Double-click PFREG.EXE and wait while the program checks for components in the status box.

Choose the Unregister button, and close any error messages that may appear. Choose the Register button to re-register all the selected applications in Windows 95, then choose Close.

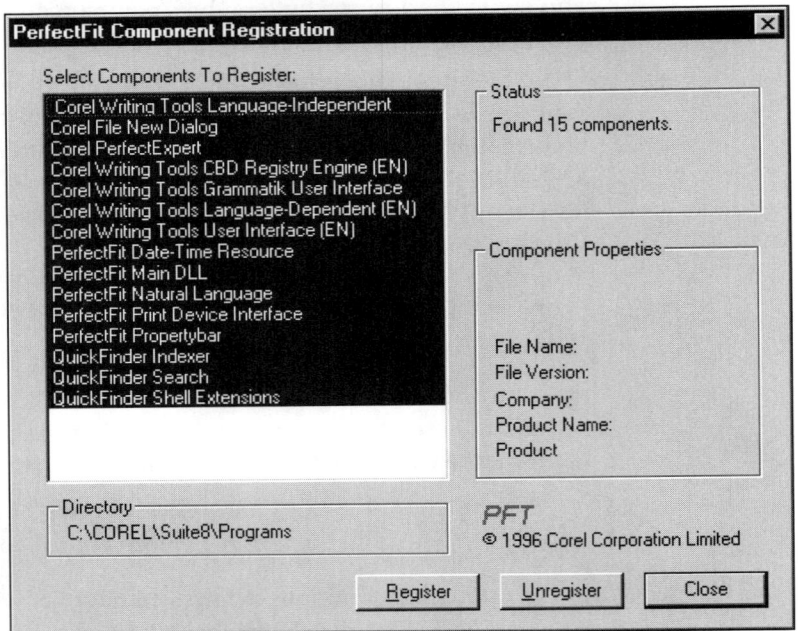

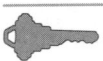 *Note:*   *Archive decompression can cause problems that PFREG may not be able to solve. If unregistering generates error messages, you may need to reinstall the Corel WordPerfect Suite.*

Check the CONFIG.SYS and AUTOEXEC.BAT Files to See Whether QEMM 8.0 Is Being Used

To check the AUTOEXEC.BAT and CONFIG.SYS files, click the Start button and then choose Run. Type **sysedit** and choose OK. Look at each line in the CONFIG.SYS and AUTOEXEC.BAT files to check for QEMM lines. QEMM is a memory manager for Windows 3.1 that has been known to cause complications for applications running in Windows 95. If any of these lines mention QEMM, type **rem** followed by a space at the beginning of the line. Typing "rem" before a line in the system files causes the line to be ignored. Save the files, restart your computer, and then try reinstalling the Corel WordPerfect Suite.

Check the CONFIG.SYS and AUTOEXEC.BAT Files for 16-bit CD-ROM Drivers

Old 16-bit drivers may interfere with the installation process. Use the System Editor (sysedit.exe) to edit your AUTOEXEC.BAT and CONFIG.SYS files. If you see a 16-bit CD-ROM driver in either of these files, type **rem** followed by a space at the beginning of the line listing 16-bit drivers and then restart your computer. For more information, contact your CD-ROM manufacturer. Insert a CD into the CD-ROM drive and use Microsoft Explorer to see if Windows 95 can read it. If Windows 95 can still read the CD-ROM drive after you add a REM command, the 16-bit CD-ROM driver may have been interfering with the Windows 95 32-bit drivers. Try reinstalling WordPerfect at this point.

Caution: *If you are not familiar with editing system files, you might be better off getting the local computer guru to help you with these steps, or you may damage your system files.*

If Windows 95 cannot see the CD-ROM drive after you "remmed" out the 16-bit command, then real-mode (16-bit) versus protected-mode (32-bit Windows 95) drivers are running. Click the Start button, choose Settings and then Control Panel, and then double-click Add New Hardware to allow Windows 95 to detect the CD-ROM driver. Follow the wizard and use the auto detect option. If the driver cannot find the driver or if problems with your CD-ROM persist, contact the manufacturer of the CD-ROM driver to obtain a 32-bit driver or to determine the suggested emulation in Windows 95. If you cannot find a suitable replacement for your CD-ROM driver, use the System Editor again to remove the REM commands you added and restart your computer so that your CD-ROM drive will work on your computer. Until you find a current driver for your CD-ROM, you will not be able to install WordPerfect.

Check the CD-ROM Settings

To check the CD-ROM settings, click the Start button and choose Settings. Choose Control Panel and then double-click System. Click the Performance tab, choose File System, and then click the CD-ROM tab. Check the "Optimize access pattern for:" line and verify that the CD-ROM is *not* set to "No read-ahead." It should be set to the type of CD-ROM installed on your machine.

If you still have problems, try the following: If your machine has 8MB of RAM, set the speed to Single spin, regardless of the actual drive speed. If your machine has 12MB of RAM, set the speed to Double spin. If your machine has 16MB or higher of RAM, set the speed to Quad speed or higher. At this point, try the installation again.

If the CD-ROM Fails, Copy the Files Manually

Copy the files from the Corel CD to the destination drive and reinstall the files over themselves. If your computer has real-mode (16-bit) CD-ROM drivers, choose "Command Prompt Only" from the Windows 95 Startup menu and use the DOS XCOPY command to copy the \COREL directory structure from the CD to the hard drive. Here's how:

1. Display the Windows 95 Startup menu by restarting the computer and pressing F8 when the message "Starting Windows 95" appears on the screen.

2. When the DOS prompt appears, copy the files by entering the command: **xcopy d:\corel*.* c:\corel /s** (where *d* represents the CD-ROM drive and *c* represents the hard drive where WordPerfect is installed). The XCOPY command will take some time (at least half an hour) to complete and will use more disk space than a Typical installation.

Note: *You can also use Windows Explorer to copy the files from the CD. Start Explorer, select the drive letter of your CD-ROM (for example, drive d:), right-click the COREL folder, and choose Copy. Select the drive letter that identifies the hard drive to which you want to copy the files (for example, drive c:), right-click on a blank area in the right window, and choose Paste. This will copy the COREL directory tree to the hard drive.*

3. Restart the computer and press the F8 key immediately when the message "Starting Windows 95" appears. Choose Safe Mode from the Windows 95 Startup menu.

4. Begin the installation again by clicking Start, choosing Run, and typing *c*:**\corel\office7\appman\setup\setup.exe** (where *c* is the hard drive where WordPerfect is installed).

5. Start a new installation and send the program to the location to which you copied the files (for example, C:\COREL).

Note: *During the installation process, the following message may appear: "Insufficient Disk Space. You do not have enough room on C to install specified components." Just continue past this message. The program is already installed, but the registering of the information needs to be completed.*

Clean the Corel WordPerfect 8 CD

Your CD may be dirty enough to prevent your CD-ROM drive from reading it properly. In some cases, washing the CD in lukewarm water with a mild detergent and then rinsing it and drying it with a soft cloth may correct decompression and lockup problems. When drying the CD, wipe outward from the center toward the edge, not around the circle as you might wipe a plate. Also check for any scratches on either side of the CD.

Resume the Installation

If your installation stops at a certain point each time you install the Corel WordPerfect Suite, try this. Start the installation again and choose Resume (*not* Redo). Perform this procedure at least three times. If Setup continues to stop at the exact same location, you may have to break down and call Corel technical support—you may have a bad CD. However, if the installation percentage indicator increases each time you resume the installation, continue to choose Resume until the installation is complete.

I got an "Invalid Page Fault" error message during install. What's wrong?

If you get the "WPI8 Caused an Invalid Page Fault in Module ABC10.DLL" error message while installing WordPerfect, you should rename the MAPI32.DLL file. There are several different versions of the MAPI32.DLL, and some versions may cause a conflict with the installation of WordPerfect.

Locate the MAPI32.DLL file, which is usually found in the C:\Windows\System folder. Rename this file to something like MAPI32.OLD. Next, use Windows Explorer to copy the MAPNT40.DLL file from the Corel WordPerfect Suite 8 CD to the folder where the renamed MAPI32.DLL file is located. This file is located in the Corel\Appman\Wkswpi8 folder on the CD. Then rename the MAPNT40.DLL file to MAPI32.DLL and try installing again.

? **I installed Corel WordPerfect 8, but when I select the Corel WordPerfect Suite 8 Setup or Corel Remove Program shortcut, an error message appears. What should I do?**

When you select the Corel WordPerfect Suite 8 Setup or Corel Remove Program shortcut from the Start menu, the following error message may appear: "The drive or network connection that the shortcut 'Corel Remove Program LNK' refers to is unavailable. Make sure that the disk is properly inserted or the network resource is available, and then try again." Make sure the Corel WordPerfect Suite 8 CD is in the CD-ROM drive. Also make sure the Corel WordPerfect Suite 8 Setup or Corel Remove Problem shortcut is pointing to the CD-ROM drive. To do this, follow these steps:

1. Right-click Start on the taskbar and then choose Open.

2. Double-click Corel WordPerfect Suite 8, Setup & Notes.

3. Right-click Corel Remove Program and then choose Properties.

4. Click the Shortcut tab and make sure the correct path (such as D:\Corel\Appman\Setup\Remove.exe) is pointing to the CD-ROM drive.

? **I installed WordPerfect 8, but the Open File dialog box does not appear when I choose File and then choose Open. What's wrong?**

If you can start WordPerfect but cannot get the Open File or Save As dialog box to appear, there is a problem with your registry. Here's how to fix it:

1. If WordPerfect 8 is open, close the application.

2. Copy the file PFREG.EXE from the \Corel\Suite8\Programs folder to the \Corel\Suite8\Shared\Compents folder.

3. Double-click PFREG.EXE in the Compents folder.

   The PerfectFit Component Registration dialog box appears. Two components should appear in the Select Components to Register window.

4. Click the Register button to register the two components. Then choose Close.

? **I installed WordPerfect 8, but I'm having display problems when moving the insertion point. What's wrong?**

There are a few known display problems in WordPerfect 8. If you are using the ATI graphics driver MACxw4 version 2.01, you may have problems with cursor movement when selecting or editing equations. Corel recommends that you contact your vendor for an updated driver.

? **I installed WordPerfect 8, but the text appears to be ragged. How can I make the text appear smooth?**

If you are using Microsoft PLUS! with the Smooth Edges of Screen Fonts option enabled, some text in WordPerfect 8 may not always appear smooth. For example, text marked by Spell-As-You-Go, merge codes, or SGML codes may appear fuzzy. To correct the problem, Corel recommends that you disable Smooth Edges of Screen Fonts. To do this, click Start from the taskbar, then choose Settings and then Control Panel. Double-click Display, click the Plus! tab, then deselect Smooth edges of screen fonts.

? **I installed WordPerfect 8, but when I try to open the Address Book, a Borland database engine error message appears. What should I do?**

If you successfully install Corel WordPerfect Suite 8 and then remove Corel WordPerfect Suite 7 (or Corel Office Professional 7) from the system, attempting to start Corel Address Book 8 results in the error message "Borland Database Engine configuration file does not exist. Please run Setup." You can correct the error by reinstalling Corel WordPerfect Suite 8, or you can reinstall the Borland Database Engine 4.0 components from the Corel WordPerfect 8 CD. Here's how to reinstall just the Borland Engine Database 4.0 components:

1. Insert the Corel WordPerfect 8 CD and choose Corel WordPerfect Suite Setup.

2. Choose Next and Yes until the Installation Type screen appears (if prompted, click Close Application to close any applications that may be open).

3. Choose Custom. Then click Next.

4. Verify the drive and path for the installation and click Next.

5. Choose Selection Options. Then choose Deselect All and click OK.

6. Scroll to the bottom of the list and select Required Components. Then click the Components button.

7. In the Required Components dialog box, make sure that everything is unchecked except Database Tools (check it to mark it, as needed).

Note: *Unchecking some of the items that may already be checked may result in messages indicating that the component is a vital part of the application. If this happens, go ahead and deselect the item anyway. These components are already installed.*

8. Click OK, Next, and then Install.

? When I run WordPerfect 8 from a Network installation, I receive the error message "Too Many Fonts Installed." What should I do?

When WordPerfect is run from a Network installation with the TrueType fonts option selected, some of the fonts will be installed as shortcuts instead of being installed to the hard drive. Because your network has a large number of fonts, Windows 95 or Windows NT will exceed the font limit for your system, causing the error. Here's how you can work around this problem:

1. From the workstation, click Start on the Windows taskbar. Choose Settings and then Control Panel.

2. Double-click Fonts.

3. Select fonts that you no longer need (hold down CTRL to select multiple items). Then choose File and then Delete to delete these fonts.

4. Choose File and then Install New Font.

5. Change the directory to indicate the network directory where the font files are located (contact your network supervisor for location information, if necessary). Select the fonts that you want installed and click OK.

CONVERSION ISSUES

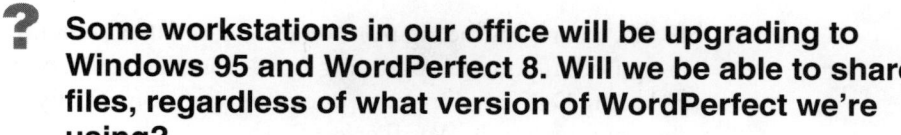

Some workstations in our office will be upgrading to Windows 95 and WordPerfect 8. Will we be able to share files, regardless of what version of WordPerfect we're using?

Yes. Files saved in WordPerfect 8 are compatible with earlier versions of WordPerfect. WordPerfect 8 can read and write WordPerfect 6.0/6.1 files, and WordPerfect 6.0/6.1 can read files saved in WordPerfect 8. However, if the WordPerfect 8 document has elements created by features that were not available in WordPerfect 6.1, those elements will not appear in the WordPerfect 6.1 document.

If some of your co-workers are still using WordPerfect 5.1/5.2, you'll probably want to save files in an earlier format. Although WordPerfect 5.2 for Windows and WordPerfect 5.1+ for DOS include conversion utilities that read files saved in the 6.0/6.1 format, you cannot be sure that everyone has the most recent upgrade of those older versions.

To save a file in an earlier format, choose File and then Save As. From the File Type list, select the format in which you want to save the file. If you want to change the default setting so that all your files are saved in an earlier format, close the Save As dialog box and choose Tools and then Settings. Double-click Files and select the file type you want from the Default save file format list.

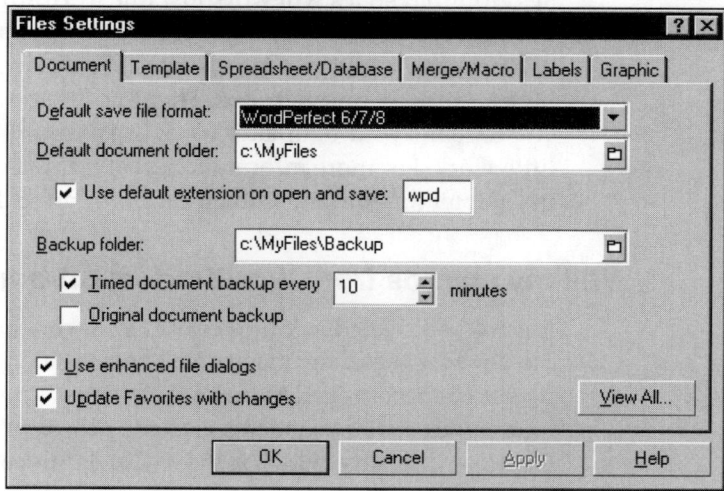

❓ Can I use the documents I created in previous WordPerfect versions?

Yes. If you are upgrading from WordPerfect 6.0 or later, no conversion is required. If you are upgrading from WordPerfect 5.2 or earlier (including DOS versions), the document is automatically converted when you open it in WordPerfect 8.

The default directory in both WordPerfect 7 and 8 is C:\MYFILES, where C represents the drive on which WordPerfect is installed. To easily access your other documents, you can either move your files to the MYFILES folder or change your default directory. To change the default directory, choose Tools and then Settings. Double-click Files and then type the location of your existing files in the Default document folder text box.

❓ Can I use the custom toolbars I created previously?

When you install WordPerfect 8, any custom toolbars you created in WordPerfect 6.1 or 7 should be automatically transferred to the WordPerfect 8 default template (WP8US.WPT). To select a toolbar, right-click the toolbar and choose the toolbar you want from the QuickMenu.

❓ Can I use my styles and templates from previous versions of WordPerfect?

Yes. Your old styles will work just fine in WordPerfect 8—just open the document containing the styles or retrieve the styles file you created in a previous version of WordPerfect. To do this, choose Format, Styles, Options, and Retrieve. Then specify the styles file you created.

To make your templates work in WordPerfect 8, you need to do a little work. For more information, see "Using PerfectExpert Projects" in Chapter 3, "Working with Your WordPerfect Document."

❓ Will my macros from WordPerfect 6.1 and 7 convert?

Macros you created in WordPerfect 7 will work just fine in WordPerfect 8. However, some of the macros you created in WordPerfect 6.0/6.1 may need to be recompiled to make them work correctly. The easiest way to use your previous macros is to copy them to your new WordPerfect 8 macros directory, which is in C:\Corel\Suite8\Macros\WPWin. You can then play them by choosing Tools, Macro, and Play and then double-clicking the macro you want.

For more information on making your macros run properly, see "Using Macros" in Chapter 13, "Macros and Templates."

? Do I need to update my Address Book in WordPerfect 8?

Corel Address Book 8 should be updated automatically with the addresses from Corel Address Book 7 when you install Corel WordPerfect Suite 8 and should include any custom fields needed for the data. However, if this procedure doesn't happen automatically, you can do it manually as long as Corel Address Book 7 is still installed on the system. Here are the steps:

1. Open Corel Address Book 7.

2. Click the tab to select the address book containing the data to be exported.

3. Choose Book and then Export.

4. If prompted, select Entire Address Book (or you can select just certain records you want exported).

5. Set the desired path and specify the filename of the ABX file to be exported. Then click OK.

6. Repeat steps 2 through 5 for other address book tabs as desired, remembering to give each a unique file name.

7. Close Address Book 7.

For more information on using the Corel Address Book, see "Corel Address Book" in Chapter 8, "Merges, Labels, and Envelopes."

? Can I use older language modules with WordPerfect 8?

If you purchased language modules for earlier versions of WordPerfect, you should update them for WordPerfect 8. For information on updating your language modules, contact your local reseller or see the Corel WordPerfect Web site (choose Help and then Corel Web Site) for more information.

ADDING AND REMOVING SUITE COMPONENTS

? I just found out I need a component that I didn't install. Do I need to reinstall the whole suite?

No. You can use the Custom installation to select additional components. The following steps describe how to add the macro component, but you can use a similar procedure to install other additional components.

1. Insert the Corel WordPerfect 8 CD and click Corel WordPerfect Suite Setup.

2. Choose Next and Yes until the Installation Type screen appears (if prompted, click Close Application to close any applications that may be open).

3. Choose Custom and then click Next.

4. Verify the drive and path for the installation and click Next.

5. Choose Selection Options. Then choose Deselect All and click OK.

6. Select the category of the component (for example, WordPerfect). Then click the Components button.

7. Select the next category of the component (for example, WordPerfect Macros). Then click the Components button again.

8. Select the components you want. Then click OK and Next until you're ready to click Install.

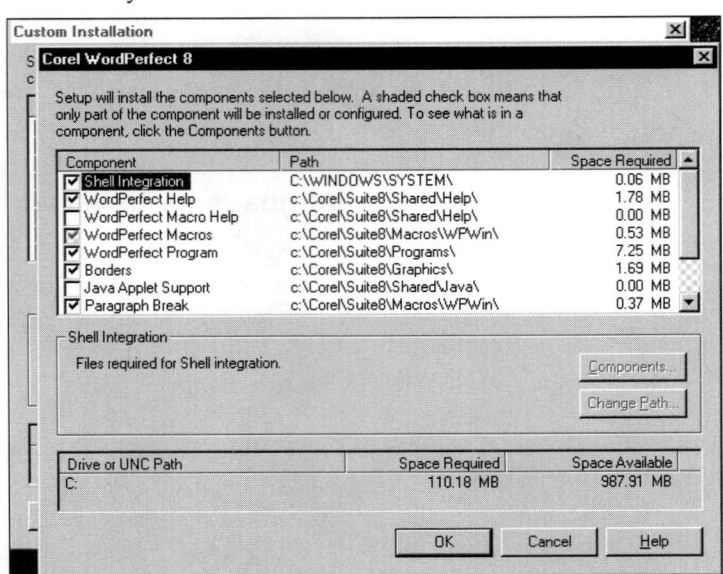

FREE COURSES JUST FOR YOU
Throughout 2003

Enjoy brushing up on computer skills/keyboard skills

Confidence skills

Remembering numbers in an easy way

Dealing with customers
(face to face/telephone skills)

Come and join us at a time to
suit you for a coffee and talk

Morgan Burns Career Training
38 Victoria Street, Bristol
0117 9221717

(5 minutes walk from the Galleries or the centre)

Learning+Skills Council
West of England

9. Continue with the installation.

? How do I remove WordPerfect 5.2 or 6.1 for Windows?

Removing programs from Windows is more complicated than simply deleting the folders and their files. When programs are installed in Windows, files are scattered all over your hard drive, and an uninstall program is required to remove them effectively. To remove non-Windows 95 programs such as WordPerfect 6.1 for Windows, you should use an uninstaller program such as MicroHelp's Uninstaller, Vertisoft's Remove-It, or Quarterdeck's CleanSweep. Your local computer store should carry these utilities.

SPEED AND PERFORMANCE ISSUES

? The Open File dialog box takes approximately 15 seconds to appear. How can I speed things up?

This problem is more common for WordPerfect 7 than for WordPerfect 8. If the Open File dialog box takes too long to appear, turn off the Preview option. Choose File and then New. Then when the File Open dialog box finally appears, click the Preview button, which is the third button from the right.

This should reduce the delay considerably.

? Changing folders takes an abnormally long time. What's wrong? Can I speed things up?

Switching folders in the File Open dialog box (or any file management dialog box) takes 30 to 60 seconds to accomplish, and this performance problem worsens as the Windows session continues. According to Corel, system resources are being used but not "given back" by the system.

To correct this problem, install the patch for KERNEL32.DLL from Microsoft. The new file date is 2/2/96 with a time stamp of 9:51 AM . The file size is still 402 KB. The update can be obtained from the Microsoft Web page at **http://www.microsoft.com/windows/software/krnlupd.htm**.

? **When I edited a table, an IPF error message appeared. What's wrong? How can I obtain more disk space?**

The error message "WPWIN7 caused an IPF in module WPWIN7.EXE at 0137 : 006218E1" may occur when you have insufficient disk space on your hard drive. If you have only 2MB of available hard drive space, for example, Windows will not have enough room to swap files effectively and so will display error messages. Free up some hard drive space by removing unnecessary files. Consider purchasing an uninstaller utility, which helps remove unwanted applications, duplicate files, unnecessary graphics, and Internet and fax debris.

? **Each time I run WordPerfect, I want to play a macro. Is this possible?**

Yes. You can add startup options (also called switches) to your command line to perform special tasks such as running a macro or opening a file when you start WordPerfect. Figure 2-3 shows a macro (/m) startup option added to the command line.

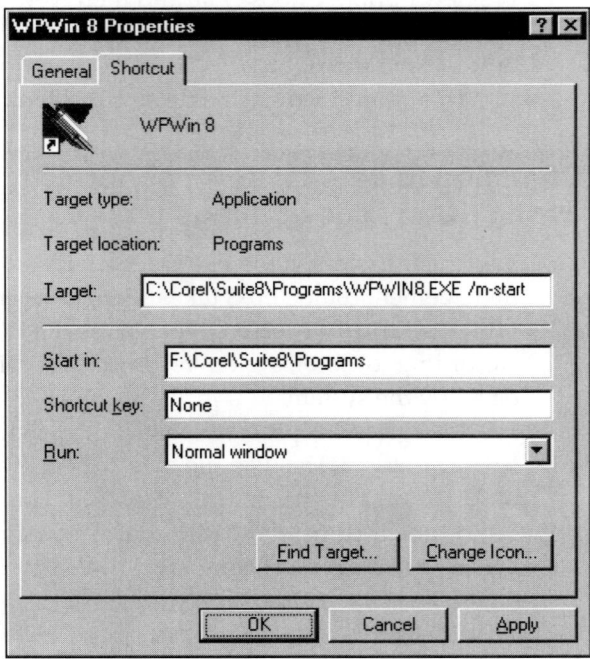

Figure 2-3.   Add a startup option to WordPerfect

To use such an option only once, click Start, choose Run, and then type **wpwin** followed by a space and the startup option. You can also add the startup option to the WordPerfect 8 shortcut. For example, the option wpwin /m-start.wcm runs a macro called START.WCM when you start WordPerfect. Here's how to set up a macro startup option:

1. Right-click the Start button on the taskbar and then choose Open. Double-click Corel WordPerfect Suite 8 (if you have a WordPerfect icon on the desktop, skip this step).

2. Right-click the WordPerfect 8 shortcut and then choose Properties.

3. Click the Shortcut tab. Then place the insertion point at the end of the path in the Target text box.

4. Press the spacebar and then type **/m-*macroname*** (where *macroname* is the name of the macro). Click OK.

 *Note:*   *Make sure you compile the macro before running it.*

Table 2-1 shows some of the startup options you can use. You set them up just like you set up the macro startup option.

Table 2-1.   Startup Options

Option	Function
:	Opens WordPerfect without displaying the startup screen.
/d-*path*	Redirects the overflow files and temporary buffer files to the specified folder (for example, /d-c:\temp).
filename	Opens the specified file from the documents folder (usually C:\MYFILES). If the file is not in the default directory, type the full pathname.
filename /bk-*bookmark name*	Opens the specified file and branches to the specified bookmark.
/l-*language code*	Identifies which entry in the Language Resource File (wp.lrs) and which language DLL file WordPerfect uses (for example, /l-SP).
/m-*macroname*	Starts the specified macro.
/mt-*macroname*	Starts the specified macro from the default template.
/nb	Turns off original document backup.
/u-*name*	Identifies the user initials for use on your network.

 **Note:**   *If you want to use more than one startup option, enter a space and then type the next option.*

GETTING HELP

? I asked the PerfectExpert how to create a table of contents, and it included information on everything but the table of contents. How do I get help in WordPerfect?

If you choose Help and then Ask the PerfectExpert, you probably won't get an answer to your question. The best way to get help in WordPerfect is to use the Help Index, shown in Figure 2-4. Choose Help and then Help Topics, click the Index tab, and then type the name of the task or feature you want to know more about.

Select the other tabs in the Help Topics: WordPerfect Help dialog box to discover more ways of using Help. For example, to find out what kinds of documents you can create, use Showcase Help. Choose Help and then Help Topics and click the Contents tab. Double-click

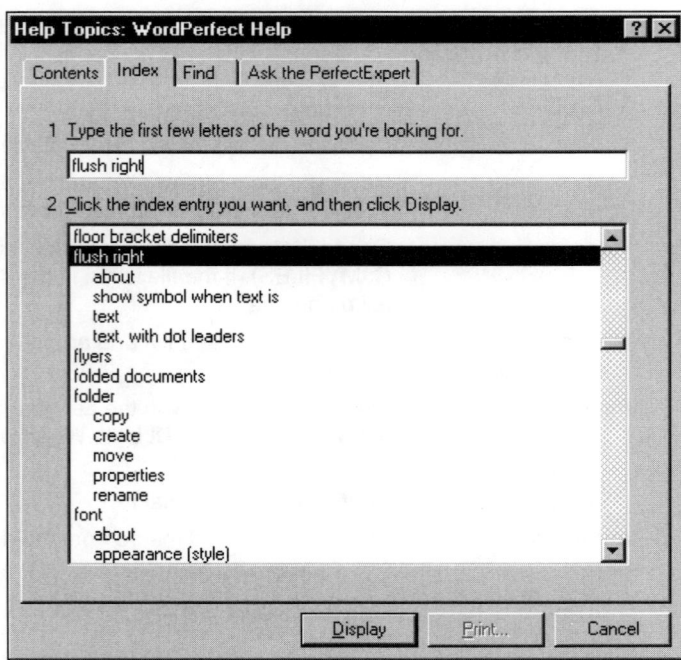

Figure 2-4.   Use the Help Index to browse through help topics

Showcase Corel WordPerfect. Click the document you want to know more about and then click the arrows in the larger representation of the document. The best way to learn is to explore.

 ***Tip:*** *To find out what any toolbar button, dialog box option, or menu command does, press* SHIFT-F1 *and then click the item you want to know more about.*

? How do I order printed manuals?

To order manuals for individual products in the Corel WordPerfect Suite, call (800) 772-6735.

? Is there a Corel WordPerfect magazine or some type of newsletter that I can subscribe to?

Yes. You can call (800) 228-9626 or write to WordPerfect for Windows Magazine, Attn: Subscription Services, 270 West Center Street, Orem, Utah, 84057-9927 to start a subscription to *WordPerfect Magazine*.

? Is there a Web site for Corel WordPerfect?

Yes. It's located at the following URL address: **http://www.corel.com**.

Working with Your WordPerfect Document

Answer Topics!

Working with Your WordPerfect Document @ a Glance

⇨ WordPerfect 8 includes some new features, such as the shadow cursor, margin guidelines, and property bar. This chapter provides answers to questions about how to use these new features as well as how to juggle different document windows, move through your document, and get your work done faster with keystrokes.

⇨ When working in WordPerfect, many people trip up on the same tasks and make the same mistakes. By taking a few precautions such as saving your documents frequently and using the right tool for the job, you can avoid many of these common pitfalls. If you learn the basics well, such as the procedures for copying, moving, and deleting text, getting your work done will be much easier. This chapter answers your questions about how to complete important tasks.

⇨ When you format a document, you change its appearance. Formatting includes common editing tasks such as changing the font, aligning text, adjusting the margins, and adding footnotes and page numbering. This chapter answers your questions about formatting.

⇨ The Find and Replace command can save you a lot of time. If you're looking for a specific reference but you're not sure exactly where it is, you can let WordPerfect find the reference for you. You can also have WordPerfect replace the text you find with other text—so if you misspell your boss's name all the way through a document, you can make sure you replace each occurrence with the correct spelling. You can even use the Find and Replace feature to search for special characters and codes. Consult this chapter when you have questions about Find and Replace.

⇨ Writing good prose is hard enough without having to worry about typing errors, misspelling, and incorrect grammar. Thanks to WordPerfect, you no longer have to fumble around with a dictionary, thesaurus, and usage guide while you type. WordPerfect includes three features—Spell Checker, Thesaurus, and Grammatik—that will increase your efficiency and accuracy while you write. This chapter helps you make better use of these proofing tools.

⇨ This chapter answers your questions about PerfectExpert Projects. A *project* is a predesigned document that is linked to a PerfectExpert panel. You just need to enter your individual information and preferences and then let WordPerfect do much of the rest of the work. For example, to send a fax you can fill in a preformatted fax cover sheet and then send the fax right from WordPerfect if you have the appropriate fax software.

THE BASICS

? What are the elements in a WordPerfect window and what is the purpose of each?

WordPerfect for Windows appears in a window, just like any other Windows application. The window includes many elements that make it easy to create, edit, print, and save your documents. Figure 3-1 shows these elements.

⇨ The *title bar* shows which document is open. When WordPerfect is not maximized or minimized, you can drag the title bar to move the WordPerfect window.

⇨ The menu bar lists commands that help you get your work done. If you don't know how to use menus yet, you're reading the wrong book.

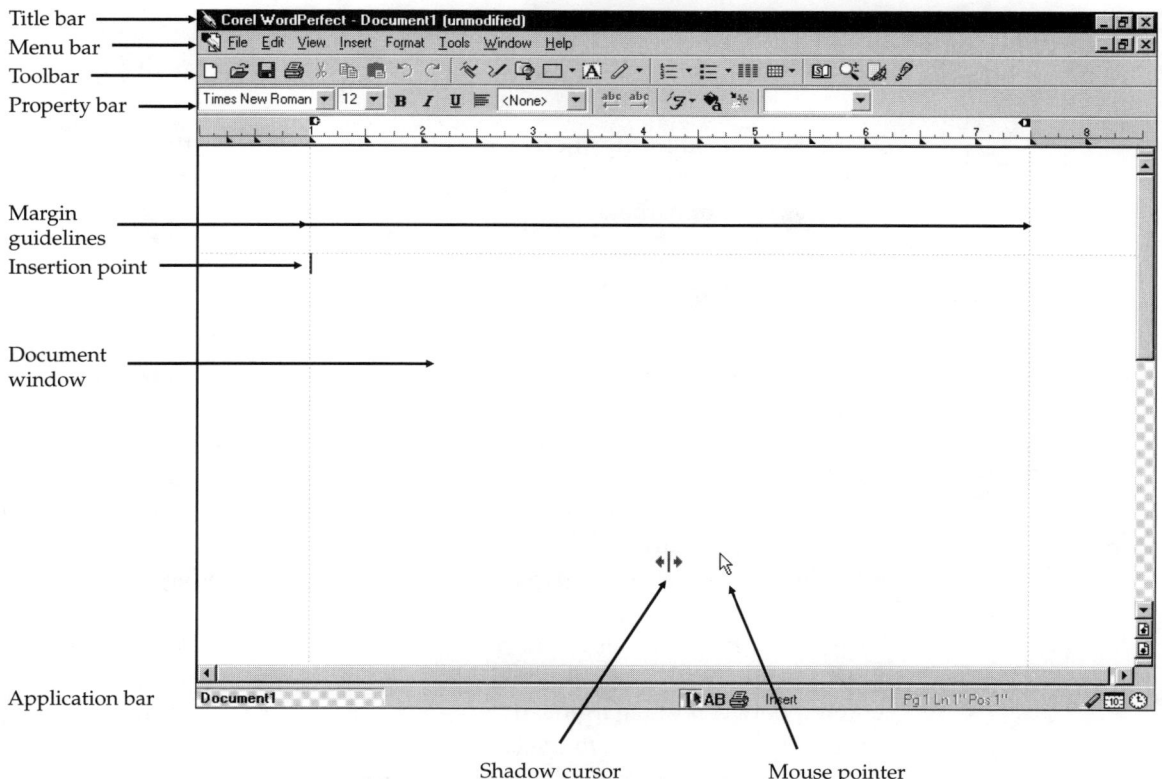

Figure 3-1. The WordPerfect application window

⇨   The *toolbar* includes buttons that you can click to perform a WordPerfect operation. Toolbar buttons provide shortcuts that simplify common tasks, such as opening and saving a document.

⇨   The *property bar* has pull-down lists and buttons for performing common functions. The items on the property bar change depending on the task you are performing. For example, when you're working on an outline, the Outline property bar appears; when you're working on a graphic, the Graphics property bar appears.

⇨   The *margin guidelines* indicate the area of your document that will be printed. You can drag these guidelines to adjust the size of the margins.

⇨   The *insertion point* indicates where text appears when you type.

⇨   The *document window* is where you type your text.

⇨   The *shadow cursor* shows where you can move the insertion point.

⇨   The *mouse pointer* lets you click, double-click, or drag across objects in your document.

⇨   The *ruler* lets you change margin and tab settings. You can display the ruler by choosing View and then Ruler.

⇨   The *application bar* (formerly called the *status bar*) shows the names of the documents you have open and provides information about the current document.

? Why does a flashing arrow appear when I move the pointer?

This is the shadow cursor. The shadow cursor lets you type anywhere in the typing area, which is inside the margin guidelines. As you drag the mouse pointer across the screen, you'll notice a flashing gray cursor that indicates where the insertion point will be when you click. Along with the shadow cursor is an arrow indicating the alignment of the text. When the arrow points to the right, for example, the text will be left-aligned at the tab stop position, with characters moving to the right as you type.

If you point the mouse at the middle of the screen, the shadow cursor appears with a two-pointed arrow. Text you type will be centered between the margins. If you point the mouse at the right margin, the arrow points to the left. Text you type will be right-aligned, with text shifting to the left as you type.

Tip: *If you use the shadow cursor to drag across a blank area of your document, a QuickMenu appears. Use this menu to insert a graphic, text box, or table into the box you've drawn. Try it!*

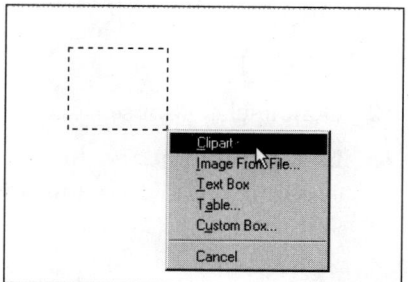

 **Warning:**   *The shadow cursor is one of those "Hey look at me" tools that marketing people love to hype. However, be aware that clicking a blank area with the shadow cursor inserts a bunch of paragraph marks called hard returns in your document, and it may insert several tab stops as well. If you overuse the shadow cursor feature, you may find these extra hard returns and tabs frustrating. Use the shadow cursor sparingly, such as for title pages and letters.*

? The shadow cursor bugs me. How do I turn it off?

To turn off the shadow cursor in WordPerfect 8, choose View and then Shadow Cursor.

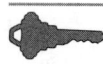 **Note:**   *To turn off the shadow cursor in WordPerfect 7, choose Edit, Preferences, Display, and then Shadow Cursor. This procedure works only with the version of WordPerfect 7 included with Corel Office Professional 7 or the updated version of WordPerfect 7 included on the Corel Care CD.*

? When I use my mouse, occasionally I can't run an application or select anything by double-clicking. Is something wrong with my mouse?

One possible reason that your double-click didn't work is that you moved the mouse between the two clicks, which means that Windows thinks you're clicking in two different places. Hold the mouse still while you double-click.

Another possible reason that your double-click didn't work is that double-clicking works only if the time between the two clicks falls within a certain range. If you click slowly, you may want to increase the double-click interval in the Control Panel. Here's how:

1. Click Start on the Windows taskbar and choose Settings and then Control Panel.

2. Double-click Mouse.

3. Look for and then set the option that controls your double-click speed (the location of this option varies according to your mouse software).

How do I turn off the margin guidelines?

To turn off the margin guidelines, follow these steps:

1. Choose View and then Guidelines.

2. Deselect Margins and click OK.

The options I need aren't on the standard toolbar. Can I select different toolbars?

WordPerfect 8 includes 15 different toolbars that you can choose from, as shown in Figure 3-2. These toolbars include buried treasures that can help you get your work done. For example, the Shipping Macros toolbar includes options for creating graphic watermarks, paragraph breaks, and reverse text (white on black), as well as for converting footnotes to endnotes and endnotes to footnotes. Other toolbars, such as the Outline Tools and Legal toolbars, help you finish specific tasks. To select a different toolbar, follow these steps:

1. Right-click the toolbar. Then select a different toolbar.

2. When you're finished with the toolbar, right-click the toolbar and select it again to turn it off.

Tip: *To find out what a button on a toolbar does, hold the pointer over the button for a moment and read the QuickTip.*

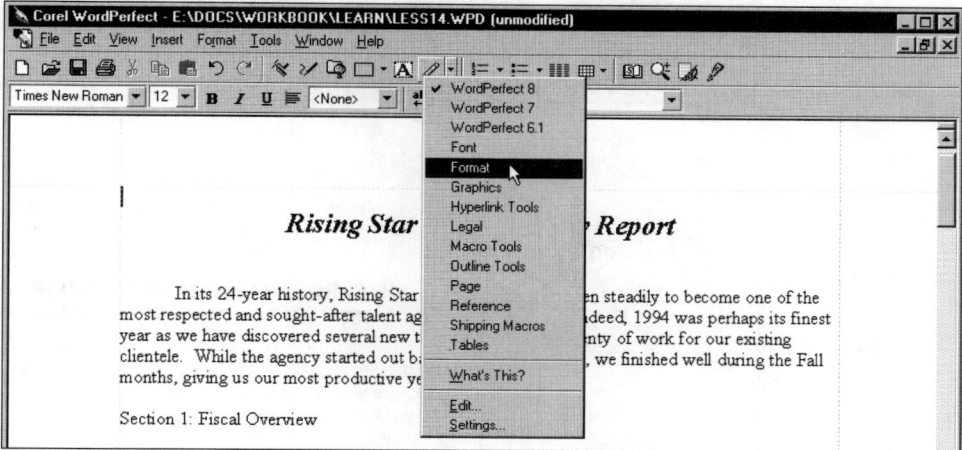

Figure 3-2.   Select the toolbar that helps you get your work done

? I turned off the main toolbar, and now there's nothing to right-click. How do I get the toolbar back?

Here's how to display the toolbar again:

1. Choose View and then Toolbars.
2. Select WordPerfect 8 and click OK.

? What happened to the QuickSpots that appeared in WordPerfect 7?

The addition of property bars in WordPerfect 8 made QuickSpots (also called hot spots) redundant. In most cases, the same options that were available using the QuickSpots in WordPerfect 7 appear on the property bars and QuickMenus in WordPerfect 8. The content of the property bar automatically changes as you work. For example, if you click a graphic, the property bar includes options that help you edit the graphic. You can also right-click text, graphics, headers, bars, or just about anything else on the screen to display a QuickMenu full of options, as shown in Figure 3-3. In most cases, these QuickMenus contain the same options found when you clicked the QuickSpot in WordPerfect 7.

Property bar ———▶

QuickMenu ———▶

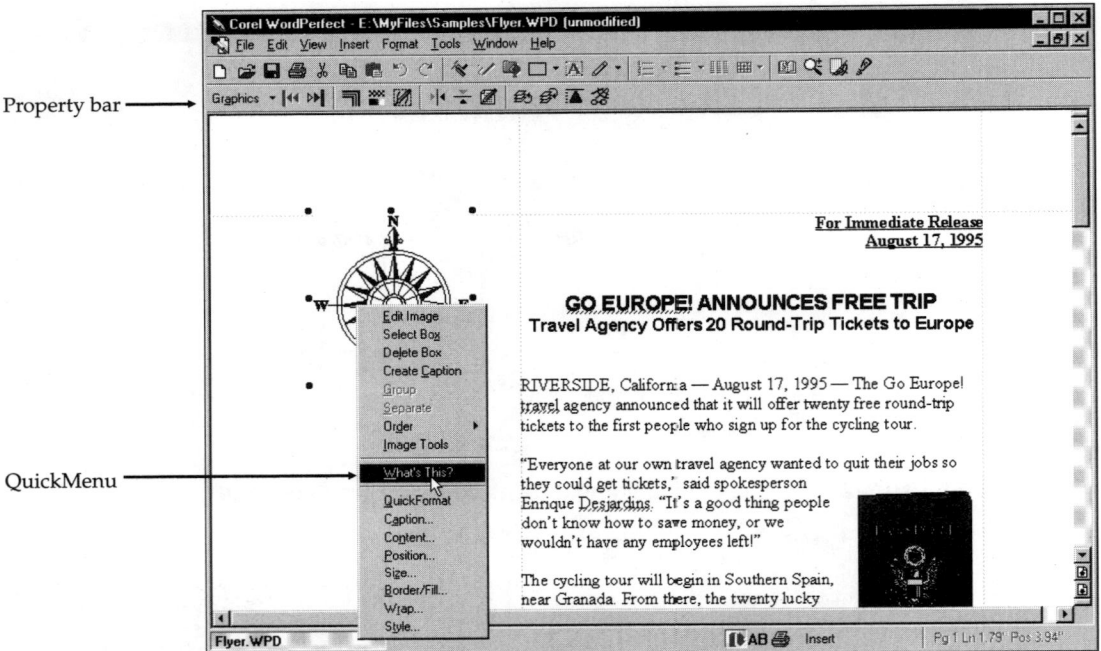

Figure 3-3.   Right-click any item in your document to bring up a QuickMenu

❓ How do I view two documents at the same time?

You can view two or more documents at the same time by choosing Window and then Cascade, Tile Top to Bottom, or Tile Side by Side. Then just click the document window you want to work in, as shown in Figure 3-4.

Note: *If you drag the title bar off the screen, you can't use the mouse to drag it to a new location. Click the window and then press* ALT-SPACEBAR *and choose Move. Use the arrow keys to move the window.*

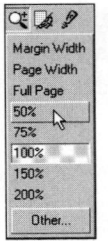

❓ My text doesn't fit on the screen. How can I view it all without changing the margins?

You can change the magnification of your document to see more or less of your text. To zoom in close, you can choose 200% magnification. If you want to see most of the text on the page, you can choose 50%

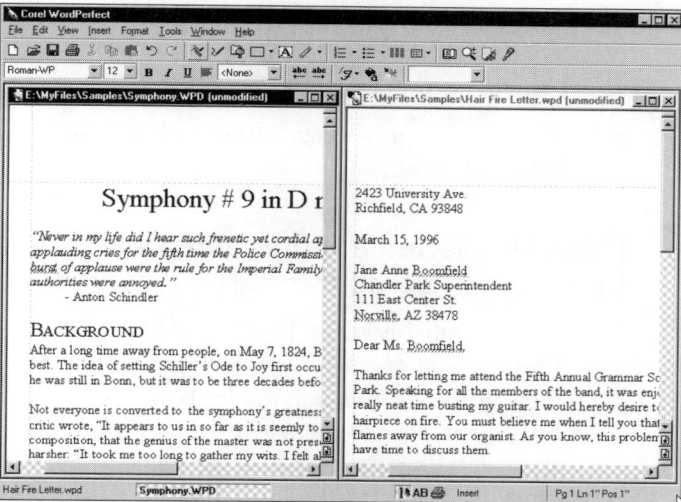

Figure 3-4.   Two documents tiled side by side

Switching Between Documents and Applications

You can open up to nine documents at one time in WordPerfect. There are three basic ways to switch between open documents:

⇨ Choose Window on the menu bar and then click the document you want to switch to.

⇨ Click the name of the document on the application bar at the bottom of the screen.

⇨ Use keyboard shortcuts. Press CTRL-F6 or CTRL-SHIFT-F6 to cycle backward and forward through the open documents.

Sometimes you may want to work in several applications at once. Here are three different ways to switch between applications:

⇨ On the taskbar, click any open application you want to use.

⇨ Hold down the ALT key and press TAB to cycle through the open applications. Release the ALT key when you get to the application you want.

⇨ Press CTRL-ESC to display the Start menu. Then select the application you want to run.

magnification. To change the magnification, click Zoom on the toolbar. Then select the magnification you want.

Tip: *You can also view two pages at the same time by choosing View and then Two Pages.*

? I know I inserted a footer and a watermark, but I can't see them when I scroll through my document. Why not?

You're probably using Draft view instead of Page or Two Page view. Page view shows how the document will look when printed. Draft view attempts to match the fonts you have chosen and displays the document close to the way it will look when printed, but it does not show certain page elements such as footers, headers, and watermarks. Working in Draft view is often faster than working in Page view. To see all the elements in your document, choose Page view from the View menu.

? How can I remove all the bars and work on a clean screen?

When you're writing, sometimes you just want to type without any menus, toolbars, scroll bars, or anything but an old-fashioned clean slate. To remove all the bars and work on a blank screen, choose View and then Hide Bars. When you want to display the bars again, press ESC.

? How do I display spaces, tabs, paragraph marks, and other nonprinting characters?

To know exactly how many spaces, tabs, and hard returns you've inserted, you can view nonprinting characters as shown in Figure 3-5. To do this, click View and then Show ¶.

Tip: *You can also specify which characters are displayed when you choose Show ¶. Choose Tools and then Settings, double-click Display, click the Symbols tab, and then select the symbols you want to display.*

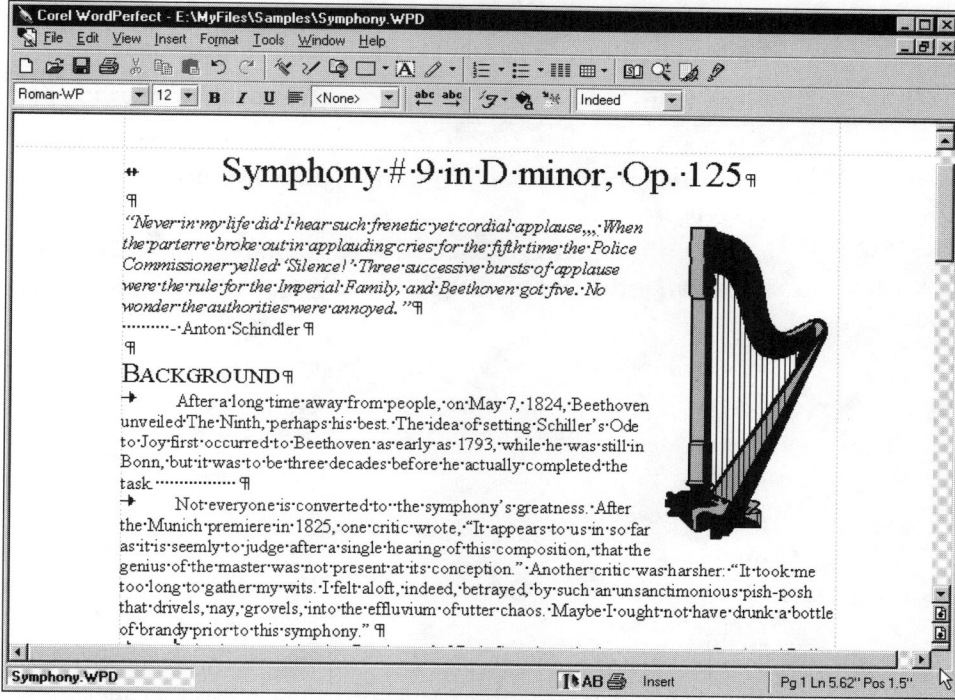

Figure 3-5.   You can view nonprinting characters such as spaces, tabs, and hard
returns

? **When I scroll using the vertical scroll bar and then start typing, the insertion point goes back to its original location. Why?**

Actually, the insertion point does not return to its previous location. When you scroll using the vertical scroll bars, the insertion point stays in the same place. After you scroll, remember to click where you want to begin typing.

? **Pressing PAGE DOWN doesn't take me to the next page. How do I move down a page?**

Press ALT-PAGE DOWN to move down a page. If you prefer keeping your hands on the keyboard, take a look at Table 3-1.

Table 3-1.   Keystrokes for Moving Through a Document

Press this:	To move the insertion point here:
CTRL-HOME	Beginning of document
CTRL-HOME, CTRL-HOME	Beginning of document before codes
CTRL-END	End of document
HOME	Beginning of line
HOME, HOME	Beginning of line before codes
END	End of line
PAGE DOWN	Bottom of screen
PAGE UP	Top of screen
ALT-END	Bottom of page
ALT-HOME	Top of page
ALT-PAGE DOWN	Top of next page
ALT-PAGE UP	Top of previous page
CTRL-RIGHT ARROW	Next word
CTRL-LEFT ARROW	Previous word
CTRL-DOWN ARROW	Top of next paragraph
CTRL-UP ARROW	Top of previous paragraph
CTRL-G	Go To dialog box

In WordPerfect for DOS, I could press CTRL-HOME twice to return to the cursor location. How can I return to the previous position of the insertion point in WordPerfect for Windows?

Unfortunately, WordPerfect for Windows doesn't have a keystroke that's quite as slick. Here's how you can return to the previous insertion point location:

1. Press CTRL-G to display the Go To dialog box.

2. Choose Last Position and click OK.

Tip: *You can create a keystroke macro that returns you to the previous position. For more information on creating macros, see Chapter 13.*

? Text scrolls too quickly when I hold down the down arrow key. Can I slow it down?

You can change the repeat rate of keystrokes from the Windows Control Panel.

1. Click Start on the Windows taskbar. Choose Settings and then Control Panel.

2. Double-click Keyboard.

3. Move the slider to select a slower repeat rate.

? I used to use WordPerfect for DOS. What can I do to get used to the new Windows keystrokes?

When switching from DOS to Windows, you need to get used to using the mouse, or you'll be frustrated (you may be frustrated anyway). It's time to learn new methods, many of which you'll come to prefer to your old DOS ways. Table 3-2 lists some of the more useful keystrokes in WordPerfect.

? WordPerfect 6.1 displayed shortcut keystrokes on the menus. How do I display shortcut keystrokes on the menus in WordPerfect 8?

Some menu commands have been assigned shortcut keystrokes. For example, pressing CTRL-P opens the Print dialog box, and pressing CTRL-S saves the document. Here's how to display these shortcut keystrokes next to the menu commands:

1. Choose Tools and then Settings. Then double-click Environment.

2. Click the Interface tab.

3. Choose Display Shortcut Keys.

WORKING WITH TEXT

? I made a mess of my document, but I don't know what I did. What can I do?

First, save the file with a different name just in case something went wrong. Next, take advantage of WordPerfect's Undo feature. By

Table 3-2.   Common WordPerfect Keystrokes

Keystroke	What It Does
ALT-F4	Exits WordPerfect.
CTRL-F4	Closes document.
CTRL-S	Saves document that's already been saved.
F3	Saves document with a different name or format (Save As).
CTRL-O	Opens file.
CTRL-P	Opens the Print dialog box.
CTRL-SHIFT-P	Prints document.
F8	Begins text selection (block).
CTRL-W	Lets you insert symbols.
CTRL-C	Copies text to clipboard.
CTRL-X	Cuts (moves) text to clipboard.
CTRL-V	Pastes text from clipboard.
F1	Displays help.
SHIFT-F1	Displays context help.
ESC	Cancels operation.
CTRL-BACKSPACE	Deletes current word.
CTRL-DELETE	Deletes rest of line.
CTRL-SHIFT-DELETE	Deletes rest of page.
CTRL-Z	Undoes action.

choosing Edit and then Undo, you can reverse the last editing change you made to your document. If choosing Undo the first time doesn't solve the problem, continue to choose Undo until the problem is fixed.

? What are the first steps I should take when a problem occurs and what can I do to help prevent problems in the first place?

When working with computers, things can—and often do—go wrong. Here are some simple ways you can prevent or overcome problems with WordPerfect:

⇨ Save often. Get into the habit of pressing CTRL-S every few minutes. It doesn't hurt anything to save the document repeatedly, and if your three-year-old child decides to unplug your computer, you won't lose much work. If you think that

Common Mistakes to Avoid

For you typists who are making the switch to computers, here are some common pitfalls to avoid:

⇨ Don't press ENTER at the end of every line in a paragraph. Let text wrap automatically and press ENTER only when you finish the paragraph.

⇨ Don't use the spacebar to indent the beginning of a paragraph or to center text. Your work may look okay at first, but if you go back and edit your document, things may get messy. To indent the first line of a paragraph, press TAB. To center a line, place the insertion point at the beginning of the line and choose Format, Line, and then Center.

⇨ Don't press the ENTER key several times to move to the next page. Again, your document will look okay at first, but after you edit your text, you'll have to deal with unwanted blank lines. Instead, press CTRL-ENTER to insert a page break.

⇨ Don't turn off your computer until after you exit WordPerfect and shut down properly. Exiting WordPerfect properly gives you a chance to save any document you're working on, and it does some other clean up work behind the scenes.

⇨ Don't rely on the Automatic Backup feature to save your files. Although Automatic Backup saves a copy of the file you're working on every 10 minutes or so, the surest way to prevent lost work is to get in the habit of choosing File and then Save (or pressing CTRL-S) every few minutes.

⇨ Don't type page numbers manually. If you manually insert page numbers at the top or bottom of the page, the numbers may move to a new position when you edit the text. Instead, use the Page Numbering feature (choose Format, Page, and then Numbering) or insert the page number in a header or footer.

⇨ Don't press TAB at the beginning of every line in a paragraph you want to indent. Instead, press F7 to indent.

⇨ If you want to break a long word at the end of a line, don't press the hyphen key followed by a space. If you do this, editing changes may force the broken parts of the word onto the same line, leading to oddities such as "misan- thropic." Instead, place the insertion point where you want the hyphen to appear and press CTRL-SHIFT— to insert a soft hyphen that will appear only if the word needs to be broken.

something may be seriously wrong with your document—for instance, it is missing text or contains strange characters—choose File and then Save As and save the document under a different name. If your original file is corrupt, saving the document with a different name may fix the problem.

⇨ Take advantage of Undo. If you make a mistake, such as deleting the wrong text, choose Edit and then Undo. If your formatting becomes out of whack, choose Edit and Undo several times until the document reverts to a satisfactory state. To look at your last editing changes, choose Edit and then Undo/Redo History. Click the last editing change you want to undo and then choose Undo.

⇨ Track down troubles with Reveal Codes. When a formatting problem occurs, choose View and then Reveal Codes to display the formatting codes. For more information on using Reveal Codes, see "Reveal Codes" in Chapter 10.

⇨ Avoid Typeover mode. By pressing the INSERT key, you toggle between Insert mode and Typeover mode. When you're in Typeover mode, text you type replaces any text following the insertion point. If you notice that typing gobbles up the following text, choose Undo and then press INSERT. The application bar at the bottom of the screen indicates whether you're in Insert or Typeover mode.

⇨ If pressing keys on the keyboard doesn't do anything, ask a few questions before you restart your computer: Is a dialog box prompting for something? Is the WordPerfect menu bar highlighted? Try pressing ESC to see if that gets you out of trouble.

? Pressing BACKSPACE takes too long to delete a paragraph. Is there a quicker way to delete text?

You can highlight, or *select*, text you've already typed so you can delete, edit, or move it, as shown in Figure 3-6. If you're switching from WordPerfect for DOS, selecting text is the same thing as *blocking* text.

There are several ways to quickly select words, sentences, and paragraphs in WordPerfect:

⇨ Select a word by double-clicking it.

⇨ Select a sentence by triple-clicking it or by clicking next to the sentence in the left margin. Drag down to select additional sentences.

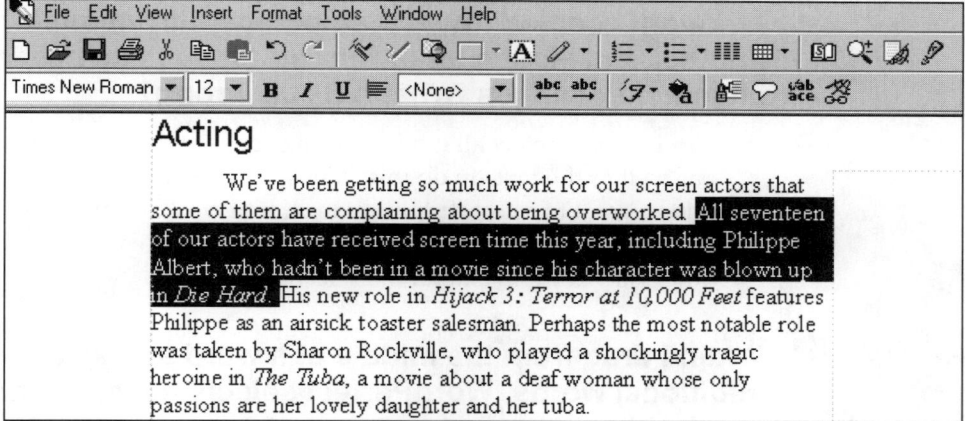

Figure 3-6.   Select text to delete, edit, or move it

⇨ Select a paragraph by quadruple-clicking it or by double-clicking next to the paragraph in the left margin.

⇨ Choose Edit, Select, and then click Sentence, Paragraph, Page, or All. You can also right-click in the left margin and choose a selection option.

? I don't like selecting text with the mouse. How do I select text using keystrokes?

Place the insertion point where you want to begin selecting text. Then hold down the SHIFT key and use the arrow keys to select text. You can also press F8 and use the arrow keys to extend the selection.

You can use the SHIFT key along with other keystroke combinations to extend the selection. For example, pressing SHIFT-HOME selects all the text between the insertion point and the beginning of the line, and pressing CTRL-SHIFT-END selects all the text from the insertion point to the end of the document.

? I selected a couple of paragraphs so I could move them, but now they're gone. What happened?

Anything you type when text is selected will replace selected text. Choose Edit and then Undo.

 *Tip:*   *To cancel a selection, click anywhere outside the selection.*

? **I thought I copied my entire document from one window to another, but I lost a lot of formatting such as headers and alignment changes. What did I do wrong?**

You need to select all the formatting codes at the top of the document as well as the text. To do this, choose Edit, Select, and then All. If you don't want to select the entire document, you can press CTRL-HOME twice to move the insertion point above the codes. Then hold down the SHIFT key and extend the selection.

? **When I drag from the middle of a word and select additional words, WordPerfect selects the entire first word. How do I select just part of a word?**

Ordinarily, text is selected word by word. Hold down ALT while you drag to select character by character. If you prefer selecting character by character all the time, do this:

1. Choose Tools and then Settings. Then double-click Environment.

2. Deselect Select Whole Words Instead of Characters and then click OK.

? **I want to select only the middle column in a table created with tabs. Is there a way to select only part of a paragraph?**

1. Drag from the first character where you want the selection to begin to the last character in the tabular column where you want the selection to end.

2. Choose Edit, Select, and then Tabular Columns.

Event	Time	Location	Sponsor
Lunch	Noon	Main Pavillion	Jeremy Candies
Canoe Racing	11:00	Easter Lake	Carter Kayaks
Horseshoe toss	1:30	Horseshoe pits	Schmaltz Beer
Horseback riding	All day	Pine Meadows Park	Jeremy Candies

 ***Tip:***   *You can also select half of a paragraph. Drag from the upper-right corner of the block to the lower-left corner. Then choose Edit, Select, and Rectangle.*

 ### When I select a word, sometimes it gets moved for no reason. What happened?

You actually moved the text with the mouse using an operation called *drag-and-drop*. This operation works just as you might expect. You select text and then drag that selection to a different place, where you drop it, as shown in Figure 3-7. If you want to copy the text while using the drag-and-drop technique, hold down CTRL.

Tip: *Choose Edit and then Undo if you drop the text in the wrong area.*

When I try to use the mouse to drag text from one document to another, I can't scroll because I'm holding down the mouse. What am I doing wrong?

Although you can drag and drop text from one document to another, you have more control if you copy and paste text using the clipboard. Nevertheless, here are two different ways you can drag and drop text across documents:

⇨ Open both documents. Then choose Window and Tile Top to Bottom (or Tile Side by Side). Before you drag and drop the text, scroll down to make sure you can drop the text without scrolling. Then select the text and drag it from one window and drop it in the other.

⇨ Open both documents. Then select the text in one document and drag it to the application bar at the bottom of the screen. As you

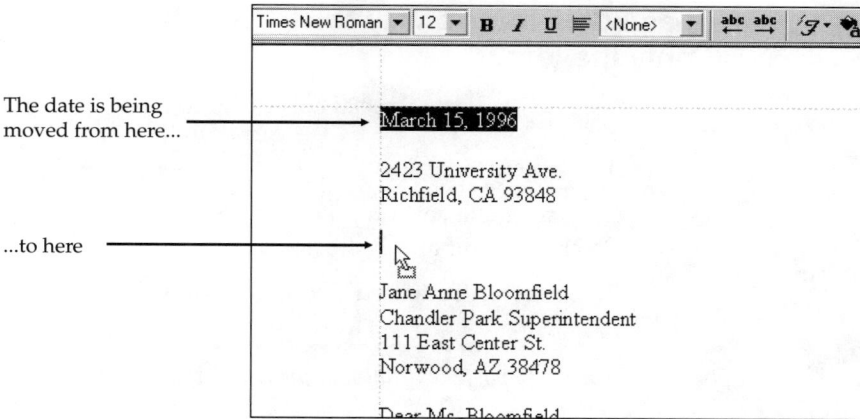

Figure 3-7.   Drag and drop text

hold the pointer over the document name on the application bar, the window of that document becomes active, letting you drop the text in that document window. If you need to scroll to a different location, hold the pointer just below the toolbar to scroll up or just above the horizontal scroll bar to scroll down.

I want to copy text from several paragraphs all at once, but pressing CTRL-C just replaces the previous copy. Can I copy more than one selection at a time?

Although you cannot select more than one block of text at a time, you can use WordPerfect's Append feature to move multiple blocks of text or graphics, in order, to another position. Here's how:

1. Select the first item you want to copy. Then choose Edit and Cut (or Copy).

2. Select the next item you want to copy. Then choose Edit and Append.

3. Continue to append items to the clipboard. Then move the insertion point where you want the text to appear and choose Edit and then Paste.

Warning: *If you choose Edit and Copy (or Cut) instead of Append, the clipboard contents will be replaced, and you'll have to start over. You may need to choose Undo several times to restore your cut text.*

When I cut or copy text from one place to another, I don't want any of the font or attribute codes or styles to be pasted. Is there a way to strip out the formatting and paste only the text?

Yes. Use the Paste Special command to paste text without attributes.

1. Copy the text.

2. Place the insertion point where you want the text to appear. Then choose Edit and Paste Special.

3. Select Unformatted Text in the list box and click OK.

Tip: *To paste text without formatting, you can also press CTRL-SHIFT-V.*

? How do I delete a page in a document?

Move the insertion point to the page you want to delete. Then choose Edit, Select, and Page. Press DELETE. You can also move the insertion point to the top of the page and press CTRL-SHIFT-DELETE.

Tip: *You can press* CTRL-BACKSPACE *to delete the current word. Press* CTRL-DELETE *to delete everything from the insertion point to the end of the line.*

TEXT FORMATTING

All about Fonts

A font consists of a *typeface*, such as Courier or Times New Roman; a *size*, such as 10 point or 12 point (72 points equal 1 inch); and *appearance*, such as regular, bold, or italics. Bold, italics, underline, and other font characteristics are also referred to as *attributes*. You can use either *monospaced* fonts or *proportionally spaced* fonts in your document.

```
Monospaced fonts (such as Courier New) use
the same amount of horizontal space for each
character in the font.
```

Proportionally spaced fonts vary the amount of horizontal space for each character in the font.

As a general rule, you should use proportionally spaced fonts in your document if you want it to look like it's been typeset. However, monospaced fonts are often used in special circumstances such as in legal documents.

Fonts can also be classified as *serif* or *sans serif*. The letters of serif fonts have curved edges, like this:

Times New Roman is a serif font.

The letters of sans serif fonts have straight edges, like this:

Arial is a sans serif font.

Sans serif fonts are commonly used for larger text, such as titles and headings. Serif fonts are commonly used for body text.

I changed the font, and now my document is all Greek to me. What did I do wrong?

Some fonts, such as Symbol, Parties MT, and Almanac MT, turn the characters into symbols. Before you select a font, look at the font beforehand to make sure your text will still be readable. Here are some common ways to change the font in your document:

⇨ Select the text you want to change. Then select an option from the property bar. When you select a font, a representation of that font appears, as shown in Figure 3-8.

⇨ Select the text you want to change and choose Format and then Font to open the Font dialog box. The Font dialog box is useful when you want to add several attributes to the text, or when you want to select a special appearance attribute, such as double underline, subscript, or superscript.

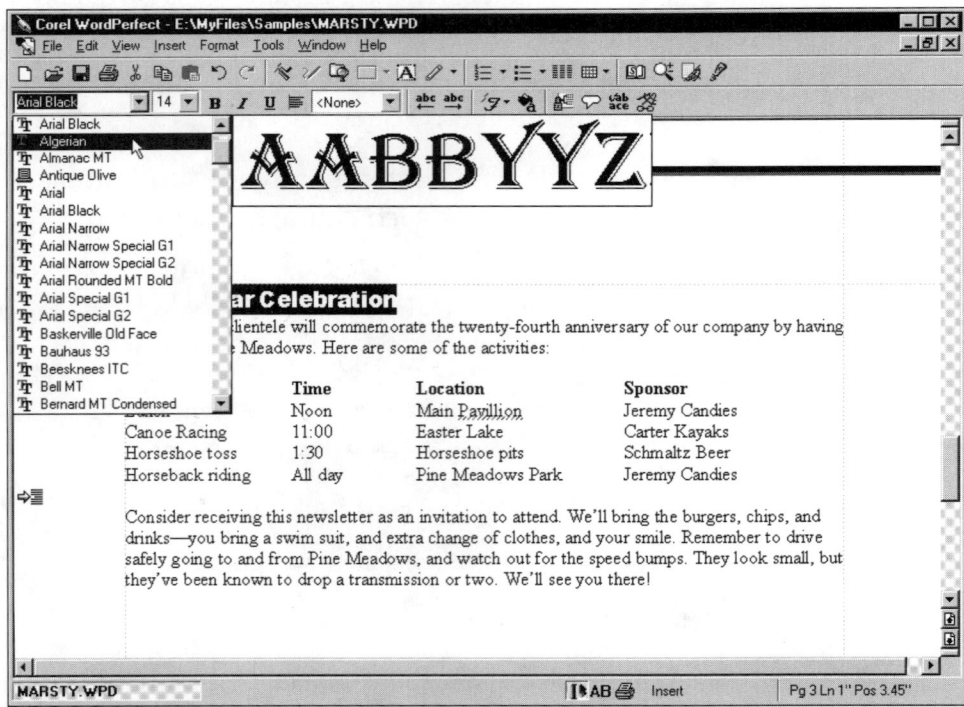

Figure 3-8.   Select a font from the property bar

Tip: *When you want to make a word bold, italic, or underlined, you don't need to select the word. For example, to make a word bold, click the word and press* CTRL-B.

When I underline text, the spaces are also underlined. Is it possible not to have spaces underlined between words?

Here's how you can remove the underlining from spaces between underlined words:

1. Move the insertion point to the top of the document.
2. Choose Format and then Font.
3. Select Text Only from the Underline pop-up list.

Tip: *If you want to use Text Only as the default option in all future documents you create, place the codes in the Current Document Style (also called the Initial Codes). Choose File, Document, and Current Document Style and select Use as Default. Then follow steps 1 through 3.*

What is the difference between the Full and All justification options?

Alignment, also referred to as *justification*, determines how text is positioned between the margins. WordPerfect provides six options for aligning text between the margins, as shown in Figure 3-9.

⇨ *Left* alignment creates an even left margin with an uneven, or ragged, right margin.

⇨ *Center* alignment centers the text between the left and right margins, with uneven left and right margins.

⇨ *Flush Right* alignment creates even right margins with an uneven left margin.

⇨ *Flush Right with Dot Leaders* inserts periods in the blank space to the left of right-aligned text.

⇨ *Full* justification adds spaces to the lines of text, except lines ending with hard returns when you press ENTER, so lines are aligned evenly on both the left and the right. This option does not affect the last line of the paragraph.

Left alignment

Center alignment

Flush right

Flush right with
Dot Leaders

Full

All

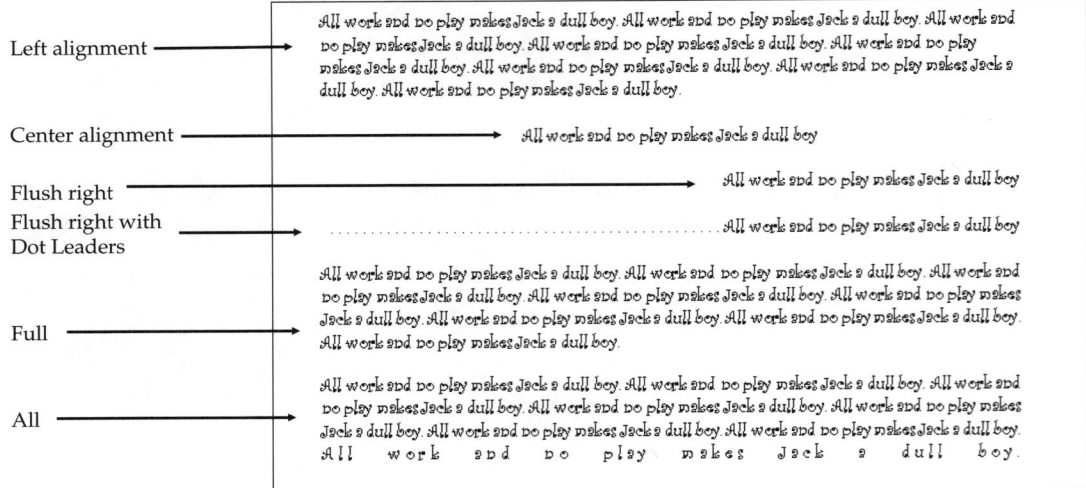

Figure 3-9.   Change the alignment in your documents

⇨   *All* justification adds spaces to align every line with the left and
right margins, including the last line of paragraphs, titles, and
other single-line paragraphs.

? I chose Format, Justification, and Center to center a heading, but now the rest of my document is centered, too. How do I center just a single line?

You can use either the property bar or menu bar to change the
alignment of text. However, there are differences between the two
main methods for changing the alignment: line formatting and
justification.

Line formatting affects individual lines or paragraphs. For
example, if you choose Format, Line, and Center and then type text,
the centering ends when you press ENTER. If you want to center
existing text, place the insertion point at the beginning of the line
and choose Format, Line, and Center (or press SHIFT-F7).

Justification, on the other hand, functions similarly to other types
of formatting such as margins and tab settings. When you click in a
paragraph and choose Format, Justification, and Center, all text is
centered until the end of the document or the next justification code.
If you are typing new text, centering remains in effect even after you
press ENTER, and you need to choose Format, Justification, and Left,

for example, to return to left justification. However, if you select text before you choose a justification option, the formatting affects only the paragraph(s) selected.

Tip: *Selecting an alignment option from the Justification button on the property bar also changes the justification. Here are the shortcut keystrokes for justification: Left* (CTRL-L), *Right* (CTRL-R), *Center* (CTRL-E), *and Full* (CTRL-J).

Pressing F7 and ALT-F7 doesn't work in a footer. How do I use left, center, and right alignment on a single line in a footer?

For some reason, these keystrokes don't work sometimes when you're in a header or footer. Instead, you need to use the menu commands. Here's how:

1. Place the insertion point on a blank line and type the text to be left-aligned.

2. Choose Format, Line, and Center and then type the text to be centered.

3. Choose Format, Line, and Flush Right and then type the text to be right-aligned.

Tip: *If you want to insert dot leaders between the words with different types of justification, press* SHIFT-F7 *twice to create centered text with dot leaders. Then press* ALT-F7 *twice to create flush right text with dot leaders.*

Bill Clampett...................	July 12, 1998	Page 42

Can I use justification to create signature lines at the bottom of a letter?

Yes. WordPerfect has a special option called End Centering/Alignment that lets you do just that. Here's how:

1. Place the insertion point on a blank line and choose Format, Line, and Center.

2. Choose Format, Line, and Other Codes.

3. Select End Centering/Alignment and choose Insert.

4. Type the text (such as **Sincerely,**).

When I switch from left justification to full justification, the new justification changes the way my lines wrap. Is there a way to disable the spacing adjustment caused by the justification.

Yes. You can change the hyphenation zone to 0. After you do so, all words should stay on the same line regardless of your justification choice. Follow these steps:

1. Choose Tools, Language, and Hyphenation (in WordPerfect 7 choose Format, Line, and Hyphenation).

2. Type **0** in the Percent Left and Percent Right text boxes and click OK.

How do I set full justification as the default format for every document?

Although you cannot change the default justification for documents you've already created, you can change the justification for all new documents you create.

1. Choose File, Document, and Current Document Style.

2. From the menu bar in the Styles Editor dialog box, choose Format, Justification, and Full.

3. Choose Use as Default and then click OK.

4. Choose Yes to have the style affect all new documents.

 Note: *In WordPerfect 7, choose Format, Document, and Initial Codes Style.*

When I press ENTER to center a document on a page, subsequent editing changes its position. How do I center a document on a page so that it stays that way for good?

When you center pages vertically, you can center only the current page, or you can center the current page and all subsequent pages.

When writing a letter, for instance, you usually want to center only the first page.

1. Place the insertion point on the first page and choose Format, Page, and Center.

2. Select Current Page and click OK.

Note: *If you're using Draft view, you cannot see a vertically centered page. To see the centered page, choose View and then Page.*

❓ I changed the margins, but only one paragraph was affected. How do I change the margins for the entire document?

In most word processors, margins affect the entire page. However, WordPerfect is flexible enough to let you change margins for individual paragraphs, as shown in Figure 3-10.

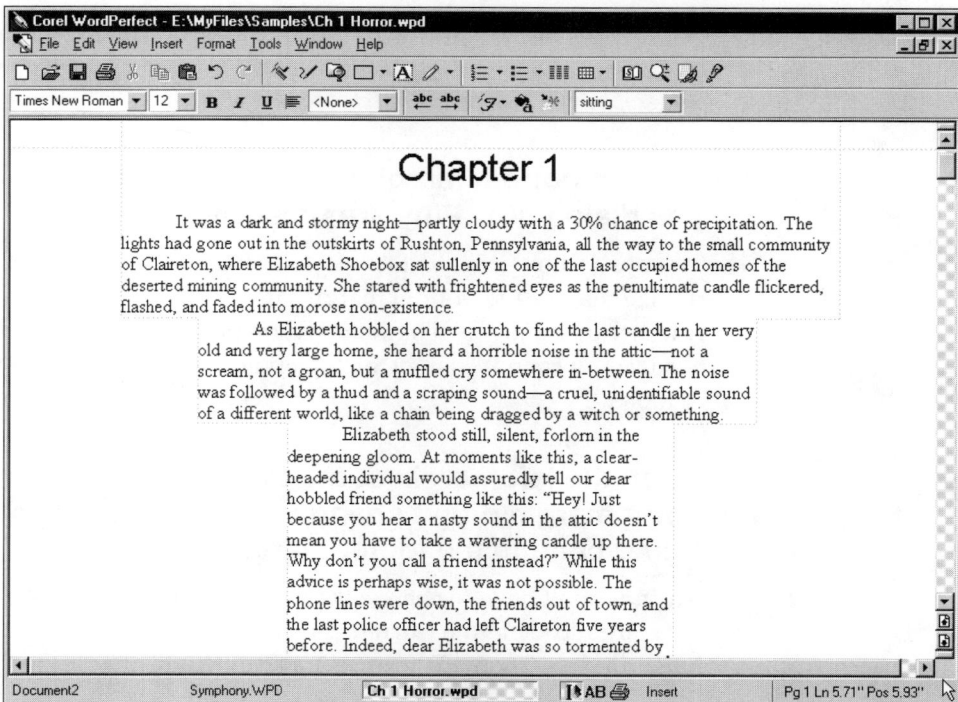

Figure 3-10.   You can change the margins for individual paragraphs

 *Note: When you change the margins, WordPerfect inserts a code at the beginning of the paragraph. The margin change affects that paragraph and all subsequent paragraphs until the end of the document or the next margin code. However, if you select text, the margin change affects only the paragraphs in which the text is selected.*

The quickest way to change the margins is to drag the margin guidelines or the margin indicators on the ruler.

⇨ To use the guidelines for the top and bottom margins, you must be in Page or Two Page view. Place the mouse pointer over one of the margin guidelines until the pointer changes to a two-headed arrow. As you drag a guideline, WordPerfect displays a QuickStatus box that shows the margin position relative to the edge of the paper.

⇨ To enter specific margin settings, place the insertion point where you want the margin change to begin and choose Format and then Margins to display the Margins dialog box. From there, you can specify the left, right, top, and bottom margins.

 *Note: If you select text before you drag the margin guidelines, only the paragraphs in which text is selected will be affected by the margin change.*

❓ The top and bottom margins are not available in the Margins dialog box. Why are these items dimmed?

One possibility is that text is selected. If text is selected, you cannot change the top and bottom margins using the Margins dialog box. Another possibility is that the insertion point is in either a footer or header. You cannot change the top and bottom margins in a header or footer.

❓ I changed the left margin at the top of the document, but the footer margin didn't change. Do I have to go into the footer and change the footer margin?

No, you don't have to change the margin in the footer. Instead, place the margin code in the Current Document Style (formerly called Initial Codes). Then the formatting change will affect other formatting elements such as footnotes, headers and footers, and watermarks. Here's what you need to do:

1. Choose File, Document, and Current Document Style.

2. From the menu in the Styles Editor dialog box, choose Format and then Margins.

3. Specify the margin changes. Then click OK.

4. Make sure Use as Default is *not* selected, unless you want the change to affect all new documents. Then click OK.

 ***Note:***   *In WordPerfect 7, choose Format, Document, and Initial Codes Style.*

I added a page number at the bottom of the page, but I still want the text to end one inch from the bottom of the page. Can I do that?

If you still want your text at the bottom of the page to have a one-inch margin after you insert a page number or footer, change the bottom margin to a smaller amount, such as 0.6". Depending on the size of your page number or footer, you may have to adjust the bottom margin setting up or down.

I changed the line height, and now my text overlaps. What's wrong?

When you change the line height to a fixed value by choosing Format, Line, and Height, the line height will remain constant regardless of how large or small the font is. If you select a large font with a small line height, your text will overlap. Unlike fixed line height, line spacing is automatically adjusted to work with the current font size. Unless you're concerned with subtle design touches, don't use the line height option—use line spacing instead. Here's how:

1. Place the insertion point where you want the new line spacing to begin.

2. Choose Format, Line, and Spacing.

3. Type the amount of spacing (such as 2) you want and click OK.

? ### I want to use 1.3 spacing within paragraphs and double-spacing between paragraphs. How do I do that?

This is a common request of designers who want to add a subtle design touch, as shown in Figure 3-11. The Paragraph Format dialog box includes options that let you change the spacing between paragraphs so that you don't have to rely on pressing ENTER to create spacing.

1. To change spacing *within* paragraphs, choose Format, Line, and Spacing. Then specify the amount of spacing (such as **1.3**).

2. To change spacing *between* paragraphs, choose Format, Paragraph, and Format. Then in the Number of Lines text box specify the spacing (such as **2**) you want and click OK.

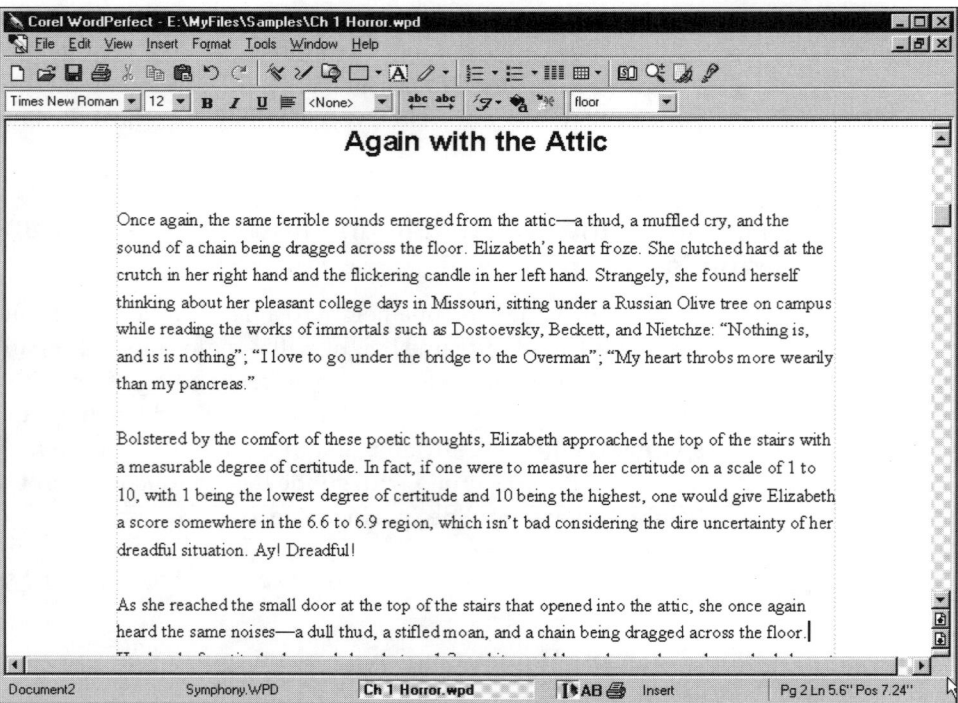

Figure 3-11.   In addition to changing line spacing, you can change the spacing between paragraphs

? **Why do several lines move when I press TAB?**

QuickIndent helps you indent a paragraph after you have typed several lines. When you press TAB at the beginning of any line in a paragraph except the first, you indent the entire paragraph. If the first line of the paragraph does not begin with a tab, that line is not indented, creating a hanging indent. If you press TAB in the middle of the first line, the rest of the paragraph will be indented at that point.

Note: *To turn off QuickIndent, choose Tools and then QuickCorrect. Then click the Format-As-You-Go tab. Deselect QuickIndent and click OK.*

? **I'm writing a book, and I'm tired of pressing TAB at the beginning of every paragraph. Any suggestions?**

You can use the First Line Indent option to automatically indent paragraphs. Here's how:

1. Choose Format, Paragraph, and Format.

2. Specify the distance (such as **0.5"**) in the First Line Indent text box. Then click OK.

? **There is too much space between the margin and the tab indent. How do I change the location of tabs?**

Tab stops, also called *tab settings*, control the distance moved when you press the TAB key, and they can also affect the way paragraphs are indented. For example, you can set tab stops that align characters on the right, that align characters on the decimal point, and that center text at the tab setting. You can also use these same tab stops with dot leaders. Figure 3-12 shows some of the tab settings.

	LEFT	CENTER	RIGHT	DECIMAL
	Ben	Ben	Ben	67.24
	Alice	Alice	Alice	4.878
	Ignacio	Ignacio	Ignacio	323.3
	Ben	Ben	Ben	67.24
	Alice	Alice	Alice	4.878
	Ignacio	Ignacio	Ignacio	323.3

Figure 3-12.   Types of tab stops

There are two ways to set tabs: using the ruler and using the Tab Set dialog box.

⇨ To set a tab using the ruler, choose View and then Ruler if the ruler is not already displayed. Simply click the tab line of the ruler, just below the desired position of the tab in the ruled line. For example, to set a tab at the 1.25" marker, click as shown here:

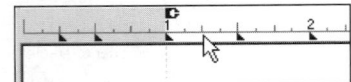

Left-aligned tabs are set by default. To choose a different type of tab stop, right-click the tab line of the ruler to see the QuickMenu, as shown in Figure 3-13. After you select the type of tab, click the tab line of the ruler to insert the tab stop. You can drag tab stops to move them, and you can drag them off the ruler to delete them.

⇨ To set a tab using the Tab Set dialog box, shown in Figure 3-14, choose Format, Line, and Tab Set. Select the tab type and position and then click Set. When you're done, click OK.

 *Note:*   *Setting tabs is similar to setting margins or line spacing. If you change the tab settings when the insertion point is in the middle of a paragraph, the tab setting affects that entire paragraph and all subsequent paragraphs until the next tab setting change. If you select text, the tab setting affects only the paragraphs in which text is selected.*

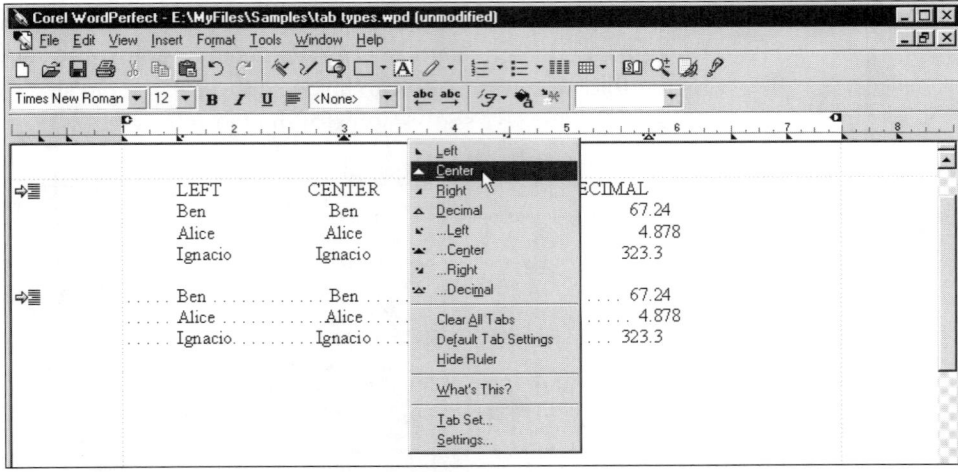

Figure 3-13.   Right-click the tab line to change the type of tab stop

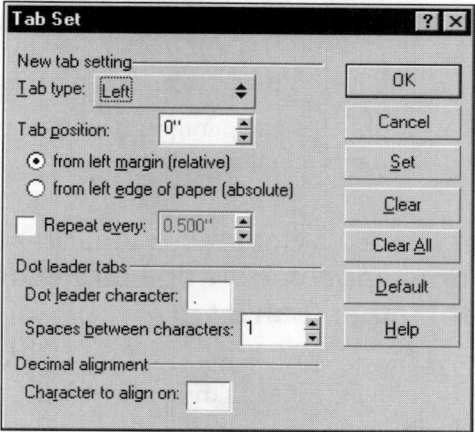

Figure 3-14.   The Tab Set dialog box

   *Tip:*   *To get more information about an option in the Tab Set dialog box, click ? (the question mark button on the title bar). Then click the option you want more information about. You can also press* SHIFT-F1 *and click an option, or you can right-click an option.*

After I changed the tab settings, an icon appeared in the left margin. What is it?

After you change your tab settings, an icon appears in the left margin. You can click this icon to display a tab line. You can use the tab line to add, delete, or change the tab stops in the text, just like you use the ruler. You can also right-click this icon and choose Cut, Copy, or Delete.

. . . . . Ben	. . . . Ben	. . . Ben.	67.24
. . . . . Alice	. . . Alice	. . . Alice.	. 4.878
. . . . . Ignacio.	. . Ignacio	. . Ignacio.	323.3

How do I return to the default tab settings?

After you make tab setting changes for a tabular column, for example, you may not want the changes to be in effect for the rest of the document. To return the tab settings to their default positions, right-click in the paragraph and then choose Default Tab Settings.

? How do I copy tab settings from one place to another?

1. Right-click the tab icon in the left margin and choose Copy.

2. Right-click the paragraph where you want the tab settings to be copied and choose Paste.

? After I insert a dot leader tab, pressing F7 doesn't make the dots appear. How do I create dot leaders with an indent rather than a tab?

When you create menus, agendas, and other such items, you may want to indent to a tab stop with a dot leader, as shown in Figure 3-15. Here's how:

1. If you haven't already done so, define the dot leader tab setting. Right-click the tab line on the ruler, select a tab type with a dot leader, and then click the tab bar where you want the dot leader tab to appear.

2. To indent the text to that position, press TAB, SHIFT-TAB, and then F7.

? Why does the hanging indent format end after I press the ENTER key?

In some word processors, the hanging indent is automatically reactivated for the next paragraph. When you use WordPerfect's hanging indent feature, only the current paragraph is affected.

Concert Schedule

Friday, August 6, 1998 . . . . Symphony Hall . . . . This concert will feature some of the major works of the Baroque musicians

Saturday, August 14, 1998 . . . . Palomar Collage . . . . Listen to a rousing rendition of the pieces of John Phillips Sousa

Thursday, August 26, 1998 . . . . Civic Center . . . . Hear the inspiring melodies of 20th century artists, including Ravel and David Lee Roth

Figure 3-15. You can create an indent with a dot leader

However, there are a couple of options for easily formatting multiple paragraphs.

⇨ You can apply the hanging indent to each paragraph in one step if the paragraphs are already typed. To do this, select the paragraphs for which you want to use a hanging indent and then choose Format, Paragraph, and Hanging Indent (or press CTRL-F7). Each selected paragraph will be formatted with a hanging indent.

⇨ If you'd rather have the hanging indent automatically inserted each time you press ENTER at the end of a paragraph, you can create a simple chained style. Follow these steps to create the style:

1. Choose Format, Styles, and Create.

2. In the Style Name text box, type a name such as **Hanging**. In the Description text box, type **Continuous Hanging Indent**.

3. Make sure the Enter Key Will Chain To option is selected and set to <Same Style>.

4. Click the insertion point in the Contents text box and press CTRL-F7.

5. Click OK to return to the Style List dialog box.

6. To have this style available in every document, choose Copy from the Options drop-down list, choose Default template, and click OK. Then click Close.

❓ I pressed TAB but the insertion point didn't move. Why not?

There might not be any more tab settings to the right of the insertion point. Look at the ruler to check the tab settings. If you want to restore the original tab settings, right-click the paragraph and choose Default Tab Settings.

❓ I use parentheses to display negative numbers in a tabular column. How do I align positive numbers and negative numbers in parentheses, as shown here?

WRONG	RIGHT
118	118
(43)	(43)
373	373
(1353)	(1353)

You can create this effect by using a decimal tab and changing the decimal alignment character from a period to a closing parenthesis.

1. Set the decimal tabs in your tabular columns.

2. Select the tabular columns. Then choose Format, Line, and Tab Set.

3. Choose Decimal from the Tab Type pop-up list.

4. Select the period in the Character to Align On text box. Then type a closing parenthesis to replace it.

5. Click OK.

? I changed the decimal alignment character from a period to a hyphen, but the procedure didn't work. Why not?

When typing text in your tabular columns, you need to use hard hyphens instead of normal hyphens as alignment characters.

1. Set the decimal tabs in your tabular columns.

2. Select the tabular columns. Then choose Format, Line, and Tab Set.

3. Choose Decimal from the Tab Type pop-up list.

4. Select the period in the Character to Align On text box. Then type a hyphen to replace it.

5. Click OK.

Now when typing your text in your tabular columns, press CTRL-HYPHEN to insert hard hyphens.

? Can I use one of the symbol characters as the dot leader character?

You can select a new character for the dot leaders, including characters from the character sets in the Symbols dialog box.
To select a new dot leader character, follow these steps:

1. Choose Format, Line, and Tab Set.

2. Select the existing character in the Dot Leader Character text box.

3. Type the new character; or press CTRL-W to display the Symbols dialog box, select the symbol you want, and click Insert and Close.

 **Note:**   *If you want more than one space inserted between the characters, insert that number in the Spaces between Characters text box. Click OK when you're finished.*

The new dot leader character is used from that point forward in your document whenever you insert a dot leader tab. You can also quickly insert a row of dot leaders from the insertion point to the right margin by pressing ALT-F7 twice. To insert dot leaders from the insertion point to the center of the page, press SHIFT-F7 twice.

? How do I change the size of the dots in the dot leaders? How do I change the distance between dots in the dot leader?

Changing the size of the dots in the dot leader is easy. Just select the dot leader and choose a different font size. To change the distance between dots in the dot leader, do the following:

1. Place the insertion point in the paragraph where you want the changes to take effect.

2. Choose Format, Line, and Tab Set.

3. Type a number in the Spaces between Characters text box and then click OK.

? How can I convert text in uppercase letters to lowercase letters and vice versa without deleting and retyping?

WordPerfect has a shortcut key that quickly toggles the case of selected text. To use this feature, select the text you want to convert and press CTRL-K. If the text was originally in lowercase letters (or mixed uppercase and lowercase), it is converted to all uppercase letters. Similarly, if the text was in all uppercase letters, it is converted to lowercase. However, when converting to lowercase, WordPerfect still capitalizes the first word in each sentence, as well as any instances of the single letter *I* in the text. Each time you press CTRL-K, the case of the selected text is toggled.

You can also change the case of text in WordPerfect by selecting the text and choosing Edit and then Convert Case and selecting the option you want, such as Lowercase. This method gives you the additional option of Initial Capitals, which capitalizes each word in the selection. This option works well for capitalizing headlines and titles.

? **I set up the margins, paper size, and everything for a booklet. Then I copied the text from another document and lost all my formatting. How can I retain my formatting when inserting copied text?**

When retrieving text into a newsletter, booklet, or other highly formatted document, use the Paste Simple option. After you copy the text, place the insertion point where you want the new text to appear and press CTRL-SHIFT-V.

If you don't want to use Paste Simple, click a blank line before you paste. After the text is pasted, move to the beginning of the pasted text, turn on Reveal Codes (choose View and then Reveal Codes), and then delete the formatting codes you don't need.

? **In Word for Windows, I can press CTRL-ENTER to go to the next line on a page without creating a new paragraph. How do I do this in WordPerfect?**

This feature is not as important in WordPerfect since formatting elements such as margin settings and line spacing do not turn off when you press ENTER. Nevertheless, you can move to the next line in WordPerfect without starting a new paragraph by pressing CTRL-SHIFT-L. This procedure is helpful when you are working with features such as outlines and bulleted lists.

? **I need to write a 500-word essay. How can I find out the word count?**

Choose File and then Properties. Then click the Information tab.

FIND AND REPLACE

? **Is there a quick keystroke for Find Next and Find Previous?**

Yes. After you close the Find and Replace dialog box, you can search for the most recently specified text by pressing SHIFT-F2 to find the next occurrence or ALT-F2 to find the previous occurrence.

Tip: *You can use the QuickFind buttons to find text quickly. Click anywhere in the word that you want to locate or select a phrase. Then click either the QuickFind Next or QuickFind Previous button on the property bar.*

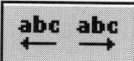

I misspelled my boss's name about twenty times in my document. How do I replace the misspelled name?

Suppose your boss's name is "Jan Punkin" and you wrote it as "Jan Pumpkin." You can use the Find and Replace dialog box, shown in Figure 3-16, to change the error. Here's how you can replace the misspelled words and save your job:

1. Move the insertion point to the beginning of the document.

2. Choose Edit and then choose Find and Replace.

3. Type the misspelled word (such as **Pumpkin**) in the Find text box.

4. Type the properly spelled word (such as **Punkin**) in the Replace With text box.

5. Click Find Next to locate the first occurrence of the word.

6. Click Replace to replace the occurrence, Find Next to skip to the next occurrence without replacing the word, or Replace All to replace all occurrences without checking.

Note: *If you replace text that should not have been replaced, choose Edit and then Undo.*

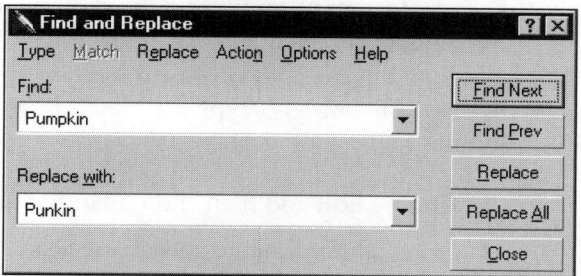

Figure 3-16.   Search for and replace text, characters, and codes

❓ I'm using Find and Replace to find a word I know is in my document, but WordPerfect can't find it. Why not?

Here are several reasons WordPerfect may not find the word you're looking for:

⇨ You may have mistyped the word, either in the document or in the Find and Replace dialog box.

⇨ The insertion point may be after the occurrence of the word. Continue to click Find Next until you're sure you've searched the entire document.

⇨ The word you're looking for may be in a header, footer, or footnote. Make sure Include Headers, Footers, Etc. in Find Option is selected on the Options menu.

⇨ WordPerfect may be searching for the text in a specific case or font. Make sure neither Case nor Font is selected on the Match menu.

❓ I found *car*, *carpet*, *carry*, *incarcerate*, and other words containing car. How can I find just *car*?

In this case, WordPerfect is searching for *car* regardless of whether it's a whole word or just part of a word. To search only for *car*, use the Whole Word option.

1. Choose Edit and then choose Find and Replace.

2. Before you begin your search, choose Match and then Whole Word from the dialog box menu.

❓ When I import an ASCII file, why can't I use Find and Replace to convert double hyphens to em dashes?

During document conversion, hard hyphens often appear instead of hyphens. You can check this by turning on Reveal Codes (choose View and then Reveal Codes). A hard hyphen appears as - and a normal hyphen appears as [-Hyphen]. Here's how you can replace hard hyphens with long dashes.

1. Choose Edit and then choose Find and Replace.

2. To search for the two consecutive hard hyphens, press CTRL-HYPHEN twice in the Find text box.

3. Click the Replace With text box and then press CTRL-W. Type **m-** and then click Insert and Close.

4. Click Replace All.

? Is there a way to use the Find and Replace feature so that the text being searched for is replaced with the same text but in bold?

Yes. You can include font attributes in a find and replace operation to search for specific text and replace it with the same text with a different attribute, such as bold. For example, you can quickly change your resume or curriculum vita so that whenever your last name appears in the bibliography, it is bold. Follow these steps:

1. Place the insertion point in the document where you want to begin searching.

2. Choose Edit and then Find and Replace.

3. In the Find text box, type the text you want to search for, such as **Harrison**.

4. In the Replace With text box, type the text you want to replace the original text with—in this case, also **Harrison**.

5. Choose Replace and then Font.

6. In the Replace Font dialog box, choose Bold and click OK.

7. To automatically replace every occurrence, click Replace All to begin the find and replace operation. To verify each replacement, instead click Find Next until an occurrence you want to replace is highlighted; then click Replace.

? I formatted my headings in Univers, but they need to be formatted in Arial. Can I find and replace fonts without changing the text?

Maybe, depending on how you formatted your text. If you have applied font changes to selected text, you will not be able to replace fonts effectively. One of WordPerfect's shortcomings is that it does not allow you to replace general paired codes (codes with a beginning and an end), such as bold, italics, and font changes made to selected text, unless you include the text to be searched for and replaced.

Note: *If you used styles to format your headings, you should edit the style instead of using Find and Replace.*

If you inserted the font codes without selecting text, here is how you would find text in one font and replace it with another font:

1. Choose Edit and then choose Find and Replace.
2. From the dialog box menu, choose Type and then Specific Codes.
3. Select Font in the list and click OK.
4. Specify the font you want to find (such as Univers) from the Find Font drop-down list.
5. Specify the font you want to use as the replacement (such as Arial) from the Replace With drop-down list.
6. To automatically replace every occurrence, click Replace All to begin the find and replace operation. To verify each replacement, click Find Next until an occurrence you want to replace is highlighted; then click Replace.

? I changed the left margin from 1 inch to 3 inches in several places in my document. How do I use Find and Replace to change the 3-inch margins to 2-inch margins?

You can use the Specific Codes option to change formatting such as line spacing and margins, as shown in Figure 3-17.

1. Choose Edit and then Find and Replace.
2. From the dialog box menu, choose Type and then Specific Codes.
3. Select the specific code (such as Lft Mar) in the list and click OK.

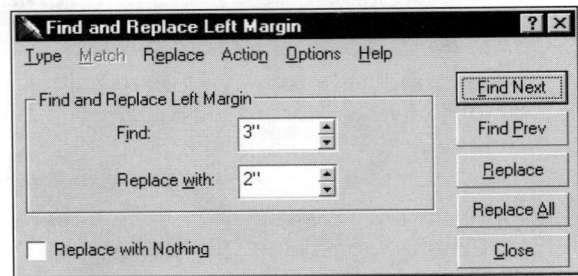

Figure 3-17.   Find and replace specific codes

4. Specify the find value (such as **3"**) in the Find text box and the replace value (such as **2"**) in the Replace With text box.

5. To automatically replace every occurrence, click Replace All to begin the find and replace operation. To verify each replacement, click Find Next until an occurrence you want to replace is highlighted; then click Replace.

? I want to find each occurrence of *c.m.* and replace it with *cm³*. How do I do this?

You cannot add the superscript font directly to the text you type in the Replace With text box. Instead, you must use the Replace Codes option to add the superscript, as shown in Figure 3-18. Here's how:

1. Choose Edit and then choose Find and Replace.

2. Type the text you want to find (such as **c.m.**) in the Find text box.

3. Type the replacement text (such as **cm**) in the Replace With text box.

4. To add the superscript code, choose Replace and then Codes. Select Suprscpt On in the Replace Codes list box and choose Insert. Type the number to be superscripted (such as **3**). Then select Suprscpt Off in the Replace Codes list box and choose Insert & Close.

5. To automatically replace every occurrence, click Replace All to begin the find and replace operation. To verify each replacement, click Find Next until an occurrence you want to replace is highlighted; then click Replace.

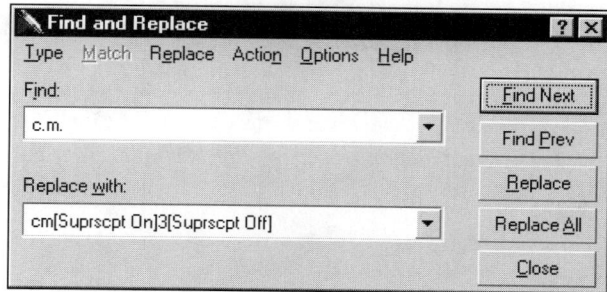

Figure 3-18. Find and replace codes

 ***Tip:***   *Instead of bothering with the Codes dialog box, you may just want to format the text in your document the way you want it (such as cm^3) and then copy and paste it into the Find and Replace dialog box.*

? Why are some codes dimmed in the Replace Codes list box?

Not all the codes listed in the Find Codes list box are available as replacement codes. While it makes sense to search for a general [Lft Mar] code regardless of its value, it doesn't make sense to replace a code with a nonspecific [Lft Mar] code. You can use the Specific Codes option to choose a replacement code.

? I misspelled my boss's name in three different ways: *Livingsten*, *Livingstein*, and *Livingston*. Her real name is *Livingstone*. How can I replace all the misspelled words?

You can use a wildcard search to search for the misspelled name. Since you typed the first part of the name correctly, you can type **Living** and then add the code [*(Many Char)] to search for additional letters. Here's how:

1. Choose Edit and then choose Find and Replace.

2. Type the beginning of the text you want to find (such as **Living**) in the Find text box.

3. To add a wildcard, choose Match and then Codes. Select *(Many Char) in the Find Codes list box and choose Insert & Close.

4. Type the replacement text with (such as **Livingstone**) in the Replace With text box.

5. To automatically replace every occurrence, click Replace All to begin the find and replace operation. To verify each replacement, click Find Next until an occurrence you want to replace is highlighted; then click Replace.

 Note: *You can also use the code [?(One Char)] to search for words with a single wildcard character. For example, enter **ca[?(One Char)]** to find cat, cab, and car.*

? When I open a text file, all the lines end with a hard return. How do I replace [HRt] codes with [SRt] codes?

This problem is surprisingly common. When you import documents from the Internet or from other common resources, you may find that each line ends with a hard return when opened in WordPerfect. However, instead of using Find and Replace to make the lines wrap naturally, open the file using a different file format. Here's how:

1. Choose File and then Open. Then double-click the text file you want to open.

2. In the Convert File Format dialog box that appears, select ASCII TEXT CR/LF to SRt (DOS) from the drop-down list and click OK.

Note: *If you have already saved the file as a WordPerfect document, you may want to save the file as an ASCII DOS Text file and then open it again. To do this, choose File and then Save As. Then select an option from the File Type pop-up list. However, keep in mind that you'll lose your document's formatting.*

THE PROOFING TOOLS: SPELL CHECKER, THESAURUS, AND GRAMMATIK

? Just what are WordPerfect's Spell Checker, Thesaurus, and Grammatik?

WordPerfect's Spell Checker points out misspelled words, duplicate words, and irregular capitalization. The Thesaurus offers lists of synonyms and antonyms to choose from. Grammatik proofreads your document for grammatical accuracy and offers readability suggestions.

? Why do wavy lines appear below some of the words and phrases in my document?

WordPerfect includes several new features for checking your spelling and grammar on the fly, including Spell-As-You-Go, Grammar-As-You-Go, and Prompt-As-You-Go, shown in Figure 3-19. You can use these tools to check your spelling and grammar while you type, or you can turn them off.

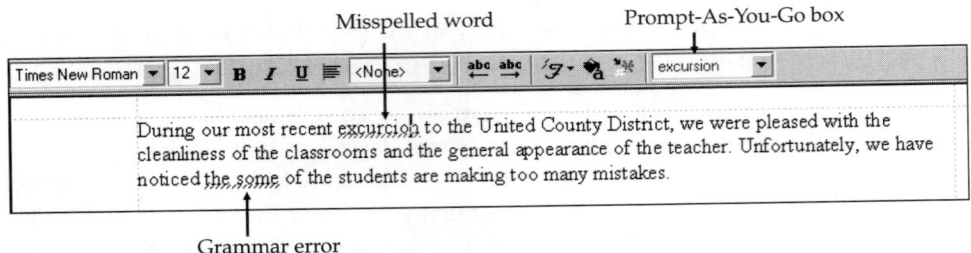

Figure 3-19.   WordPerfect flags possible spelling and grammar errors on the fly

The Spell-As-You-Go feature automatically checks your spelling as you type your document, placing a wavy red line under words it cannot find in the dictionary. You can leave the wavy lines where they are and correct your errors later, or you can fix them as you work. If you know the proper spelling, you can press BACKSPACE and correct the error, or you can right-click the misspelled word to see the Spell-As-You-Go QuickMenu. You can then select one of the suggested spellings at the top of the document, or you can choose Skip in Document if the word is spelled properly.

WordPerfect also includes Grammar-As-You-Go. With this feature turned on, you'll see wavy blue lines under possible grammatical errors. Right-click the error to see the rule of grammar that is possibly being broken and a suggested correction. To turn on Grammar-As-You-Go, choose Tools, Proofread, and Grammar-As-You-Go.

Tip: *You can also use the Prompt-As-You-Go list box to check spelling and grammar. Depending on where your insertion point is placed, this option displays spelling suggestions, alternative words, or synonyms for words in the Thesaurus. You can click a word in your document and then click the Prompt-As-You-Go drop-down list and select a replacement word.*

❓ I don't like all the wavy lines in my document. How do I turn off Spell-As-You-Go?

Choose Tools, Proofread, and then Off.

 **Tip:**   *If you want to turn off Grammar-As-You-Go but leave Spell-As-You-Go turned on, choose Tools, Proofread, and then Spell-As-You-Go.*

❓ When I type *MHz*, it is changed to *Mhz*. How can I avoid this?

This "correction" is actually a result of the Format-As-You-Go feature, which corrects common mistakes while you type. For example, if you type "let's tell CLarence to add 1/2 cup of milk," WordPerfect will change it to "Let's tell Clarence to add ½ cup of milk." In most cases, these changes are desirable, making you feel like you're a better typist than you really are. However, with words such as MHz, WordPerfect thinks you're making a mistake when you aren't. Here are two ways to correct this problem:

⇨ If you don't expect to use the troublesome word often, type the rest of the sentence and then go back and change the word to the way it's supposed to be (such as from *Mhz* to *MHz*). After you make the change, click outside the word. Be sure not to press the spacebar after you retype the word or you'll cause the same change to recur.

⇨ You can also add the word to your QuickCorrect entries. Follow these steps:

1. Click Tools and then QuickCorrect.

2. In the Replace box, type the word using the spelling proposed by the Format-As-You-Go feature.

3. Type the correct spelling in the With box and then click OK.

For more information, see "QuickCorrect and Format-As-You-Go" in Chapter 10.

❓ The Spell Checker always stops on my last name. How can I prevent that from happening?

The Spell Checker compares the words in your document to a list of words in its dictionary. By adding words to the dictionary, you can prevent the Spell Checker from flagging uncommon words you use often. Here's how:

1. Choose Tools and then Spell Check.

2. When the Spell Checker stops on your last name, choose Add.

 Tip: *If Spell-As-You-Go is turned on, you can right-click the word and choose Add.*

 Note: *The Spell Checker uses word lists when checking for errors. You can add words to a list so the Spell Checker will skip, replace, or display alternatives for them. You can create multiple user word lists. User word lists must include the extension .UWL. The main word list that ships with WordPerfect is called Wt80xx.uwl (where xx is the code for your language, such as US). Each document has its own user word list to which you can add words and phrases that pertain to that document.*

? Oops! I added a misspelled word to the Spell Checker dictionary. How can I retract a word added to the Spell Checker dictionary?

We've all had those nights when *Califrnia* looked good enough to be added to a dictionary. Here's how to delete a word mistakenly added to the Spell Checker dictionary:

1. Open a blank document and choose Tools, Spell Check, and No.

2. Choose User Word Lists from the Options drop-down list (use the Customize drop-down list in WordPerfect 7).

3. Select the incorrect word from the Word/Phrase list and click Delete Entry.

? Whenever I spell-check a WordPerfect document, the Spell Checker always starts from the beginning of the document—no matter where my insertion point is. How do I get the Spell Checker to start from a specific location in my document rather than from the top?

When you choose Tools and then Spell Check, the Auto Start feature automatically starts spell-checking the entire document from the beginning. If you don't want to spell-check the entire document from beginning to end, you have two options. First, you can select the text you want to spell-check before starting the Spell Checker. Second, you can turn off the Auto Start feature and have the Spell Checker dialog box displayed before each spell check begins, allowing you to select the options you want.

Here's how to disable the Auto Start feature:

1. Open a blank document window and choose Tools and then Spell Check.

2. Choose No to keep the Spell Checker open.

3. From the Options drop-down list, deselect Auto Start (in WordPerfect 7, deselect Auto Start from the Customize drop-down list).

Now, when you want to spell-check a document, choose Tools and then Spell Check. By default, WordPerfect is set to spell-check the entire document from the beginning. If that's what you want, choose Start. Otherwise, from the Check drop-down list, choose the option you want to use, such as Page or To End of Document.

Tip: *To spell-check a portion of text, select the text before you begin spell-checking.*

? I have a document that includes a section of foreign language text. Spell Checker stops at each word, and I must click the Skip button. Can I disable Spell Checker for just a portion of a document?

Yes. Here's how you can disable the writing tools for a section of text:

1. Select the text that you want the Spell Checker to skip.

2. Choose Tools, Language, and Settings (just choose Tools and then Language in WordPerfect 7).

3. Check Disable Writing Tools (in This Portion of the Text) and then click OK.

A Writing Tools: Disable code will be inserted before the selected text, and a Writing Tools: Enable code will be inserted after it. Next time you use Spell Checker, this section of text will be ignored.

? I'm writing a document in Spanish. How can I spell-check it?

If you want to use language tools such as Spell Checker and Grammatik to proofread text in another language, you must have the word list (dictionary) for that language. Corel Language Modules, which include language tools and word lists, are available for many languages.

You can use up to 10 user word lists and 10 main word lists for proofreading. For example, you can use both the U.S. English main word list and the Canadian French main word list when you proofread a U.S. English document.

Here's how you can make sure the right word lists are available:

1. Open Spell Checker.

2. Click Options and then User Word Lists.

3. Select the language from the Language drop-down list. Then click Add List to use additional word lists with that language.

4. Select the filename for the word list and then click Open.

? I have a supplemental dictionary I used in WordPerfect 6.1 that contains an extensive list of words. Can I use this dictionary with WordPerfect 8?

You can add the user word lists from WordPerfect 6.1 or 7 to WordPerfect 8. Here's how:

1. Open the Spell Checker.

2. Click Options and then User Word Lists.

3. Click Add List.

4. Select the wt61*xx*.uwl file (where *xx* represents the language) usually found in the Windows directory. Then click Open.

5. Click Close.

Note: *An X appears in the check box next to each active word list.*

How do I look up an antonym for a word?

The Thesaurus includes synonyms for most words and antonyms for many words. Here's how you would find the antonym for the word *caught*, as shown in Figure 3-20:

1. Click the word in your document for which you want to find an antonym. Choose Tools and then Thesaurus.

2. Scroll down the list of synonyms until you reach the antonyms.

Tip: *If you want to see synonyms for one of the words in the word list, double-click the word to display a new list in the next panel. If you want to see a definition of the word, select Options and then Show Definitions.*

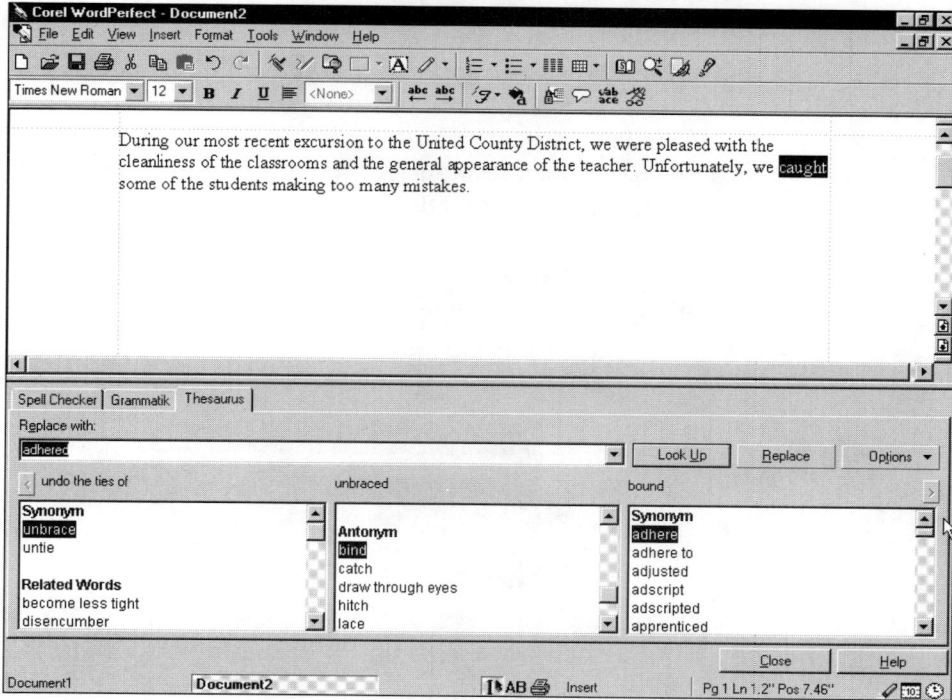

Figure 3-20.   Use the Thesaurus to look up synonyms and antonyms

? **I'm writing an article for a scientific journal. Can I change Grammatik's checking style to better fit this type of document?**

WordPerfect includes 10 grammar checking styles you can choose from, shown in Figure 3-21. You can select any of these checking styles to suit the needs of your current document. Here's how to change the checking style:

1. Choose Tools and then Grammatik.

2. Choose Options and then Checking Styles.

3. Select a different checking style, such as Technical or Scientific. Then click Select.

? **When I open Grammatik, a message appears telling me the dictionary couldn't be located. How do I find the dictionary?**

When this message appears, click Browse. Then look for the WT80EN.MOR file, which is usually found in C:\Corel\Suite8\Programs. After you locate the file, the error message will no longer appear when you open Grammatik.

If you cannot find the file, click the Start button on the taskbar and then choose Find. Search your hard drive for the WT80EN.MOR file. If you still cannot find the dictionary, perform a Custom installation and reinstall Grammatik.

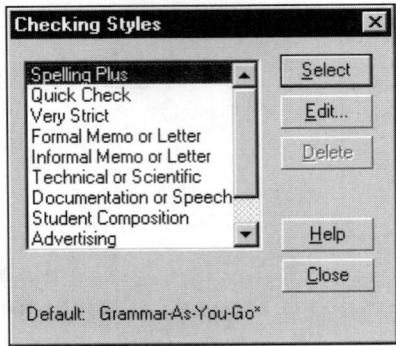

Figure 3-21.   Select a Grammatik writing style

? **The passive voice is used by me too often. How do I tell Grammatik to flag passive sentences?**

You can either select a different checking style, such as Very Strict, or you can edit the checking style you're using. Here's how to edit a checking style:

1. Choose Tools and then Grammatik.

2. Choose Options (in WordPerfect 7, choose Customize) and then choose Checking Styles.

3. Select the checking style you're using (Spelling Plus is the default style). Then choose Edit.

4. Select the options you want in the Rule Classes list box.

5. Choose Save to edit the current style or choose Save As to create a new style.

? **Grammar-As-You-Go doesn't flag passive sentences. Why not?**

Grammar-As-You-Go has its own writing style, which you can edit. Here's how:

1. Choose Tools and then Grammatik.

2. Choose Options (in WordPerfect 7, choose Customize). Then choose Checking Styles.

3. Select Grammar-As-You-Go in the list box. Then choose Edit.

4. Select the options you want in the Rule Classes list box.

5. Choose Save.

USING PERFECTEXPERT PROJECTS

? **What is a PerfectExpert project and how do I create one?**

A *project* is a predesigned document that is linked to a PerfectExpert panel. You just need to enter your personal information and preferences and let WordPerfect do its work. For example, if you need to send a fax, you can fill in a preformatted fax cover sheet and then send the fax right from WordPerfect if you have the appropriate fax software. You can select from dozens of projects, shown in Figure 3-22, that help you get your work done in WordPerfect and the other applications in the Corel WordPerfect Suite.

You can begin a new project in three ways:

⇨   Click Corel PerfectExpert on the DAD bar on the Windows taskbar. The DAD bar includes buttons that launch Corel WordPerfect Suite applications such as WordPerfect, Quattro Pro, Presentations, and Corel PerfectExpert.

⇨   Choose Corel New Project on the Corel WordPerfect Suite 8 menu (the Start menu).

⇨   In WordPerfect, Quattro Pro, or Presentations, choose File and then New.

You can narrow the list of selections by selecting a category at the top of the drop-down menu. The categories group projects according to application, such as WordPerfect or Quattro Pro, and according to

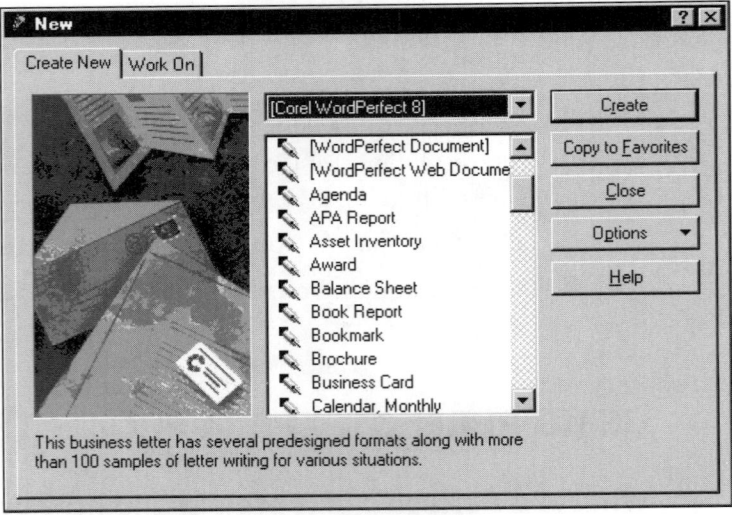

Figure 3-22.   Select from a host of PerfectExpert projects

task, such as Budget or Education, as shown in the following illustration:

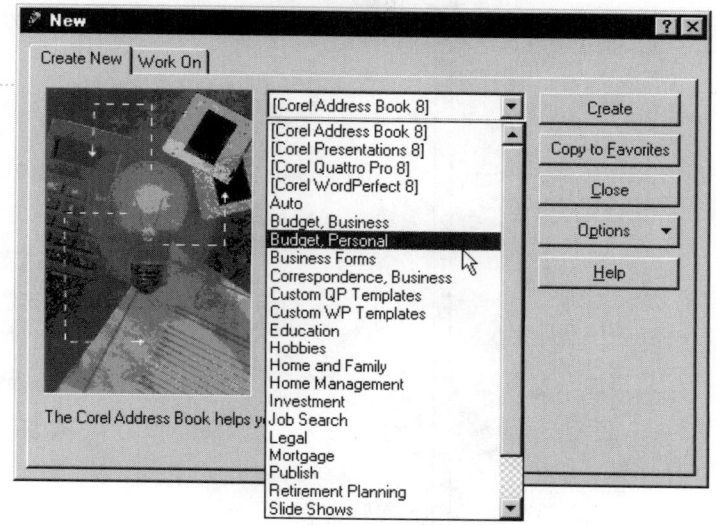

? I want to create a letter as I did with the Letter Expert in WordPerfect 7. What do I do in WordPerfect 8?

When you use the Business Letter project to create a business letter, you can select the style of the letter, and you can even include prewritten text on a number of subjects, such as a response to bill error complaints. Here's how you can use the PerfectExpert, shown in Figure 3-23, to create a letter:

1. Choose File and then New.

2. Select Letter, Business in the list box. Then click Create.

3. Select and change the elements (such as To, From, and Closing) you want to be modify. Then click Finished.

4. Select any options in the PerfectExpert panel needed to complete the letter, including any Finish options.

5. Click the X in the upper-right part of the panel to close the PerfectExpert.

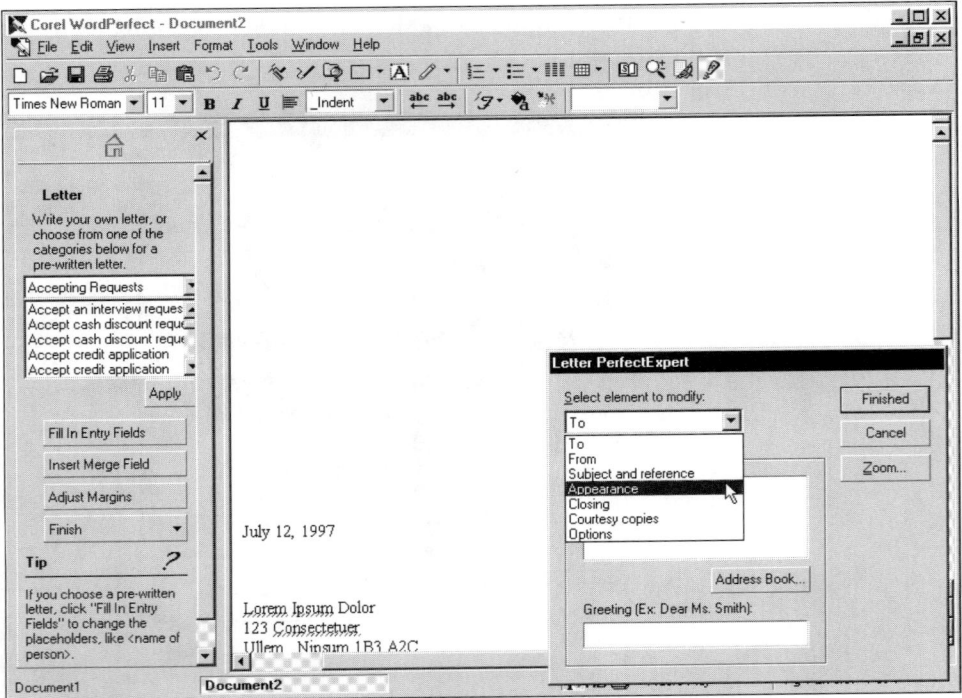

Figure 3-23.   Creating a quick business letter

 ***Tip:*** *The best way to learn about the power of PerfectExpert projects is to experiment. You'll be surprised at how quickly you can create all sorts of documents, from calendars and business cards to invoices and graph paper.*

 ***Note:*** *You can still create templates and add them to categories in the New dialog box. If you created templates in previous versions of WordPerfect, you can still use the templates in WordPerfect 8. For more information on working with templates, see "Working with Templates" in Chapter 13.*

? I tried to create business cards, but I received an error message about the CD-ROM drive. What's wrong?

When you installed WordPerfect 8, only some of the projects were copied to your hard drive. If you insert the Corel WordPerfect Suite 8 CD into the CD-ROM drive, you'll be able to run any of the projects listed. However, you can also perform a Custom installation to add the rest of the projects to your hard drive. For more information, see "Adding and Removing Suite Components" in Chapter 2.

? I work for three different people. How do I change the personal information in a template?

The first time you filled out your personal information when working on a project, WordPerfect designated the listing in the Address Book as your personal information. However, that doesn't mean you're stuck with that personal address for all future projects you create. Here's how you can designate a different listing in the Address Book as your personal information:

1. Choose File and then New.

2. Choose Options and then Personal Information.

3. Click OK to close the message box that tells which listing is currently assigned to the Personal Information.

4. Select a different name in the Address Book. Then click Select.

Note: *If you change your personal information and the change does not take effect for the next project you create, exit and restart WordPerfect.*

? When using a template created in WordPerfect 6.1, I receive a message saying, "To use this template in WordPerfect 8, you need to edit it." Why do some templates need to be edited?

When using a WordPerfect 6.1 template in WordPerfect 8, you may also see the message "This template was created for use with WordPerfect 6.x and does not use the new universal Address Book used in WordPerfect 7. Do you want to convert this template for use with WordPerfect 7?" These messages appear only when you use templates that include prompts or that use data stored in the Personal Information address book.

Because of some differences in the way template prompts are handled in the two versions, some WordPerfect 6.1 templates with prompts need to be edited and saved again to make them compatible with WordPerfect 7 or 8. Templates that do not have prompts do not need to be converted. Here's how to convert a template in WordPerfect 8:

1. Copy the template to the Custom WP Templates folder usually located in C:\Corel\Suite8\Template (or C:\Corel\Office7\Template in WordPerfect 7).

2. Choose File and then New. Select the template in the list box and then choose Options and Edit WP Template.

3. When asked to convert the template, choose Yes.

4. Edit, save, and close the template.

 *Note:* *If the message "Macro tconvert.wcm not found" appears, you did not include all the macros when you installed Corel WordPerfect Suite 8. You can either perform a Custom installation and include all the macros (see "Adding and Removing Suite Components" in Chapter 2), or you can delete the prompts causing the problem and add new prompts using the Build Prompts option on the property bar.*

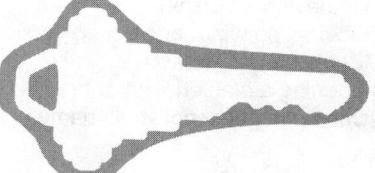

File Management

Answer Topics!

FIle Management @ a Glance

⇨   Every program, graphic, spreadsheet, database, or WordPerfect document is stored in files on your computer disk. The number of files can quickly mushroom into the thousands. Managing so many files can be difficult. You may need to delete old files to make room for new ones, copy groups of files to backup disks, or find a file whose name you've forgotten. You may need to edit a co-worker's document created in Microsoft Word and work on files downloaded from the Internet. You may also want to save versions of files so that if you don't like your most recent changes, you can revert to a previous version. How do you manage your files efficiently? This chapter tells you what to do.

⇨   You can use QuickFinder to search for files by name or by content. For example, if you know the name of a document but not where it's stored, you can search for the document name anywhere on your hard drive or network. If you can't remember the name of the document but you know it deals with microbiology, for example, you can search for all files containing the words "cell membrane"—a phrase most of us look for at least once a month. If you need help with QuickFinder, this chapter answers your questions.

⇨   By learning how to back up and save your documents effectively, you can avoid a lot of pain and suffering. This chapter answers your questions about file backup and includes a list of troubleshooting procedures that you can work through when things go wrong with files.

WORKING WITH FILES

❓ I'm upgrading from DOS. What is the difference between a folder and a directory?

Folders and directories are the same thing. The Microsoft people just thought they'd use *folder* to make things easier to understand, and when you think about it, *folder* does make more sense than *directory*, metaphorically speaking. Figure 4-1 illustrates a few basic Windows and DOS terms that you should know.

❓ I want to save a file as Bob.ltr, but WordPerfect renames it Bob.ltr.wpd. How can I fix this?

A quick solution to this problem is to place quotation marks around the filename: for example, "Bob.ltr ". When quotation marks are used, the .WPD extension is not added. However, in Windows 95, using the proper extension is needed to associate a file with a program. For example, if you double-click the Bob.ltr file from the Windows Explorer or from My Computer, Windows 95 won't know which program the file is associated with. Also, if you do not use the .WPD extension for WordPerfect documents, you cannot print them from the Open File dialog box without opening them. As a general rule, you're better off using the .WPD extension.

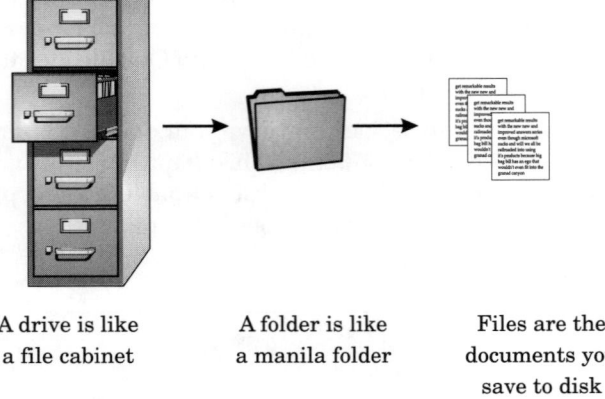

A drive is like   A folder is like   Files are the
a file cabinet   a manila folder   documents you
                                               save to disk

Figure 4-1.   The relationship among drives, folders, and files

File Management Terms You Should Know

In WordPerfect 8, it's easy to create a document, save it, print it, and open it to use it again. However, navigating your way through the file management buttons and menus can sometimes be confusing, especially if you're accustomed to DOS. Here are some tips and definitions that should help:

⇨ A *file* is a single document or part of a program. There are two basic types of files: *program files* and *data files*. Program files are the pieces that make up a program. Data files are documents, spreadsheets, and other items that programs can create.

⇨ The *drive* is device where all files are stored. The A: drive and the B: drive are usually reserved for floppy disks. The C: drive is usually your hard drive. If your hard drive is partitioned, the D: and E: drives may also be hard drives. Additional drive letters may be designated for CD-ROM drives, backup drives, and network drives. Make sure you know which drive letters are assigned to which drives in your system.

⇨ Each disk drive can be subdivided into numerous *folders*, also known as *directories*. Each folder can contain files and other folders. Folders inside other folders are sometimes called *subfolders* or *subdirectories*.

⇨ The *path* specifies the exact route to a particular file, including the drive, folder or folders, and filename. For example, the path

```
C:\Corel\Suite8\Template\Calendar.wpt
```

says, "Go to drive C:, then go to the Corel folder, then go to the Suite8 folder, then go to the Template folder, and then go to the file named Calendar.wpt."

⇨ Dialog boxes that let you open or save documents, graphics, and other files are referred to as *file management* dialog boxes. The Open File dialog box displays the documents found in your default document folder. However, you can change the default document folder by choosing Tools | Settings | Files and then typing the new path in the Default document folder text box.

⇨ You can save WordPerfect 8 documents using any name of any reasonable length. The name can consist of multiple words and spaces. In fact, you may often want to save documents by their actual titles. For example, you can use "Senegart Industries Quarterly Report.wpd" as a document name. Although you are no longer limited to eight-character DOS names for your documents, you can still add the DOS period and three-letter extension at the end of a document name to group and identify documents. If you don't add the .WPD extension, WordPerfect adds it for you. If you want to type a document without an extension, type the document name enclosed in quotation marks, such as **"Letter to bill"**.

⇨ The File Open dialog box is similar to the Windows Explorer. You can right-click a file or folder and select an item from the shortcut menu that appears. You can use this method to delete, rename, print, cut, copy, and paste files, and you can also view a file's properties.

⇨ If you haven't made any changes to a document since the last time it was saved, "(unmodified)" appears next to the document name at the top of the document window. If "(unmodified)" doesn't appear, you should save the document before you exit WordPerfect, unless you've made unwanted changes.

 *Note:* *If you need to create lots of files that have extensions other than .WPD, you can turn off this option. Choose Tools | Settings | File and then deselect Use Default Extension on Open and Save.*

❓ What is the difference between a WordPerfect Compound File and a WordPerfect 6/7/8 file?

The WordPerfect Compound File format is the native file format for OLE 2 servers. This format permits full implementation of the Windows 95 shell integration features. The WordPerfect Compound File was called the WordPerfect 7 file format in WordPerfect 7.

Here are some of the advantages of using a WordPerfect Compound File:

⇨ OLE objects open more quickly.

⇨ By default, a file is associated with an application by its extension. However, if a file has an extension without an entry in the registry, then Windows 95 will read information from the Compound document section and launch the appropriate application.

⇨ If you have an OLE 2 browser application, you have the capability to browse, modify, and share embedded WordPerfect Compound documents without starting WordPerfect. The actual ability to browse, modify, and share information depends on your browser application.

⇨ If a WordPerfect document is encrypted, WordPerfect saves the OLE object information in the prefix rather than in the Compound document. This is done so users cannot use a third-party browser to look at embedded objects in a password-protected document. Not all applications implement this security feature.

⇨ Possible future advantages include capabilities to move documents from one place to another without losing links and to allow more than one person to work on a document at the same time.

Here are some of the disadvantages to using the WordPerfect Compound File format instead of the WordPerfect 6/7/8 format:

⇨ The file size increases by 3 to 5K.

⇨ A Compound file opens more slowly. The delay is usually only less than 1 second, but the time may be longer when opening large files.

⇨ WordPerfect 5.1 and 6.1 cannot open documents saved in the WordPerfect Compound File format.

❓ How do I make a file read-only so another file can't be saved over it?

If you want others to be able to open a file without being able to save over the current version, you can make the file read-only. To make a file read-only, close the file in WordPerfect and then choose File |

Open. Right-click the filename and choose Properties. Select Read-only and click OK.

 ## I remember the password, but I can't open a password-protected document in WordPerfect 6.1. Why not?

In WordPerfect 7 or 8, you can select a case-sensitive password that can be read only in WordPerfect 7 or 8, or you can select a case-insensitive password that can be read by any version of WordPerfect. Here's how you can open a document in WordPerfect 8 and change the password so WordPerfect 6.1 can read it:

1. Choose File | Save As.

2. Type the name of the document in the File Name text box.

3. Select Password Protect and then choose Save.

4. Select Original Password Protection. Then type the password and click OK.

5. Retype the password to make sure you typed it correctly.

Warning: *Make sure you write down the name of the password in a safe place where you can find it. If you cannot remember the password, you will not be able to open or view the document.*

 ## I added a password to a file, but I can't remember the password. Can you help?

No. You're out of luck. If I were a mean person, I would wag my finger at you and say, "You should have written down the password." I like to think I'm above that—but you really should have written down the password.

Note: *I have heard rumors that some people out there have the ability to break password-protected documents. I don't know who these people are, but if your document is really important, you may want check around the computer underworld before giving up.*

? While formatting a newsletter, I like to store several versions of a file. Does WordPerfect have a "Revert to Saved" or "Discard Edit" feature?

WordPerfect 8 has a feature called Version Control. As you edit a document, you may not want to keep all of your changes, especially when tinkering with design-intensive documents such as newsletters and brochures. If fact, sometimes you may even want to store several versions of the same document so you can select among them as the need arises, as shown in Figure 4-2. With Version Control, you can save different versions of a document in the same file.

Here's how to save versions:

1. Open and save the document you're working on.

2. Choose File | Version Control | Save Current.

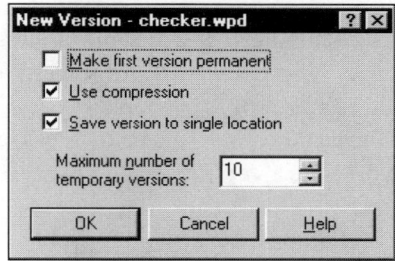

3. Select Make First Version Permanent if you don't want the first version to be replaced.

4. If you want to save the versions in a different file, deselect Save Version to Single Location.

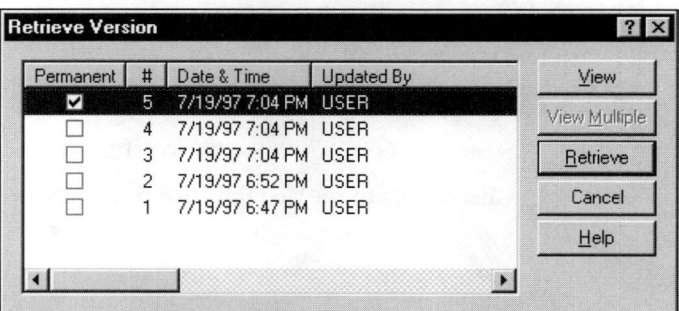

Figure 4-2.   After you have saved several versions of a file, you can revert to any of them

5. Click OK.

6. When you're ready to save an edited version of the document, choose Save Current again.

The options on the Version Control submenu are dimmed, and I can't save any versions. What's wrong?

If you can't use Version Help, you need to perform a Custom installation to add the Versions component (under Accessories). See "Adding and Removing Suite Components" in Chapter 2.

When I try to save a version after making several changes, the message "Working file is not newer than latest version" appears. What should I do?

If this problem occurs in WordPerfect, one solution is to save the file as a WordPerfect Compound File. Choose File | Save As and then type a new filename and select WordPerfect Compound File from the File Type drop-down list. If you save the file as a WordPerfect Compound File, this error message should no longer appear when you save a version.

Note: *You cannot open a file saved as a WordPerfect Compound File in a version of WordPerfect before WordPerfect 7.*

How do I retrieve a version?

When you want to see, edit, or print a version of a document, you can select the version from the Retrieve Version dialog box, shown earlier in Figure 4-2.

1. Open the file.

2. Choose File | Version Control | Retrieve Current.

3. Select the version you want to return to and then click Retrieve.

4. Choose Yes to replace the current document or No to create a new document based on the version you selected.

 ***Note:***   *When you choose not to save versions in a single location, they are stored in the C:\Corel\Versions folder with this syntax: C$$DIRECTORY$$FILENAME$WPD.cv. You cannot open this file or retrieve versions from it directly.*

? I moved a version of a file to a different folder, but an error message appeared when I tried to retrieve an earlier version. What did I do wrong?

You should use the Corel Versions option to delete, copy, or move a file. If you simply move the saved file, WordPerfect won't know where the versions are stored, and you'll see the message *"filename does not contain version information to be retrieved."* Here's how to move a file correctly:

1. Choose File | Open (or open Windows Explorer).

2. Right-click the file you want to move or delete. Then click Corel Versions | File | Move.

3. Specify the new name and location of the file and choose Save.

? How do I merge two documents together—that is, how do I retrieve the contents of one file into another file?

WordPerfect has three commands that let you open or create documents. To open a previously saved file, choose File | Open. To retrieve the contents of a file into the current document, choose Insert | File.

1. Open the first document. Then place the insertion point where you want the next document to be retrieved.

2. Choose Insert | File. Then double-click the name of the file you want to insert.

If you really want to use the Merge feature to create form letters and assemble documents, see Chapter 8.

? **When I choose New from the File menu, a dialog box appears. How do I just open a new blank document?**

 To open a new document based on a project, such as a business letter or a fax cover sheet, choose File | New and then select the project. However, if you just want to open a new blank document, click the New Blank Document button on the toolbar or press CTRL-N.

? **I would like the descriptive names I used in files created in WordPerfect 6.1 to become the filenames in WordPerfect 8. How can I convert them?**

If you have only a few files that need to be renamed, you may just want to rename the files in the File Open dialog box or in Windows Explorer. However, if you used Document Summary to add descriptive names to lots of documents in WordPerfect 6.1, you can use the Longname.wcm macro to convert these descriptions to the actual filenames in WordPerfect 8.

 *Note:* *Longname.wcm is not included by default with the Typical installation. You must use the Custom installation to select this macro. For more information, see "Adding and Removing Suite Components" in Chapter 2.*

1. Choose Tools | Macro | Play.

2. Double-click Longname.wcm.

3. Select the files you want to rename (you may need to select a different folder). Then click OK.

? **An error message appears when I play the Long Filename macro included with WordPerfect. What's wrong?**

When you run the Longname.wcm macro in WordPerfect 8, selecting the files from the list and clicking OK returns the following error message: "DLLLoad error (Status: 1157, Library: 'SHWIN70')." The WordPerfect programmers forgot to update this WordPerfect 7 macro to work in WordPerfect 8. Here's how you can fix this problem:

1. Choose Tools | Macro | Edit and then double-click Longname.wcm.

2. Go to line 337 and look for the following:

```
'DLLCall Prototype WfsPathSplit ("SHWIN70";
"WfsPathSplit"; Void; {AnsiString (Filename); &An-
siString (A); &AnsiString (B); &AnsiString (C);
&AnsiString (D)})'
```

3. Replace SHWIN70 with **PFIT80** and then click Save and Compile.

4. Close the macro and then replay it. The macro should work fine.

❓ In Word, I can use SHIFT to close the open documents. Is it possible to close all open documents in WordPerfect at the same time?

You can use the Closeall macro to close all open documents. Here's how:

1. Choose Tools | Macro | Play.

2. Double-click Closeall.wcm.

You will be prompted to save any changes in documents that have not been saved.

Tip: *If you want to close all your documents more quickly, you can assign the Closeall macro to a keystroke, or you can add the Close All button to the toolbar. See Chapter 13 for more information.*

❓ In WordPerfect 6.1, I stored my favorite folders in QuickList. What happened to QuickList?

QuickList has been replaced by the Favorites option, which is a Windows 95 standard. You can use the Favorites option to display the directories and files you use most often, as shown in Figure 4-3.

To view the Favorites list from the Save As or Open File dialog box, click the Favorites button.

To add a folder to the Favorites option, specify the directory. Then click the Add Current Location to Favorites button.

To add a file, select the file and then click the Add Selected Item(s) to Favorites button.

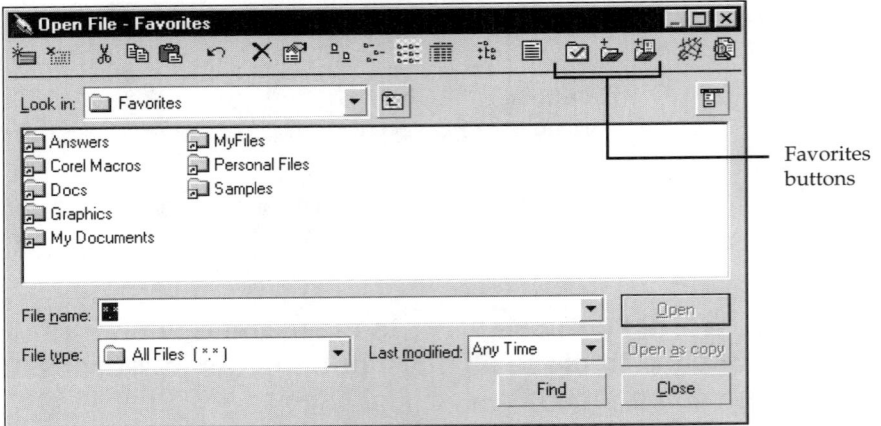

Figure 4-3.   Use the Favorites option to display your favorite folders and files

❓ I deleted a folder in Favorites, but the folder is still on my hard drive. What's the deal?

Items added to the Favorites list are Windows shortcuts, as indicated by the arrow in the folder. Shortcuts are representations of the folders or files, not the folders or files themselves. You can delete a Favorites shortcut by right-clicking it and choosing Delete. However, the actual folder or file the shortcut refers to remains on the disk until you delete it directly.

❓ How do I mark several files to be opened, moved, copied, or deleted?

Hold down the CTRL key to mark the files. Then right-click the selected files to bring up a shortcut menu full of Windows 95 file options, as shown in Figure 4-4.

Tip: *To copy or move files, right-click the selected file and then choose Cut or Copy. Move to the folder where you want the files to appear and then right-click a blank area of the list box and choose Paste from the shortcut menu.*

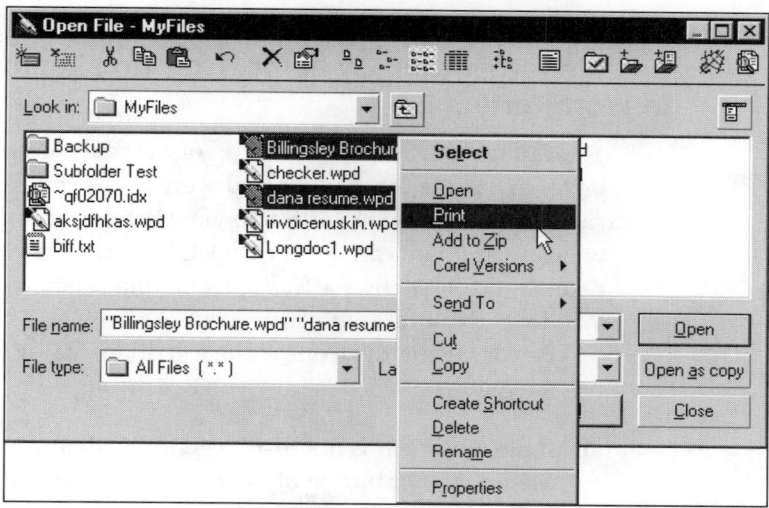

Figure 4-4.   Use the shortcut menu to open, move, and delete files

? I accidentally deleted an important file from my hard drive. How do I get it back?

First of all, make sure you don't empty the Windows 95 Recycle Bin. If the file is still in the Recycle Bin, you can restore it. Double-click the Recycle Bin, select the file you deleted, and choose File | Restore.

If you have emptied the Recycle Bin, don't do anything else on your computer, such as saving, opening, or printing other files. You may be able to use a commercial undelete utility to salvage your file. If the file was saved on a network, check with your network supervisor to see if you can retrieve the deleted file from a network backup file.

? Can I create new folders for my documents without leaving WordPerfect?

Yes. Here's how you can create new folders (also called directories):

1. In a file management dialog box such as Open File, move to the folder in which you want the subfolder to appear.

2. Right-click a blank area of the list box and choose New | Folder from the shortcut menu.

3. Type a name for the folder and then press ENTER.

 **In previous versions of WordPerfect, I could list my files by date rather than by name. How do I list my files by date in WordPerfect 8?**

You can use the buttons at the top of the Save As and Open File dialog boxes to change the way your files are displayed. For example, you can select the Preview button to view the documents in a Viewer window, and you can select the Details button to view the file size and date. Figure 4-5 shows a Tree view (similar to the view you see in Windows Explorer) with large icons.

Besides using the icons at the top of the dialog box, you can also use the menu bar. Here's how you can arrange files by date:

1. If the menu bar is not displayed in the dialog box, click the Toggle Menu On/Off button at the right side of the dialog box.

2. From the dialog box menu bar, choose View | Arrange Icons | By Date.

Note: *Changes made to the column widths or sort order in the File Open dialog box are not saved when the dialog is closed. Currently, there is no way to save the file arrangement in the File Open dialog box.*

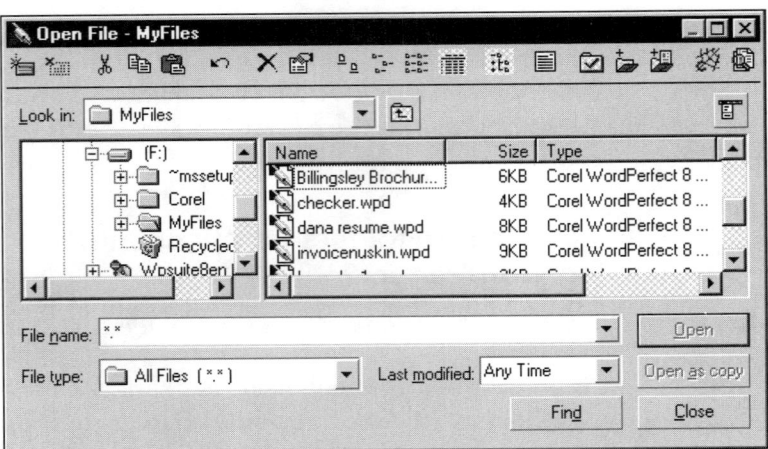

Figure 4-5.   You can view folder contents in different ways

? I don't need all this stuff in the Open File and Save As dialog boxes. How can I get rid of all these options?

The default file management dialog boxes, such as the Open File and Save As dialog boxes, are enhanced with lots of additional options such as a Preview button and search options. Here's how you can display simpler Windows 95 file management dialog boxes:

1. Choose Tools | Settings and then double-click Files.
2. Deselect Use Enhanced File Dialogs and then click OK. Then click Close.

? How do I open a document created in another word processor?

WordPerfect has many conversion filters for common word processors such as Word, Write, and Ami Pro. To open a file created in another word processor, try this first:

1. In WordPerfect, choose File | Open. Then double-click the file you want to convert.
2. Select the type of file format you want. Then click OK.

If that doesn't work, you may need to open the file in the other word processor, save the file in Rich Text Format (RTF), and then open it in WordPerfect. If you can't figure out how to save the file in a different format, copy the text in the document using the other word processor and then choose Edit | Paste Special in WordPerfect to bring in the text.

? I'm trying to convert a Lotus Works file. How do I do that?

There are currently no conversion filters available for Lotus Works. In Lotus Works, save the file as a text file or in RTF. Then open the file in WordPerfect.

? I run WordPerfect 5.1 on my home computer, but I use WordPerfect 8 at work. Why can't my home computer read the files I bring home from work?

WordPerfect 8 uses a different file format than WordPerfect 5.1. However, WordPerfect 8 comes with a special converter that lets it open files saved in WordPerfect 5.1. The latest versions of WordPerfect 5.1 for DOS (5.1+) and Windows (5.2) have converters for files created in WordPerfect 6, 7, and 8, which you can order by contacting Corel. If you cannot obtain the upgrade for these older versions, you can always save the WordPerfect 8 document in the 5.1 format. Here's how:

1. Choose File | Save As.

2. Select the WordPerfect 5.1/5.2 format from the Save As Type drop-down list.

3. Type a name for the file in the File Name text box and then click OK.

? When I open a WordPerfect 5.1 file, text runs through a text box. Why?

This is a problem in the conversion process. WordPerfect 5.1 and WordPerfect 8 don't provide the same text wrapping options. In 5.1, text wrapping is either on or off, whereas WordPerfect 8 offers a variety of wrapping options, such as contour wrapping.

A workaround for this problem is to set the Wrap option in WordPerfect 8 to Neither Side. Here's how:

1. Right-click the edge of the text box and choose Wrap.

2. Select Neither Side and then click OK.

? I save text files from the Web and edit them in WordPerfect. How do I get rid of the hard returns at the end of every line?

When you import documents from the Internet or from other common resources, you may find that each line ends with a hard return when opened in WordPerfect. To get rid of the hard returns, open the file using a different file format. Here's how:

1. Choose File | Open. Then double-click the text file you want to open.

2. In the Convert File Format dialog box that appears, select ASCII TEXT CR/LF to SRt (DOS) from the drop-down list and then click OK.

FINDING FILES WITH QUICKFINDER

? **WordPerfect 6.1 provided a QuickFinder button in the Open File dialog box. Where is the QuickFinder option in WordPerfect 8?**

In WordPerfect 8, the QuickFinder feature has been incorporated into the file management dialog boxes, such as the Open File and Save As dialog boxes. You type the filename or text you're looking for in the File Name text box, specify the drive or folder where you think the file is located, and then you choose Find. See the answer to the next question for details.

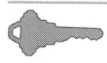

Note: *The Find option will not appear in your file management dialog boxes if you have turned off the Use Enhanced File Dialogs file setting. To use enhanced dialog boxes, choose Tools | Settings, double-click Files, and then select Use Enhanced File Dialogs.*

? **I can't find a file, but I know I saved it somewhere on my hard drive. How do I find it?**

You can use the QuickFinder feature—which appears as the Find button on the Save As and Open File dialog boxes—to search for files by name or by content. For example, if you know the name of a document but not where it's stored, you can search for the name of your document anywhere on your hard drive or network. If you can't remember the name of the document but you know it deals with potted meat products, for example, you can search for all files containing the words "potted meat."

You can use the file management dialog boxes to search for files, as shown in Figure 4-6. Here's how to search for a file:

1. Open any of the file management dialog boxes such as Save As or Open File.

2. Specify the lowest folder in your hard drive tree structure, such as c: or c:\MyFiles, where you think you saved the file (subfolders are automatically included).

Select the drive
or folder to
search in

Type the
filename or
contents

Figure 4-6.   You can search for names of files or for text in documents

3. Type the name of the file (such as **Letter to Betsy.wpd**) in the File
   Name text box. If you don't know the filename, type text that's in
   the file, such as **Dear Aunt Betsy**.

Tip: *You can use wildcards for single letters (?) and multiple letters (*)
when searching for files. For example, type* ***.wpd** *to search for all files with a
.WPD extension; type* **rep*.*** *to search for any file beginning with "rep."*

4. If you know when you saved the file, select the time period (such
   as Yesterday or Last Year) from the Last Modified text box to
   narrow your search.

5. If you know the type of file you're looking for, such as a
   WordPerfect document, select the file format from the File Type
   drop-down list.

6. Choose Find to locate the file you want.

Note: *The time required to find the file depends on how much you
narrowed your search and how fast your computer is. You may have to wait a
while. You know the search is complete when the Stop Find button changes to
the Back button.*

I'm looking for a file on my company network, but the network volume does not appear on the Look In drop-down list. How can I get the network volume to appear?

To see the folders on a network, you may need to map the drive first so that it will appear on the Look In drop-down list. Click the Map Network Drive button, then specify the drive letter and the shared folder you want to map the drive letter to. For more information on mapping network drives, see your Windows 95 documentation or ask your network supervisor.

 **Note:**   *If the drive will not map to the path you specify, you may not have rights to that location. See your system administrator.*

 How do I search for files that contain *rain* but not *forest*?

You can use the search operators in the File Name text box to focus your file searches. These operators are described in Table 4-1.

Table 4-1.   Search Operators

Operator	Word Pattern	What It Finds
And (&)	rain & forest	Files containing *rain* and *forest*
Or (│)	rain │ forest	Files containing *rain* or *forest* or both words
Not (!)	rain ! forest	Files containing *rain* but not *forest*
Exact phrase (" ")	"rain forest"	Files containing the phrase *rain forest*
Followed by (..)	rain .. forest	Files containing *rain* before *forest*
Group	(rain, forest, Brazil)	Files containing *rain*, *forest*, and *Brazil* in any order
Match single character (?)	rain?	Files containing *rain* plus a single character, such as *rains*
Match multiple characters (*)	rain*	Files containing *rain* plus additional characters, such as *rains*, *raining*, and *rained*

? Searching for files takes a long time on my computer. How do I index files to make the search go faster?

You can use QuickFinder Manager, shown in Figure 4-7, to create a Fast Search file (previously called a *search index*). A Fast Search file groups together folders and subfolders you search in often, such as your MyFiles folder or your C: drive. You can also use QuickFinder Manager to edit, delete, or update an existing Fast Search file.

Once you create a Fast Search file, you can use it for subsequent searches. Searching a Fast Search file is much quicker than searching each individual file. The next time you search for a file in the folder you've specified in your Fast Search file, WordPerfect automatically performs a Fast Search operation.

1. Click Start on the taskbar. Then choose Corel WordPerfect Suite 8 | Tools | QuickFinder Manager 8.

2. Choose Create.

3. Type the pathname of the drive or folder (such as **c:** or **c:\MyFiles**) you want to search in (subfolders are automatically included).

4. Select Manual Update or Automatic Update. Then click OK and close QuickFinder Manager.

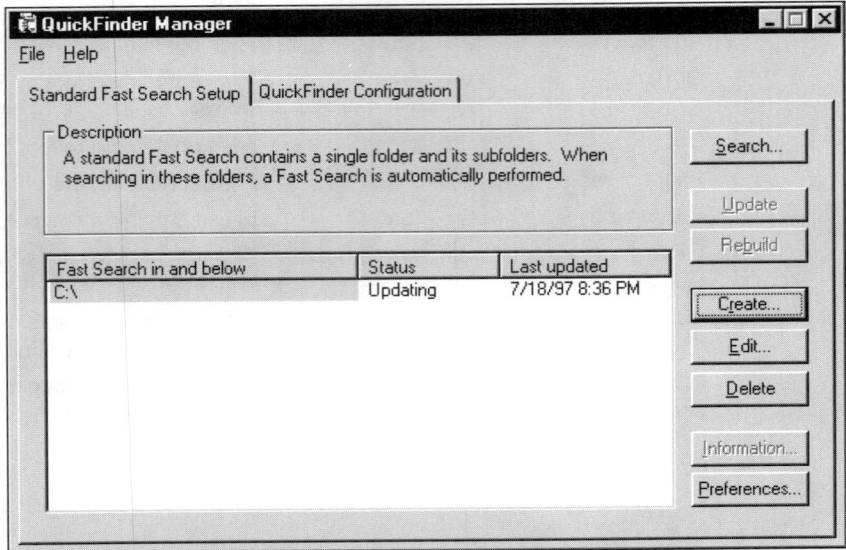

Figure 4-7.   You can use QuickFinder Manager to create a Fast Search file

 *Note:*   *If you select Automatic Update, the Fast Search file is updated at the specified interval. However, if you don't want to take up system resources with this option, you can select Manual Update and then update the Fast Search file yourself by opening the QuickFinder Manager and selecting Update. Just remember to update your Fast Search file before you search.*

❓ I know the file is out there, but QuickFinder can't find it. What's the deal?

If you are absolutely certain that a particular file exists, follow these suggestions to troubleshoot:

⇨ First, make sure the Look In text box displays the correct drive or folder. Make sure the search criteria are correct for the file you are looking for and make sure the File Type drop-down list displays the correct file format.

⇨ The file you are looking for may be hidden. To show all files, including hidden files, open the Windows Explorer and then choose View | Options | Show All Files.

⇨ If you created a Fast Search file that requires manual updating, choose Start from the taskbar and then choose Corel WordPerfect Suite 8 | Tools | QuickFinder Manager 8. Select the Fast Search file and then choose Update.

⇨ Search the hard drive for previously created .IDX files and rename them. In some instances, .IDX files generated by previous versions of WordPerfect can interfere with a search.

FILE BACKUP AND TROUBLESHOOTING

❓ I've noticed when opening files that there is a document saved with the extension .BK!. I didn't create this document. Where did this come from?

You have the Original Document Backup option turned on. After you save a file, the original file is saved with a .BK! extension. Each time you save the file, the BK! file is replaced. This option protects you if you accidentally replace a file that you want to keep. Follow these steps to turn Original Document Backup on or off:

1. Choose Tools | Settings and then double-click Files.

2. Select or deselect Original Document Backup and click OK. Then click Close.

? The electricity went out while I was working on a file. How do I recover what I was working on?

WordPerfect includes several options for backing up files, including Timed Backup and Original Document Backup. However, don't rely on these backup options to protect against data loss—nothing works as well as pressing CTRL-S every few minutes to save files the good old-fashioned way.

WordPerfect backs up every open document you're working on every 10 minutes, which means that the most you'll lose is 10 minutes worth of work. If you've been working on a document for more than 10 minutes when the computer shuts down, just start WordPerfect again, and you will be prompted to save, open, or delete the backup files. These backup files are stored in C:\MyFiles\Backup. You can use the File Settings dialog box (choose Tools | Settings | Files) to change the backup interval or specify a different location, as shown in Figure 4-8.

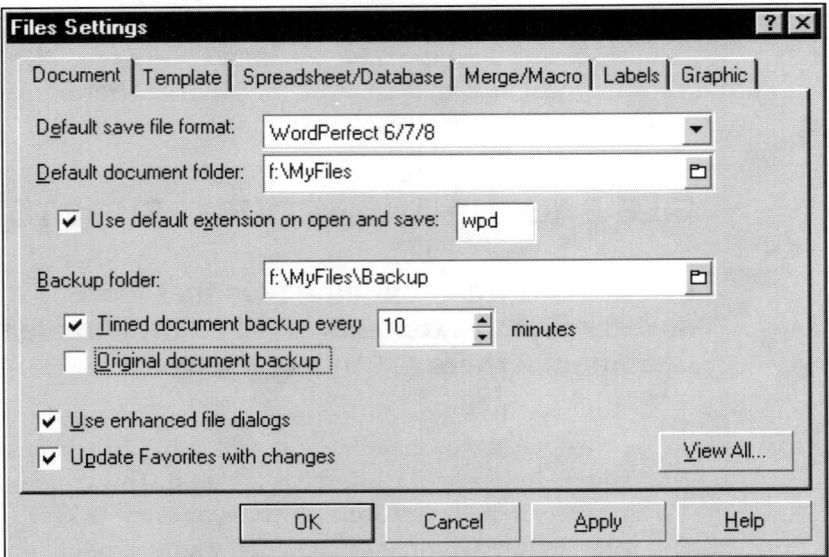

Figure 4-8.   Use Files Settings to change backup options

Tip: To protect against hard drive failure or some other mishap, you should also back up your important documents on a reliable floppy disk or other storage media.

I tried to launch WordPerfect by clicking a WordPerfect document in Windows Explorer, but a dialog box appeared asking me which application I wanted to use. How do I make the computer know it should use WordPerfect?

When you install WordPerfect 8, the extensions .WPD, .WCM, and .WPT are added as associations to WordPerfect. If you're using another extension such as .LTR, you need to add an association so that Windows will open WordPerfect when you launch a document with that extension. Here's how:

1. In Microsoft Explorer, click the name of the file you want to open. Then hold down SHIFT and right-click the filename.

2. Choose Open With and then select wpwin8 from the list of programs. This will create an association between WordPerfect and the file's extension.

3. Select the Always Use This Program to Open This Type of File check box. Then click OK.

I would prefer *not* to have the files listed at the bottom of the File menu. Can I turn this feature off without affecting the files themselves?

The File pull-down menu in WordPerfect displays a list of the last nine documents you opened. This makes it easy to open a file you were recently working on: you can simply select that filename from the File menu or press the number displayed next to the file you want to open. If you don't want this list of filenames displayed, you can turn off this feature. Turning off this display does not affect the actual files in any way. Here's how you can turn off this feature:

1. Choose Tools | Settings and double-click Environment.

2. Click the Interface tab, deselect the Display Last Open Documents on the File Menu check box, and click OK. Then click Close.

Note: *If you're using WordPerfect 7, choose Edit | Preferences and double-click Environment. Deselect the Display Last Open Filenames check box and click OK. Then click Close.*

Tip: *The Open dialog box also displays a list of the files you've most recently opened. Choose File | Open and then click the drop-down arrow to the right of the File Name text box. A list of the documents you've most recently opened is displayed. To open one of these files, select it from the list and click Open. Unlike the list on the File pull-down menu, the list in the Open dialog box cannot be turned off.*

? I tried to save a file from WordPerfect onto a floppy disk and received the following error message: "WPWIN error, can't open file." What's wrong?

First, make sure you have enough room to save the file on the disk and make sure the disk is not write-protected. Then try to save the file to a different floppy disk. Also, there is a limit to the number of files you can place in the root directory on a floppy disk. On 360K and 720K disks, that limit is 112 files. On 1.2 M and 1.44M disks, the limit is 224 files. You can get around this limitation by creating subdirectories on the floppy disk and then saving files in the subdirectories.

? When I tried to save a file, I received the message "Invalid Folder Identifier." What did I do wrong?

Even with the long filename capabilities of Windows 95, certain characters still cannot be used in a filename. These characters are \ / : * ? " < > and | . Be sure to use a name without any of these characters.

? I'm using Windows NT 4.0, and many of my files are becoming corrupt. What should I do?

Microsoft Corporation has verified that two different problems in Windows NT 4.0 can cause data or file corruption. Both problems have been corrected in the latest Windows NT 4.0 U.S. Service Pack. You can download the latest Service Pack from Microsoft's various download services, such as the following:

http://www.microsoft.com/syspro/technet/tnnews/features/
nts4sp3.htm

?

When opening a file with a long filename from a Novell server, I receive this message: "A Selected Item is Not Accessible." What should I do?

This problem occurs only if you run a Novell NetWare server that supports Long Filename (OS2 Name Space). Rename the file using the 8.3 naming convention (an eight-character name followed by a three-letter extension: for example, Letter.wpd) to open the file without any errors.

Layout and Design

Answer Topics!

Layout and Design @ a Glance

⇨   Whether you're writing a form letter to send your customers, creating a sales report, or laying out a 20-page newsletter, the formatting features in WordPerfect let you give your documents a professional appearance. No matter how good the contents of your document, if it isn't appealing to the eye, your audience may skip your text. This chapter answers your questions about page formatting and layout techniques to help you create documents that are both eye-catching and readable.

⇨   You can add a header, a footer, or page numbering to include running text and page numbers on every page of document. If you're printing on both sides of the page, you can create a balanced effect by adding two headers or footers in your document: one for odd pages and the other for even pages. This chapter answers your questions about how to use these features in your documents.

⇨   This chapter provides tips on how to organize your text using bulleted lists, numbered lists, and outlining and how to customize your lists using various number and bullet styles.

⇨   You can automate your formatting with document styles. Instead of adding the same types of formatting to similar elements in your document, you can group these formatting codes into one style. This chapter provides tips on how to use styles to give your documents a more consistent look and feel—and to speed up your work.

⇨   You can use columns to make articles in newsletters and brochures easier to read and more visually appealing. This chapter shows you how to avoid some of the tricky problems that may surface when you use columns.

⇨   This chapter shows you how to take advantage of typesetting features such as hyphenation, kerning, and letter spacing to add visual appeal to your documents.

⇨   You can spruce up the appearance of your documents with drop caps, page and paragraph borders, watermarks, and other subtle design touches. The desktop publishing section of this chapter helps you push the limits of a word processor.

HEADERS, FOOTERS, AND PAGE NUMBERING

? I want to place different headers on odd and even pages. Where is the option that lets me do this?

WordPerfect lets you use up to two headers and two footers on each page, although you will usually use only one header or footer per page. You can make headers and footers appear on all pages or just on even or odd pages.

When you create a header or a footer by choosing Insert | Header/Footer, the Header/Footer property bar, shown in Figure 5-1,

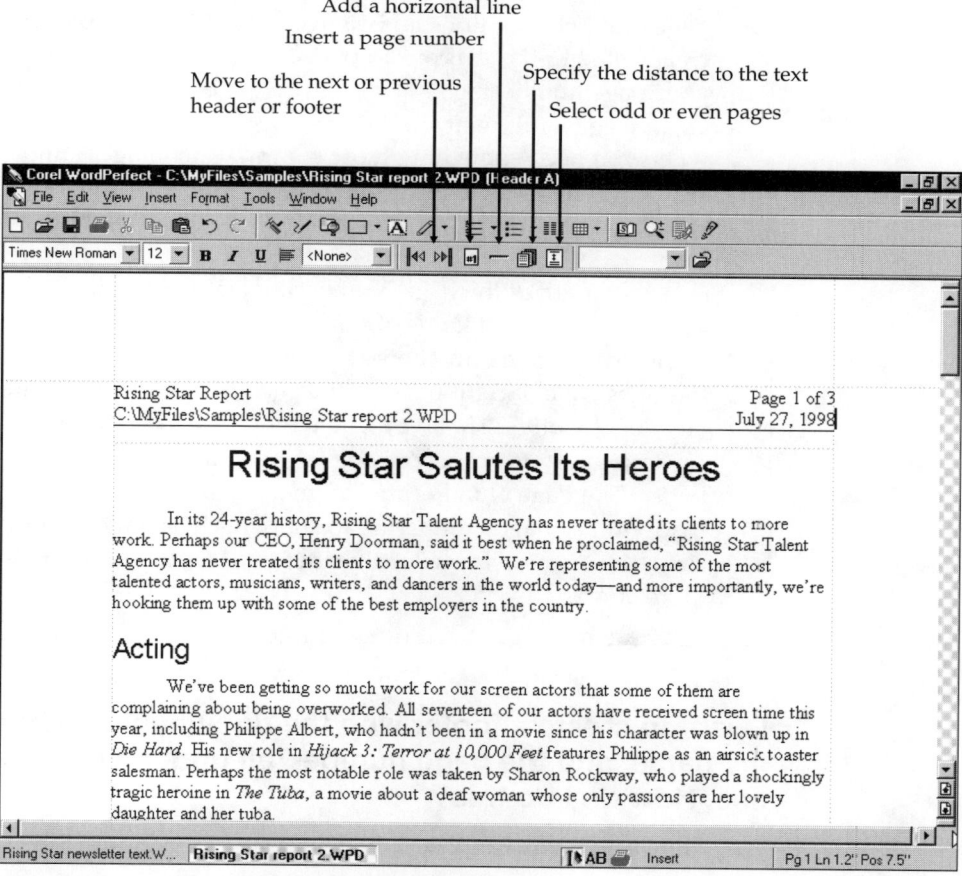

Figure 5-1.   The Header/Footer property bar

appears. You use this bar to format your header or footer. For example, this bar provides options for adding page numbers and horizontal lines, and changing the distance between the header or footer and the text, and positioning headers on odd or even pages.

Using Page Numbering versus Headers and Footers

When should you use WordPerfect's Page Numbering feature, and when should you use a header or footer? Both options let you place running information anywhere at the top or bottom of pages, and both options let you insert text. For example, you can create a footer that has only a page number, or you can add text to your page numbering.

As a general rule, you'll want to use headers and footers when you need something more complex than page numbers. If you just want to include running page numbers in your document with little or no text, you may prefer to use the Page Numbering feature.

A strength of the Page Numbering feature is that it lets you easily create special kinds of numbering. For example, when you want to place page numbers at the left edge of left pages and at the right edge of right pages, use Page Numbering rather than Headers/Footers. That way, you won't have to set up two separate headers or footers: one for odd pages and one for even pages. The Page Numbering feature also includes several ready-to-use page numbering formats, such as "Page x of y." You can also use these formats in headers and footers, but it requires more effort.

? **I want to create a footer with the document title, the date, my name, and the page number, all under a horizontal line. How do I do this?**

Here's how you can insert the footer shown in Figure 5-2.

1. Choose Insert | Header/Footer.

2. Select Footer A and choose Create.

3. Click the Horizontal Line button on the property bar and then press ENTER.

4. Type the document title. Then choose Format | Line | Flush Right (or press ALT-F7).

5. Type **Page**. Then click the Page Numbering button and choose Page Number.

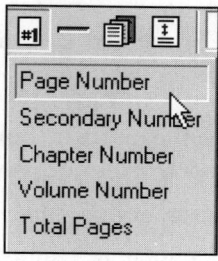

6. Press ENTER and type your name. Then choose Format | Line | Flush Right again.

7. Choose Insert | Date/Time and select the date format you want to use (select Automatic Update if you want the date to be current whenever you open or print the document). Then choose Insert.

8. Click the Close button on the property bar to return to your document.

 *Note:*   *You can view your headers and footers only in Page or Two Pages view. You cannot view them in Draft view.*

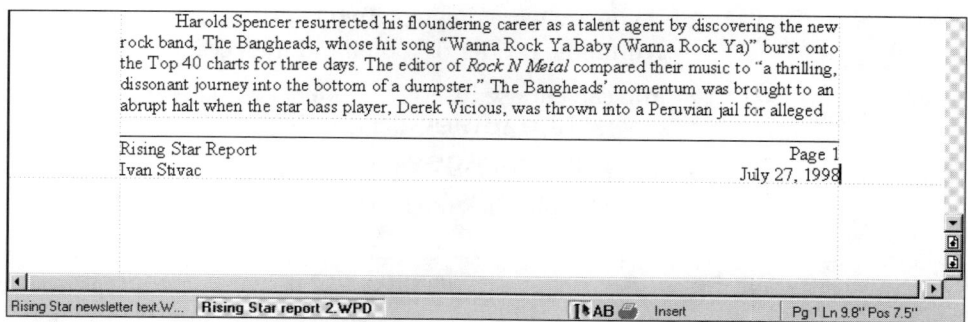

Figure 5-2.   Commonly used footer

 **I started a header on page 2, but it appears on the first page, too. How do I suppress a header on the first page?**

By default, WordPerfect displays the header, footer, or page numbering on every page beginning on the page where the insertion point is placed through the end of the document. However, when you edit your text, your header or footer code may move up or down a page. The best way to remove the header from the first page is to start the header at the top of the document and then suppress it on the pages where you don't want it to appear. Here's how to suppress a header or footer:

1. Place the insertion point on the page where you want the header or footer to be suppressed.

2. Choose Format | Page | Suppress.

3. Select the item you want to suppress and then click OK.

Note: *If you want to discontinue a header or footer for the remainder of the document, place the insertion point on the page where you want the header or footer to stop (the insertion point must be outside the header or footer). Choose Insert | Header/Footer, select the item, and then choose Discontinue. To discontinue page numbering, choose Format | Page | Numbering, select No Page Numbering from the Position drop-down list, and then click OK.*

 I can't see my header on the page. How do I edit it?

When you want to make changes to a footer or header, you can do so in any of the following ways:

⇨ If you are using Page or Two Page view, you can simply click within the header or footer and then edit the text.

⇨ You can choose Insert | Header/Footer, select the item you want to edit, and then choose Edit.

⇨ You can turn on Reveal Codes (choose View | Reveal Codes) and then double-click the header or footer code.

Tip: *If you can't see the footer, use the vertical scroll bar to scroll down.*

 **I don't see an option for deleting a footer. How do I delete a footer?**

To delete a footer or a header, place the insertion point on the page where you inserted the header or footer code. Turn on Reveal Codes (choose View | Reveal Codes) and then drag the code out of the Reveal Codes window to delete it.

Tip: *If you can't find the header or footer code, you can search for it. Choose Edit | Find and Replace | Match | Codes. Then double-click the item (such as Header A) you're looking for and choose Find Next. If you can't find Header A, try finding Header B.*

 **Is there a quick way to add the filename to a footer?**

When you work with a lot of document printouts, you may wonder where the file was saved. Adding a header or footer containing the filename will save you from looking through folders for a specific file. You can insert either the filename (such as Letter.wpd) or the path and the filename (such as C:\MyDocs\Letter.wpd). Here's how to create a header or footer that displays the filename:

1. Save the document.
2. While editing or creating the header or footer, place the insertion point where you want the filename to appear.
3. Choose Insert | Other | Filename (or Path and Filename).

Note: *If you insert the filename in the header or footer without first saving the document, a filename code will be inserted in the header or footer code, but nothing will appear until you save the document.*

I'm printing on both sides of the page. How can I place all the even page numbers on the left side of the footer and all the odd page numbers on the right side?

You can use Footer A and Footer B to create facing pages as shown in Figure 5-3. In Footer A, the page number is left-aligned, and the chapter title is flush right. In Footer B, the chapter title is left-aligned, and the page number is flush right.

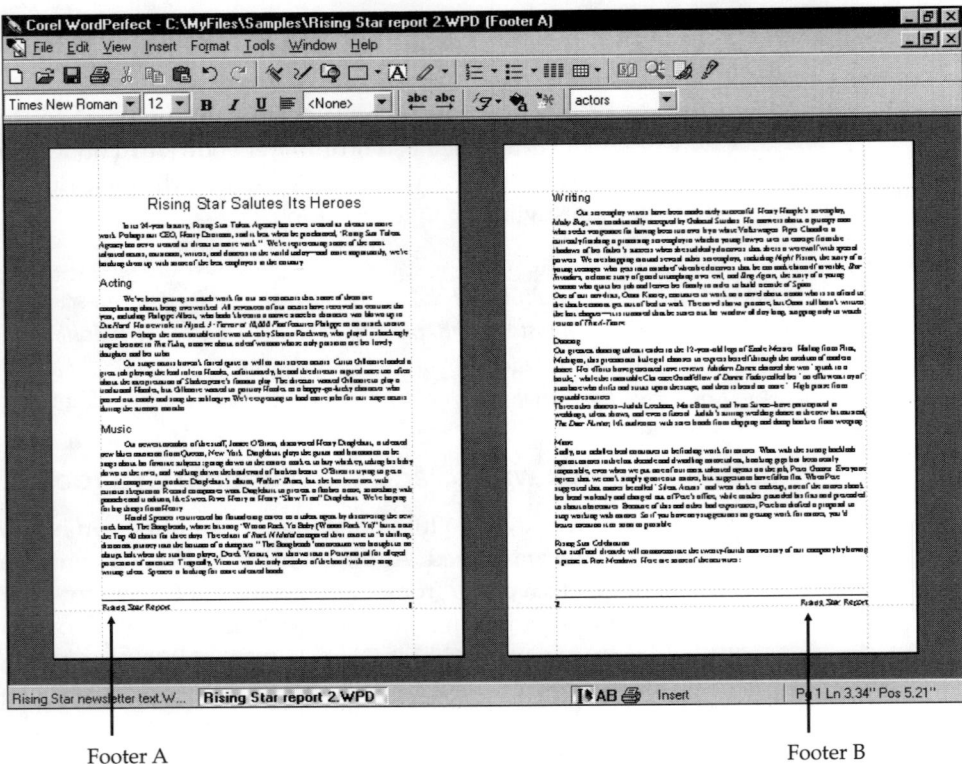

Footer A   Footer B

Figure 5-3.   Create facing footers

When creating Footer A, use the Header/Footer Placement button to make sure Footer A appears only on even pages. Make sure Footer B appears only on odd pages.

Tip: You can use the Page Numbering feature to creating a mirroring effect. Choose Format | Page | Numbering and then select one of the Alternating options from the Position drop-down list. For example, if you want even numbers placed at the bottom of left-hand pages and odd numbers placed at the bottom of right-hand pages, you can select Bottom Outside Alternating or Bottom Inside Alternating.

? How can I make sure that each chapter in my book starts on an odd page?

You can use the Force Page feature to make sure the first page of a chapter stays on an odd- or even-numbered page. If necessary, WordPerfect will insert a blank page to make the chapter start on an odd or even page. Here's how you can force a page:

1. Place the insertion point on the page that you want to remain odd or even.

2. Choose Format | Page | Force Page.

3. Select Current Page Odd or Current Page Even. Then click OK.

Tip: *If you use a document style to format your chapter titles, it's a good idea to place the Force Page code in the style. That way, you won't have to insert it on every chapter title page—the style will do it for you. See "Working with Styles" later in this chapter.*

? I changed the left margin at the top of the document to 1.5 inches, but the footer left margin is still at 1 inch. What do I do?

All document default settings are applied to a new header or footer, including the default font, margin, and tab settings. When you change the fonts or margins in your document, these changes do not affect the header or footer. However, you can format the text in the header or footer just like the current document. One solution is to insert a 1.5-inch left margin code in the footer. Often a better solution is to add the left margin code in the Current Document Style. Any formatting code you place in the Current Document Style will also affect headers and footers. Here's how:

1. Choose File | Document | Current Document Style.

2. From the Styles Editor menu bar, choose Format | Margins.

3. Type **1.5"** in the Left text box. Then click OK twice to return to your document.

? I use several headers in my document, and I want to use a font that is different from the rest of the document. How can I change the style for all headers in the document?

You can edit the Header A or Header B system style. For more information, see "Working with Styles" later in this chapter.

? How do I use roman page numbers in footers?

You can select various types of numbering to use in your headers and footers, such as uppercase or lowercase letters or roman numerals. Here's how to insert roman numerals:

1. Create the header or footer with a page number as usual.

2. Move the insertion point where you want roman numerals to begin. Then choose Format | Page | Numbering.

3. Select No Page Numbering from the Position drop-down list.

4. Choose Custom Format.

5. Select a number style (such as I,II,III,...) from the Page list box. Then choose Insert in Format.

6. Click OK twice.

? Every few pages, I want to change a word or two in the header. Can I do this without retyping the entire contents of the header?

Not really. When you edit the header, the changes you make affect the entire header, even on previous pages. Instead, you need to create a new header each time you want new text to appear. However, you don't have to retype all the information for every header. Instead, you can copy and paste the header code and then edit the copied code. This procedure is not all that quick, but it's faster than re-creating each header. Here's how to copy the header code:

1. Move the insertion point to the top of the page where you inserted a header and then choose View | Reveal Codes.

2. Place the Reveal Codes cursor just before the Header A (or Header B) code and then press SHIFT-RIGHT ARROW to select it.

3. Press CTRL-C to copy the code.

4. Place the insertion point at the beginning of the new section where you want to create a new, changed header. Then press CTRL-V to paste the code. Repeat this paste operation for all sections.

5. Edit the header on the pages where you copied the header codes.

? How do I number pages in a header with both a chapter number and page number, such as 1-1, 1-2, 2-1, 2-2, and so on?

Just as you can have WordPerfect print the current page number, you can place a chapter code at the beginning of each chapter and have WordPerfect insert the current chapter number and page number into a header or footer. If you want to get really fancy, you can throw volume numbers into the mix to create a 1.1.1, 1.1.2, 1.1.3 effect. Here's how to insert the chapter number and page number:

1. Place the insertion point in the header or footer where you want the page number to appear.

2. Click the Page Numbering button on the property bar and select Chapter Number.

3. Type whatever punctuation you want, such as a period or dash.

4. Click the Page Numbering button on the property bar and select Page Number.

   At the beginning of each chapter or section, you need to let WordPerfect know the current chapter number.

5. To change the chapter number, choose Format | Page | Numbering.

6. Choose Set Value and then select the Chapter tab.

7. Type the number of the current chapter (you may also want to click the Page tab and change the page number if you want numbering for the new chapter to start at page 1) and then click OK.

? Why are my headers printing on top of each other?

Headers occupy the same space on the page, whether they are designated as Header A or as Header B. Header A and Header B are designed for use on odd and even pages, not for use on the same page, although you can place them both on a page. To keep headers from printing on top of each other, do one of the following:

⇨ If you want the information to appear on every page, make sure all your information is in either Header A or Header B—not in both. Then delete the header code that you do not want.

⇨ If you want to create a facing pages effect, make sure Header A is assigned to odd-numbered pages and Header B is assigned to even-numbered pages. Edit your header using the Header/Footer Placement button on the property bar.

Note: *If you add a new footer with the same letter—for example, if you add Footer A a second time—the new footer will replace the previous footer from that page onward.*

? When I create a header, the rest of the text in the document moves down. How can I move the header above the top margin so that the document text stays put?

The header appears below the top margin by default. If you want the main document text to be below the top margin and the header above it, you can drag the Header/Footer guidelines. To drag the top guideline of the header, you must turn off your margin guidelines. Here's how to move the header above the top margin:

1. Create the header and make sure the insertion point is outside the header.

2. Choose View | Guidelines. Deselect Margins and make sure Header/Footer is selected. Then click OK.

3. Move the mouse over the top guideline until the line and arrow symbol appears. Then drag the guideline up to its new position.

4. Choose View | Guidelines again. Then select Margins and click OK.

Warning: *Do not move the header too far above the margin. Most printers cannot print to the edge of the paper. If the header or footer extends into this area (called the unprintable zone), your printer won't be able to print it, even though you can see it in Page View.*

? Why doesn't my header appear on the first page of my document?

One possible reason is that you didn't place the insertion point on the first page when you inserted the header. The header or footer code must be somewhere on the first page for the header to appear there. You can use Find and Replace to search for the header code elsewhere in your document and then paste it into page 1. Choose Edit | Find and Replace | Match | Codes. Then double-click the item (such as Header A) you're looking for and choose Find Next. If you can't find Header A, try searching for Header B. Once you find the header code, select it and press CTRL-X to cut it. Then move the insertion point to the first page and press CTRL-V to paste the code.

Another possible reason your header doesn't appear on the first page is that it may be suppressed. Place the insertion point on the first page and choose Format | Page | Suppress. Make sure the header you want displayed (Header A or Header B) is not selected.

? How do I place the page number of the *next* page at the bottom of the current page?

This may sound like an odd request, but this numbering convention is common is some business sectors. Someone once asked me how to create a Canadian "military footer" in which (.../2) is on page 1, (.../3) is on page 2, and so on. I was about to tell her to go away, but then I remembered that you can achieve this effect using a secondary page number in a footer. Here's how:

1. Place the insertion point on the first page of the document (or on the page that you want numbered as page 1).

2. Choose Format | Page | Numbering. From the Position drop-down list, select the location where you want the number to appear. Then choose Set Value.

3. Click the Secondary tab and then type **2** in the Set Secondary Page Number text box. Select the Let Number Change as Pages Are Added or Deleted option and then click OK twice.

4. While creating or editing the footer, type any text before the secondary number, such as **(....**

5. Click the Page Numbering button. Then select Secondary Number and type any additional text, such as a closing parenthesis.

 *Tip:*   *On the last page of your document, discontinue or suppress the footer so you don't imply that there are additional pages.*

I want a page number at the bottom of the first page and in the upper-right corner of all remaining pages. What do I do?

One way to accomplish this is to insert one page numbering code on the first page and another page numbering code on the second page. The second page numbering code overrides the first, so in most cases, this works just fine. However, when editing text, you may accidentally bump the second page numbering code onto a different page. To make sure the second page numbering code always starts on page 2, you can use Delay Codes. Here's how:

1. Move the insertion point to the top of the document.
2. Choose Format | Page | Numbering.
3. Select Bottom Center from the Position drop-down list.
4. Select the type of numbering in the Page Numbering Format list box and then click OK.
5. With the insertion point still on the first page, choose Format | Page | Delay Codes.
6. Click OK to skip one page.
7. In the Define Delayed Codes window, choose Format | Page | Numbering.
8. Select Top Right from the Position drop-down list.
9. Select the type of numbering in the Page Numbering Format list box and then click OK. Click Close.

I don't want page numbering to start until the fifth page of the document, and I want the introductory material to be numbered with small roman numerals. How do I do this?

In this case, you need to insert two different page numbering formats, and you need to reset the value to 1 at the beginning of the first section, after the introductory material such as the title page, table of contents, and so forth. Here's how you do this:

1. Move the insertion point to the top of the document.

2. Choose Format | Page | Numbering.

3. Select i or -I- from the Page Numbering Format list box, select the position, and then click OK.

4. Place the insertion point on the page where you want the new numbering scheme to begin.

5. Choose Format | Page | Numbering.

6. Select the page numbering format (such as 5 or -5-) and position and then choose Set Value.

7. Type **1** in the Set Page Number text box, select Always Keep Number the Same, and then click OK twice.

Note: In this scenario, you want to select the Always Keep Number the Same option so that Chapter 1 always begins on page 1. If you did not select this option, adding more pages to the introductory material might cause the chapter to start on page 2 or 3.

I started new page numbering at the beginning of each chapter, but now I can't use the Multiple Pages Print option to print a range of pages, such as pages 1 through 4 of Chapter 2. What am I doing wrong?

Each time you restart page numbering, WordPerfect treats the following pages as a new section. Thus, to print pages 1 through 4 from the second group of page numbers, you type **2:1-4**. Here are the steps:

1. Choose File | Print and then click the Multiple Pages tab.

2. Type the number of pages you want to print, such as **2:1-4**, in the Page(s)/Label(s) text box. Then choose Print.

*Tip: If your document includes chapter, volume, or secondary page numbers, you can indicate a section to be printed by typing the appropriate number in the Chapter, Volumes, or Secondary Pages text box. For example, type **2** in the Chapter text box and **1-4** in the Page(s)/Label(s) text box to print pages 1 through 4 of Chapter 2.*

Is there a way to insert "extra" pages in a document and have them numbered with letters, such as 16A, 16B, and 16C? After these pages are inserted, the page numbering should continue with regular numbers (17, 18, 19, and so on).

You can insert page numbers containing letters, such as 16A and 16B, in the middle of a document and then have the regular page numbers continue by setting up a custom page numbering format. Follow these steps:

1. Place the insertion point on the page where you want to start the lettered numbering.

2. Choose Format | Page | Numbering and then select Custom Format.

3. Press DELETE to delete the current text in the Custom Page Numbering Format text box. Type the page number that should appear with the letters, such as **16**.

4. In the Secondary Pg list box, select the A,B,C,... option. Then choose Insert in Format and click OK.

5. Choose Set Value and click the Secondary tab. Then type **1** in the Set Secondary Page Number text box and click OK twice.

   The additional pages in the document are now numbered 16A, 16B, 16C, and so on. The first number always stays the same, and the letter is automatically incremented with each new page. Now you have to restart page numbering after the special set of numbers.

6. Place the insertion point on the page where the regular numbers should start again.

7. Choose Format | Page | Numbering.

8. In the Page Numbering Format list box, select the type of page numbering you were using before the custom numbering began.

9. Choose Set Value. Then type the number (such as **17**) at which regular page numbering should resume and click OK twice.

LISTS AND OUTLINES

❓ What kinds of lists can I create in WordPerfect?

Lists are a great way to organize information. In WordPerfect, you can create many kinds of lists, as shown in Figure 5-4.

You can use the Outline/Bullets and Numbering feature to create bulleted and numbered lists. When you begin a list, WordPerfect automatically turns on the Outlining feature and displays the Outline property bar. One of the advantages of using sequenced lists, such as numbered lists or outlines, is that if you change the order of the items, the numbers to the left of each paragraph are updated automatically.

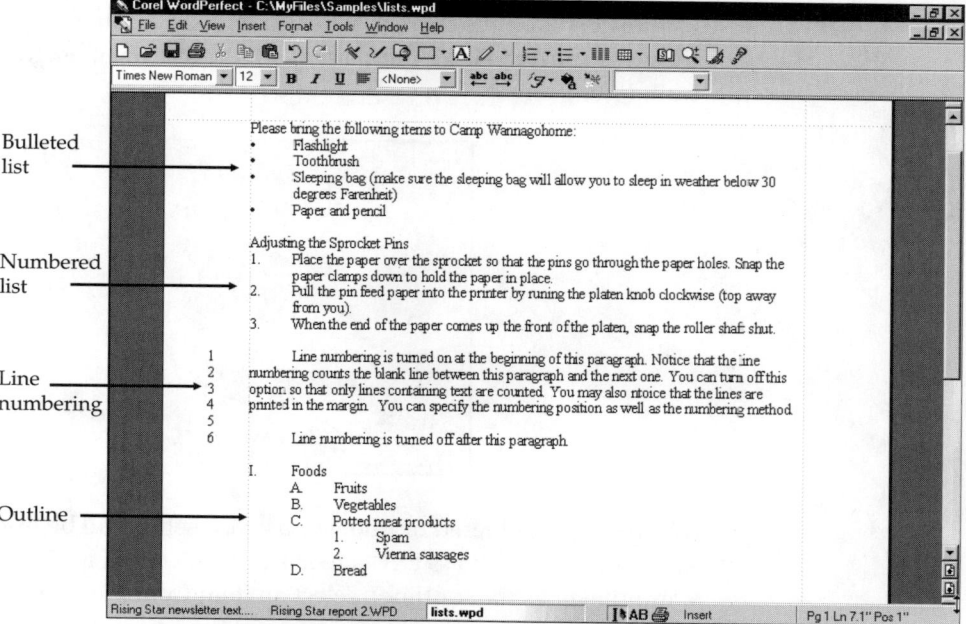

Figure 5-4.   Different kinds of lists

 ## What's the quickest way to create a bulleted or numbered list?

You can create numbered or bulleted lists in three ways. You can use the Numbering and Bullets buttons on the toolbar, you can start lists while you type using Format-As-You-Go, or you can use the Bullets and Numbering dialog box.

Tip: *When creating lists, you can start typing the list from scratch, or you can type the text first and then apply the bullets or numbers afterward.*

Using the Toolbar

The toolbar provides two buttons to help you create lists:

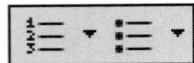

To begin a list using the toolbar, either click the Numbering or Bullets list button to use the current list of numbering or bullet types, or click the arrow next to either button and select the type of list from the pull-down menu.

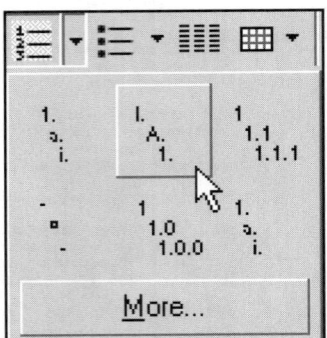

The type of numbered or bulleted list you select will be inserted at the start of each line. Press ENTER to start the next item in the list. To create a multilevel list (an outline), select an item from the Numbering drop-down list and then press TAB to move up one level or SHIFT-TAB to move down one level. To end the list, press ENTER-BACKSPACE.

Tip: *If you don't want an item to be included in the list, click it and then click the Numbering or Bullets icon on the toolbar. If you want to use a different bullet or number, select the text and then select a new bullet or numbering type.*

 *Note:* *To create a blank line between bulleted or numbered items, move the insertion point to the end of the first item and press* ENTER *twice.*

Using Format-As-You-Go

The QuickBullets option of the QuickCorrect Format-As-You-Go feature will sense when you are starting a list and take over from there.

➪ To start a bulleted list, type an asterisk (*) followed by a TAB. WordPerfect replaces the * with a small bullet followed by an indent. When you press ENTER, WordPerfect starts the next item in the list. When you're done with the list, press ENTER-BACKSPACE. You can also use other characters to start the list with different bullets, such as o, O, ^, >, +, or -.

➪ To start a numbered list, type the first number, letter, or roman numeral. Type a period and then press TAB. WordPerfect inserts an indent following the number. When you press ENTER, WordPerfect will begin the paragraph with the next number in the sequence. If you change the order of items in the list, the numbers are updated automatically.

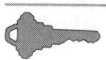 *Note:* *You cannot use Format-As-You-Go to create a multilevel (outline) list. Instead, select an option by using the Numbering button on the toolbar.*

 *Tip:* *After you turn off a numbered list, you can turn it on again by typing the next number followed by a period and a tab.*

Using the Bullets and Numbering Dialog Box

If you want more bullet and list options, use the Bullets and Numbering dialog box, shown in Figure 5-5. Follow these steps to create customized lists:

1. Place the insertion point where you want the list to begin or select the text.

2. Choose Insert | Outline/Bullets and Numbering.

3. Select an option from the Numbers, Bullets, or Text tab. Then click OK.

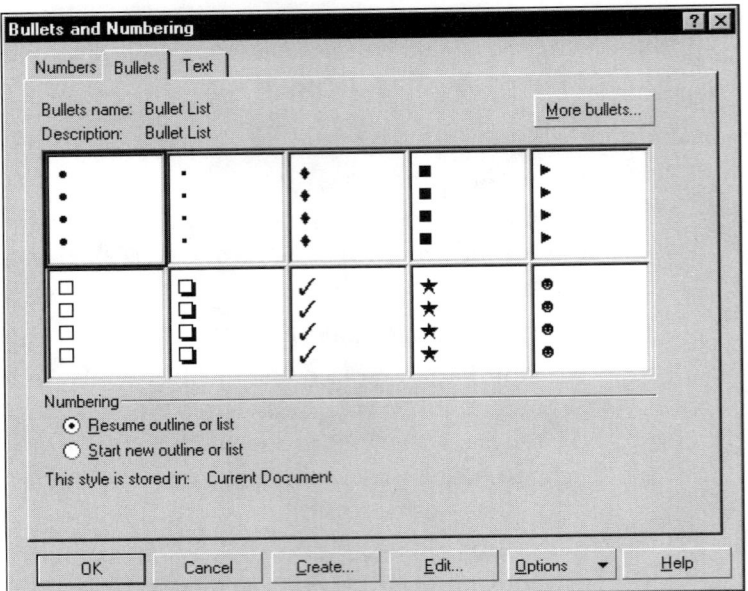

Figure 5-5.   The Bullets and Numbering dialog box

❓ I want to create numbered steps for a technical manual. How do I restart numbering for a new set of steps?

Use any of the methods above to create the list. When you're ready to start a new list, place the insertion point on the line where you want the new list to begin and then use one of the following procedures:

⇨ Type the number, letter, or roman numeral followed by a period and a tab. After you press TAB, you are asked if you want to resume the previous list or start a new one. Choose Start New List.

⇨ Choose Insert | Outline/Bullets and Numbering. Select the type of number list you want, select Start New Outline or List, and then click OK.

❓ Typing a number and a period and then pressing TAB starts a numbered list. How do I prevent this?

Sometimes you may want to type numbers at the beginning of a line without starting a numbered list. You can turn off the QuickBullets option in the QuickCorrect dialog box. Here's how:

1. Choose Tools | QuickCorrect and then click the Format-As-You-Go tab.

2. Deselect the QuickBullets option and then click OK.

 ***Tip:*** *Even if you turn off this option, you can still use keystrokes to create lists. Press* CTRL-H *to start a numbered list. Press* CTRL-SHIFT-B *to start a bulleted list.*

I just want to insert a bullet at the insertion point. How do I insert a bullet without starting a list?

To insert a bullet, choose Insert | Symbol (or press CTRL-W). Explore the various options on the Set pop-up list until you find the symbol you want to use. Iconic Symbols and Typographic Symbols have lots of bullet choices. Select the character you want to insert and then choose Insert and Close.

All the bullet characters appear as hollow squares. What's wrong?

Bullets are WordPerfect characters. When hollow squares appear, it means that not all the WordPerfect characters were installed properly. Perform a Custom installation and make sure the WordPerfect Character Sets option, under Required Shared Components, is selected. For more information, see "Adding and Removing Suite Components" in Chapter 2.

I set tabs earlier and now my bulleted list doesn't look right. How do I fix it?

The tab settings you specify at the beginning of your document affect the rest of the document until you create new tab settings. You can return the tabs to their default settings by placing the insertion point in the first item in your list and choosing Format | Line | Tab Set | Default and then clicking OK.

Bulleted and numbered lists automatically indent text one tab setting after the bullet or number. You can change the distance between the bullet or number and the text:

1. Select the list.

2. If the ruler is not displayed, click View | Ruler.

3. Drag the appropriate tab marker (usually set at the 1.5" mark) on the ruler to a new position. Then click anywhere in your document to deselect the list.

? How do I number lines in paragraphs without creating a list?

Use the Line Numbering feature to number lines in the left margin of your document. This option is useful for legal documents, macros, poetry, and any other documents that you may want to refer to by line number.

1. Place the insertion point where you want the line numbering to begin.

2. Choose Format | Line | Numbering.

3. Select the numbering method.

4. Select Turn Line Numbering On and then click OK.

 **Note:**   *Line numbering is turned on until the end of the document or until you turn it off by choosing Format | Line | Numbering and deselecting the Turn Line Numbering On option.*

? Where is the Outline feature in WordPerfect 8? Can I still use Outline mode?

In WordPerfect 8, an outline is a multilevel bulleted list. When you are working with a list, the Outline property bar includes buttons that help you create your outline, as shown in Figure 5-6. You can use items on this property bar to promote and demote outline items, show and hide families, set paragraph numbers, and modify the outline format. To create an outline, follow these steps:

1. Choose Insert | Outline/Bullets and Numbering.

2. Select the type of outline you want to use in your document and then click OK.

3. Type the first outline item. Press ENTER to add another item. Press TAB to demote the item to the next level or SHIFT-TAB to promote the item to the previous level.

4. To end the outline, press ENTER-BACKSPACE.

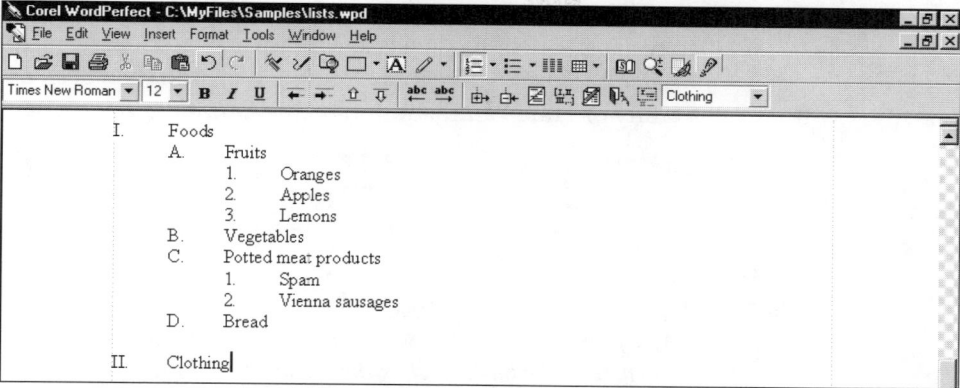

Figure 5-6.   Outline property bar

Outline Terms You Should Know

⇨ An *outline item* is a paragraph of an outline. Press TAB to move to the next outline level or SHIFT-TAB to move to the previous level.

⇨ *Body text* is text that is not numbered as part of the outline, but appears between outline entries. To type body text, press ENTER twice and then move the insertion point back up to the blank line. When you're ready to continue adding to the outline, move the insertion point down to the next outline item and begin typing.

⇨ A *family* consists of a heading at any level and all the subheadings and text under it.

⇨ An *outline definition* is a group of styles, each of which uniquely defines the appearance of the number and text for each level of the outline. WordPerfect provides several predefined outline definitions that you can use or edit. You can also create your own outline definitions.

How do I collapse and expand outlines?

One of the advantages of working with an outline is that it lets you visualize the organization of topics and subtopics, showing you at a glance how subjects are related. You can expand or collapse an outline to see as many of the levels as you want. To collapse or expand a family, click anywhere in the outline item and then click the Show Family or Hide Family button on the Outline property bar.

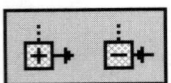

 *Tip*   *To collapse the entire outline to a specific level—for instance, to display just the first- and second-level headings—place the insertion point anywhere in the outline, click the Show Levels button, and select the lowest level you want displayed (for example, Two).*

? I hid an outline, and now the Outline property bar and my entire outline have disappeared. How do I get them back?

This is one of those goofy things in WordPerfect that can drive you nuts. If you click the Show Levels button and select <None>, your outline disappears, but so does the Outline property bar, which is the only way to bring back the levels! Here's a rather clunky workaround. Place the insertion point at the end of the hidden outline and then resume the outline by choosing Insert | Outline/Bullets and Numbering. Select the type of outline you're using, select Resume Outline or List, and then click OK. Then click the Show Levels button and select Eight to redisplay all the levels of the outline you created.

? The outline icons don't appear next to the outline I created. How do I move outline families?

First you need to turn on the icon display. Then you'll find it easy to select families and move them from one place to another within an outline. As you do so, the order is automatically updated. Here's how to select and move outline families:

1. Make sure the insertion point is in one of the outline items. Then click the Show Icons button on the Outline property bar.

2. Click the icon next to the family you want to move and then drag it to the new location, as shown in the following illustration.

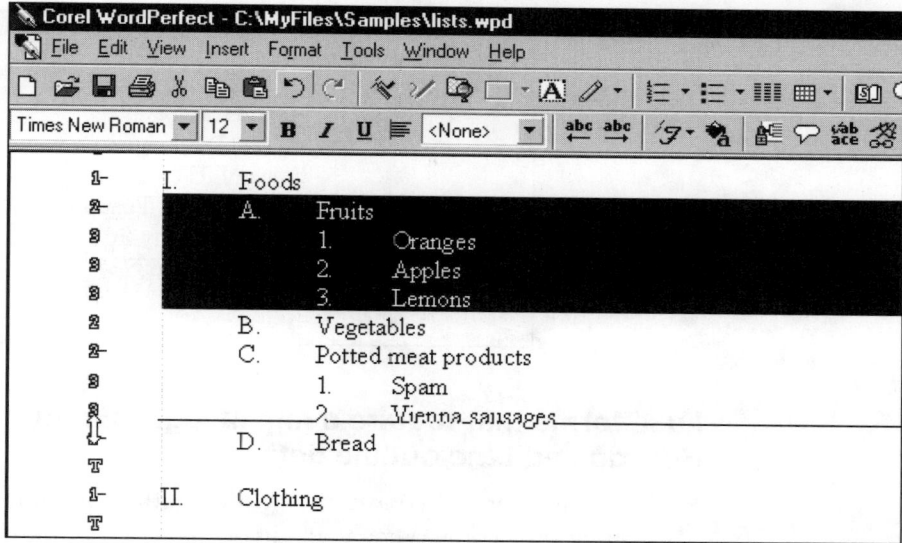

 I pressed ENTER-BACKSPACE to type body text. How do I resume the outline?

The best way to type body text between outline items is to press ENTER twice and then move the insertion point back up to the blank line and type the paragraph. Then you can simply click the next outline item to resume outlining. However, if you've already discontinued your outline, here's how to resume it:

1. Choose Insert | Outline/Bullets and Numbering.

2. Select the type of outline you're using.

3. Select Resume Outline or List and then click OK.

Tip: *To start renumbering in an outline, click the Set Paragraph Number button on the property bar, type the level you want to start at, and click OK.*

How do I keep multiple lines ending with hard returns together in the same outline level?

Press CTRL-SHIFT-L to create this effect. The insertion point will move down one line and the line will be indented, but a new number will not appear.

```
I.      Auto Repair Companies
        A.      Good Car Care
                3232 N. Bingham Dr.
                Albany, NY 12421
        B.      Super Duper Tune-ups
                873 University St.
                Omaha, NE 68734
```

? I use forms that require a mix of legal and outline types. How do I edit the outline definition?

You can either edit one of the existing outline definitions, or you can create a new one. When you edit or create an outline definition, you work with eight different styles that comprise the outline definition. Here's how to edit the styles in an outline definition:

1. Choose Insert | Outline/Bullets and Numbering.

2. Select the type of outline that most closely resembles the outline you need and then choose Edit.

3. Select the level you want to change. Then select the number or bullet you want to use from the Number/Bullet drop-down list.

4. Repeat step 3 for any level style that needs to be edited. Then click OK.

? I changed the outline definition for one document, but when I start a new document and turn on the Outline feature, the definitions don't appear. How can I save my settings for use in other documents?

After you create a new outline definition or modify an existing one, you can make your custom definition available in all your new documents. For example, if you modify the Legal outline definition and want to use it for other documents as well, you can save the edited outline definition to the default template. Here's how:

1. Open a document in which you have edited outline definitions or created new ones.

2. Choose Insert | Outline/Bullets and Numbering.

3. From the Options pop-up menu, choose Setup.

4. Select Default Template and then click OK twice.

Any custom outline definition that you created will now be available in your other documents. Any outline definition (such as Legal) that you edited will replace the corresponding default outline definition.

I include chapter numbers in my outline. However, when I change the order of the chapters in my outline, the chapter numbers stay the same. How can I automatically number chapters?

You can create a counter for your chapter titles. A counter is a numeric item in your document that can be increased or decreased sequentially. Page numbers and figure captions are counters, and you can also create your own. Three main steps are required to create counters: First you must create a counter style, then you must set the initial counter value (usually to 0), and then you must display the counter in the document.

Note: *Counters can be confusing because they first increase and then appear. This means that if you set your initial counter value to 1—which seems logical—your first displayed counter number will be 2.*

Here's how you can create a counter for chapter titles:

1. Place the insertion point at the beginning of the document or wherever you want your counter to start.

2. Choose Insert | Other | Counter and then choose Create.

3. Type a name for the counter, such as **Chapters**.

4. To change the numbering method for a counter level, click a method in the Single Level Method drop-down list. Then click OK.

5. Select the counter you just created and then choose Value. To start numbering at 1, set the value to 0. Click OK and then click Close.

6. Place the insertion point where you want your first counter to appear, such as after the first chapter title, and then choose Insert | Other | Counter | Increase and Display. Repeat this step for each chapter title.

If you change the order of your chapters, the counters will reflect the changes and display the correct numbers in order.

WORKING WITH STYLES

Why Styles?

Styles provide an easy way to format similar types of text, such as headings, titles, lists, subtitles, and quotations. Styles provide two benefits: consistency and flexibility. By defining a set of formats in a style, you can easily apply the formats to similar portions of text. Using the same style to format chapter titles, for example, will ensure that all titles look the same.

However, one of the greatest benefits of styles is that they can be updated so easily. If you edit a style, all the text formatted with that style will change automatically. So if you type a long document with 20 subtitles all formatted the same way, you can edit the subtitle style, and all 20 subtitles will be changed instantly. With the time you save, you can run to the nearest donut shop and buy some jelly donuts.

WordPerfect comes with a set of predefined heading styles that you can use to format your headings. These heading styles are useful for creating a table of contents or using the Outline feature to format text, but they aren't very pretty—you may want to edit them to include different fonts and formatting, or you may want to create your own heading styles. WordPerfect also includes system styles that format different elements in your document, such as headers and footers, footnotes, and graphics boxes.

? I've already formatted a hanging indent paragraph, and I want to quickly use the same formatting in three other paragraphs. What's the fastest way to do this?

You can either create a style based on the paragraph (called a QuickStyle), or you can use the QuickFormat feature. Although the QuickFormat feature is faster, creating a QuickStyle offers more flexibility. For example, you can copy QuickStyles—but not QuickFormat styles—to other documents.

⇨ To create a QuickStyle, place the insertion point in the formatted paragraph and then choose Format | Styles. Choose QuickStyle, type a style name and description, and click OK. Then click Close. For example, to use the hanging indent paragraph style you created as the style for other hanging indent paragraphs, place the insertion point where you want to apply the style and then select the style from the Styles drop-down list on the property bar.

⇨ When you format text using QuickFormat, WordPerfect creates a temporary style that you can use to format other similar paragraphs. Here's how to use QuickFormat:

1. Place the insertion point in the paragraph that has the formatting you want to copy.

2. Click the QuickFormat button on the toolbar.

3. To copy the paragraph format, select Headings and then click OK.

 *Note:*   *Selecting the Headings option copies the paragraph formatting, such as the style, alignment, font, and other attributes. Selecting the Selected Characters option copies only the font and attributes, not the paragraph formatting such as styles and alignment.*

4. Click the other paragraphs you want to format.

5. Click the QuickFormat button on the toolbar again to turn it off.

 *Tip:*   *A separate QuickFormat style (QuickFormat1, QuickFormat2, and so on) is created each time you use the QuickFormat feature. If you want to apply this same format to another paragraph later, place the insertion point in the paragraph and select, for example, QuickFormat1 from the Styles drop-down list on the property bar.*

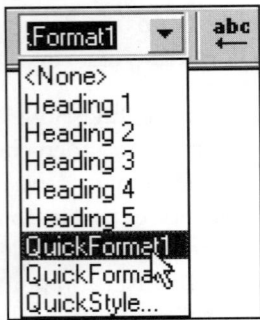

Can I edit the QuickFormat style?

Yes, you can edit the QuickFormat style, but only for the current document.

1. Choose Format | Styles.
2. Select the QuickFormat style you want to edit and then choose Edit.
3. Add or remove any formatting in the Contents box and click OK. Then click Close.

When creating a hanging indent style, I can't press SHIFT-TAB to insert a back tab. What should I do?

The problem here is that pressing SHIFT-TAB takes you to the previous option in the Styles Editor dialog box rather than inserting a back tab. Instead, use the menus in the Style Editor. Choose Format | Paragraph | Back Tab (or Hanging Indent).

I have created lots of styles. Now I want to apply them to other documents. How do I use styles in other documents?

There are two main ways to use styles you create in other documents: saving the styles in the default template and saving the styles in their own file.

⇨ You should save styles to the default template if you intend to use them in most other documents you create. This option is especially useful if you edit the heading system styles and want to use them in other documents. To save styles in the default template, choose Format | Styles and then choose Setup from the Options menu. Select Default Template and click OK.

Types of Styles You Can Create

There are three main types of styles: paragraph, character, and document.

⇨ A *paragraph (paired) style* is used for titles, headings, and other text in which the entire paragraph is formatted. A paired style can be toggled on and off, like boldfacing or italics. When you create a paragraph style, you can select what happens when you press the ENTER key after typing the paragraph. Pressing the ENTER key can turn off the style, resume the same style in the next paragraph, or chain to a different style.

⇨ A *paragraph (paired-auto) style* is the same as a paragraph (paired) style, with one added attraction: you can edit the style directly in the document. Simply select some text to which the style has been applied and then edit it. The style will be updated with the changes, as will other text formatted using that style.

⇨ A *character (paired) style* is used for words and phrases within a paragraph, although you can apply a character style to an entire paragraph. You can apply this style to selected text, or you can turn on the style, type the text, and then press the RIGHT ARROW key to turn off the style.

⇨ A *character (paired-auto) style* is a character style that you can edit directly in the document. To change the style, just select and then edit some of the text formatted with that style.

⇨ A *document (open) style* does not have an end. As with tab or margin settings, when a document style is turned on in one place in a document, it remains in effect until the end of the document, or until you override it by inserting other formatting codes.

⇨ You should save styles in a styles file if you want to use them just in certain documents. For example, you may want one set of styles for newsletters, another set of styles for reports, and another set of styles for books. These sets of styles, sometimes called *style sheets*, are saved in their own files. Here's how to save a set of styles you created:

1. Open the document containing the styles you created.

2. Choose Format | Styles.

3. Choose Save As from the Options menu.

4. Specify whether you want to save User Styles, System Styles, or Both.

Note: *If you have edited system styles, such as Heading, Footnote, and Watermark styles, and you want to include these styles in other documents, make sure you select either System Styles or Both when you save the styles. If you just want to save the styles that you created, select the User Styles option.*

5. Type a filename (such as **Report.sty**) and click OK.

Note: *When you want to retrieve the style, open the document in which you want to use the style and then choose Format | Styles | Options | Retrieve. Specify the filename (such as Report.sty) and click OK.*

? Can I display only the headings in a document?

When working in a long document, it's useful to be able to collapse the document into an outline so that you can see only one or two levels of headings. This capability is especially useful when you're copying and pasting information from other documents. To expand and condense your document, you can use the Heading system styles along with the Outline/Bullets and Numbering feature. The Outline property bar will then appear when the insertion point is in a heading.

Here's how you can edit your document to include outline headings:

1. Save your document with a different name so that you have a backup in case you make unwanted changes to your document.

2. Place the insertion point in the first title or heading in your document.

3. Choose Insert | Outline/Bullets and Numbering.

4. Select the Text tab. Then select Headings and click OK.

 Note: *If you used your own styles to format your headings, the formatting in the new style will override the formatting in the old style. You can use the Styles Editor to edit the heading styles.*

5. To apply the heading styles to additional headings, select the heading style (such as Heading 1 or Heading 2) from the Select Styles drop-down list on the property bar.

6. To collapse your document, click a heading so that the Outline property bar appears, then click the Show/Hide Body Text button to hide the body text in the document. You can select a level (such as One or Two) from the Show Levels button to display different heading levels. You can also click the Show Family and Hide Family buttons to collapse and expand the contents under individual headings.

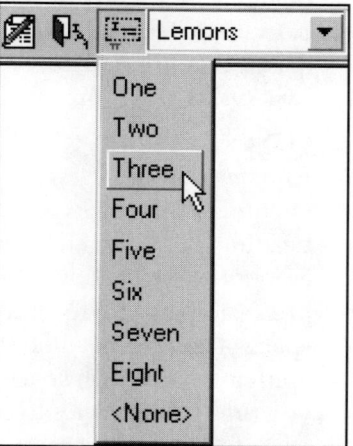

 Tip: *If you want to change the heading styles, you can edit them in the Styles Editor. Choose Format | Styles, select the heading whose style you want to change, and choose Edit.*

Ideas for Heading Styles

One of the most common uses for styles is to format headings. In my humble opinion, the heading styles that come with WordPerfect don't quite measure up. I like to use a sans serif font such as Arial for my headings, and I like to insert other formatting codes as well. You can edit the heading styles to add your own fonts and formatting, or you can create your own heading styles. However, if you use the heading styles to build outlines and create a table of contents, you'll be better off editing the default heading styles.

Regardless of whether you decide to edit the system styles or create your own heading styles, here are some features that you may want to include:

⇨ *Conditional End of Page.*   Sometimes a heading will end up at the bottom of one page, with the first paragraph of text beginning on the next page. You can insert a Conditional End of Page code to ensure that at least a few lines of text accompany the heading. To do this, make sure the insertion point is in the Contents window. From the Styles Editor menu bar, choose Format | Keep Text Together. Select the check box below Conditional End of Page, type **4** in the text box, and click OK. This ensures that the next four lines of text after the heading remain with the heading.

⇨ *Paragraph Spacing.*   When using headings in single-spaced documents, people commonly press ENTER twice before the heading and twice after the heading, creating an equal amount of space above and below the heading. You can add a professional touch to your documents by adding slightly less space below the heading than above it. You do this by applying paragraph spacing to the heading. For example, if you press ENTER twice to add two lines before the heading, you can apply paragraph spacing of 1.25 lines after the heading. In the Styles Editor, choose Format | Paragraph | Format. Type **1.25** in the Number of Lines text box and then click OK.

⇨ *Mark Table of Contents.* If you're editing one of the predefined heading styles, this option is already added for you. The great benefit of this feature is that you can define and generate a table of contents without having to mark each heading. To add a Mark Table of Contents code to a style you're creating, first select Show 'Off Codes' in the Styles Editor so you can insert the paired Mark code. Make sure the insertion point is placed after any formatting codes (so they aren't included in the generated table of contents). Then hold down SHIFT and press DOWN ARROW to select the Off codes. Choose Tools | Reference | Table of Contents and then choose Mark 1 to indicate a first-level heading, Mark 2 to indicate a second-level heading, and so on. Choose Close to close the Table of Contents property bar.

⇨ *Force Page.* When you create some documents, such as books or long reports, you might want each new chapter to begin on an odd-numbered page. You can use a Force Page code to ensure that each section begins only on a right or only on a left page. Place the insertion point in the Contents window of the Styles Editor and choose Format | Page | Force Page. Select Current Page Odd or Current Page Even and then click OK.

My newsletter uses a Q & A format. How do I chain styles so that turning off one style turns on the other?

To make your job easier when you create a question-and-answer section as shown in Figure 5-7, you can chain styles so that turning off one style turns on the other. Here's how:

1. Create the Question style. You may want to type text (such as a large **Q:** in the question style) in the contents window. To do this, type the **Q:** first, then select it, and then apply formatting.

Tip: *If you want the rest of the question following the Q: to be formatted in italics or bold, select Show 'Off Codes,' select the Off code, and press* CTRL-I *or* CTRL-B.

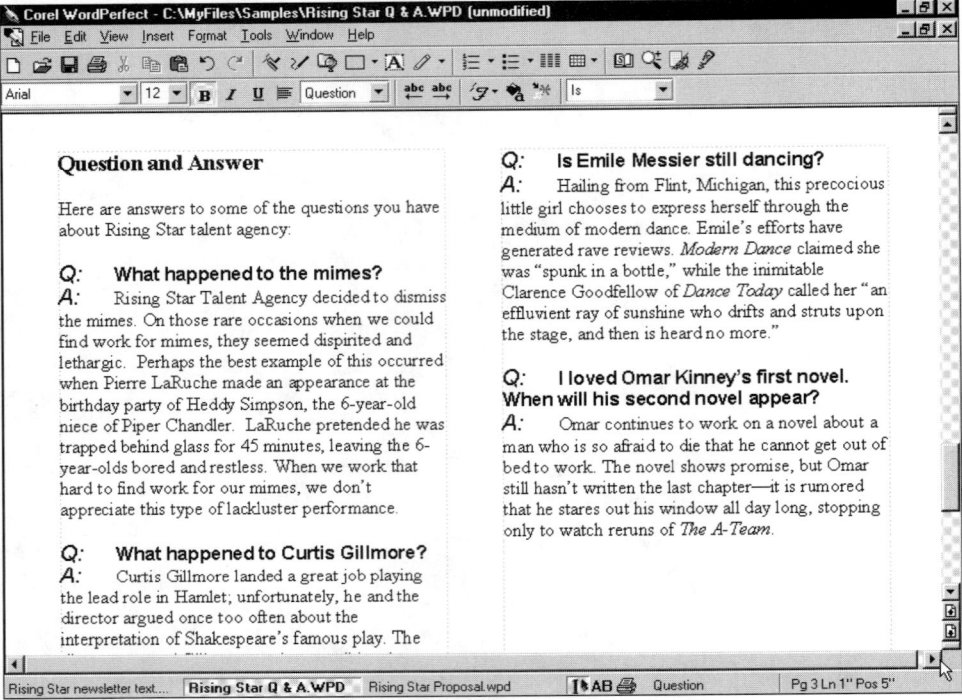

Figure 5-7.   Chained styles for a Q & A format

2. Create the Answer style in a similar way. You may want to add an extra line after the question. To do this, select Show 'Off Codes,' move the insertion point after the Off code, and press ENTER.

3. From the Enter Key Will Chain To drop-down list, select Question. Then click OK.

4. Edit the Question style. In the Styles Editor, select Answer from the Enter Key Will Chain To drop-down list.

Note: When you type your last answer, pressing ENTER will format the next paragraph in the Question style, and you'll feel like you're stuck in an endless loop. To turn off the style, choose Format | Styles and then double-click <None>.

Tip: If you want to start a new line in an answer without switching to the Question style, press CTRL-SHIFT-L.

 **I want to use my company letterhead in various letters and memos. Can I insert the logo and text into a style?**

Yes. The easiest way is to open the document containing the letterhead, turn on Reveal Codes, and copy all the codes—including the logo and company name—and paste them into a style you create, as shown in Figure 5-8.

 *Tip:*   *To view graphics and text in the Styles Editor, deselect the Reveal Codes check box.*

Note: *Another way to store your letterhead for use in other documents is by using the QuickWords feature, which saves text, graphics, and formatting. For more information, see "QuickCorrect and Format-As-You-Go" in Chapter 10.*

 **How do I delete a style without deleting the formatting from my documents?**

In the Style List dialog box, choose Delete from the Options pop-up menu. You have two options. If you select Including Formatting

Figure 5-8.   Create a style containing your letterhead

Codes, the style and the formatting are deleted. If you choose Leave Formatting Codes in Document, the style is deleted, but the formatting remains.

WORKING WITH COLUMNS

? **I want to use columns and then leave the bottom third of the page blank below the columns. Is there a way to stop the columns evenly without adding column breaks?**

You can create four types of columns: balanced newspaper columns, newspaper columns, parallel columns, and parallel columns with block protection. Creating balanced columns will help you achieve the look you want. Figure 5-9 shows some examples of WordPerfect's column types.

? **The column gutters are too wide. How do I change the spacing between columns?**

If you want evenly spaced columns, using the Columns dialog box is the best way to change the gutter space. Choose Format | Columns and then type a number (such as **0.25"**) in the Space between Text box.

If you're a carefree, format-with-your-hair-on-fire type, you can use the mouse to change the column gutters and widths. If the column

Newspaper columns   Balanced newspaper columns   Parallel columns

Figure 5-9.   Different kinds of columns

guidelines are not visible, choose View | Guidelines and make sure Columns is selected. Place the pointer over the column guideline until the pointer becomes a two-headed arrow divided by a single line. Then drag the guideline right or left. If you're dragging the left column guideline, you can hold down CTRL to keep the column size the same.

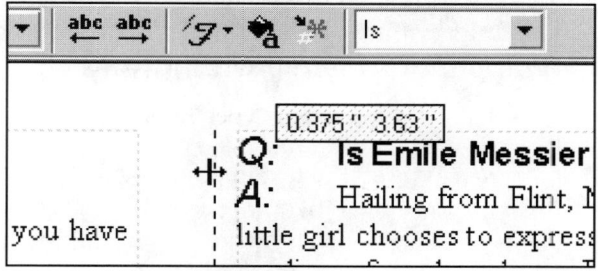

 ***Tip:*** *To change the width of both columns on either side of a gutter, place the pointer over the gutter until the pointer becomes a two-headed arrow between double lines. Then drag the gutter right or left.*

? I used the mouse to change the column gutters, and now they're all messed up. How can I make the columns evenly spaced again?

Place the insertion point anywhere in the columns and choose a different number of columns from the Columns button on the toolbar. Then click the button again and select the correct number of columns. You may want to use the Columns dialog box next time to adjust the spacing more accurately.

? How do I switch from a three-column to a two-column format on the same page?

You need to define two sets of columns. The first set of columns should be balanced newspaper columns. Here's how to set up your page:

1. To make sure the first set of columns is balanced, place the insertion point anywhere in the columns and choose Format | Columns. Then select Balanced Newspaper and click OK.

2. Place the insertion point at the beginning of the text where you want the two-column format to begin and then press CTRL-ENTER to insert a column break.

3. To define a new set of columns, select 2 Columns from the Columns button on the toolbar.

Column Tips

Here are some tips that will help make your columns look better:

⇨ Type all the text in your document before creating your columns. If you're cutting and pasting text from other documents, try using Paste Simple (CTRL-SHIFT-V) to insert the text without formatting.

⇨ Change the default 1" left and right margins to 0.5" margins to make more room for text. Also, the default 0.5" tab setting is too large a value in many columns. Try inserting a new tab stop that is 0.25" from the left margin.

⇨ To add or delete a column, simply place the insertion point in a column and then click the Columns button and select a different number.

⇨ To end a column and start typing in a new column, move the insertion point where you want to begin a new column and press CTRL-ENTER to insert a column break.

⇨ Use these keystrokes to move around your columns:

ALT-RIGHT ARROW	Moves one column to the right
ALT-LEFT ARROW	Moves one column to the left
ALT-END	Moves to the last line in a column
ALT-HOME	Moves to the first line in a column

? How do I add vertical lines between columns?

You can use the Border/Fill feature to insert lines between and around columns. Here's how:

1. Choose Format | Columns.

2. Choose Border/Fill.

3. In the Available Border Styles box, select either Column All or Column Between. These options are located on the last row of the box. Then click OK twice.

Tip: *If you want to insert a line between only two of the columns, or if you want to create other special effects, use the Draw Line feature. Choose Insert | Shape | Draw Line and then click and drag where you want the line to appear. You may want to use Two Page view or change the magnification to see more of the screen.*

Note: *If you decide you don't want column borders, choose Format | Columns | Border/Fill and then select Off at the beginning of the first row in the box.*

? The column border runs through my text box. How do I get rid of the column border in the box?

When you span a graphic, text box, or table across columns that have a border, the border runs through the graphic, text box, or table, creating a rather unpleasant visual effect, as shown in Figure 5-10. This problem has existed since the DOS versions of WordPerfect, but for some unknown reason, the programmers at Corel have neglected to fix it.

The safest way to work around this problem is to use the Draw Line feature instead of column lines to create your column borders. Another method is to create a white vertical line that blocks the column line, by following these steps:

1. Make sure the image, text box, or table is in its final location.

2. Choose Insert | Shape | Custom Line.

3. Select Vertical Line, select a thicker line from the Line Thickness pop-up list, change the length to roughly the size of the image you want to cover, and then click OK.

4. Click the line to select it and then drag it over the line you want to hide. If necessary, use the sizing handles to adjust the height and width of the line.

5. With the drawn line still selected, select the white color from the Line Color button on the property bar (or select the background color you're using).

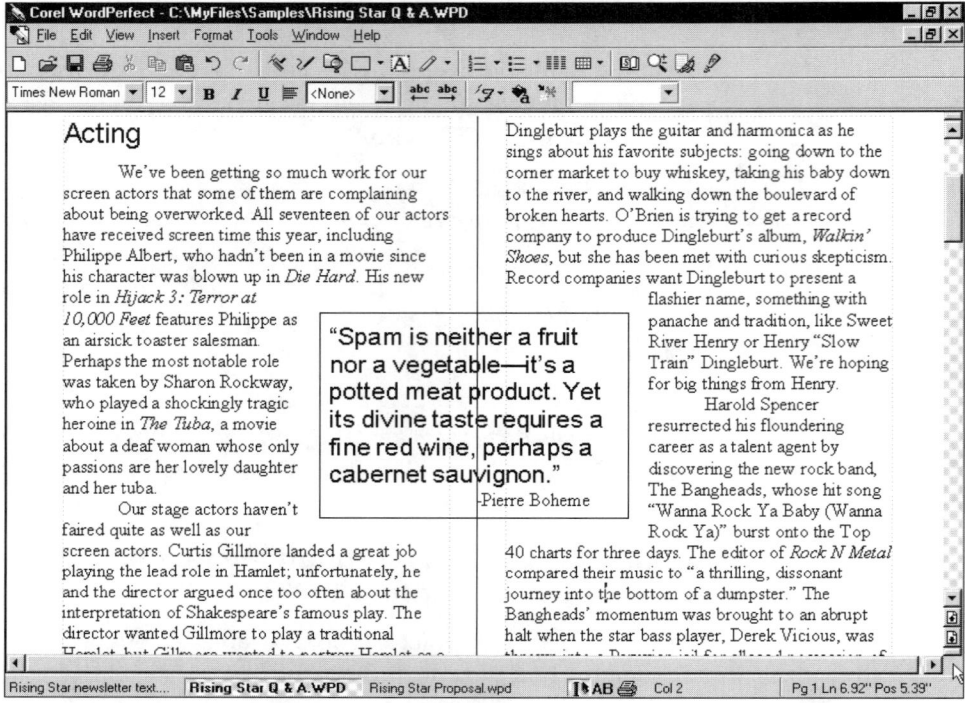

Figure 5-10.   Column borders will run through text boxes that span two columns

 *Note:*   *If the image looks okay on the screen but doesn't print properly, try printing the document graphically. This takes a little longer, but it should resolve the problem. Choose File | Print and then select the Details tab. Select Print Text as Graphics and then choose Print.*

Another method is to add a white fill and move the graphics box to the front. Here's how:

1. Make sure the image, text box, or table is in its final location, then select the object (click the edge of the text box to select it).

2. Click the Box Fill button on the property bar and then choose More.

3. Select any fill style (such as 5%) from the Available Fill Styles box. Then select White from the Foreground pop-up palette and click OK.

4. With the image or text box still selected, click the Graphics button on the property bar and select To Front.

 **Note:**   *The problem with using this method is that the text box may not be displayed properly. If this is the case, just click the text box, and it will reappear.*

How do I add a heading to a three-column newsletter that spans two of the columns?

To create a heading that spans two of the columns in a three-column format, as shown in Figure 5-11, place the heading in a text box. Then you can size and position the box perfectly.

1. With the insertion point anywhere in the columns, choose Insert | Text Box.

2. Type the heading in the text box.

Figure 5-11.   Spanning columns with a text box

3. Right-click the frame of the text box and then select Position.

4. Select Page from the Attach Box To drop-down list.

5. Select Left Column from the Horizontal From drop-down list.

6. In the Across Columns Text boxes, type **1** and **2**. Then click OK.

7. Right-click the frame of the text box and then select Size. For the Width value, select Full. Then click OK.

8. Right-click the frame of the text box and then select Border/Fill. Select No Border and then click OK.

Note: *You may need to edit the size of the heading in the text box so that it spans the columns correctly. Click within the text box, select the text, and adjust the size. You may also want to center the heading in the text box.*

TYPESETTING

My columns have a lot of white space, and many words need to be hyphenated to make the columns look better. Can I hyphenate automatically?

Yes. WordPerfect has a hyphenation feature that can be useful when working with tables and columns. Hyphenation can help you place more words on a line, and it can prevent too much white space at the ends of lines. In fully justified text, hyphenation can keep words from spacing out awkwardly.

Tip: *Instead of turning on hyphenation, you may be better off hyphenating manually. Place the insertion point in a long word that may need to be broken and then press* CTRL-SHIFT- - *to insert a soft hyphen. A soft hyphen appears only if the word needs to be broken.*

If you insist on turning on hyphenation, here's how to do it:

1. Place the insertion point in the paragraph where you want hyphenation to begin.

2. Choose Tools | Language | Hyphenation.

3. To hyphenate fewer words, increase the hyphenation zone percentages. Decrease the percentages to hyphenate more words. Then click OK.

Tip: *You will be prompted* (ad nauseam) *to hyphenate words. To see what each option in the Position Hyphen dialog box does, right-click it.*

Note: *To control how often WordPerfect prompts you for hyphenation, choose Tools | Settings and then double-click Environment. Click the Prompts tab and then select an option from the On Hyphenation pop-up menu. You can also deselect the Beep On Hyphenation option.*

Warning: *If you share documents electronically, turning on hyphenation may get you on everyone's Most Hated list. Even though you may understand how to use this feature, other people may wonder why the document keeps beeping at them.*

? I'm creating a flyer that has to be on one page. What's a fast way to get all the text on one page?

Use the Make It Fit feature to make the text fit on the number of pages you specify. When I taught English in college, some students beefed up their paper by using a large font and increasing the margins to hit the five-page mark. They would have loved the Make It Fit feature!

1. Choose Format | Make It Fit.

2. Type the number of pages you want to end up with in the Desired Number of Pages text box.

3. Select the items that can be adjusted and then choose Make It Fit.

? Placing a long dash (—) between two words often causes both words to wrap to the next line. How can I prevent this?

When you need to break words after a long dash or a slash, you can insert a Hyphenation Soft Return code (called an Invisible Soft Return code in older versions of WordPerfect) after the long dash. This inserts a nonprinting code that allows the text to wrap after the long dash. Here's how:

1. Place the insertion point after the long dash.

2. Choose Format | Line | Other Codes.

3. Select Hyphenation Soft Return and choose Insert.

Note: If you use long dashes frequently, you may want to create a keystroke macro or a QuickWord that inserts a long dash followed by the Hyphenation Soft Return code. To insert this code, choose Format | Line | Other Codes and then select Hyphenation Soft Return.

? I like to keep phone numbers together on the same line. How can I prevent phone number from breaking at the end of a line?

Instead of typing a normal hyphen between the numbers, press CTRL-HYPHEN to insert a hard hyphen. Your phone number will not be broken at the end of the line.

? I print letters using preprinted letterhead for the first page. How do I make sure the second page uses the correct top margin code?

When the first page of your letter is printed on letterhead, you'll want to use a larger top margin, such as 3", to leave room for the letterhead. On subsequent pages, however, you'll want the normal top margin of 1". However, if you insert the 1" margin code at the top of the second page, the code may move to a different page if you edit the text. Here are two ways to solve this problem:

⇨ Instead of changing the margin on the first page, insert an Advance code that pushes your text down from the top of the page. Place the insertion point at the top of the letter and then choose Format | Typesetting | Advance. Select the From Top of Page option. Then type a number (such as **3"**) in the Vertical Distance text box and click OK. This leaves room for the preprinted letterhead.

⇨ You can use Delay Codes to make sure the second margin code appears at the top of the second page. Move the insertion point to the top of the document and then change the top margin for the first page. Choose Format | Page | Delay Codes. Click OK to skip one page and then change the margin to 1" in the Define Delayed Codes window. Choose Close on the property bar when you're done. Now the 1" margin change will start on page 2.

 **I have a set of tabular columns that gets broken at the bottom of the page. Is there a way to keep these columns together on one page without inserting a page break?**

Yes. If you insert a page break or press ENTER enough times to push the item onto the next page, editing your document will likely cause spacing problems. A better approach is to use the Block Protect option in the Keep Text Together dialog box, shown in Figure 5-12.

1. Select the text that you want to keep together.

2. Choose Format | Keep Text Together.

3. Select the check box under Block Protect and then click OK.

Tip: *You may want to insert a Widow/Orphan code in the Current Document Styles to turn on this option for all your documents. Choose File | Document | Current Document Style. In the Styles Editor, insert the Widow/Orphan code (choose Format | Keep Text Together and then select the check box under Widow/Orphan). Select Use as Default and then click OK.*

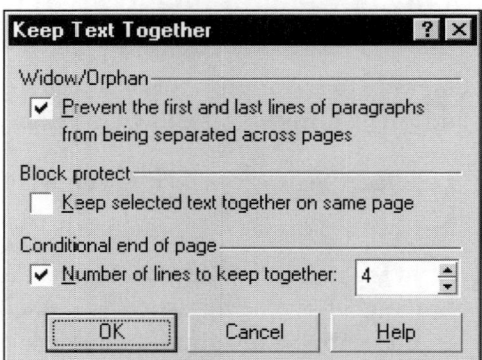

Figure 5-12.   Keep Text Together dialog box

In my newsletter headline, the "Y" and the "o" are too far apart. How can I move the letters closer together?

In most of the text you type, proportionally spaced fonts look good. However, when you increase the size of the text for a title or headline, certain letter combinations can create an unprofessional-looking gap.

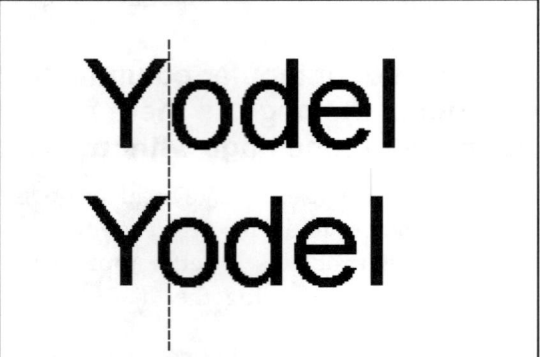

Here's how to use manual kerning to adjust the spacing between two letters:

1. Place the insertion point between the two letters.

2. Choose Format | Typesetting | Manual Kerning.

3. Click the counter arrows next to the Add/Remove Space option to adjust the letters.

 I want my newsletter title to span the entire page. How do you stretch a word or phrase across the page?

One way to accomplish this is to use a combination of letter spacing and All justification, as shown in Figure 5-13.

1. Select the headline or title you want to stretch.

2. Choose Format | Typesetting | Word/Letter Spacing.

3. In the Percent of Optimal text box under Letterspacing, select a higher percentage, such as 150%. You may need to adjust this setting a few times until the text almost fills the line. Then click OK.

4. With the text still selected, choose Format | Justification | All.

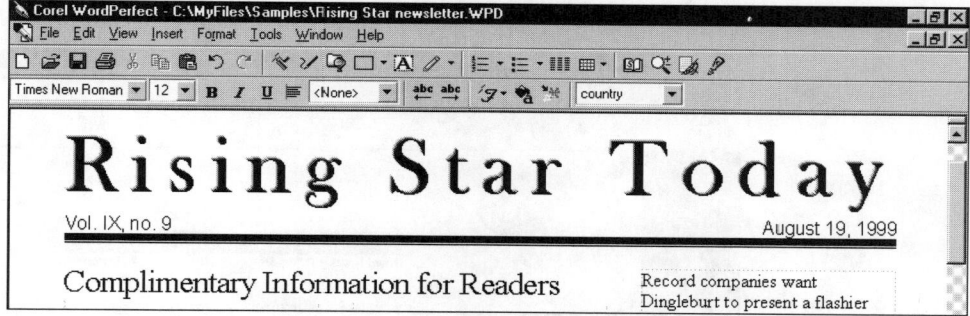

Figure 5-13.   Use All justification to stretch a title across the page

---

   *Tip:*   *An easier and fancier way to achieve the same results is to use a TextArt design. Choose Insert | Graphics | TextArt and then select a shape and colors for your title.*

DESKTOP PUBLISHING

My boss says my documents are too drab. How can I spruce up my documents?

WordPerfect is a word processor, not a desktop publisher. However, WordPerfect includes so many features that help you dress up your documents that it feels like a desktop publishing program. You can add watermarks and drop caps, rotate text, and print text in different colors. Experiment with these features to create a document design that even your boss loves. Figure 5-14 shows some of the design touches you can add to your documents.

When I'm adjusting the size of a headline, I like to increase or decrease it by a point until I get it right. Is there a quick way to nudge fonts?

WordPerfect includes two macros that can help you: Fontup.wcm and Fontdn.wcm, both located on the Shipping Macros toolbar. The Shipping Macros toolbar (called the Design Tools toolbar in WordPerfect 7) includes several layout and design options that help you adjust font size, create reversed text and graphical watermarks,

Reversed text

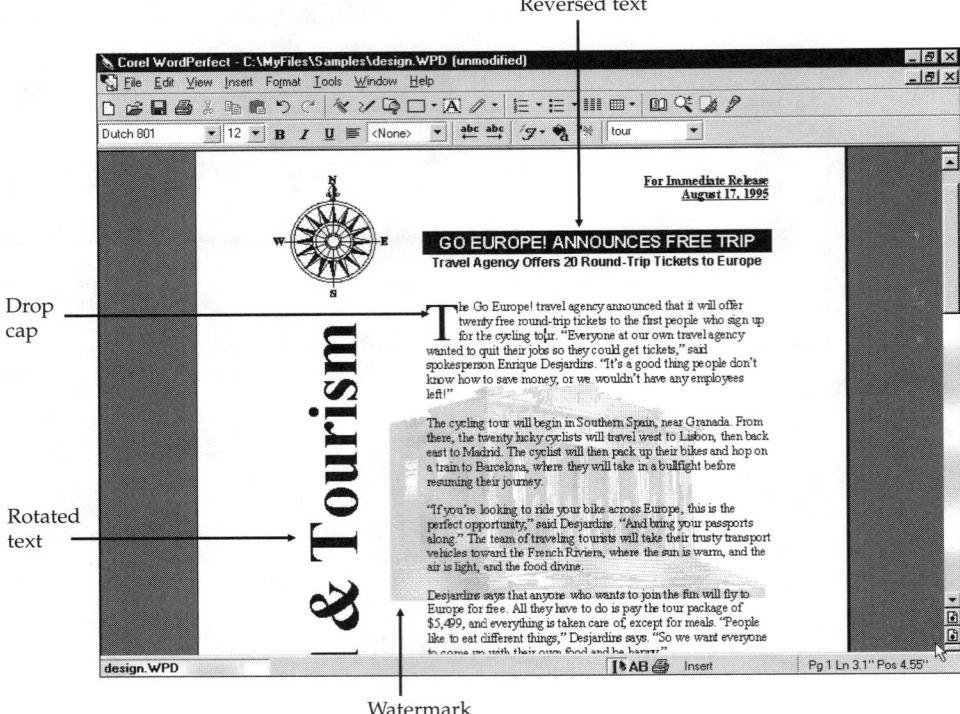

Drop cap

Rotated text

Watermark

Figure 5-14.   Add spice to your documents

and more. To see for yourself, right-click the toolbar and then select Shipping Macros.

1. Select the text you want to adjust.

2. Click the Font Up and Font Down buttons on the Shipping Macros toolbar until you achieve the effect you want.

 *Note:*   *If the message "Macro not found" appears, you need to use the Custom installation option in Setup to install the macros. See "Adding and Removing Suite Components" in Chapter 2.*

How do I rotate text?

To rotate text, you need to create a text box. Here's what you need to do:

1. Choose Insert | Text Box and then type and format the text you want to rotate.

2. Right-click the border of the text box and then choose Content.

3. Select 90 degrees (or 270 degrees) and then click OK.

4. Size and position the text box by dragging the border or the sizing handles.

 *Note:*   *When you click inside a text box containing rotated text, the text appears in an editing window. After you edit the text, choose Close to return to the document.*

How do I create white-on-black (reversed) text?

There are several ways to create reversed text. One way is to add a black paragraph fill to the text and then change the font to white. A similar approach is to place the text in a text box and then change the background to black and the text to white. Both of these methods can be tricky because at one point, the text is the same color as the background. However, the easiest and most versatile method is to use the Reverse Text macro. Here's how:

1. Select the text you want to reverse.

2. Choose Tools | Macro | Play and then double-click Reverse.wcm.

3. Select the text color and fill style.

4. Specify whether you want to place the text in a text box or use a paragraph fill. Then click OK.

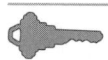 *Note:*   *After you create reversed text, you may not be able to see the results at first. Click outside the area. If that doesn't work, scroll down and then scroll back up.*

WordPerfect includes several precreated text watermark images, such as "Approved" and "Confidential." How do I create watermarks with different text?

Although you cannot easily change the watermark graphics that are included with WordPerfect, you can create watermarks containing any text you want. Once again, you have several choices.

⇨ One method is to choose Insert | Watermark | Create. Type and format the text any way you want it. You'll want to use a large font and center the text. When you're done, click the Close button. Any text you type in this screen is automatically shaded for use as a watermark.

⇨ Another option is to use the Watermark macro. Choose Tools | Macro | Play and then double-click Watermrk.wcm. Select Text and click OK. Type the text you want in the watermark (such as **For Approval**) and then click OK. If you want to change the font and size, choose Yes. You can then make additional changes to your watermark document.

⇨ A third option is to use TextArt in your watermark. TextArt gives you the added advantage of being able to rotate the text 45 degrees. Choose Insert | Watermark | Create and then choose Insert | Graphics | TextArt. Type the text in the Type Here box and then select any pattern or shading option you want. If you want to rotate the text, click the Rotation button and then rotate the text. Click Close and then size the TextArt box.

Tip: *To make the watermark lighter, click Shading on the Watermark property bar. Change the text or image shading from 25% to, say, 15%. Then click OK.*

My color watermark will not print in black and white. Why not?

If your watermark image prints in color, you need to edit the watermark image to make it a black-and-white image. You may also want to adjust the brightness of the graphic image.

1. Choose Insert | Watermark | Edit.

2. Right-click the watermark image and then choose Image Tools.

3. Choose Edit Attributes, select B & W attributes, select the Black and White check box, and then click OK.

4. To adjust the brightness, select an option from the Brightness palette in the Image Tools dialog box.

I just want the watermark on one page of a multipage document. Can I do that?

Like headers and footers, watermarks are included on every page until you discontinue them. To discontinue a watermark, place the insertion point on the page where you want the watermark to stop. Then choose Insert | Watermark | Discontinue.

❓ How can I add an ornate page border around a certificate?

You can insert two types of page borders: the standard border types found in the Border/Fill dialog box or the fancy border types. Figure 5-15 shows examples of both types.

1. Place the insertion point on the page where you want the border to appear.

2. Choose Format | Page | Border/Fill.

3. Select Line or Fancy from the Border Type drop-down list.

4. Select the type of border you want to insert and then click OK.

Fancy page border   Standard page border

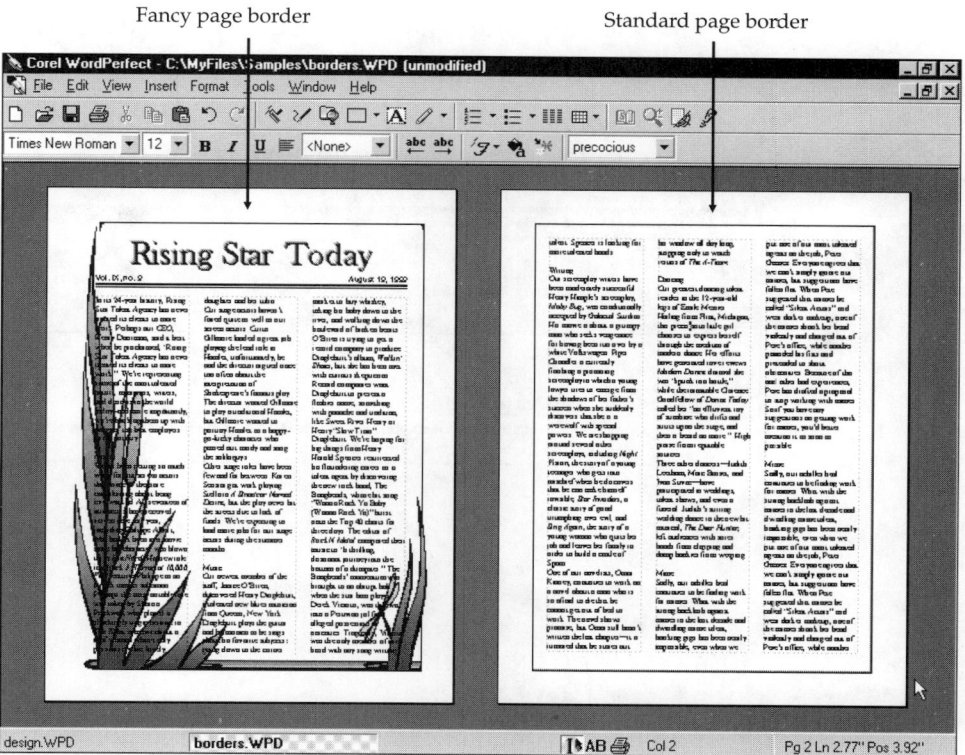

Figure 5-15.   Page borders

 **Note:**   *If you would like to use other .WPG images as fancy page borders, click the yellow directory icon, locate the folder containing the image you want to insert, and click OK. Any .WPG image in the folder you select will appear in the Page Border/Fill dialog box.*

❓ I'd like to size a paragraph border to enclose a heading so that the border doesn't go all the way across the page. How do I do this?

One of the frustrating things about using paragraph borders is that the border affects the entire paragraph from margin to margin instead of affecting only the text. You can change the right margin of the heading to control the paragraph border. Here's how:

1. Type and format your heading and press ENTER.

2. Select the heading and then choose Format | Paragraph | Border/Fill.

3. Select the border and fill you want to use and then click OK.

4. If the ruler is hidden, choose View | Ruler.

5. Select the heading and then drag the right margin icon on the ruler toward the end of your heading.

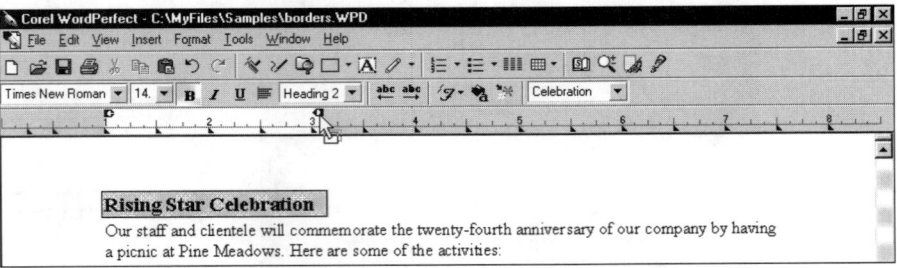

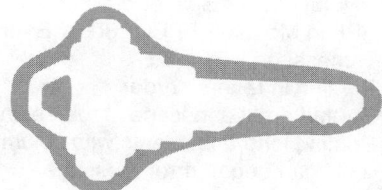

6 Answers!

Printing, Fonts, and Paper Sizes

Answer Topics!

Printing, Fonts, and Paper Sizes @ a Glance

⇨ One of the first things you learn when you begin using WordPerfect is how to print a document. Unfortunately, it's not always as easy as clicking the Print button. Pages don't always print in the right order, or gobbledygook comes out of the printer, or a number of other printing problems may occur. Browse through this chapter to learn about how you can print documents without errors.

⇨ If you print envelopes, labels, or postcards, or other documents that use special paper sizes, consult this chapter to learn how your printer handles special paper sizes and what to do if things go wrong.

⇨ If you don't like Times New Roman, you can select a different default font for all new documents. You can also change the font size ratios, use different fonts when converting documents, and print a sample of your fonts. This chapter tells you how.

⇨ Do you need to print a document on both sides of the page, but you don't have a fancy duplex printer? Do you want to print an eight-page booklet with all the pages in the right order so that it can be folded in half? Duplex and booklet printing let you take full advantage of your printer—and if you have questions about how to use these features, look in this chapter for answers.

PRINTER TROUBLESHOOTING

❓ How do I cancel a print job?

By the time you looked this up, your print job has probably already finished. But don't waste time reading this paragraph! Here's the easiest way to cancel a print job:

1. On the WordPerfect menu bar, click File | Print | Status.

2. Select the job you want to cancel. Then choose Document | Cancel Printing.

 *Note:* *If you print to a network printer, you can cancel only your own print jobs.*

❓ What happened to Print Preview?

WordPerfect 8 displays your documents exactly as they will appear when printed, so a separate Print Preview feature would be redundant. You can use Two Pages view to preview your documents, as shown in Figure 6-1. You can also select Full Page or any other magnification option from the Zoom drop-down list on the toolbar.

❓ How do I install my new printer so WordPerfect can print to it?

After you attach the printer to your computer, you must install a *printer driver*. A printer driver is a file that contains the information needed to enable programs such as WordPerfect to communicate with the printer. Once you install a printer driver in Windows, you can

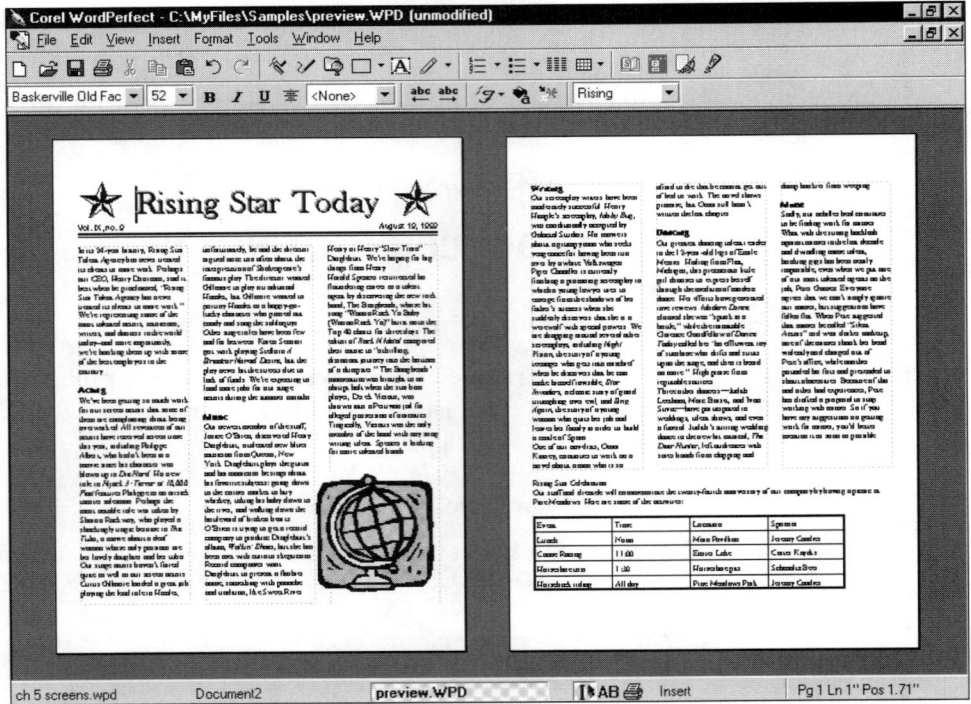

Figure 6-1.   Use Two Pages view to preview documents

print to your computer from any Windows application. Follow these steps to install the Windows printer driver:

1. Place the Windows 95 CD in your CD-ROM drive. (If you're on a network, the Windows 95 CD files may be available on a network drive or on your hard drive.)

2. Click Start on the taskbar. Then choose Settings | Printers.

3. Double-click Add Printer. Then follow the steps displayed by the Add Printer Wizard.

 *Note:*   *WordPerfect 8 no longer uses WordPerfect printer drivers. You must use the Windows printer drivers.*

❓ My printer is pulling paper from the wrong tray. How can I fix this?

You can use the Edit Page Size dialog box, shown in Figure 6-2, to specify the paper tray used with each page size you select.

1. Open the document and make sure the correct printer is selected.

2. Choose File | Page Setup.

3. Select the paper definition you want to use and then choose Edit.

4. Select the tray you want to use from the Source drop-down list. Then click OK twice and print the document.

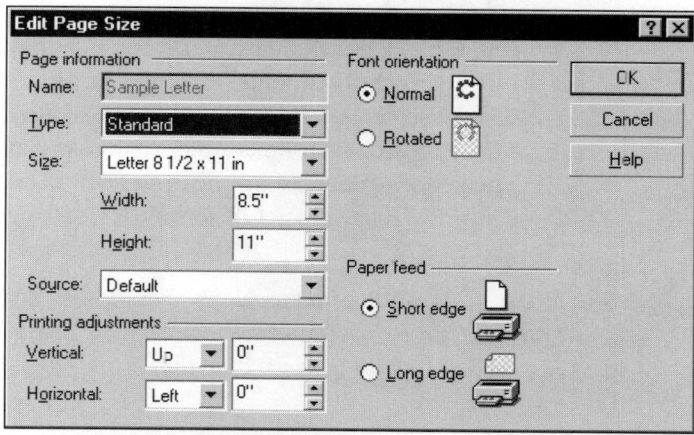

Figure 6-2.   Use the Edit Page Size dialog box to specify the paper tray

? **I just bought a printer with two paper trays: letter size and legal size. Can I specify different paper sizes within a multipage document? Can WordPerfect select the proper tray?**

Yes to both questions. For example, you may want the first page of your document to print from the tray that contains normal letter-size paper and then the rest of the document to print from the tray that contains legal-size paper. Here's how to do this:

1. Move the insertion point to the beginning of the document.

2. For the first page, choose File | Page Setup. Then select the Letter paper size and choose Edit. Make sure the proper tray is listed in the Source drop-down list and then click OK twice.

3. Choose Format | Page | Delay Codes and then press ENTER to skip one page.

4. In the Delay Codes window, choose File | Page Setup. Then select the Legal paper size and choose Edit. Make sure the proper tray is listed in the Source drop-down list and then click OK twice.

5. Click Close to close the Delay Codes window.

? **I use Draft quality printing most of the time. Can I make this the default print quality setting?**

You can change default printer settings in several ways. You can save your printer settings in WordPerfect, or you can use the Named Settings option.

⇨ If you make the same printer setting changes for most of your WordPerfect documents, you may want to save these as the default settings. Choose File | Print. Make any changes to the printer options—for example, change the quality of resolution. Then choose Save as Application Default from the Settings drop-down list. Click OK to save the settings you select.

Note: *If you run into problems with the settings you select, you may want to revert to the default settings. In the Print dialog box, select Retrieve Application Default Settings from the Settings drop-down list.*

⇨ If you find yourself changing the same printer options for a specific kind of document, you can use the Named Settings feature to save the settings. To save the current printer settings, make any changes you want in the Print dialog box. Then choose Settings | Named Settings. Type a name for the settings (such as **Draft Copy**) and then choose Add. After you add a named setting, you can select it from the Settings drop-down list in the Print dialog box.

Tips for Troubleshooting Printer Problems

Sometimes you send a job to the printer and nothing happens. Other times, it prints only half the document, or it prints unrecognizable characters. Here are some suggestions for solving the printer problems:

⇨ If nothing prints, do the obvious. Make sure the printer is turned on, online (ready to print), and loaded with paper. Make sure the paper isn't jammed in the printer. If you're printing to a network printer, make sure the network isn't down.

⇨ Check the print status to see if your jobs are backed up. Choose File | Print and then click the Status button.

⇨ If the printer prints gobbledygook, make sure the proper printer is selected. Choose File | Print and then check the Current Printer drop-down list to make sure the correct printer is selected. For example, if a PostScript printer is selected but you're printing to an HP LaserJet III, your printouts will be gibberish. Delete the print job, choose the correct printer, and give it another shot.

⇨ Try printing from a different Windows program, such as Notepad or WordPad. If the same printing problem occurs, the problem is the Windows printer driver, not WordPerfect. In this case, you may want to try an emulation or alternate compatible printer driver. For example, using an Epson FX-80 driver to print to an Okidata printer has been known to solve problems. If the emulation works, you may need to reinstall or replace the driver. Consult your printer manual for suggested emulations that work best with your computer.

⇨ Lack of printer memory can result in incomplete jobs, especially for long, complex documents with lots of graphics. If your laser printer isn't finishing a job, or if your printer is returning memory errors, try printing your document with a lower resolution. Choose File | Print and then select the Details tab. Select a lower resolution from the Resolution drop-down list.

⇨ Turn off both the computer and the printer to clear the buffer and then try again. Hey—sometimes it works!

⇨ Sometimes printing problems are the result of a corrupt file. Copy and paste the text into a blank document and then try printing again.

⇨ Try printing the document graphically. Choose File | Print, select the Details tab, and then select the Print Text as Graphics option.

⇨ You may be using an outdated version of your printer driver. Check your printer manufacturer's Web site to see if there is a more current version of your printer driver that you can download.

? **My computer at work doesn't have the same fonts as my home computer. When I print the document at work, the formatting gets messed up. What can I do to prevent this problem?**

You can use the Print to File option. This sends the print job to a file on your hard drive. You can then print this file from a different computer—even from a computer that doesn't have WordPerfect installed on it—and still retain your formatting. Here's how to print to a file:

1. Choose File | Print and then select the Details tab.

2. Select Print to File and then specify the file to which you want to print.

3. Choose Print.

4. After you copy the file to a disk, you can print the file using a DOS command. For example, if you save a file named Report.prn to the C:\MyFiles folder, and if the computer you're using prints to the printer named LPT1, type the following at the DOS prompt:

```
copy/b c:\myfiles\report.prn lpt1
```

I need to print on preprinted forms, but I can't be very precise using ENTER and TAB. Is there a way to print correctly on preprinted forms?

You can use the Advance feature to print on preprinted forms. Here's how:

1. Use a ruler to measure the distance from the top and left to each area of the preprinted form you need to fill in. Note these measurements on a piece of paper.

2. Choose Format | Typesetting | Advance.

3. Select From Left Edge of Page and then type the distance you measured. Select From Top of Page and then type the distance you measured. Then click OK.

4. Insert an Advance code for each area of the form that needs to be filled in.

5. Test print using a photocopy of the original form to make sure you got everything right.

Tip: *If you'll be printing on this form often, you can insert keyboard merge prompts so you can easily use your settings again. For more information see "Advanced Merge Operations" in Chapter 8.*

In WordPerfect 6.1, I could print from the Open File dialog box. For some files in WordPerfect 8, I can't do this. Why not?

Printing files from the Open File dialog box is like printing from Windows Explorer. Windows needs to know what program a file is associated with, so if you're using extensions other than .WPD, such as .LTR or .12, Windows doesn't know which program you're trying to print from, even though you're in WordPerfect. Use the .WPD extension in your filenames, and you'll be able to print documents just fine without opening them first.

Tip: *To print multiple documents from the Open File dialog box, use* CTRL *to select the documents and then right-click a selected item and choose Print.*

How do I print just one part of my document?

You don't have to print your entire document. Here are several methods you can use to print sections of a document:

⇨ Select the text you want to print and then choose File | Print. Make sure Selected Text is selected in the Print dialog box and then choose Print.

⇨ To print a single page, place the insertion point anywhere on the page and then choose File | Print. Select Current Page and choose Print.

⇨ To print a range of pages, choose File | Print. Select the Multiple Pages tab and then type the range of pages you want to print. The dialog box gives examples.

My Epson Stylus Pro printer prints a bunch of blank pages. How can I fix this?

When printing to an Epson Stylus Pro or Epson Stylus Color II, IIs, Pro, or Pro XL from WordPerfect for Windows, the printer will sometimes eject blank pages. To correct the problem, make sure the print resolution set in the Windows printer driver matches the print quality set in WordPerfect. For example, if the Windows printer driver is set to print to 720 dpi, the WordPerfect Resolution setting must be High. If the Windows printer driver is set to 360 dpi, the WordPerfect Resolution setting must be Medium. If the Windows printer driver is set to 180 dpi, the WordPerfect Resolution setting should be Draft.

Tip: *To change the resolution settings for your Epson Stylus printer, click Start on the taskbar and then choose Settings | Printers. Right-click the printer driver you're using and then choose Properties. Then choose Details | Setup | Print Mode/Options. You can then change the resolution.*

❓ My Okidata ML-391 Plus printer does not print from WordPerfect 8 using the Windows 95 printer driver provided on the Windows 95 CD. How do I print?

Okidata recommends using an Epson driver as its emulation. The Okidata Web site (http://www.okidata.com) suggests using only IBM, Epson, or Microline drivers as emulations. Okidata also indicates that it will not be creating a driver for the ML printers for Windows 95. Try the Epson FX-80 printer driver as a workaround; this emulation has worked for some people.

❓ When I attempt to print a document, I receive the error message "Failed Platform Function: SetBKMode" or "Out of Disk Space." What should I do?

You're probably out of disk space. Empty the Recycle Bin and free up as much disk space as possible (at least 10 MB), and your documents should print without error.

❓ When I print documents with full justification, I receive the error message "IPF in Module PFPPOP80.EXE." What's the problem?

If this error message appears when you attempt to print files with full justification, or if your printer spits out a bunch a blank pages during your print job, you may need to update WordPerfect 8. You can use Corel WordPerfect Suite 8 Service Pack #1 to fix this problem. Download Service Pack #1 (wp8sp1.exe) from the following Web address:

```
ftp://ftp.corel.com/pub/WordPerfect/wpwin/8
```

Warning: *Service Pack #1 works only in English versions of Corel WordPerfect Suite 8.*

❓ I use an HP DeskJet 500 to print. Each page comes out of the printer face up, which means that after the document is printed, the last page is on top. Can I print in reverse order?

It's annoying to have to shuffle the order of your printed pages, especially if your document is long. Here's how to print in reverse order, so page 1 is face up on the top of the pile of printed pages:

1. Choose File | Print and then click the Details tab.

2. Select Print in Reverse Order and then choose Print.

 *Tip:*   *You may want to save Print in Reverse Order as the default setting so you don't have to select this option every time you print. Select this option in the Print dialog box and then choose Settings | Save as Application Default.*

? Pages print in Landscape mode when Portrait mode is indicated on the screen. I have to select Landscape mode to print in Portrait mode, and sometimes the options are dimmed. What's wrong?

When goofy things happen with the Portrait and Landscape mode settings, WordPerfect was not registered properly during setup. Even if you uninstall and reinstall the Corel Suite, the problem will likely remain. You can fix this problem by deleting the PerfectPrint folder in the Registry Editor, but it's not a good idea to tinker with the registry unless you know exactly what you're doing. Call Corel's customer support, and a technician will walk you through the steps for editing the registry to fix this problem.

? When I print a long document that contains columns, the text prints in the gutter space between the columns. What's the problem?

When you print a large document (50+ pages) that is formatted with columns, the text will print outside of the first column and into the gutter space between the next column. The problem will occur only when you print the full document using a Windows printer driver capable of printing at 600 dpi (such as the HP LaserJet 5Si/5Si MX and HP LaserJet 4/4M). To work around this problem, you can divide the large document into several smaller documents, or you can print the document using a lower resolution, such as 300 dpi.

? When I try to print part of my document on legal-size paper on my HP LaserJet 4 Plus printer, the error message "LC Load Legal" appears. How can I fix this problem?

This problem occurs in other Windows applications as well. According to the *HP LaserJet Series 4 Printer Manual,* you need to turn the knob in the paper tray to Legal instead of Letter. When the knob is set to the appropriate size and type of paper, the message will not appear.

? Graphic lines print very slowly on my HP LaserJet 4 printer. Is there a way to speed up printing?

You can try changing the spool settings in the Windows 95 printer setup.

1. Click Start on the taskbar and then choose Settings | Printers.
2. Right-click the printer name and then choose Properties.
3. Click the Details tab and then choose Spool Settings.
4. Select the Spool Print Job So Program Finishes Printing Faster option.
5. Select EMF from the Spool Data Format drop-down list.

? How can I get my highlighting to print on my HP LaserJet 4+ printer?

Highlighting may not print to an HP LaserJet 4+ if the printer driver's dithering option for graphics has been changed from Coarse to None. Setting the dithering option to Coarse will solve this problem, not only for WordPerfect, but for other Windows programs as well.

1. Click Start on the taskbar and then choose Settings | Printers.
2. Right-click the printer name and then choose Properties.
3. Click the Graphics tab and then select Coarse.

? Why won't my Canon BJC-610 print multiple copies?

You need to deselect the Collate option in the printer driver Properties dialog box.

1. Click Start on the taskbar and then choose Settings | Printers.
2. Right-click the printer name and then choose Properties.
3. Click the Paper tab and then deselect Collate.

? The Print dialog box doesn't show the options for collating copies. Can I still collate pages when I print multiple copies?

In previous versions of WordPerfect, the two collating options were a permanent part of the Print dialog box. In WordPerfect 8, these options appear only if you increase the number of copies to more than one, as shown in Figure 6-3.

? My printer prints only text, not graphics or lines in a table. How can I print everything?

Only the text of a document will print if the Print Text Only option is selected. This option is useful for printing drafts of a document, but you need to deselect it when you want to print the final, complete draft of your document. Choose File | Print, select the Details tab, and then deselect Print Text Only.

? My printer prints a blank page at the end of a print job. What's the problem?

First, make sure there aren't any stray hard returns or hard page breaks that may have created an extra page at the end of the

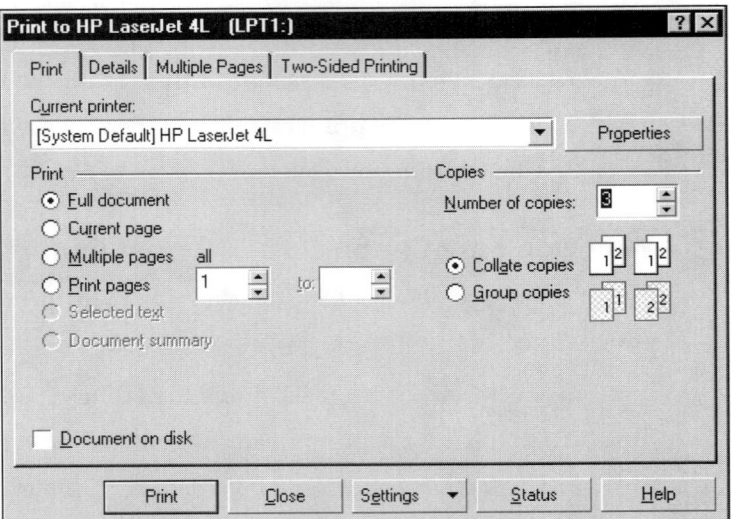

Figure 6-3.   After increasing the number of copies to more than one, you can indicate whether to collate or group the printed pages

document. If you're on a network and a blank page appears at the end of every print job, the problem is the network printer setup. Network printers often separate print jobs with a blank page with little or no regard for the environment or the pocket book. WordPerfect has no control over this setting. Convince your system administrator to change the network printer properties so these separator pages are no longer printed.

? **I store many of my older files on floppy disks so they don't clutter up my hard drive. Before I print the list of files, can I change the margins and include information such as a description, date, and size for each file?**

In WordPerfect, you can format a file list before printing by displaying it in the Windows 95 WordPad program and then saving and opening the file in WordPerfect.

1. Choose File | Open and then select the folder that you want to print.

2. If the menu doesn't appear across the top of the dialog box, click the Toggle Menu On/Off button.

3. WordPerfect prints the file list exactly as it appears in the Open File dialog box, so before printing, make any desired changes to the information displayed.

4. To print the list to a WordPad document, choose File | Print File List. Select Display in WordPad and click OK.

5. In WordPad, choose File | Save As and then type a filename using an .RTF extension (for example, **C:\MyFiles\FileList.rtf**) to indicate where you want to save the file. Then exit WordPad.

6. In WordPerfect, select the .RTF file you just saved and choose Open. Click OK to convert the file from Rich Text Format. Now you can format the list as you want, changing the margins, font, or tab settings, for example, before printing it.

USING DIFFERENT PAPER SIZES

? When I try to print labels to my IBM Lexmark 4079 printer, the error message "Out of paper or ink low" appears, even though the paper and ink are both fine. How can I fix this problem?

Changing the paper source to Default will eliminate this error message and allow the labels to print correctly. Here's how to change the paper source to Default:

1. Choose File | Page Setup.

2. Select the paper size definition you are using and then choose Edit.

3. Select Default from the Source drop-down list and then click OK twice.

? When I print labels using my ink jet printer, I am frustrated by the 0.5" bottom margin—I hardly have room for the label text. What can I do?

If you have an ink jet or laser printer, the best thing to do is use labels especially designed for laser or ink jet printers. These labels allow enough room for the printer's minimum margins, eliminating the need to add a large margin to each label. Ink jet and laser printers have a minimum bottom margin that must be accounted for on the sheet of labels; ink jet printers usually have greater minimum margins than laser printers, sometimes as high as 0.667". Labels especially created for ink jet and laser printers have an unprintable margin area along the bottom of the label sheet to accommodate the printer's minimum margin. Other types of labels, such as those designed for copiers, don't have any space around the labels.

If purchasing labels especially designed for ink jet and label printers is not an option, you can edit the label definition so the last row of labels is not used. Of course, you'll waste a row of labels on every sheet, but at least you won't have to use a tiny font to fit your text on each label. Here's how to edit the label definition:

1. Choose Format | Labels.

2. Select the labels you're using from the list and choose Edit.

3. In the Labels per Page Group box, decrease the number in the Rows text box by 1.

Warning: Some printers can generate enough heat to cause the labels to peel off and get stuck in the printer. To be safe, you may want to purchase only labels specifically designed for laser printers.

Tips on Using Special Paper Sizes

When you're printing any size of paper other than 8.5" by 11"—whether you're printing label sheets, envelopes, legal paper, diskette labels, or postcards—you need to learn the capabilities of your printer. Here are some tips on how to print special paper sizes more effectively:

⇨ Learn how your printer handles special paper sizes. Most of the newer ink jet and laser printers have a manual feed slot or tray that's designed for printing envelopes, labels, and other nonstandard types of paper.

⇨ To prevent your paper from getting wrinkled, many newer printers let you turn a knob or open a door so your paper prints straight through the printer and comes out the back. Read your printer manual to find out how your manual feed tray works.

⇨ Some printers have separate trays for special paper sizes. If you have one of these printers, make sure the labels or envelopes or other items in the tray are in the correct position. Be careful not to fill the tray too full—you might cause a paper jam.

⇨ Some printers have only one paper tray. Before you print, you need to pull out and empty the paper tray and then insert the special paper, such as envelopes, label sheets, or postcards. Adjust the paper tray guide and reinsert the tray. Print a sample or two to make sure you inserted the special paper correctly. Don't overstack your paper tray.

⇨ Printing your special paper with the wrong definition can be a costly mistake. Test print labels and other items on a blank sheet of paper and hold the test copy against your special paper to make sure everything lines up. You can draw an arrow on the test sheet to indicate how you inserted it in your printer so you know exactly which direction to insert the special paper.

? **When I print envelopes, addresses print in the wrong direction and get cut off. What's wrong?**

You may be inserting the envelopes in the wrong direction, or the font orientation and paper feed options may not be set up properly. On most laser printers and many ink jet printers, the short edge of the envelope should feed into the printer first, and the font needs to be rotated for the address to print with the correct orientation. Here's how to change the Page Setup options for envelopes:

1. Choose Format | Page | Page Setup (Page Size in WordPerfect 7).

2. Select the envelope definition you're using and choose Edit.

3. If your printer requires you to feed the short edge of the envelope into the printer, make sure Rotated is selected. If your printer requires you to feed the long edge of the envelope into the printer, make sure Normal is selected.

Note: *Consult your printer documentation or printer manufacturer for information on the proper method of inserting an envelope into the printer.*

USING TYPE FONTS

? **How do I print a sample of all the fonts available on my system?**

To create a document containing sample text in every font available on your printer, you can play the Allfonts macro. Choose Tools | Macro | Play and then double-click Allfonts.wcm.

Note: *If the Allfonts macro does not appear in the Play Macro dialog box, you may need to perform a Custom installation to select all the WordPerfect macros. See "Adding and Removing Suite Components" in Chapter 2.*

? **I printed a sample of all the fonts available on my printer, but when I display WordPerfect's font list, some of the fonts are missing. Why? How can I use all the fonts on my printer?**

If the fonts you're missing are TrueType fonts, make sure they are installed in the Fonts dialog box on the Windows Control Panel.

1. Click Start on the taskbar. Then choose Settings | Control Panel.

2. Double-click Fonts.

3. To add fonts, choose File | Install New Font. Select the fonts you want to install and then click OK.

 *Note:*   *If you're missing fonts that are not TrueType fonts, make sure that you have selected the printer that has the fonts you want to use. Available fonts depend on which printer is selected.*

When I convert documents from other word processors, weird font changes occur. How can I prevent this?

When converting a document from another file format, WordPerfect attempts to match the fonts in the original document as closely as possible. The name of the original font appears on the property bar, and both the original and replacement fonts are displayed in the Reveal Codes. You can use the Font Map feature, shown in Figure 6-4, to determine how your fonts are converted when you open documents that were formatted with different fonts than those you now have available.

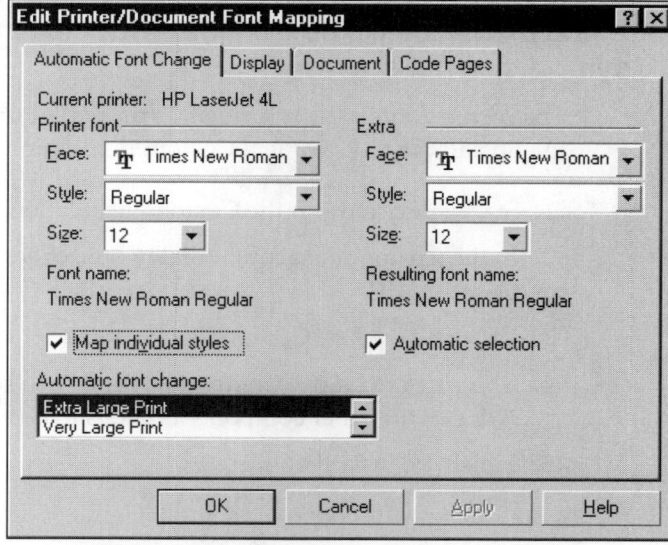

Figure 6-4.   Use the Font Map dialog box to convert the fonts in a document

To convert the fonts in a document created in another format, follow these steps:

1. Choose Format | Font | Font Map and then click the Automatic Font Change tab.

2. Select the font you want to replace in the Face drop-down list.

3. To change settings for font sizes and styles, click Map Individual Styles.

4. Select the replacement font settings in the corresponding Face drop-down list.

Note: *You can also specify conversion default settings for WordPerfect 4.2, DCA, and DisplayWrite fonts. Choose Tools | Settings and then double-click Convert. Choose Options and then select either WP 4.2 Fonts or DCA/DisplayWrite Fonts. To change a font on the list, select the font and click Edit.*

Tip: *You can also display a document in a font different from the one used to print it. Choose Format | Font | Font Map and then click the Display tab. Select a font from the Face drop-down list under Printer Font and then select the display font from the Face drop-down list under Display Font.*

The Symbol dialog box displays little boxes instead of symbols. What's wrong?

The correct fonts were not installed properly during setup. You need to reinstall the fonts using a Custom installation. Here's how:

1. Start Setup and run the Custom installation.

2. In the Custom Installation dialog box, choose Selection Options | Deselect All.

3. Choose Required Components and then choose Components.

4. Choose PerfectFit | Components and then select Symbol Fonts. None of the other components needs to be reinstalled.

5. Finish the installation.

? **Can I change the font size used for attributes such as very large, subscript, and superscript?**

In WordPerfect 6.1 for Windows, you could use the Preferences dialog box to change the size ratio of attributes such as subscript and superscript. Since WordPerfect 8 does not include a Print option in the Preferences dialog box and Windows 95 does not provide a printer property to set the size ratio, the only way to manipulate the size is to use the Font Map feature. The Font Map feature is normally used for conversion purposes; for example, when you convert a document, you can specify which fonts replace which other fonts. However, this feature will meet your needs here, too.

1. Choose Format | Font.

2. Choose Font Map.

3. From the Printer Font Face drop-down list, select the font you want to use for the attribute.

4. From the Automatic Font Change list, select the attribute (such as Very Large Print or Superscript) you want to change.

5. Select Map Individual Styles.

6. On the right side of the dialog box under the name of the attribute, specify the size of the font to use.

? **I want to change a font from one point size to another, but the font point size doesn't change correctly. What's wrong?**

Suppose you're trying to change the font from 16-point Arial to 12-point Times New Roman, but the font remains too large or too small. However, when you try to change the font in other parts of the document, it works fine. In this case, it's useful to turn on Reveal Codes (View | Reveal Codes) to see if any codes may be preventing correct size change. For example, if a Very Large attribute is attached to the font, removing this attribute may allow the font size to change correctly.

? **I don't like Times New Roman. Can I change the default font for all new documents?**

Yes. Although you cannot change the default font for documents you've already created, you can change the default font for all new documents you create. Keep in mind that changing the default font also affects features such as footnotes, headers and footers, and page numbering.

1. Choose Format | Font | Default Font.

2. Select the font face, style, and size.

3. Select Use as Default if you want this font to apply to future documents you create. Then click OK twice.

 *Note:*   *If the Default Font option is dimmed, you selected text before you opened the Font dialog box. Make sure that no text is selected when you open the Font dialog box.*

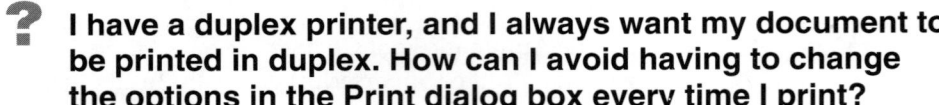

DUPLEX AND BOOKLET PRINTING

 **I have a duplex printer, and I always want my document to be printed in duplex. How can I avoid having to change the options in the Print dialog box every time I print?**

Unless you insert the printing codes into the document, any two-sided printing options you select in WordPerfect affect only the current print job. Here's how you can insert codes into your document:

1. Choose File | Page Setup and then click the Two-Sided Settings tab.

2. Select either Flip on Long Edge or Flip on Short Edge, depending on how you plan to bind the document.

3. If you want to adjust the binding width to create more space for the bound edge of the document, select Inside Margin or Outside Margin, and then type the amount of the offset (such as **0.25"**) in the Margin to Adjust for Binding text box. Then click OK.

4. When you're ready to print the document, choose File | Print and then click the Two-Sided Printing tab.

5. Select Use Document Settings and then choose Print.

Note: *Because the printing code is inserted into the document, the screen display will reflect the printing offset. The margins will appear the same size as they are set, but the page size will be reduced by the size of the offset margin.*

 **I don't have a duplex printer, but I need to print on both sides. How do I do this?**

Printing on both sides of the page is a great way to save paper—if you do it right. If you do it wrong, you may end up wasting paper instead. You can use the Two-Sided Printing tab of the Print dialog box, shown in Figure 6-5, to print front and back. For example, you can print the odd pages first, turn the pages over, and then print the even pages on the backs of the odd pages. (With some printers, you may want to print the even pages first and then the odd pages so you don't have to collate the printed pages.)

Warning: *Some laser printer manufacturers advise against printing on both sides of the paper because the toner might come off on the rollers. Be sure to check your printer manual and warranty.*

1. Before you begin, make sure you know which direction your printer feeds paper. Draw an arrow on a piece of paper so you can see the feed direction and then print on this sample page so that you can figure out which direction to insert the paper.

2. Choose File | Print and then select the Two-Sided Printing tab.

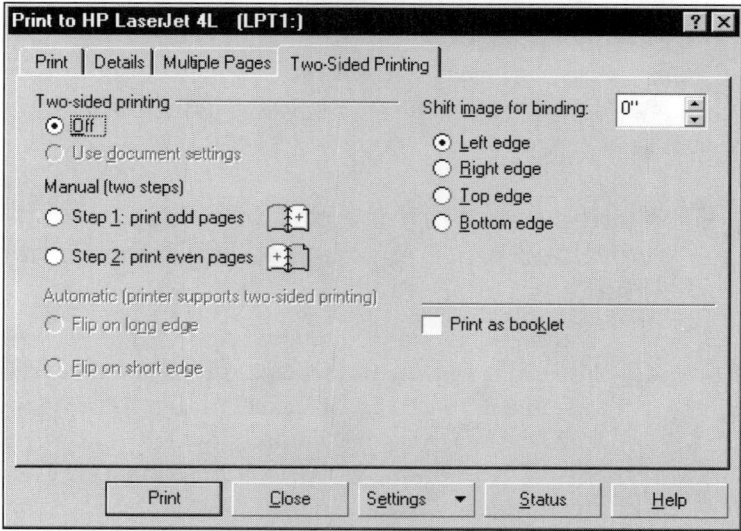

Figure 6-5.   You can use the Two-Sided Printing tab to print in duplex

3. If you intend to bind the document, specify a distance (such as **0.25"**) in the Shift Image for Binding text box. For odd pages, select Left Edge as the binding edge.

 ***Note:***   *The binding amount is added to the margin. For example, if you specify a 0.25" binding amount on the left side of a page with 1" left and right margins, the left margin will be 1.25" and the right margin will be 0.75".*

4. Select Step 1: Print Odd Pages. Then choose Print to print the odd pages in the document.

5. Reload the pages in your printer. How you do this depends on the type of printer you have. Use the sample page you created in step 1 to figure out which direction to insert the paper. On some printers, you'll want the first page facing down so the back (blank side) of the last page is on top. On other printers, you'll want the first page facing up.

6. Choose File | Print and then select the Two-Sided Settings tab.

7. If you selected a binding width for the odd pages, specify the same distance (such as **0.25"**). For even pages, select Right Edge as the binding edge.

8. Select Step 2: Print Even Pages. Then choose Print.

 ***Tip:***   *When the second side has finished printing, you may need to reorder the stack so that the first page is on top. If your document has an odd number of pages, the last page may still be in the printer.*

❓ My document printed on both sides even though two-sided printing is turned off in the Print dialog box. What's wrong?

You probably inserted the two-sided printing codes in the document. You can either use Reveal Codes to delete these codes from your document, or you can instruct WordPerfect to ignore them. To tell WordPerfect to ignore them, choose File | Print and then click the Two-Sided Printing tab. Select Off so that Use Document Settings is deselected.

Tips for Formatting Duplex Documents

Here are some formatting tips to use when printing duplex documents:

⇨ If you're using footers with page numbers, you may want to create two footers: Footer A and Footer B. Create Footer A for odd pages and place the page number on the right side. Create Footer B for even pages and place the page number on the left side. If you're using page numbering, use one of the alternating options to make sure the numbers all appear on the outside or inside of the duplex job. For more information, see "Headers, Footers, and Page Numbering" in Chapter 5.

⇨ In manual duplex printing, if you add a binding offset for documents that are going to be bound, make sure you select Left Edge for odd pages and Right Edge for even pages. To prevent text from being pushed too far into the margin, you may want to increase your left and right margins to 1.25".

⇨ You can use a Force Page code (choose Format ⎸Page ⎸ Force Page) to ensure that a particular page is odd- or even-numbered.

How do I print an eight-page booklet that has pages 1 and 8 on the same piece of paper, pages 2 and 7 on the same piece of paper, and so on?

Figure 6-6 shows what the booklet will look like when printed. You can divide your pages so that each physical printed page will contain two or more *logical* pages. In this example, one printed page contains two logical pages; however, each logical page has its own numbering. When it's time to print the document, you actually want to print logical page 1 on the same physical page as logical page 8. Page 2 prints with page 7, page 3 with page 6, and page 4 with page 5. You will then be able to fold the physical pages to create a booklet with the logical pages in the correct sequence. To accomplish this, you can use the Booklet printing option.

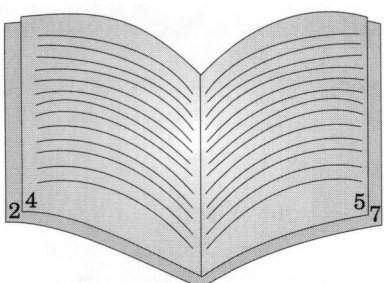

Figure 6-6.   You can use the Booklet option to create a printed booklet

Here are the steps for setting up and printing a booklet:

1. Set up your document in Landscape mode by choosing File | Page Setup, clicking the Size tab, and then selecting the Landscape option.

2. To divide your pages, click the Divide Page tab in the Page Setup dialog box. Then type **2** in the Number of Columns text box and click OK.

3. Add text and formatting to your booklet. You may want to use alternating page numbers to keep all the page numbers on either the outside or inside of the pages in the booklet.

 ***Tip:***   *You can view the booklet in Two Pages view to make sure everything looks okay.*

4. When you're ready to print, choose File | Print and then click the Two-Sided Printing tab.

5. Select Print as Booklet.

6. If you want to print on both sides of the page, select one of the Manual or Automatic options.

7. Choose Print. If you selected a Manual duplex option, you'll need to reinsert the printed pages in the printer.

? **While printing a booklet, I'm asked to reinsert page 1 before sending any part of the print job. What's wrong?**

Some printer drivers, such as the HP DeskJet 850c and Canon BJC-600 printer drivers, may prompt you to reinsert page 1 before any part of the print job has been printed. The job will not come out of the printer until you click OK and reinsert page 1. You can work around this problem by using the Manual options in the Print dialog box (choose File | Print | Two-Sided Printing) to send the front side (the odd pages) of the booklet as the first print job and then the back side (the even pages) as the second print job.

7 Answers!

Tables

Answer Topics!

Tables @ a Glance

⇨ WordPerfect's tables features help you organize information in coherent rows and columns. Tables also provide the bonus of helping you create more attractive documents. You can add and delete rows, change the numeric format of cells, add lines and shading, and even perform calculations using the numbers in your tables. This chapter answers your questions about how to use WordPerfect's many table features.

⇨ This chapter helps you use WordPerfect's advanced table features to create floating cells and import spreadsheets. After you format a table just the way you want, you don't have to repeat those steps for any similar tables you create. Instead, you can save the table style and then reuse it for the other tables. You can also merge data into tables and create forms from tables.

⇨ WordPerfect tables are powerful enough to be used as spreadsheets. You can use formulas not only to add and subtract figures in cells, but also to find the average, round off numbers, and calculate monthly payments on a loan. For tips on how to perform calculations on tables, turn to this chapter.

CREATING AND FORMATTING TABLES

? **WordPerfect 8 doesn't have a Table menu. How do I create tables?**

 One way to create a table is to place the insertion point where you want the table to appear, choose Insert | Table, and then specify the number of rows and columns you want. An easier way is to select the number of rows and columns you want in the table by using the Table QuickCreate button on the toolbar.

In WordPerfect 8, the Table menu has been replaced by the Tables property bar, shown in Figure 7-1. When you click within a table, the

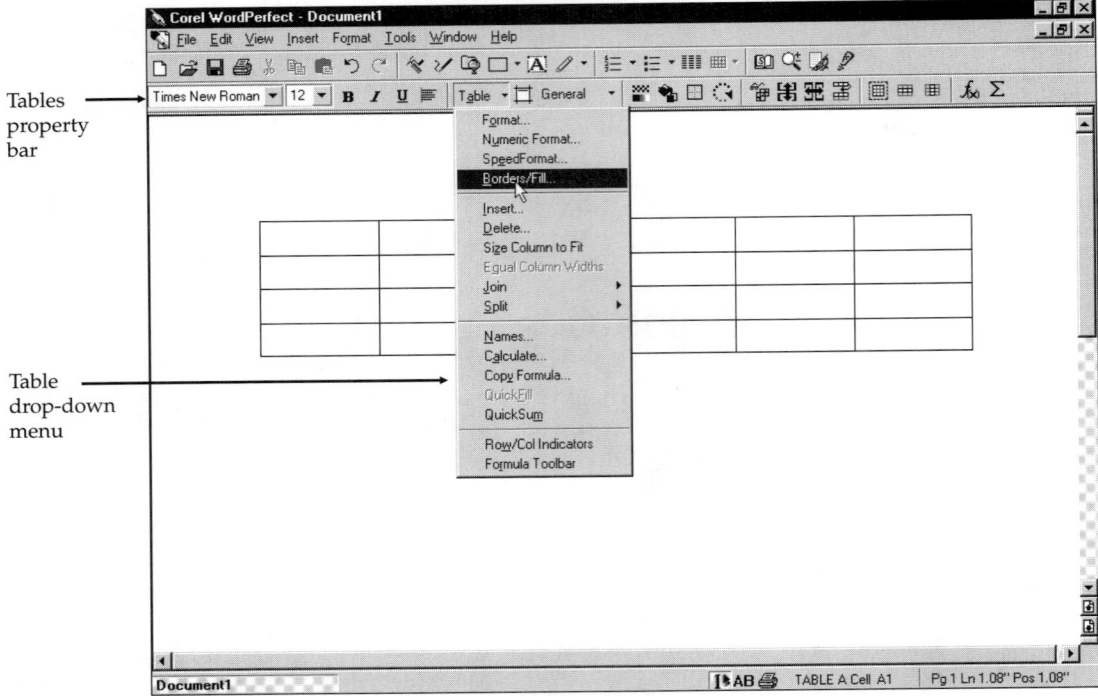

Tables
property
bar

Table
drop-down
menu

Figure 7-1.   The Tables property bar appears when you click within a table

Tables property bar displays all the options formerly found on the Table menu. Click the Table Menu button to view a list of options.

Tip: *If you prefer using the Table menu in WordPerfect 8, you can select the WordPerfect 7 menu by right-clicking the menu bar and choosing WordPerfect 7 Menu. However, keep in mind that you'll be missing several options found only in WordPerfect 8, and the documentation will be wrong. You're better off using the toolbar.*

? How do I drag to create a table?

In WordPerfect 8, you can create a table by dragging to create a box in a blank area of your document and then choosing Table from the QuickMenu.

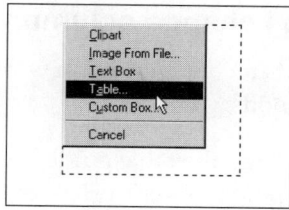

You can then specify the number of rows and columns, which appear inside the box you drew.

The advantage—or disadvantage, depending on what you're trying to do—of this approach is that the table appears inside a graphics box. You can size and move the graphics box and wrap text around it; you can even create two or more tables and place them side by side.

Can I use keystrokes to quickly insert and delete rows?

Yes. Table 7-1 lists all the important shortcut keystrokes for editing tables.

Table 7-1.   Shortcut Keystrokes

Keystroke	What It Does
TAB	Moves to the next cell
SHIFT-TAB	Moves to the previous cell
TAB (in last cell)	Adds a new row
CTRL-F12	Opens the Format dialog box
CTRL-TAB	Inserts a tab within a table
CTRL-, Decreases the column width	
CTRL-.	Increases the column width
ALT-RIGHT ARROW	Moves to the next column
ALT- LEFT ARROW	Moves to the previous column
HOME, HOME	Moves to the first column in the row
END, END	Moves to the last column in the row
CTRL-SHIFT-DOWN ARROW	Selects the table column
CTRL-SHIFT-RIGHT ARROW	Selects the table row
CTRL-SHIFT-RIGHT ARROW, DOWN ARROW	Selects the entire table
ALT-INSERT	Inserts a row above the current cell
SHIFT-ALT-INSERT	Inserts a row below the current cell

 **How do I change column widths in a table?**

You can change column widths in WordPerfect using any of these methods:

⇨ Drag the table guidelines. To drag a column guideline, move the pointer over the line until the cursor changes to a two-headed arrow. Then drag the line to a new position.

 Tip: *Hold down* CTRL *to drag a guideline and all guidelines to the right along with it.*

⇨ Use keystrokes. Place the insertion point anywhere in the column and then press CTRL-, (comma) to make the column narrower or CTRL-. (period) to make the column wider. The angle brackets on these keys, < and >, indicate the direction the column margin moves.

⇨ If you want all columns to be equal in width, select the row that contains those columns and then click the Equal Columns button.

⇨ To reduce the amount of white space in the columns of a finished table, select the columns you want to size and then click the Size Column to Fit button.

 Note: *If you add text after sizing columns to fit, the new text will be forced into the existing column. You may then want to click the Size Column to Fit button again.*

⇨ To use precise measurements for a table column, right-click a cell or a group of selected cells and then choose Format. Click the Column tab and then type a measurement in the Width text box.

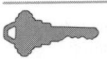 **How do I rotate text along the side of a table?**

You can rotate text in 90 degree increments, as shown in this table.

	Juanita	Denzel	Joshua	Maria	Carlton
May 17	✕				✕
May 24			✕		
May 31		✕			

To rotate text in a table, do one of the following:

⇨ Place the insertion point in a cell or select a group of cells in which you want rotated text. Then click the Rotate button on the Tables property bar. Each time you click this button, the text rotates 90 degrees in a clockwise direction.

⇨ Select the cells to be rotated and then right-click the table and choose Format. Select the rotation direction from the Rotate drop-down list.

Note: *The rotated text is inserted inside a text box in the cell. To edit the text, double-click the rotated text and then make any changes in the editing window. When you're done, click Close.*

❓ How do I format the numbers in a table so that two decimal places are displayed and negative numbers appear in parentheses?

You can display the numbers in tables in different ways. You can display numbers in exponential format (such as -1.4e+05), as currency (such as $14,500), or as dates (August 14, 1998). After you change the numeric format, any numbers you type in your table will be converted to that format. You can change the numeric format of individual cells or columns cells, or you can change all the cells in a table. You can also customize any of the numeric formats to suit your needs.

To format numbers so that two decimal places are displayed and negative numbers appear in parentheses, follow these steps:

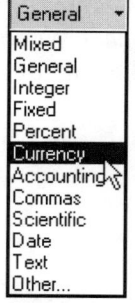

1. Select the cell or cells you want to format.

2. Right-click the selection and choose Numeric Format.

3. Click the Cell, Column, or Table tab at the top of the dialog box.

4. Select Accounting to display two decimal places with dollar signs inserted and negative numbers placed in parentheses.

5. If you want to customize the number format, select the format and then click Custom. Select the options you want, and then click OK twice.

Tip: *You can also select a number type from the Numeric drop-down list on the Tables property bar. The button shows you which numeric format is in effect in the cell where the insertion point is located.*

❓ Why are some cells aligned properly but not others?

A table has two levels of alignment formatting: cell formatting and column and table formatting. Cell formatting takes precedence over column and table formatting. Column and table formatting have equal priority, so whichever you set last is the formatting in effect. If you've changed the alignment of a specific cell, you can change the alignment of the column or table until the cows come home, but the changes won't affect the formatted cell—you must change the cell format.

For example, suppose you want a column of numbers decimal-aligned with a centered heading at the top of the column. Simply set the column format to Decimal and the cell format for the column heading to Center. Since the cell format overrides the column format, the heading is centered. If you want to change the alignment of the heading in that column, you must change the cell format, not the column format.

Things become tricky when a column contains several different cell formats. To see the current settings for the cells in a column, select the cells and then right-click the selection and choose Format. Click the Cell tab. If the Horizontal text box says Mixed, the cells have different justification options. Select an alignment option for the selected cells, and the change will take effect.

❓ I have a really long table that spans several pages. How do I repeat the headings at the top of every page?

You can label your column headings as header rows. Then WordPerfect will make sure they appear at the top of every page, even if you add or delete rows. If you want to use more than one row of column headings, the rows must be adjacent. For example, you can set rows 1 *through* 3 as header rows, but not rows 1 *and* 3. When you set up a header row, the cell address in the application bar appears with an asterisk (*).

Follow these steps to set up a header row:

1. Select the row or rows.

2. Right-click the selection. Then choose Format.

3. Click the Row tab, select Header row, and then click OK.

 **Note:**   *When you sort rows in a table, header rows are not included in the sort.*

❓ Why did a row in my table move to the next page?

Table rows adjust so they're as tall as the tallest cell in the row. Because table rows can't straddle page breaks, if one cell in a row has enough text to wrap to the next page, the entire row is moved. This can leave a big space at the bottom of the page. Here are some ways to fix this problem:

⇨ Check each cell in the row to make sure it doesn't contain extra hard returns.

⇨ Edit lengthy text down to a reasonable size. If this doesn't work, use a smaller font size for the text in that cell.

⇨ If the text is still too long, try splitting the row into two rows and then cut and paste text from one cell into the cell below it. To split a row, select it, click the Table drop-down list on the property bar, and choose Split | Cell. Select Rows and click OK.

Tip: *If your table is being broken by a page break, you can make sure the table stays together on one page by selecting the entire table and choosing Format | Keep Text Together | Block Protect.*

❓ Why does text disappear when I'm typing in a table?

Either the table has a fixed row height and now you're out of space, or the cell you're typing in has filled the entire page. Your text isn't gone—it's simply stored as hidden text. When more space is available, the text will become visible.

If your table has a fixed row height, you can increase the height value or use the Automatic option so that the row height adjusts to accommodate the amount of text you type. To change the row height, click within a row or select a group of rows, right-click the row or selection, and choose Format. Then either select Automatic or increase the value in the Fixed text box. Another solution is to format the text with a smaller font so that it fits without disappearing.

If the text you type in a cell disappears because it fills the entire page, you have several options. You can increase the top and bottom margins on the page, use a smaller font size for the text in the cell, resize the column so you have more room, or split the row and place some of the text in the next row.

? **Why does the insertion point move to the next cell when I press ENTER? I can type only one line.**

You have the row set to accept only a single line of text, which is useful for inserting numbers, but not so useful if you need to add paragraphs of text. Here's how to change this:

1. Select the rows you want to change. Then right-click the selection and choose Format.

2. Click the Row tab, select Multiple Lines, and click OK.

? **How do I remove all the lines in a table?**

1. Right-click the table and then choose Borders/Fill.

2. Click the Table tab.

3. Select X (None) for the table border.

4. Select X (None) for the default cell lines. Then click OK.

Tip: *After you remove the table lines, you'll probably want to view the table gridlines to see what you're doing. Choose View | Guidelines and make sure Tables is selected.*

? **How do I convert tabbed columns to tables?**

If you create columns using the TAB key and then wish you had used the Tables feature instead, it's not too late to change. Here's how you can convert tabular columns to tables:

1. Make sure the columns are evenly aligned, with plenty of space between columns. Make sure there is only one tab stop between each tabular column, or the extra tab stops will be converted into blank cells.

2. Select the tabular columns. Don't include the final hard return, or you'll end up with an extra row in your table.

3. Click the Tables button on the toolbar and then choose Tabular Columns.

 *Tip:* *If you end up with unwanted blank cells when you convert tabular columns to a table, choose Edit | Undo. Make sure you delete the extra tab stops, and then try again.*

? How do I "dress up" a table to make it look nice?

You can use the SpeedFormat feature, shown in Figure 7-2, to turn your plain table grid into a work of art. SpeedFormat works best for tables with a header row and a Totals column, but you can use it to format any kind of table quickly. For example, you can use the Column Fill Single option to shade every other column or the Row Fill Single option to shade every other row.

1. Right-click the table. Then choose SpeedFormat from the QuickMenu.

2. If you want to get rid of all previous formatting, including any formatting changes you have made to individual cells, select Clear Current Table Format before Applying. This option is useful when changing SpeedFormat styles.

3. Select a style and then choose Apply.

 *Note:* *If you want to apply formatting just to the table as it now is, without applying the format to any additional cells you create, select Apply S on a Cell by Cell Basis. For example, if this option is selected when you shade alternate rows, the shading pattern will not continue when you add or remove rows. In most cases, it's best to leave this option turned off.*

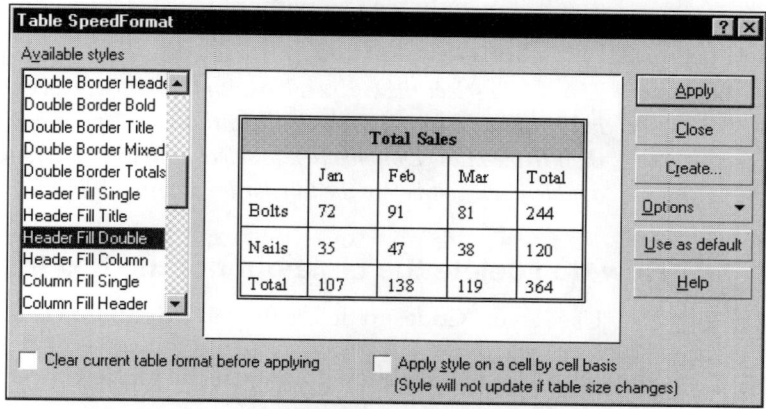

Figure 7-2. Use the SpeedFormat dialog box to quickly create tables that please the eye

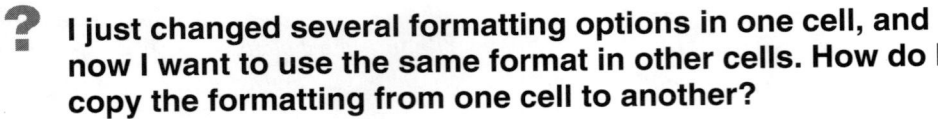 **I just changed several formatting options in one cell, and now I want to use the same format in other cells. How do I copy the formatting from one cell to another?**

While SpeedFormat lets you change the look of a table to a predefined format, the QuickFormat feature works well for copying formatting from one cell to another. Although QuickFormat is commonly used to format headings quickly, you can also use it to format tables. Most of the formatting, including alignment, border styles, and fill styles, will be copied. Here's how:

1. Click the formatted cell.

2. Click the QuickFormat button on the toolbar and then click OK to copy the cell formatting.

3. Click any cells you want to format.

4. When you're finished, click the QuickFormat button again.

When I select a table and try to cut it, the text disappears, but the table structure remains. How do I cut and paste the entire table?

One way to cut and paste the entire table is to select the hard return before or after the table before you cut it. Another way is to select the entire contents of the table and then choose Edit | Cut. When asked what you want to cut or copy, select either Row or Column and click OK. You can then paste the entire table somewhere else in your document. If you select Selection in the Cut or Copy Table dialog box, you'll copy only the text without the structure.

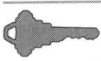 *Tip: To select the entire table with the mouse, place the pointer next to the left border of any cell in the table until the pointer becomes a left arrow and then triple-click. Double-click to select only the row. To select only a column, double-click just below the top border of any cell in the table.*

How do I delete the table but not the text inside the table?

Use Reveal Codes to delete the table definition code:

1. Place the insertion point near the top-left corner of the table and then choose Edit | Reveal Codes.

2. Place the Reveal Codes cursor just to the left of the Tbl Def code and then press DELETE.

3. In the Delete Table dialog box, select Table Structure (Leave Text) and then click OK.

 **In a table, the TAB key takes me to the next cell. How do I quickly insert dot leaders after text in a table column?**

To move the text to the next tab stop in a table cell, you can press F7 to indent the whole paragraph, or you can press CTRL-TAB to move just the first line to the next tab stop. Use the ruler to format that next tab stop as a decimal tab (see "Text Formatting" in Chapter 3).

Tip: *To insert a tab with dot leaders in the center of a cell, press SHIFT-F7 twice. To insert a flush right tab with dot leaders in a cell, press ALT-F7 twice.*

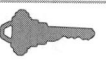 **A table formatted in Landscape mode appears in the middle of my document. When I change the page orientation to print this table, the footer also prints in Landscape mode. How do I print a table in Landscape orientation and still keep the footer in Portrait orientation, so it appears in the same place on all the pages of my document?**

The best way to print the table in Landscape mode is to put it in a graphics box and rotate it. Then you don't have to worry about page codes. The only drawback to this approach is that you need to edit the table in a special editing window for rotated text, but that's not such a big deal:

1. Select the table and then choose Edit | Cut. When prompted, select Column or Row and then click OK.

2. Choose Insert | Graphics | Custom Box.

3. Select Table and click OK.

4. Double-click inside the table box and then choose Edit | Paste.

Note: *If the error message "Too much text for the current context" appears, just click OK. The rest of the text is formatted as hidden text. When you resize the table, everything will reappear.*

5. Right-click the graphics box border and then choose Content. Select 90 degrees and click OK.

6. Right-click the graphics box border and then choose Size. Set the Width and Height values to Full (or specify custom dimensions). Then click OK.

Tip: *To edit the rotated table, click inside it and then make the editing changes in the editing window. Click Close when you're done. To edit the graphics box, right-click just outside the table and use the QuickMenu to make changes.*

? I added a thick border around my table, but now when I type in the table, there is not enough space between the thick left border and the text. How can I add more room?

When you add thick borders, WordPerfect does not adjust the amount of distance between the cell border and the text in the cell—but you can change the distance easily enough. Here's how:

1. Right-click the column with the thick border and choose Format.

2. Click the Column tab.

3. Under the Inside Margins in Column group, increase the distance specified in the Left text box and then click OK.

Tip: *If the bottom row is too close to the border, right-click the row and choose Format. Click the Row tab and then increase the distance specified in the Bottom text box in the Row Margins group.*

? I have a table with more than 200 rows that spans several pages. What's a quick way to number table rows?

You can use the QuickFill feature to number all the rows in a table. QuickFill looks for a pattern in the text you're typing and then continues that pattern through the rest of the selected text. For example, if you want to list all the months in the top row, type **Jan** and **Feb** in the first two columns, select the rest of the row, and choose QuickFill. The rest of the months (Mar, Apr, May, and so on) are inserted automatically.

Here's how you can number the rows in a long table:

1. Type **1** in the first column of the first row and then type **2** in the first column of the second row.

2. With the insertion point in the first column, press CTRL-SHIFT-DOWN ARROW to select the entire column.

3. Right-click the column and then select QuickFill.

Tip: *Besides using QuickFill to fill in months, you can also use it to fill in numbers (1, 2, 3, and so on, or 12, 24, 36, and so on), years (1998, 1999, 2000, and so on), and dates (Oct. 5, 1998, Oct. 6, 1998, and so on). You can also repeat the same number or letter in each cell.*

On the screen, my table includes nice, thick lines, but when I print, only the text appears. How do I print table lines?

The Print Text Only option is probably selected in the Print dialog box. When this option is selected, graphics and table lines do not print. To fix this problem, choose File | Print and then select the Details tab. Deselect Print Text Only and then choose Print.

I'm trying to add a new row in my table, but the table will not expand to another page. What's wrong?

If you used the Drag to Create feature to create the table, the table is inserted in a graphics box, and graphic boxes cannot span more than one page. If the table or a table cell needs to extend across more than one page, you need to cut the table from the graphics box, delete the graphics box, and then paste the table into your document.

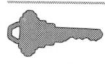

Note: *If you want cells to be divided across a page, make sure the option that allows cell to be split at a page break is turned on. Select the rows you want to allow to be broken, right-click the table, and then choose Format | Row | Divide Row across Pages.*

I want to order the rows in a table according to the information in the third column. How do I sort a table?

In WordPerfect 8, you can use the Sort Table button on the property bar to sort table rows based on the column in which cells are selected. You can sort in *ascending* (a, b, c... or 1, 2, 3...) or *descending* (c, b, a... or 3, 2, 1...) order using *alphanumeric* or *numeric* criteria. To sort text such as names or addresses, you'll want to select either Alpha Ascending or Alpha Descending. To sort numbers, you'll want to select either Numeric Ascending or Numeric Descending. If, for example, you perform an Alpha Ascending sort on numbers, "1,800,000" will be sorted before "490,000" because "1" comes before "4." If you perform a Numeric Ascending sort, "1,800,000" will come after "490,000" because it's a larger number.

1. Select the cells in the column that you want to sort by. If you have a Totals column in the last row, you won't want to sort that row.

2. Click the Sort Table button on the property bar and then select the type of sort you want to perform.

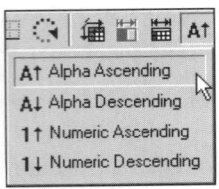

 Note: *If you want to sort your table rows using more complicated criteria, use the Sort feature. For more information, see "Sorting Lists" in Chapter 10.*

USING ADVANCED TABLE FEATURES

 **I created two tables, but now I want to combine all the information in one table. Can I join tables?**

You sure can. Here's how:

1. Make sure the two tables are stacked directly above and below each other, with no text or extra hard returns between them.

2. Make sure the two tables have the same number of columns (they don't need to be the same width—WordPerfect will resize the columns in the second table, which means you may have to resize the columns after you join the tables).

3. Place the insertion point in the upper table.

4. Click the Table drop-down menu on the property bar and then choose Join | Table.

？ Can I place text beside a table?

You can place text beside a table in several ways. In all cases, make sure the table is narrower than the margins, or you will not be able to type text.

⇨ Create a large cell on one side of the table by joining column cells and removing the top, bottom, and right lines of the cell. Type the text in the resulting single, large cell. The text will appear as though it is beside the table.

⇨ Create two columns. To do this, select the table and then select 2 Columns from the Columns drop-down menu on the toolbar. Drag the gutter to size the columns so that the table fits in one column and the other column is available for the text you type.

⇨ The most flexible approach is to place the table in a graphics box so the text can wrap around the box, as shown in Figure 7-3. To do this, select the table, press CTRL-X, select Row or Column, and click

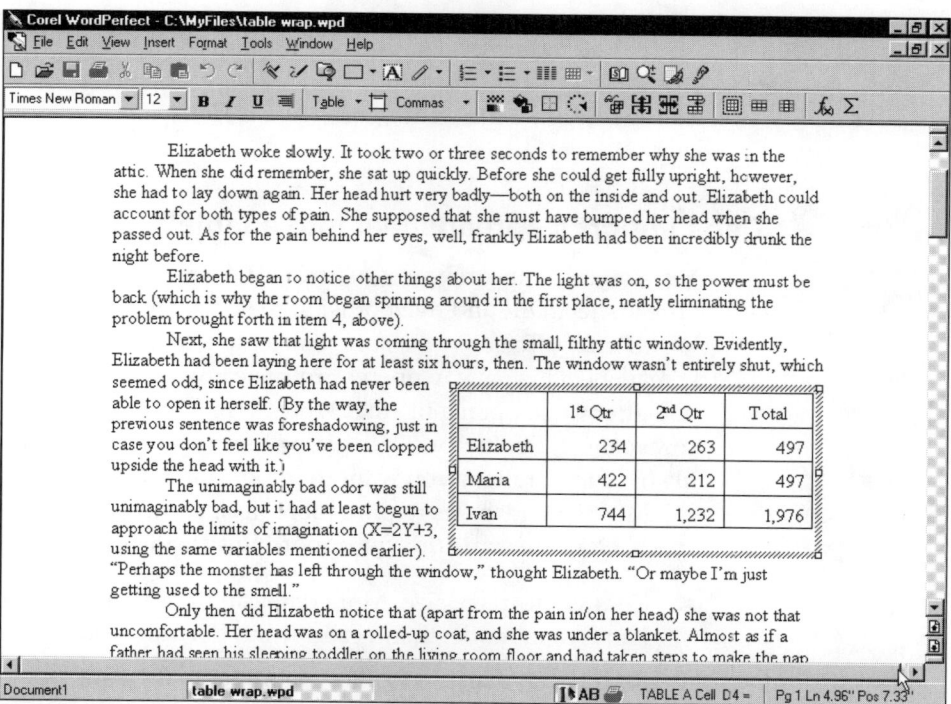

Figure 7-3.   When you create a table in a graphics box, text can easily wrap around it

OK. Choose Insert | Graphics | Custom Box, select Table, and click OK. Double-click inside the box and then press CTRL-V. You can move the table box by dragging the box border, and you can size it by dragging any of the sizing handles.

Tip: You can also use the columns or graphics box methods to place two tables side by side.

How do I center my table between margins?

In WordPerfect 8, you can specify whether your table is left-aligned, centered, or right-aligned. Of course, if your table takes up the full margin space, its alignment doesn't really matter. Here's how to center a table between the margins:

1. Right-click the table and then choose Format.
2. Click the Table tab and then select Center from the Table Position on Page drop-down list.

Note: This method does not work if your table is in a graphics box. If your table is in a graphics box, right-click the graphics box border and choose Position. Select Center of Margins from the Horizontal drop-down list and click OK.

Can I import a spreadsheet into a table?

Yes. You can import Excel, Quattro Pro, Lotus, PlanPerfect, Spreadsheet DIF, and most other spreadsheet formats into WordPerfect. To convert a spreadsheet to a table, open or insert the spreadsheet just as you open or retrieve any other document. When you attempt to open a file that WordPerfect recognizes as a spreadsheet, the Import Data dialog box appears. You can specify the file or named ranges you want to import into your document.

Most spreadsheets require more horizontal space than vertical space. Here are some tips for importing spreadsheets effectively:

⇨ Change the page size. More data can fit horizontally on a page, in Landscape mode, than vertically, in Portrait mode.

⇨ Reduce the margins to allow more room for data.

⇨ Use a small font, such as 8-point Arial.

? I used the Border/Fill option to add a gradient fill, but it doesn't look right in the table. How can I fix it?

When you add a gradient fill to a table cell, the fill may not be displayed correctly on screen. The gradient fill patterns don't appear in the document window the same way they print; instead, the background color you selected appears as a solid color in the table cell. However, when you print the page, the fill will be the correct gradient pattern.

? I use the same format every time I create a particular type of table. Can I create a table style?

Yes. You can use the SpeedFormat option to save the style for use in other tables. For example, you can create a table with a thick outside border with dotted inside lines and a double line above the Totals row. You can also format all cells except those in the left column and top row so they are right-aligned and use the Currency option. Then you can save this formatting for use in other tables you create. Here's how:

1. Create and format the table, specifying justification, text size, lines, fills, and any other options.

2. Right-click the table and then choose SpeedFormat.

3. Choose Create, type a name for the style, and click OK.

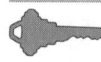 *Note:* *By default, the table style you create is saved in the default template, where it can be used by all other documents. If you want to save the table style to a file for use on other computers, click Options and Save As in the Table SpeedFormat dialog box.*

? How can I reference a value located in another table in the same document?

If you use lots of tables in your documents, you may want to refer to figures in the cells of other tables. For example, if you have several tables containing subtotals, you may want to create a table that includes a grand total calculated by referring to the bottom line in the other tables.

Here's how to refer to other table cells:

1. Place the insertion point in the cell where you want the value of the referenced cell to appear.

2. Right-click the table and choose Formula Toolbar from the QuickMenu.

3. Click the Formula entry window on the Formula toolbar and then click the cell in the table that you want to reference. The address of the reference cell should appear in the Formula Entry window.

4. Click the green check mark to the left of the Formula Entry window. The information in the reference cell should appear in the target cell.

5. Click Close to close the Formula toolbar.

? I need to calculate data in a paragraph, but I don't need a table. How can I do the math without using a table?

One of WordPerfect's unique features is the *floating cell*, which lets you use table functions and formulas in the body of your text. A floating cell consists of a pair of codes surrounding the kind of information that you often put in table cells. Floating cells can even be formatted like table cells, and they can reference table cells or other floating cells. The mortgage loan letter shown in Figure 7-4 includes four floating cells. The final figure was calculated based on the first three figures.

Here's how to create a floating cell:

1. Choose Insert | Table, select Floating Cell, and choose Create.

2. If necessary, specify a format (such as Currency or Percent) for the floating cell by choosing Table on the property bar, selecting Numeric Format, selecting the format you want, and then clicking OK.

3. Type the data or insert a formula in the floating cell. To reference another cell, click the Formula Entry window on the Formula toolbar and then click the table cell or floating cell you want to reference.

4. When you're done typing the floating cell information, press END or RIGHT ARROW to move past the floating cell code.

Note: *WordPerfect automatically names floating cells—for example,* *FLOATING CELL A—that you insert in the document. If you want a more* *descriptive name, such as "Interest Rate," choose Names on the Formula* *toolbar and then type the name.*

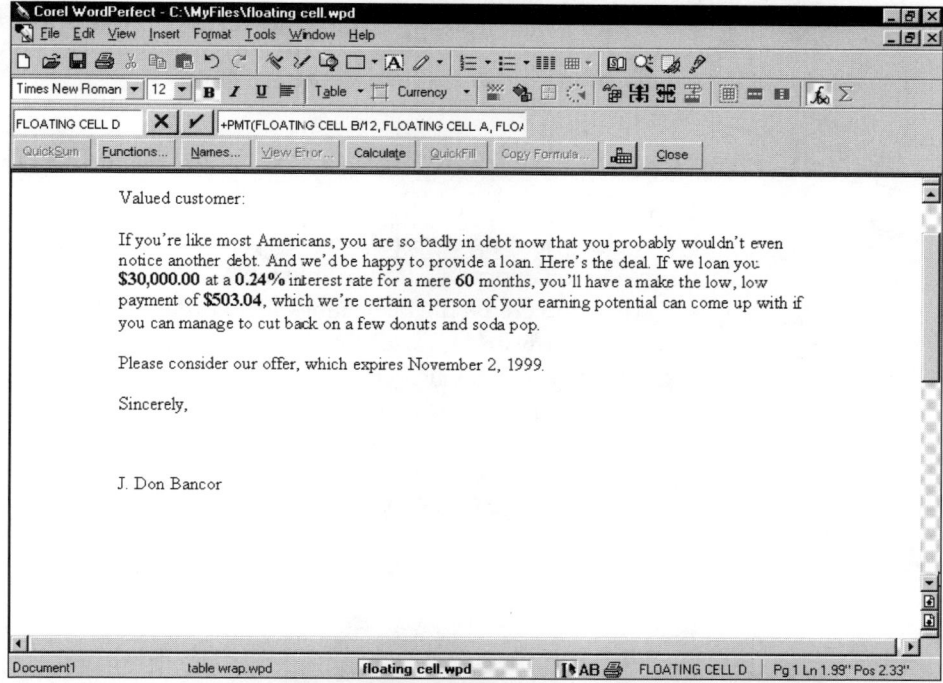

Figure 7-4.   You can use floating cells to perform calculations in your document text

I need to save a file in ASCII format to upload to a BBS. What's the best way to convert a table?

Here's how to save a table in ASCII delimited format:

1. Make sure the table is not located in a graphics box. If it is, cut and paste the table into your document and then delete the graphics box.

2. Select the entire table without selecting the hard return above or below the table. Then press DELETE.

3. Select Convert Contents to merge data file and then click OK

4. Choose File | Save As.

5. From the File Type drop-down list, select ASCII (DOS) Delimited Text.

6. Type a filename and then choose Save.

Note: *To import this file into WordPerfect, choose Insert |*
Spreadsheet/Database | Import and then select the file.

 ## I need to create a custom invoice form. How do I do this?

To create an invoice or other forms, you can create irregular columns
in a table by joining and splitting cells as necessary. Figure 7-5 shows a
sample invoice form created from a table.

After you create the basic table structure you need, use the
QuickSplit Row and QuickSplit Column buttons on the property bar
to shape your form. Click either QuickSplit Row or QuickSplit
Column and then click the cell you want to split. Click the button
again to turn it off.

To join cells, select the cells you want to join. Then choose Table
on the property bar and click Join | Cell.

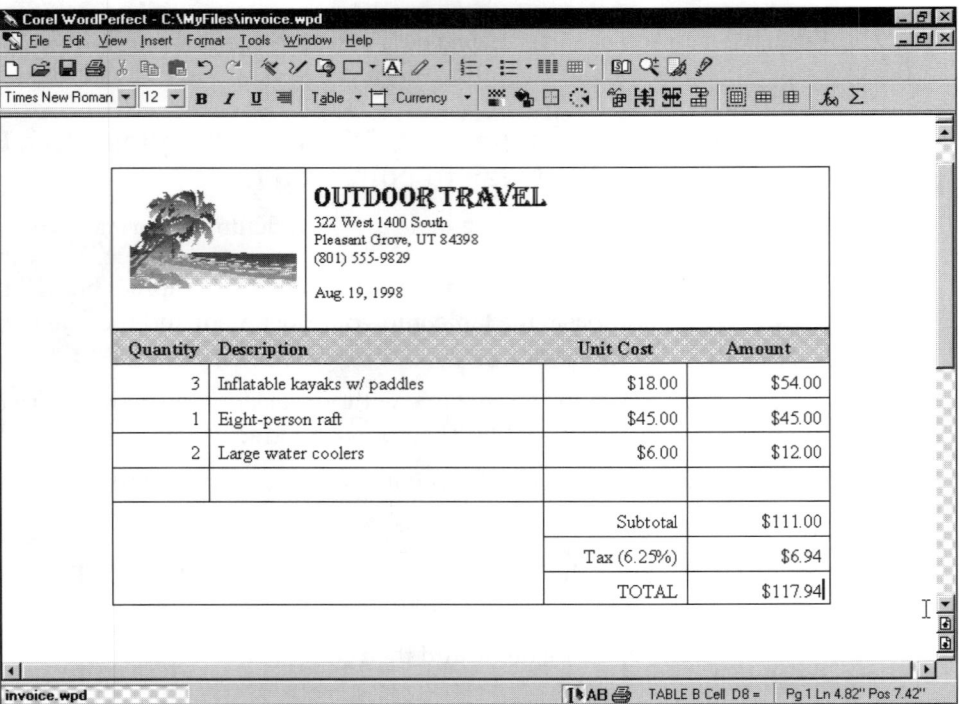

Figure 7-5.   This invoice was created from a table

Tip: *Another way to create irregular columns is to create one table immediately below another. When printed, the two tables will look like a single table.*

I created a form with a table, but I don't want users to be able to change certain cells. What can I do?

Here is how you can lock cells in a table so they can't be edited:

1. Select the cells you want to lock.

2. Right-click the selection and then choose Format.

3. Click the Cell tab and then select Lock Cell to Prevent Changes.

Note: *If the Disable Locks in All Cells option on the Table page of the Properties for Table Format dialog box is selected, your cells will not be locked. This option is useful when you want to temporarily unlock locked cells so you can edit them without having to unlock each cell individually. Remember, however, to turn off this option when you're done.*

How do I insert a check box into a form?

Check boxes are a great way to add flair to forms. When you add a check box with WordPerfect's Checkbox macro, clicking the box will place an X in it, and clicking it again will remove the X. The current font size determines the size of the check box.

Follow these steps to insert a check box into your document:

1. Choose Tools | Macro | Play.

2. Double-click Checkbox.wcm.

Warning: *If you press* TAB *after inserting a check box at the beginning of the line, you'll start a list, and you'll lose the ability to check and uncheck the box. Click away from the check box or press* END *to move past the hypertext codes.*

Tip: *If you just want to insert a check box graphic without the hypertext codes, press* CTRL-W. *Then in the Number text box, type either* **5,24** *(to insert an unmarked check box) or* **5,25** *(to insert a marked check box) and choose Insert and Close.*

PERFORMING CALCULATIONS IN TABLES

 I want to add each column of numbers and place the sums in the Totals row. What's the fastest way to add the numbers in a column?

 You can use the QuickSum feature to quickly add the numbers in a column or row. Place the insertion point in the blank cell in the bottom row (to add a column) or in the right-most column (to add a row) and then click the QuickSum button.

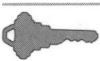 *Warning:*   *The QuickSum feature adds only the cells directly above the cell. If your table contains any blank rows, any cells above the blank rows will not be added.*

 I am continually changing the values in a column of numbers and adding and deleting rows. What's the best way to calculate the sum of this column?

If you use QuickSum (or the SUM function) to add the numbers in a column, WordPerfect adds only the current range of cells. If you add rows later, for example, the sum will not reflect those new numbers unless you recalculate the total. A better approach is to use the Subtotal function, which automatically recalculates the sum of the column of numbers directly above it every time a value is added, deleted, or changed. To insert a subtotal, place the insertion point in the cell where you want the subtotal to appear and then type **++** (or type + in the formula entry line on the Formula toolbar). When you move the insertion point outside the cell, the numbers in the column will be added.

Tip: *Subtotal adds the numbers above it until it encounters a cell that contains text or another Subtotal. If you want to add subtotals to create a grand total, type* **==** *in a cell at the bottom of the column that contains the subtotals.*

? I used + to add the numbers in a column, but the column heading (1998) was added with the rest of the numbers. How can I prevent this?

You can tell WordPerfect to ignore certain cells when you are calculating data.

1. Select the cells that should be ignored.

2. Right-click the selection and then choose Format.

3. Click the Cell tab and select Ignore Cell When Calculating. Then click OK.

4. Right-click the table and then choose Calculate.

? How do I calculate the average of a group of numbers in my table?

You can use the Formula toolbar to insert formulas in your document. You can average cells, calculate monthly payments, and insert a host of other spreadsheet functions in your WordPerfect tables. Figure 7-6 shows cells selected for use in the Average (AVE) formula in the Formula Entry window on the Formula toolbar.

1. Right-click the table and then choose Formula Toolbar.

2. Place the insertion point in the cell where you want the calculated averages to appear.

3. Click Functions on the Formula toolbar. Then select the function (such as AVE for averages) and choose Insert.

4. To specify which cells you want to average, either type the cell addresses (such as **b2:b8** to find the average of all cells between B2 and B8) or drag across the cells you want to average to insert the addresses automatically.

5. To insert the formula in the cell where you placed the insertion point, click the Check button to the left of the formula.

Tip: *To display the cell addresses (such as A2, B4, and so on) for a table, click the Row/Column Indicator button on the Formula toolbar.*

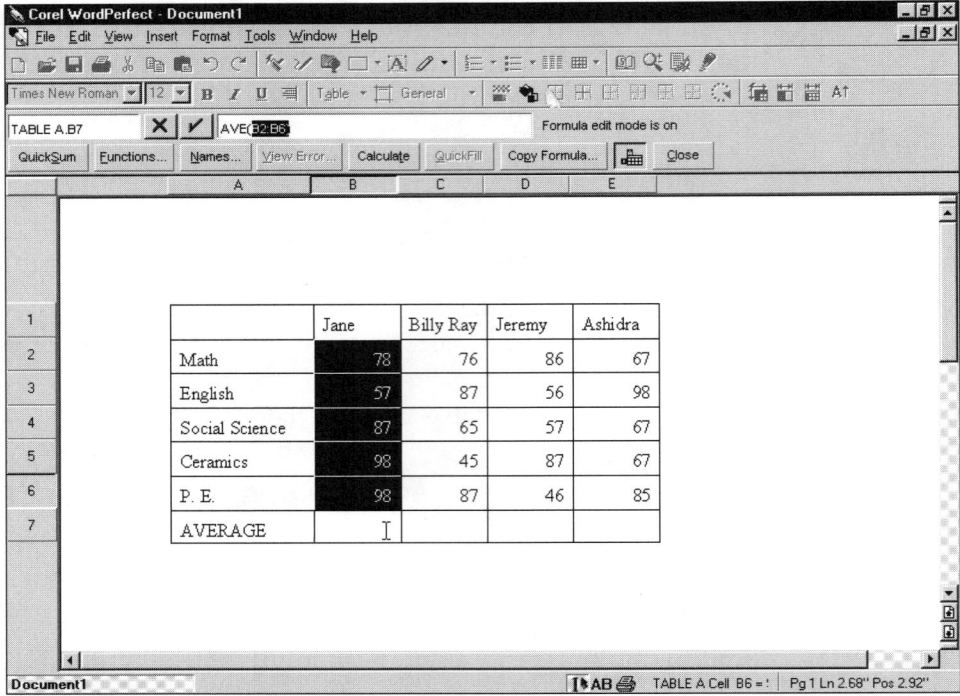

Figure 7-6.   You can use the Formula toolbar to perform numerous types of calculations

Is there a quick way to copy a formula across an entire row or column of cells?

You can easily copy formulas to other cells so you don't have to insert the same formula in each cell. Here's how:

1. If the Formula toolbar is not displayed, right-click the table and then choose Formula Toolbar.

2. Place the insertion point in the cell containing the formula.

3. Click Copy Formula on the Formula toolbar.

4. To copy the formula to the right across the same row, select Right and then type the number of cells (not including the cell in which the formula already appears). To copy the formula down cells in a column, select Down and type the number of cells below the source cell.

Tip: *If you want to copy the formula to cells that are not adjacent to the cell containing the formula, select the entire cell (not just the number in the cell), then press* CTRL-C. *Select Cell and choose OK. Then paste the formula in the the cell or cells where you want the formula to appear.*

When I type a2*b2 in a cell, the numbers are not multiplied. How do I multiply the numbers in two cells?

When you type **a2*b2** in a cell, WordPerfect thinks you're typing text. To quickly perform a calculation in a cell, you must precede the expression with = or +. For example, to multiply cell a2 by cell b2, you can type **=a2*b2** or **+a2*b2**; when you move to the next cell, WordPerfect will perform the multiplication. You can also type formulas using this method. For example, typing **=AVE(a2:a4)** directly in a cell averages the numbers in cells A2, A3, and A4.

When I calculated the monthly payment for a mortgage in a table, the numbers came out too large. What am I doing wrong?

When you calculate monthly payments, several things can go wrong. The most likely problem is that you failed to divide the interest rate by 12. Another possibility is that you incorrectly specified the loan rate; for example, on an 8% loan, you may have specified the percentage as 8 or 0.8 instead of 0.08. Yet another possibility is that you forgot to make the principal a negative number. Figure 7-7 shows a sample monthly payment.

Here's how to use the PMT function to calculate loan payments:

1. Insert the loan data into the table as shown in Figure 7-7.

2. Format the data cells with the proper numeric formats. To change the Interest Rate cell to a percentage, right-click the cell containing the interest, choose Numeric Format | Percent and then click OK. Use the same method to change the Principal and Monthly Payment cells to Currency.

3. Right-click the table and choose Formula Toolbar.

4. On the Formula toolbar, click Functions and then double-click the PMT function.

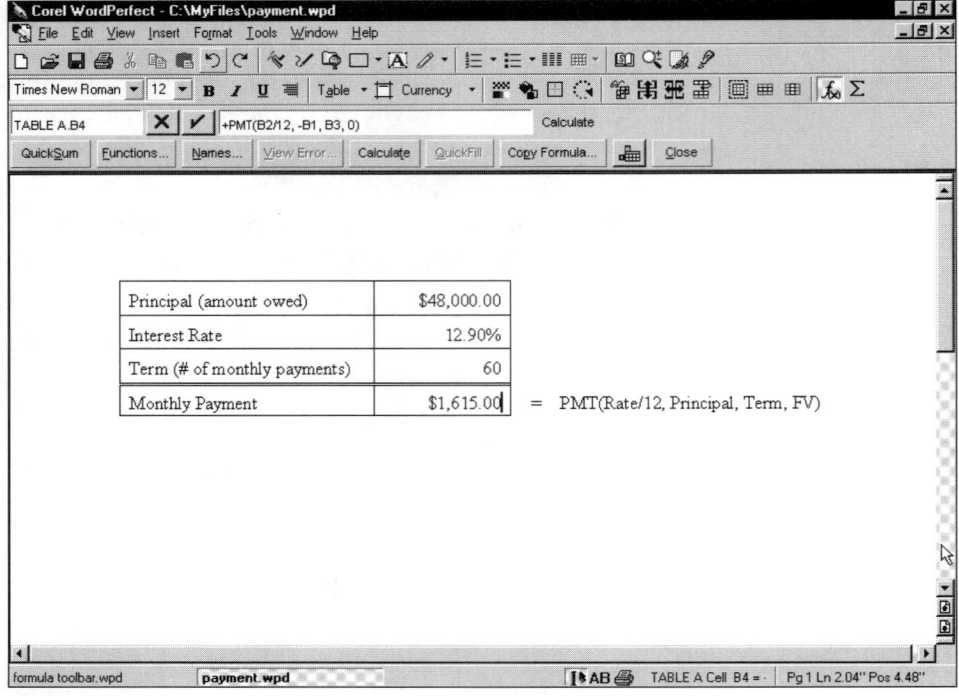

Figure 7-7.   Check your entries to avoid mistakes when calculating the monthly
payment on a loan

5. Replace the payment expressions with the appropriate cell
addresses. Remember to make the principal a negative number
and remember to divide the interest rate by 12 since it's
compounded monthly.

Note: *In the PMT function, Rate% is the interest rate, PV is the present
value (principal), Periods is the number of payments, FV is the future value
(0 at end of the loan), and [Type] is the type of loan.*

I changed some figures in the table that were referenced by a formula. Why didn't WordPerfect recalculate the numbers?

If you change data, right-click the table and choose Calculate.
WordPerfect will then recalculate all values in all tables in your
document.

You can have WordPerfect recalculate a single table, or all tables, automatically when you change data. However, this may slow you down when you're working in tables. To turn on automatic calculation, choose Table from the property bar and then choose Calculate. Under Automatic Calculation, select Calculate Table or Calculate Tables in Document. Then click OK.

? **I'm trying to calculate the total hours worked and I've used Hour(C2)-Hour(B2) in my table, but this formula calculates only full-hour increments. How do I calculate hours to the minute?**

Here's how you can calculate to the minute:

1. Select the cells in your table that contain the start time, end time, and total hours worked.

2. Right-click the selection and choose Numeric Format.

3. Select Date/Time and then choose Custom.

4. Select one of the formats containing only the time (such as 19:21:38—which represents 7:21 p.m.) from the drop-down list and then click OK twice.

5. Insert the start time and end time in the first two cells. Make sure you type either 24-hour time or include am or pm (for example, you can type either **17:00** or **5:00 pm**).

6. Click the Total Hours column and type a formula (such as **=C2-B2**) that subtracts the end time cell from the start time cell.

Troubleshooting Table Calculation Problems

To avoid errors when performing calculations in your tables, watch for these common problems:

⇨ If you add or delete rows or columns, use the Formula toolbar to update the range in any formula containing references to cells whose numbers have changed.

> ⇨ If a column heading contains numbers, such as a date, these numbers may be added to the subtotal or sum at the bottom of the column. To prevent this problem, select the heading cells, right-click the selection, and choose Format | Cell | Ignore Cell When Calculating.
>
> ⇨ Make sure that cells containing numbers are not formatted as text. Turn on the Formula toolbar and click the cells that contain numbers. If the numbers don't appear in the Formula toolbar, check the number type for the cell (right-click the cell and choose Numeric Format). Try changing the number type to Fixed or something other than General. You can also delete the cell and retype the number.
>
> ⇨ Remember that only one number can be calculated in a cell. Anything after a hard return will be ignored in the calculations.
>
> ⇨ If your Sum formula performs calculations on a large range, try adding a Sum or Subtotal calculation part way through the range to see if that portion is adding correctly. If you can determine where the calculations are off, you can then troubleshoot that area.

? I thought I deleted a formula, but when I tabbed to the next cell, the message "Replace formula?" appeared. How do I delete a table formula?

This message is intended to prevent you from accidentally deleting or typing over a formula. One way to avoid this message is to select the entire cell before you press DELETE. To select the cell, place the insertion point just below the top border of the cell until the pointer become an up arrow. Then click. When you press DELETE, the formula is deleted for good.

 ***Tip:*** *If you never want this error message to appear, choose Tools | Settings, double-click Environment, click the Prompts tab, and then deselect Confirm Deletion of Table Formulas.*

? When I typed a formula, the message "Reference to cell outside of table" appeared. What should I do?

In this case, you included an address in your formula that's not part of your table. For example, if your table contains only three columns and your formula refers to cell D1, this message will appear.

This problem is usually the result of confusing rows and columns. In a cell address (such as D4), the letter refers to the column and the number refers to the row. To help you remember this, you can turn on the row and column indicators. Right-click the table and choose Formula Toolbar. Then click the Row/Column Indicator button.

? When I type a formula, the message "Circular reference" appears. What's wrong?

A circular reference occurs when a formula references its own cell. For example, if you create the formula A1+A2 in cell A2, you have created a circular reference. In this case, either move the insertion point to cell A3 or refer to the correct cells you're trying to add.

? I don't want zeros (0.00) to appear in cells when I perform calculations and the result is zero. How can I remove the zeros?

You can use an IF statement that tells WordPerfect to leave a cell blank if the amount is zero. For example, if your formula is A7*E7, use the following statement:

```
IF(A7*E7=0,NA(),A7*E7)
```

Here's what this formula says: If the amount equals zero, do not insert any value. Otherwise, insert the calculation result.

Merges, Labels, and Envelopes

Answer Topics!

Merges, Labels, and Envelopes @ a Glance

⇨   You can use the Corel Address Book to store names, addresses, phone numbers, e-mail addresses, and other useful information about people you contact. You can then insert any of these addresses directly into your WordPerfect document or generate labels, merge letters, and envelopes based on the Address Book entries. You can also add your own name, address, and personal information to the Address Book so your personal information can be included in project documents. This chapter helps you make full use of the Address Book.

⇨   Merging is the process of combining information from two files. The most common use of the Merge feature is to create form letters: First you create a data file containing contact information. Then you create a form file with fields that reference the data information, allowing you to generate form letters. You can also use Merge to create fill-in-the-blank forms. If you have questions about how to use the Merge feature, consult this chapter.

⇨   Besides creating simple form files, you can use advanced merge techniques to direct the operation of your merge. For example, you can use the Keyboard command to pause the merge while you type information. This chapter offers guidelines for using these advanced features.

⇨   WordPerfect includes nearly 200 label definitions, which means that when you want to create labels, most of the work has already been done. All you need to do is select the right definition and type your labels. If you've stored addresses in a merge data file or in your Address Book, you can generate labels in seconds—and if you have any questions, you can turn to this chapter.

⇨   This chapter also helps you use WordPerfect's envelope form, which
automatically addresses envelopes using the return address you specify
and the mailing address in your letter. If you've stored addresses in a
merge data file or in your Address Book, you can quickly generate
envelopes.

COREL ADDRESS BOOK

❓ What is the difference between My Addresses and Frequent Contacts?

The Address Book has two pages, My Addresses and Frequent
Contacts, as shown in Figure 8-1. Type contact information on the
My Addresses page. When you first use a particular entry in the My
Addresses list—for instance, by using it to dial a person's phone
number or by inserting the address into a WordPerfect document—
the address is copied to the Frequent Contacts page. The Address
Book keeps track of how often you use each entry and records the
date of the most recent use.

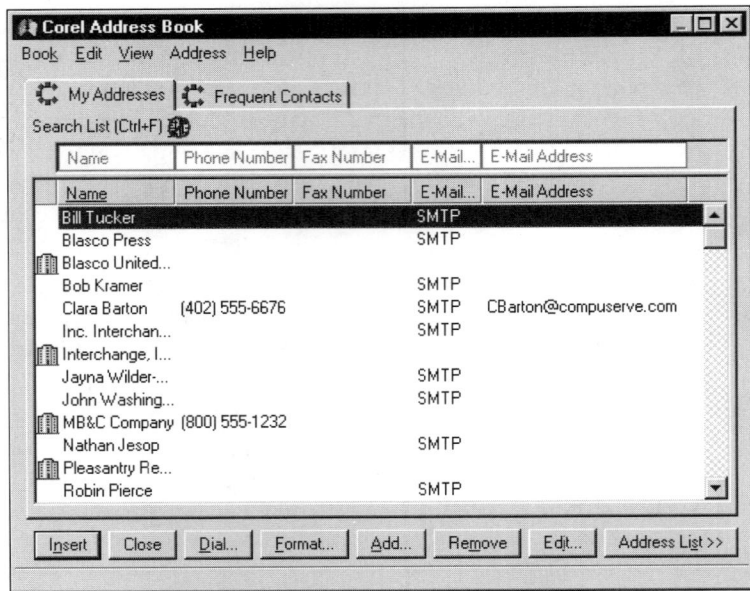

Figure 8-1.   Store contact information for clients and others in the Corel Address
Book

 *Note:*   *If you've created an Address Book in Microsoft Exchange, your Address Book may contain additional pages. When the Address Book is installed, Corel searches for any other available messaging systems and then links them to theWordPerfect 8 settings. This also means that when you add names to the Address Book through WordPerfect, these names will be available to all other applications that recognize the messaging system.*

When I insert an address from the Address Book, only the name and address appear. How do I insert the company name as well?

When you choose Insert to add an Address Book entry to your document, by default only the name and address appear. However, you can customize the format of the Address Book insertion to include other information. Here's how:

1. Choose Tools | Address Book and then select an entry that contains the type of information you want to include.

2. Choose Format.

3. Select one of the predefined formats, such as Name and Company, or choose Custom and select your own entries.

I want to import data exported from Corel Address Book 7 as an .ABX file, but not all of the fields correspond to fields in Corel Address Book 8. What should I do?

Before you begin the import process, you need to create custom fields in Corel Address Book 8 to accommodate any unmatched fields.

1. Open Corel Address Book 8 from within WordPerfect 8.

2. From the Address Book, choose Edit | Custom Fields.

3. Choose New and then type a field name that exactly matches the one in the Address Book you're importing. Then click OK.

4. Repeat step 3 for all custom fields to be added and then click OK.

5. Import the Address Book.

? The message "Invalid field name" appeared when I tried to import an Address Book data file. What's wrong?

Your fields didn't match up properly. The most probable cause is that a field in your merge data file contains too much information—for instance, the city, state, and zip code may all be entered in the same field. To fix this problem, open the merge data file in WordPerfect and look at the fields. Do one of the following:

⇨ Split up some of the fields in the data file before importing it. For example, create separate City, State, and Zip Code fields.

⇨ When mapping data fields, select Ignore Field for any field that's too large. You can then fill in the missing information by editing the entries in the Address Book.

⇨ Add one or more custom fields to your Address Book to accommodate the large field. To create a custom field, choose Edit | Custom Fields in Address Book, click New, type a name for the field, and click OK.

To import your database file into the Address Book, follow these steps:

1. Choose Tools | Address Book. Then choose Book | New.
2. Type a name for the new Address Book and then click OK.
3. Choose Book | Import.
4. Select Merge Data/Notebook File and then click Next.
5. Specify the file name and then click Next.
6. Map the data file fields to corresponding fields in the Address Book. For example, you may need to map "Company" to "Organization" and "Zip" to "Zip Code." If any field names in the two Address Books match, the fields are mapped automatically. If a field in the imported file does not have a match, "Ignore Field" is displayed. Highlight each item marked with "Ignore Field" and then select an appropriate field in the Address Book fields list.
7. Click Finish.

? How do I import Sidekick data into the Address Book?

Here are the steps for importing Sidekick data into the Address Book:

1. Save the cardfile in Sidekick in a format the Address Book can import: With the cardfile on your screen in Sidekick, choose Tools | Export Cardfile. Type a name for the file in the Source text box, using an .SDB file extension. Select the Comma Delimited (*.CSV) option from the File Types drop-down list under the Target. Specify a name for the exported cardfile in the Target text box. Choose Export.

2. Start the Address Book and choose Book | New. Then type a name for the book and click OK.

3. Choose Book | Import, select ASCII Delimited Text and then click Next.

4. Specify the Sidekick file you just saved and then click Next.

5. Continue with the expert until you are finished importing the Sidekick data.

How do I share an Address Book on a network?

You can place your Address Book data on a network, either to share it with others or for your own use. If an Address Book is to be shared with other users, Corel recommends that you make it read-only or give other users read-only rights.

To place your Address Book on a network, you need to move the Database folder. In WordPerfect 8, the database is typically located on this path: C:\Corel\Suite8\Shared\Address\Database.

Each user will then need to specify the database location from his or her own machine. You may want to teach others using the network how to specify the network Address Book location from their personal workstations. Each user should follow these steps:

1. Open the Address Book and then choose Edit | Settings.

2. Make sure the preferred profile is Corel 8 Settings and then click the Services tab. (If you change the preferred profile, you will need to exit your applications and restart the Address Book.)

3. Select Corel Address Book 8 and then click Properties.

4. Specify the location of the network Address Book and then click OK.

Note: *If you want to maintain a local Address Book in addition to the networked one, you will need to change the path each time you want to change to a different Address Book database.*

5. Close the Address Book and restart it to make the changes take effect.

Note: *Be aware that the My Addresses and Frequent Contacts books are hidden, which means that only the person who creates the data in these books will be able to see that data. Shared data will need to be added or copied to a custom book to be visible by other users.*

? We're sharing an Address Book on the network, but not all the information appears. What's wrong?

If you have full rights to a network database, you should be aware that the Microsoft driver for NetWare contains a bug that causes a disk-caching problem so that incomplete information is written to the database. If you are using the Microsoft driver for NetWare, you must disable the write-behind cache option in Windows 95. To do this, each user must click Start on the taskbar and then choose Settings | Control Panel, double-click System, click the Performance tab, choose File System, click the Troubleshooting tab, and then select Disable Write-Behind Caching for All Drives.

? I need to type the name Maria de la Peña in my Address Book. I pressed CTRL-W to insert the tilde, but nothing happened. How do I insert special characters?

The WordPerfect Address Book is a separate application and is not linked to the WordPerfect character sets, so when you press CTRL-W, nothing happens, not even if you press it a whole bunch of times, which I'm sure you did. It's kind of clunky, but here's a workaround: insert the character in a WordPerfect document and then cut and paste the character into the Address Book.

? When I try to start the Address Book, the message "Unable to Load Corel Address Book..." appears. What's wrong?

If you're starting Corel Address Book 8 from within WordPerfect 8 for Windows, this message may appear . You may have chosen not to install Microsoft Exchange or the Corel Address Book when you set up WordPerfect. You can install the Corel Address Book by performing a Custom installation.

This message also may appear because the registry contains a reference to the CD ROM drive for the CRLAB8.DLL component of the Address Book.

Warning: *To remove this reference, you must edit the registry. However, editing the registry can be tricky, and you can run into unpredictable snares along the way too numerous to write about in this book. I hate to say this, but you should call Corel technical support and have them walk you through the registry changes.*

If you think you know enough about editing the registry to try it on your own, here's what to do:

1. To open the Windows registry, click Start on the taskbar and choose Run. Then type **regedit** and click OK.

2. Back up the registry before you edit or make changes (choose Registry | Export Registry File).

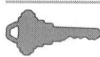

Warning: *If you're not familiar with this backup process, exit now or you may seriously mess up your system settings.*

3. Search for CRLAB8.DLL in the registry. There should be a few references to this filename. Check the paths and make sure none are pointing to the CD ROM drive or any location other than the place where WordPerfect 8 was installed.

Is there a way to print the Address Book?

Not directly, but you can do it with the help of the Address to Merge macro (adrs2mrg.wcm). This macro converts the addresses in the Address Book to a merge data file. You can then print the addresses or merge the data with a form file.

1. Choose Tools | Macro | Play.

2. Double-click adrs2mrg.wcm.

3. Specify which book (such as My Addresses or Frequent Contacts) you want to merge and then click OK.

4. To print a quick list of the names, choose Hide Codes from the Options drop-down list on the Merge bar and then choose Print from the same Options drop-down list.

Tip: *If you want more control over the format of the printed list, you can create a form file containing only the records you want to print. If you want to print the addresses without page breaks, choose Print from the Options list on the Merge bar.*

MERGES AND FORM LETTERS

? Should I use the Address Book or a merge data file to enter addresses?

Either will work. If you don't want to retype all your address information, you can use a database or the Address Book as your data source, or you can convert your address information into a merge data file. Merge data files offer more flexibility during a merge than do external data sources such as the Address Book or a database.

Follow these steps to convert Address Book data to a merge data file:

1. Choose Tools | Macro | Play.

2. Double-click adrs2mrg.wcm.

3. Specify which book (such as My Addresses or Frequent Contacts) you want to convert and then click OK.

? My Address Book doesn't contain the names of the people I want to send form letters to. How do I create a merge data file from scratch?

If you haven't typed any of your addresses yet, here's how you can use the Merge dialog box, shown in Figure 8-2, to create a merge data file:

Definitions: *A field contains a single information item for a person, such as the name, address, or phone number. A record consists of all the fields for that person.*

1. Choose Tools | Merge.

2. Choose Create Data, select New Document Window, and then click OK to create the data file in a new document window.

3. Add the names for the fields you want in your records. Break the fields into small categories, such as First Name, Last Name, and

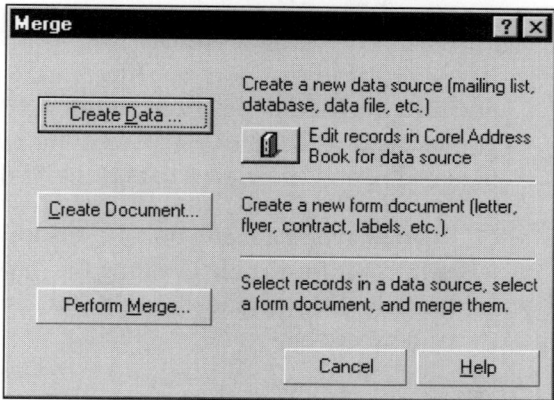

Figure 8-2.   You can use the Merge dialog box to create a merge data file

Zip Code. If you create fields that contain several categories of information, such as City, State, Zip, you may have some headaches later if you want to convert the data file or add bar codes.

4. If you want the records placed in table rows, select Format Records in a Table. Table rows make data sorting easier, but try not to tamper with the table structure, or you may mess up the merge.

5. When you've added all the names, click OK.

6. Type the specific address information in the fields you created.

7. Choose New Record for each new entry and then choose Close. Click Yes to save the changes.

Tip: *You can add or edit the field names in the data file at any time. Open the data file, choose Quick Entry on the Merge bar, and select Field Names.*

When I press ENTER in the Quick Data Entry dialog box, the insertion point moves to the next field. How do I create a two-line address in a data file?

In the Quick Data Entry dialog box, pressing ENTER takes you to the next field. However, you can press CTRL-ENTER at the end of a line to start a new line in the same field. Although it looks like the first line disappears, it's still there, as you can see if you click the Up button next to the field text box.

? How do I convert a written letter into a form file?

If you've already written the letter, you're only a few steps away from having a form letter, shown in Figure 8-3. You need to tell WordPerfect you're creating a form file, replace some specific information with field codes, and associate a data file with the letter. Here's how:

1. If you haven't already done so, create the data file containing the address information. Creating the data file first lets you associate the data file with the form file and insert field names more easily and precisely.

2. Open the letter.

3. Choose Tools | Merge and then choose Create Document (choose Form in WordPerfect 7).

4. Select Use File in Active Window and then click OK.

5. Specify the data file name, Address Book, or ODBC data source and then click OK.

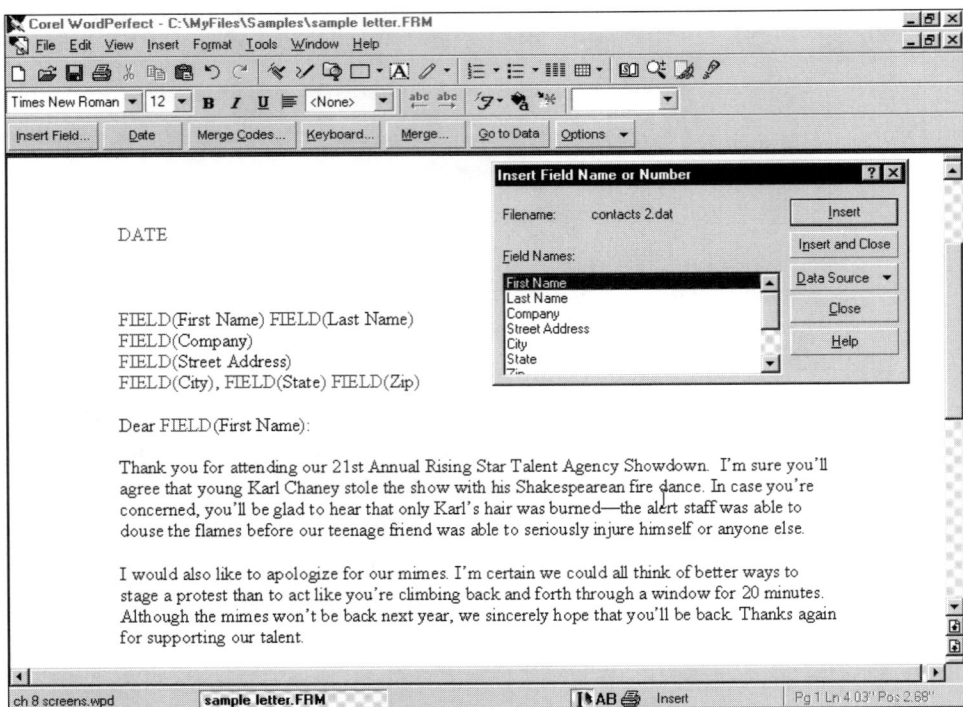

Figure 8-3.   You can easily convert a letter to a form file

6. Click Insert Field on the Merge bar and then delete the name and address and replace them with field codes. You can place more than one field on a line—for example, FIELD(First Name) FIELD(Last Name). Remember to enter the proper punctuation and spacing between fields.

Warning: Delete the text first and then insert the field codes to replace it. If you select the text to be replaced and then insert the field name, the text itself will appear as the field name instead of being replaced by the correct field name—for example, FIELD(84604) may appear instead of FIELD(Zip).

Tip: If you need to edit the letter after you insert the merge codes, you can hide the merge codes to make editing easier. On the Merge bar, choose Options | Display as Markers. You can also choose Options | Hide Codes, but you'll be more likely to delete a code.

I associated a data file with a form file, and now I want to use a different data file. How do I unassociate a data file from a form file?

After you associate a data file with a form file, you're not stuck with that data file forever. You can switch to a different data file, or you can even select no association.

1. With the form file open, choose Tools | Merge | Perform Merge.

2. In the text box next to the Data Source button, specify the data file you want to use, or click the Data Source button and choose None.

Warning: If you change to a different data file, your field names may not match up properly in your form file. You may need to open the form file and reinsert the field names. To do this, click Insert Field on the Merge bar, select Data File from the Data Source drop-down list, and specify the new data file.

When I try to merge my files, the message "Field names don't match" appears. What's wrong?

Several things could have gone wrong. After you added the field names to the form file, you may have made changes to the field names in either the data file or form file, or you may have associated a different data file with different field names. Open the data file and form file and check the field names.

If you make changes to both the data file and form file, remember to save the modified files before you merge. Unless you specify otherwise, WordPerfect uses the files on the disk, not the files on the screen, in the merge. After you save the changes, make sure the field names are consistent and then try the merge operation again.

? Some of my fields contain the wrong information. How can I search the merge data file to make sure records have the right field information?

If you used the Quick Data Entry dialog box to insert records in your data file, it's unlikely that the data file contains errors, unless you typed the wrong text in the wrong field—for example, if you typed **CA** in the Zip Code field. If you created the data file manually, in WordPerfect 5.1, for instance, or if you added columns to your data table or ENDFIELD codes to your merge file without using Quick Data Entry, many more types of errors are possible. You may have missing fields, fields without an ENDFIELD code, and fields containing the wrong data.

Here's how you can use the Quick Data Entry dialog box to make sure your records are okay:

1. Open the data file.

2. Check the FIELDNAMES record at the top of the document to make sure all the fields are properly separated by semicolons. If you added ENDFIELD codes to your records, make sure the corresponding field name is included in the FIELDNAMES record.

3. Make sure your ENDFIELD and ENDRECORD commands appear in a different color. A common mistake is to insert an ENDFIELD or ENDRECORD code simply by typing these names in all capital letters. When you manually insert fields or records, you must click the End Field or End Record buttons on the Merge bar so that an actual merge code is inserted.

4. Choose Quick Entry on the Merge bar and then click Next to scroll through the records. Scan each record to make sure it contains the right information in the right fields.

? **I used a table to create my data file, and I can't get my merge to work. What can I do?**

Open the data file and make sure there aren't any codes between the Open Style and Table Definition codes. Choose View | Reveal Codes and then cut and paste any formatting codes into the Current Document Style (choose File | Document | Current Document Style).

? **When I use one of my data files, the merge is really slow, and sometimes my system locks up when I try to select records for the merge. What's wrong?**

If your merge is slow, you may have formatting codes at the top of your document. For example, your document may contain paper size, page centering, margin, and alignment that must be placed at the beginning of each letter in your merge. To speed up the merge, cut and paste these codes into the Current Document Style (choose File | Document | Current Document Style).

If the merge is still significantly slow, your data file may be corrupt. Try turning off Undo/Redo History, which can cause problems in merge data files. To do this, choose Edit | Undo/Redo History, choose Options, deselect Save Undo/Redo Items with Document, and then click OK. Save the data file and then try the merge again.

If that doesn't fix the problem, you may be able to salvage a corrupt data file by saving it in the ASCII (DOS) Delimited Text format and then importing the file back into WordPerfect. Here's how:

1. Save the file by choosing File | Save As, selecting ASCII (DOS) Delimited Text from the File Type drop-down list, and choosing Save. Then close the file.

2. Import the file by choosing Insert | Spreadsheet/Database | Import. From the Import As drop-down list, select Merge Data File. Select the file and then click OK.

3. Add the field names again by choosing Merge Codes on the Merge bar, double-clicking FIELDNAMES in the Merge Codes list box, and then adding the field names.

4. Do any clean up work for records that may not have converted properly. Save the data file and then try the merge again.

? **When I put the page numbering code at the beginning of my form file, all of my merged letters are numbered consecutively, as if they are a single document. How do I make each merge letter start with page 1?**

When you merge a multiple-page letter, the page numbers don't automatically start over with each new record. For example, if you're merging a three-page letter, the first page of the second merged letter will be numbered as page four. Besides inserting the page numbering code, you need to set the page number value to 1. Here's how:

1. Open the form file and then place the insertion point at the beginning of the document.

2. Choose Format | Page | Numbering.

3. Choose Set Value, type **1**, and click OK.

4. Save the form file and then run the merge again.

? **How can I remove page breaks during a merge?**

In most cases, such as when you create form letters, you want each record to be divided by a page break. However, if you are merging a list of names into a document performing a similar task, you may not want the page breaks between records. Here's how to remove the page breaks between records:

1. Choose Tools | Merge and then choose Perform Merge.

2. Choose Options.

3. Deselect Separate Each Merged Document with a Page Break and then click OK.

4. Choose Merge to merge the documents.

Tip: *If you don't separate each document with a page break, a page break may fall at an awkward place in some of your merged items (for example, in the middle of a label). If you don't want this to happen, select the fields in your form file before you merge and choose Format | Keep Lines Together. Under Block Protect, select the items you don't want split and then click OK.*

 **Sometimes I want to send mail to only one person, or to only a small group of people, in my data file. How do I select records from my data file?**

Before you merge documents, you can mark the records you want to include in the merge, as shown in Figure 8-4.

1. Choose Tools | Merge | Perform Merge.

2. Make sure the correct data source is displayed and then choose Select Records.

3. Select the Mark Records option.

4. Select the records you want to merge and then click OK.

Tip: *If you want to specify a range of records to merge, choose Tools | Merge | Perform Merge | Select Records and then select Record Number Range and specify the range. Records are numbered sequentially in the data file from beginning to end.*

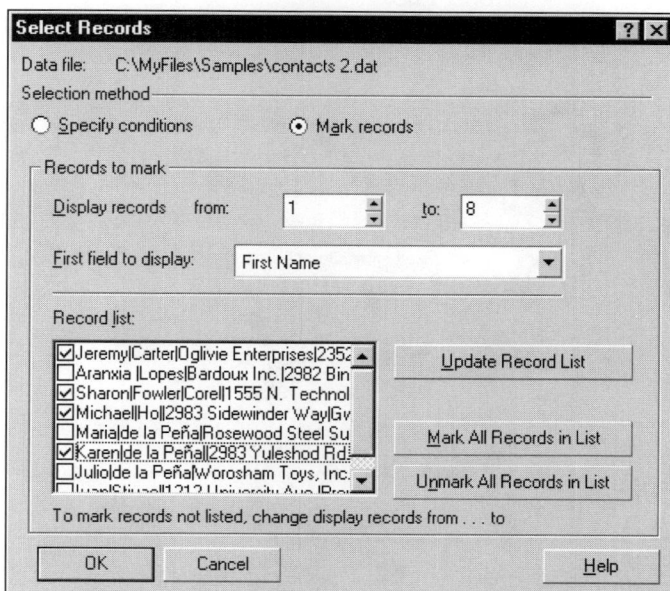

Figure 8-4.   You can select the records you want to merge

I have a list of addresses in a data file, but I want to send letters only to people named Arroyo living in California. Is there a way to extract only records that meet certain criteria?

Sometimes you may want to include only people who meet certain conditions in a merge operation. For example, you may want to send letters only to people who live in California, or only to people whose last name is Arroyo, or only to people named Arroyo who are also living in California. Instead of editing your data file to include only the records you want, you can specify the conditions of your merge so that only the records that meet the criteria will be included, as shown in Figure 8-5. Here's how:

1. Choose Tools | Merge | Perform Merge.

2. Make sure the correct data source is displayed and then choose Select Records.

3. From the first Field drop-down list, select the field (such as **Last Name**) you want to use in your condition.

4. Below the field, type the condition (such as **Arroyo**) in the Cond 1 box.

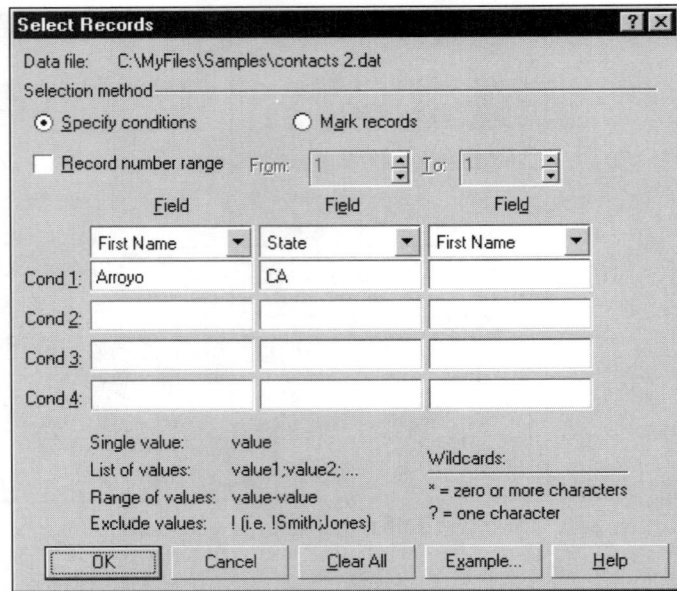

Figure 8-5.   You can specify conditions to merge only certain records

5. Use the same procedure to set any other conditions you want to use. You can specify additional fields within Cond 1 to create an AND condition (such as people whose last name is Arroyo AND who live in California). You can also specify additional conditions to create an OR condition (such as people whose last name is Arroyo OR Washington).

 **Warning:**   *The text you insert must be an exact match of the data in your field. For example, if you type* **California** *but your data file uses state abbreviations such as CA, you won't extract the California records.*

 Tip: *WordPerfect Help provides excellent examples showing how to use wildcards and other characters to define your search criteria. Choose Example in the Select Records dialog box to learn more about how to specify merge conditions.*

 **Tip:**   *When selecting merge records by zip code, if zip codes are included with other information such as the city and state, use the * wildcard, as in *92408*, so that any text before or after the zip code will match your criterion.*

When I merge files using the Address Book as the data source, the company records are also inserted. How can I exclude these records from the merge?

If you have used the Address Book to keep track of names and addresses, there is no reason to create a separate data file containing the same names and addresses. Instead, you can use the Address Book as the data source when you merge. However, the entire Address Book is seldom a candidate for a merge. In most cases, you'll want to select the Address Book records you want to use. Here's how:

1. Choose Tools | Merge | Perform Merge.

2. Specify the form document you want to use.

3. From the Data Source drop-down list, select Address Book.

4. Choose Select Records, click each record you want to include in the Merge, and select Select Address. You can select records from any page in the Address Book.

5. Click OK and then choose Merge.

❓ I tried to perform a merge, but the output file was blank. What went wrong?

Make sure the correct form and data sources are specified. Also check any search criteria to make sure you haven't specified conditions that can't be met. In the Perform Merge dialog box, select Select Records and then click Clear All to remove all criteria. If you're merging using the Address Book and used search criteria for a previous search, exit and restart WordPerfect so that the previous search is cleared from memory.

❓ I need to merge ASCII delimited files from other programs with a WordPerfect form file, but I often just get a blank document. What's wrong?

The data files you merge must be saved as ASCII (DOS) Delimited Text files. Here are some other things to check:

⇨ Make sure the fields have field numbers instead of names. ASCII delimited text doesn't support field names.

⇨ Open the data file to verify the delimiters that separate the fields.

⇨ Use the same delimiters for each data file. Typically, quotation marks separate fields and commas separate records. You can specify the delimiter by choosing Tools | Settings and double-clicking Convert (by choosing Edit | Preferences and double-clicking Convert in WordPerfect 7).

Tip: *If you want to add records to the ASCII file, you may want to open the ASCII file as a merge data file so that it's easier to work with. Choose File | Open, double-click the ASCII file, and then select ASCII (DOS) Delimited Text from the File Type drop-down list. In the Import Data dialog box, select Merge Data File from the Import As pop-up list. Check the fields and records; some ENDRECORD, ENDFIELD, and page break codes may not have converted properly.*

? **I am unable to specify an ODBC database as a data source for my merge operations. What's the problem?**

When you attempt to associate a merge form file with an ODBC-compliant database, you may not be able to find the database when you select the Associate an ODBC Data Source option and click the Select ODBC Data Source button. If the ODBC database option does not appear when you choose Select ODBC Data Source, the database is most likely not properly registered with the ODBC applet under the Control Panel. Once the database is properly registered there, it should appear in the list and become accessible to merge operations. For additional information on how to ensure that an ODBC database is properly set up, refer to your ODBC database software documentation.

ADVANCED MERGE OPERATIONS

? **How do I pause a merge to allow keyboard input for unique information not available in the data file?**

You can use the Keyboard ([*prompt*]) command, which is also useful for creating forms and other jobs that you may not think of as merge projects because the form file is not merged with the data file. You can use this command to create fill-in-the-blank forms that pause at each blank and prompt you for the required information. The [*prompt*] parameter reminds you what to type at the location of the pause.

For example, you may want to send a form letter that grabs address information from a data file, but then also add individualized text telling each person when you are scheduled to meet with him or her. Instead of adding a new field to the records in the data file (which is also a viable option), you can add the following line to your form letter:

```
You are scheduled to meet with us on KEYBOARD(Type
the date and time:).
```

Here's how to insert a keyboard prompt in a form file:

1. Place the insertion point where you want the prompt to appear and then click Keyboard on the Merge bar.

2. Type the prompt text you want to use and then click OK.

3. When you merge, you'll be prompted to type the text for each record in your document. After you type the text, choose Continue on the Keyboard bar.

? **I created a memo that uses the Merge feature to prompt for information. However, I use some of the variable information (such as the recipient's name) in more than one place. Can I set up my form file so I just enter this variable information once and have it applied throughout my memo?**

You can use the GETSTRING command to capture keyboard input and display the result in different areas, as shown in Figure 8-6. Here's how to insert the GETSTRING command:

1. In the form file, place the insertion point where you want to insert the variable name.

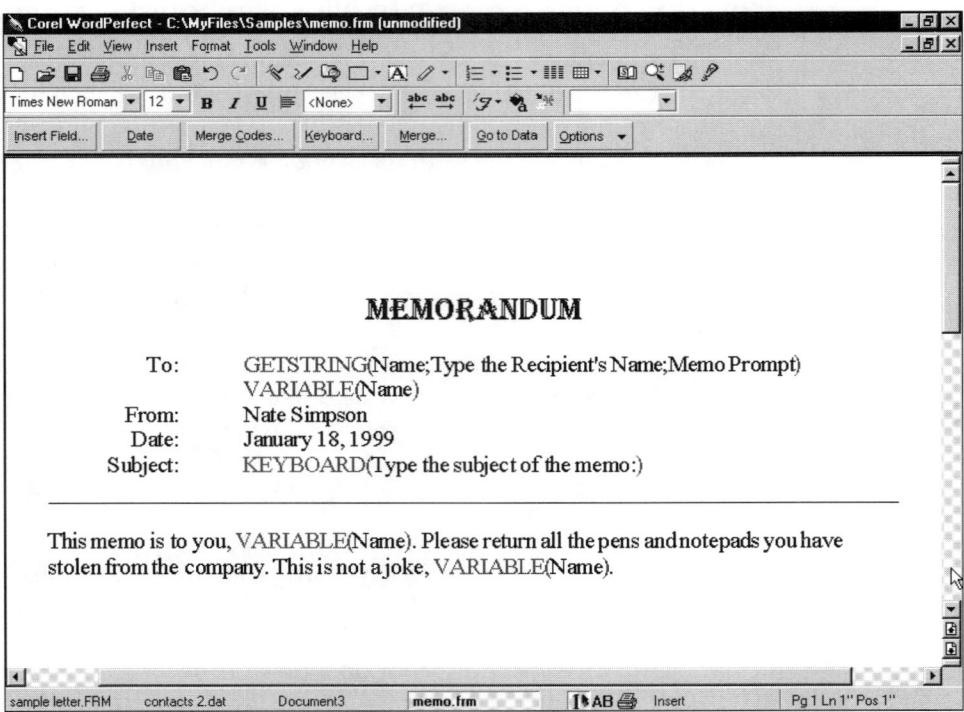

Figure 8-6.   The GETSTRING command captures keyboard input

2. Choose Merge Codes and then double-click the GETSTRING command.

3. Type the name of the variable (such as **First Name**), the prompt you want displayed (such as **Type your first name**), and the title that will appear in the title bar of the message box (such as **Prompt**). Then click OK.

4. Place the insertion point where you want the variable to appear and then double-click VARIABLE in the Insert Merge Codes dialog box.

5. Type the name of the variable and then choose Insert.

6. Repeat steps 4 and 5 at each location where you want the variable information to appear. When you are done, click Close.

How can I create a table that expands automatically as information is inserted during a merge?

First create the table and insert the merge fields into each cell. Insert the REPEATROW command in the far-right cell of the table, as shown below. Do not press ENTER in the last row before you insert this command, or you may end up with a blank line in every row.

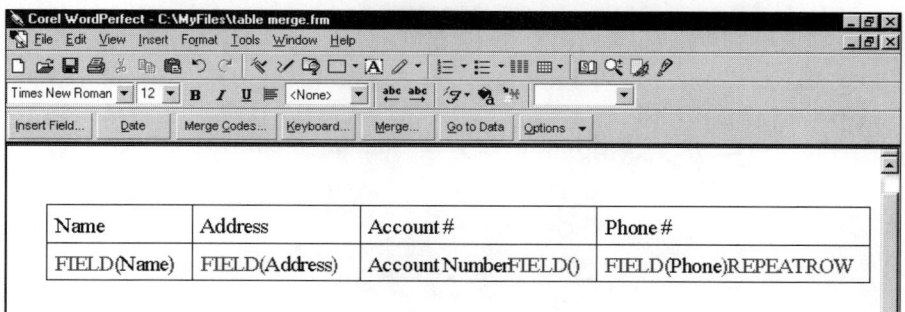

I have a checklist in a form file, and I want a checked box to appear next to the items in the checklist only if the data file field is "YES." How do I set up a conditional merge?

You can use the IF command to specify whether or not a checked box appears. Suppose you want to end up with a checklist like this:

Dear Ms. Simpson:

Our records indicate that you have the following:

☒   Computer
☐   Printer
☐   Modem
☒   Scanner

You would set up your form file like this:

Dear FIELD(Greeting) FIELD(First Name) :

Our records indicate that you have the following:

IF(TOUPPER(FIELD(Computer))=YES)☒ELSE ☐ENDIF   Computer
IF(TOUPPER(FIELD(Printer))=YES)☒ELSE ☐ENDIF   Printer
IF(TOUPPER(FIELD(Modem))=YES)☒ELSE ☐ENDIF   Modem
IF(TOUPPER(FIELD(Scanner))=YES)☒ELSE ☐ENDIF   Scanner

The first IF statement essentially says, "If the Computer field in the data file is YES, insert a checked box. Otherwise, insert a blank box." The TOUPPER command tells the statement to recognize both "yes" and "Yes" as "YES," to avoid problems in case you used different capitalization styles in your merge data file.

Here's how you would insert these conditional statements:

1. Make sure your data file includes the necessary fields.

2. In the form file, place the insertion point where you want to insert the merge code.

3. Choose Merge Codes on the Merge bar, double-click IF(expr), and click OK.

4. In the Insert Merge Codes dialog box, double-click TOUPPER(expr) and then click OK.

5. Choose Insert Field on the Merge bar, insert the field, and close the dialog box.

6. Type the rest of the expression, as shown in the preceding example. Use the Insert Merge Codes dialog box to add the ELSE and ENDIF statements.

Tip: To insert the marked check box, press CTRL-W, type **5,25**, and choose Insert and Close. To insert the blank check box, press CTRL-W, type **5,24**, and choose Insert and Close.

In my business, I regularly send invoices to the same people, but for different amounts. The form file contains a table that totals the itemized amounts at the bottom of the last column. Why can't I get the amounts in each merged invoice to total correctly?

To calculate tables during a merge, you need to use the Automatic Calculation feature. With this feature turned on, WordPerfect automatically recalculates a table whenever the amounts change, including whenever amounts are inserted during a merge. Here's how you can fix your problem:

1. Open the merge form file that contains the table.

2. Make sure you've inserted the Sum command in the cell where you want the total to appear. If you haven't, place the insertion point in that cell, right-click, and choose Formula Toolbar. Click the Edit Formula text box and type **SUM ( )**. Place the insertion point between the two parentheses and then use your mouse to select the cells that you want to add. WordPerfect automatically inserts the cell addresses, such as F1:F5. Then click the check mark to insert the formula in the cell.

3. To turn on Automatic Calculation, choose Table | Calculate. In the Automatic Calculation box, select the Calculate Tables in Document radio button. Note that this is different from choosing the Calc Document button. Then click OK.

Note: You need to select the Automatic Calculation option only once; it remains in effect for all future documents until you turn it off. However, it may slow down your work in tables.

? How can I learn more about merge programming commands?

The Corel WordPerfect 8 CD includes an entire book on merge programming commands. Here's how you can take advantage of this information:

1. Make sure the Corel WordPerfect Suite 8 CD is in the CD-ROM drive.

2. If the Corel WordPerfect Suite screen appears, click Reference Center. You can also click the Start button on the taskbar and then choose Corel WordPerfect Suite 8 | Setup & Notes | Reference Center.

3. Click Merge Programming Commands.

4. Click Contents and then click the programming command you want to know more about.

? How do I chain a second data file so I don't have to run a merge operation twice?

Chaining data files is especially useful if you have split up your data files—but you must make sure that all of your merge data files use the same field names as in the form file.

Assume that your second data file is named Address2.dat. To chain this file to your first file, you would use the Insert Merge Codes dialog box to add the following line to the top of the first data file, after the field names and before the first record:

```
PROCESSON CHAINDATA(address2.dat) PROCESSOFF
```

Figure 8-7 shows where this line should appear.

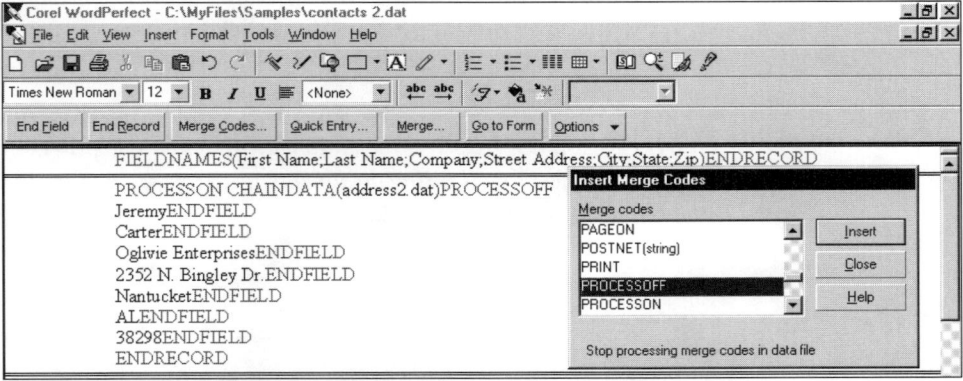

Figure 8-7.   You can insert a merge command to chain data files

? **Why can't I use the City, State, Zip field from my merge data file as a bar code in a form file?**

You can merge zip codes from a data file into a form file, but the zip code must be in its own field. You'll need to create a separate field just for the zip code. After you do so, here's how you can merge a zip code as a bar code:

1. In the form file, place the insertion point where you want the bar code to appear.

2. Select Merge Codes on the Merge bar and then double-click POSTNET(string).

3. Close the Insert Merge Codes dialog box.

4. With the insertion point between the parentheses following the POSTNET merge code, choose Insert Field on the Merge bar. Then select the zip code field from the data file and choose Insert and Close.

5. Save the form file and then merge the data and form file.

? **I want a macro to run at a certain place in the document to insert information, but the CHAINMACRO command plays the macro at the end of the merge. What's wrong?**

You can play a macro during a merge using either the NESTMACRO or CHAINMACRO command. Use the NESTMACRO command to play the macro at a certain point in your form file. Use the CHAINMACRO command to play the macro when the merge has ended.

To play a macro at a certain point in your merge, follow these steps:

1. In the form file, place the insertion point where you want to insert the command.

2. Choose Merge Codes on the Merge bar and then double-click NESTMACRO.

3. Type the name of the macro and then click OK.

Note: *You can also play a macro when the merge pauses for input due to a Keyboard command. Just play the macro as you normally would.*

LABELS

? I have all my addresses in a data file. Do I have to retype all my addresses in the labels document?

No. You can use the Merge feature to merge your addresses into the labels document. All you have to do is create a form file that contains the label definition, insert the fields in the first label as shown in Figure 8-8, and you're ready to merge. Here are the steps:

1. Choose Tools | Merge | Create Document.

2. Specify the name of the data file and then click OK.

3. Choose Format | Labels, specify the type of label you're using, and click Select.

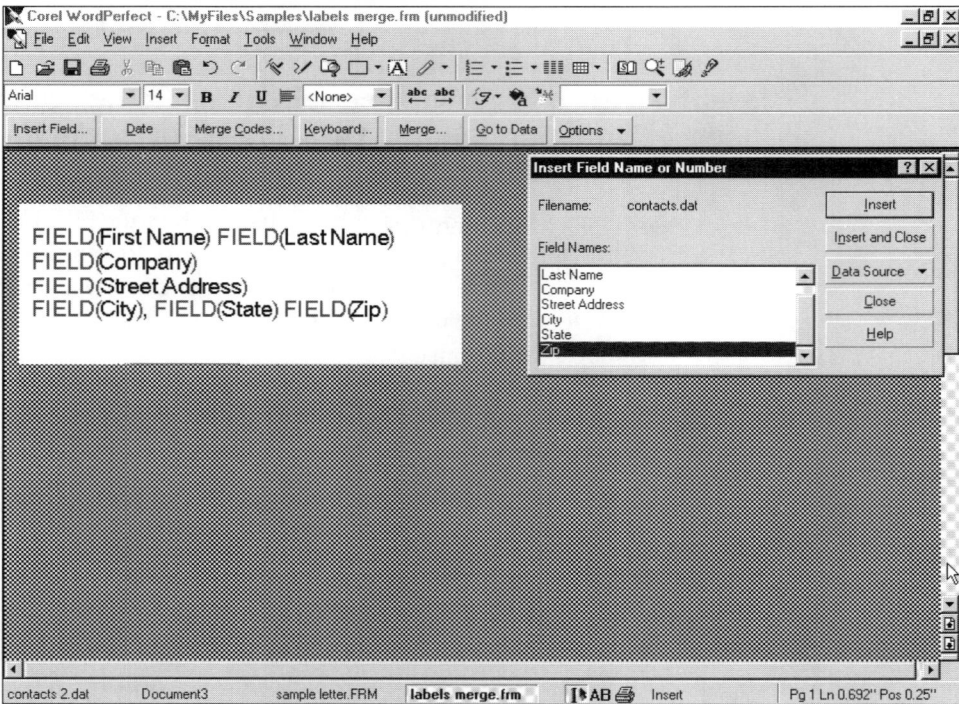

Figure 8-8.   You can use Merge to create labels

Tip: *Almost all of the label definitions are for the Avery brand. If you don't use Avery labels, scroll through the definitions until you find the definition that most closely matches your labels. Most generic brands are directly compatible with their Avery counterparts.*

4. If you want to center the labels, choose Format | Page | Center, select Current and Subsequent Pages, and click OK.

5. Choose Insert Field on the Merge bar and then insert the fields in the first label as shown in Figure 8-8. Close the dialog box when you're done.

6. Choose Merge on the Merge bar. Then choose Merge to create a set of labels based on your merge data file.

? My addresses are in the Address Book. Do I need to convert the addresses to a merge data file before inserting them in labels?

When creating labels for mass mailings using WordPerfect, you don't need to set up a merge file—or even insert any field codes—to print addresses. You can simply select your label paper size, open the Address Book, and select the addresses for which you want to print labels. Here are the steps:

1. In a blank document window, choose Format | Labels.

2. Select or create a label page size and then choose Select.

3. Choose Tools | Address Book.

4. Hold down CTRL and click the addresses for which you want to create labels. Then choose Insert.

Tip: *If you want to insert address information other than what is inserted, choose Tools | Address Book | Format and then select a different address or create a custom address with the information you need.*

Tips on Using Labels

Here are some tips to consider when working with labels:

⇨ When working with labels, leave plenty of room in the margins. Laser printers have unprintable regions ranging from 0.2 to 0.5 inches. If you don't leave enough space, part of the label text may be cut off. Choose Format | Page | Center to center the text on the labels. If necessary, you can also increase the margins.

⇨ Remember that each label is a page. Press ALT-PAGE DOWN and ALT-PAGE UP to move from label to label. You can also use the Go To command (Edit | Go To) to jump to a specific label.

⇨ When typing label information manually, press CTRL-ENTER to start each new label. If you press ENTER several times to move to the next label, you may have problems later if you try to select records, sort, and use other options.

⇨ Before you print your actual labels, print the label information on an ordinary sheet of paper and make sure everything works okay. For more information on printing labels, see "Tips on Using Special Paper Sizes" in Chapter 6.

? The labels I just bought at the office supply store aren't listed in the Labels dialog box. Can I create my own label definition?

Yes. However, before you do, make sure you're looking at the right list of label definitions. In the Labels dialog box, choose Laser or Tractor-Fed, depending on which type of printer you have, or choose both if you want to see every definition. If you still can't find the label definition, follow these steps:

1. Choose Format | Labels.

2. Select the label definition that most closely resembles the one you need to create and then choose Create.

3. Type a name for the label definition and then specify the label information such as the number of labels per page, label size, and spacing between labels. Then click OK.

4. Test print the labels on a blank sheet of paper to make sure you created the correct definition. Edit the definition as necessary.

? Why doesn't the text print on the edge of some labels?

The most likely problem is the label definition. If your printer has a wide unprintable zone, some label definitions—especially those in which labels extend to the edge of the sheet—may not print correctly. If text gets cut off in one column or row of the label sheet, you need to adjust the label definition to account for the printer's unprintable zone. Another possibility is that you inserted the label sheet in the manual feed slot too far away from the edge. Another possibility is the your printer may shift text slightly left or right.

Here's how to adjust the label definition:

1. Choose Format | Labels.

2. Select the label definition you're using and then choose Edit.

3. If your printer is shifting the label text, try changing the Top Edge or Left Edge measurement under Top Left Label.

4. Make your label size narrower by adjusting the Width measurement under Label Size. To shift the labels toward the center, increase the Left Edge measurement.

5. When you're done editing the definition, click OK. Make sure your label text still fits in each label (you may need to use a smaller font) and then try printing again.

? I use the same style of Avery labels almost every time, but I'm tired of scrolling to find its definition. How can I move the definition to the top of the Labels list?

Rename the label definition with a space or an underscore at the beginning of the label. Here's how:

1. Choose Format | Labels.

2. Select the definition you frequently use and then choose Edit.

3. Place the insertion point at the beginning of the Label Description text box, press the spacebar, and then click OK.

 **I want to create a sheet of labels with my return address on it. How can I do this without copying and pasting?**

WordPerfect provides a slick and quick way to print multiple copies of the same label to create return address labels. Follow these steps:

1. Open a blank document and choose Format | Labels.

2. Select the label definition you want to use and choose Select.

3. Type the text (such as your return address) for the label.

4. Choose Tools | Merge | Perform Merge.

5. Choose Options. Then type a value in the Number of Copies for Each Record text box and click OK.

6. Choose Merge.

 ***Note:*** *The number of copies you specify remains in effect until you exit WordPerfect. If you want to perform other merges before exiting, first choose Tools | Merge | Perform Merge | Reset.*

 **I want to print just certain labels. How can I avoid leaving blank labels on several sheets of paper?**

If you use the Print dialog box to print multiple selected labels, many blank labels will be left on the label sheets, which is a waste of good labels. One clumsy way to avoid this is to copy and paste the labels you want to print at the top of the document so that all the labels you want to print appear in consecutive order. However, if you have used a merge data file to merge labels, a better way to avoid blank labels is to select records during the merge.

 ***Note:*** *To select records, you must make sure your labels are divided by a page break. If you merged labels, this won't be a problem. However, if you typed your labels manually and pressed* ENTER *a bunch of times to move to the next label, this process won't work. You need to press* CTRL-ENTER *between labels instead.*

Here's how you can select records for your labels:

1. Choose Tools | Merge | Perform Merge.

2. Make sure the correct data source is displayed and then choose Select Records.

3. Select the Mark Records option.

4. Select the records you want to merge and then click OK.

 Records in my data file are mixed case (Jane Doe). When creating address labels, is there a quick way to capitalize everything?

You can use the TOUPPER merge code to change the text in the field to uppercase. Here's how:

1. Open the form file.

2. Select the entire field that you want in all capital letters.

Note: If a line contains more than one field, you can select all the fields on the line. However, you cannot select fields on more than one line at a time.

3. Choose Merge Codes and then double-click TOUPPER.

4. Repeat this procedure for each separate line in your merge address.

Can I insert a graphic in all my 1" x 4" labels (Avery 8161) so that I don't have to cut and paste?

Yes. One method is to insert the graphic in the merge form file before you merge. However, if you choose this method, make sure you use the Image on Disk option so the size of the merged file isn't too large. After you insert and size the graphic in the form file, right-click the graphic and choose Content. Select Image on Disk from the Content Type drop-down list and then click OK. If necessary, type a name for the image and choose Save.

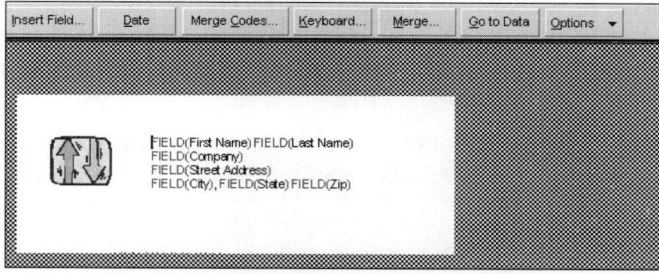

If you typed your labels manually, you can try creating a watermark at the beginning of the label file and then increase the brightness. Here's how:

1. Move the insertion point to the top of the label document and then choose Insert | Watermark | Create.

2. Insert the image in the watermark window and then size and move it as you like.

3. Right-click the image and choose Image Tools. Select a darker image from the Brightness pop-up list. Then close the Image Tools palette.

4. Click outside the image. Then click the Close folder to exit the Watermark editing window.

Note: The watermark appears behind any text. If you placed the image on the left side of your labels, you can increase the left margin and make any other adjustments, such as reducing the font size, to make the label text fit on the label.

During a merge, only one label prints per page or only one record appears. What am I doing wrong?

This used to be a common problem in WordPerfect 6.1. Any margin change in the data file or form file caused one page to print per label. If this happens in WordPerfect 8, there must be a conflict with other codes. Try this:

➪ Open the data file, turn on Reveal Codes, and delete any formatting codes that may be causing problems.

➪ Open the labels form file. Besides the normal formatting codes such as Center Page, only two codes should appear on a single label: the paper size and the merge field codes. All margin codes should be part of the label definition.

➪ Make sure all merge field names in the form file match those in the data file.

➪ Remove any ENDFIELD and ENDRECORD codes that may have been placed inadvertently in the form file.

➪ In the Perform Merge dialog box, choose Reset to clear memory before choosing Merge.

 **Note:**   *If your printer still prints only one label per page, your registry may include incorrect settings. You may want to uninstall WordPerfect, use a program such as Microsoft RegClean 4.1 to clean the registry, and then reinstall WordPerfect.*

ENVELOPES

? When merging envelopes, I selected a bar code option, but none of the bar codes appeared. How do I create envelopes with bar codes during a form letter merge?

When creating form letters, you can use the Envelopes feature to generate envelopes at the end of your merge document. You add the fields for the mailing address and bar code in the Envelope dialog box, as shown in Figure 8-9.

Here's how to create envelopes for your form letters:

1. Open the form file and then choose Tools | Merge | Perform Merge.

2. Choose Envelopes.

3. If you don't have preprinted envelopes, type your name and address in the From text box.

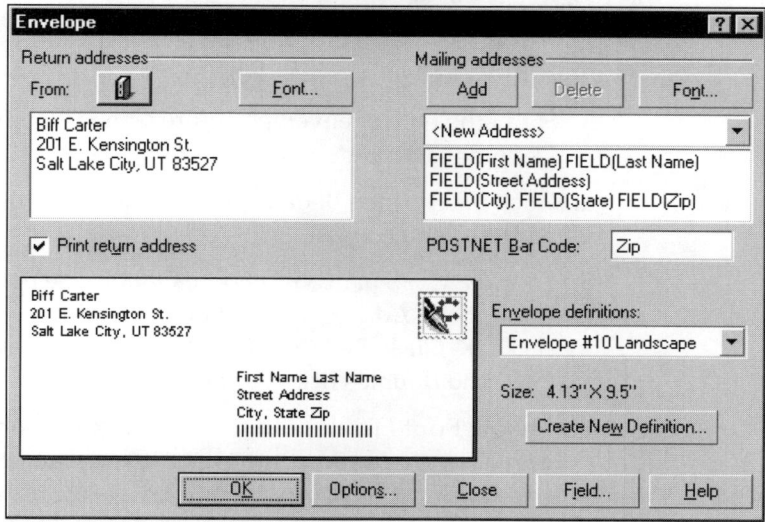

Figure 8-9.   Use the Envelope dialog box to specify the merge fields for envelopes

4. Select the type of envelope you're using from the Envelope Definitions drop-down list.

5. Click the Mailing Addresses text box and then click Field. Insert the fields in the text box as shown in Figure 8-9.

6. To add a U.S. Postal Service (USPS) bar code, choose Options. Select either Position Bar Code above Address or Position Bar Code below Address. Then click OK. Click the POSTNET Bar Code text box, choose Field, and double-click your zip code field.

 *Note:*   *To insert a bar code, the zip code must be in its own field.*

7. Click OK. Then choose Merge.

The form letters are placed at the top of your merge document, and the envelopes are placed at the end of your merge document. For information on printing envelopes, see "Using Different Paper Sizes" in Chapter 6.

All my addresses are stored in the Address Book. How do I create an envelope using the Address Book?

You can extract a record from the Address Book to create an envelope. Here's how:

1. In a blank document window, choose Format | Envelope.

2. If you don't have preprinted envelopes, type your name and address in the From text box.

3. Select the type of envelope you're using from the Envelope Definitions drop-down list.

4. Click the Address Book icon next to the To option. Then select the address and click OK.

5. To add a USPS bar code, choose Options. Select either Position Bar Code above Address or Position Bar Code below Address. Then click OK. Click the POSTNET Bar Code text box and then choose Field and double-click your zip code field.

6. Choose Print Envelope to send the envelope job straight to your printer, or choose Append to Doc if you want to insert the envelope in your merge document.

❓ The post office requests that envelopes be addressed in all capital letters with no punctuation. Is there a quick way to format envelopes this way?

The Envelope dialog box does not provide a quick way to convert from lowercase to uppercase letters. However, you can use Small Caps, which also meets the post office requirements. Display the address in the Mailing Addresses text box, place the insertion point at the beginning of the address, and then choose Font. Select Small Caps and click OK. Although no change appears in the Envelope dialog box, the address will print in small capital letters on the envelope. If necessary, make the same change for the return address. You'll have to remove the punctuation manually.

❓ The Envelope feature grabbed the wrong address in the letter I'm sending. How do I make it grab the right address?

If your letter is open when you choose Format | Envelope, WordPerfect will grab the mailing address and insert it in the Envelope dialog box for you. However, if the letter contains more than one address, WordPerfect may grab the wrong one. If this happens, close the Envelope dialog box and then select the mailing address before you choose Format | Envelope. Selecting the address beforehand ensures that the right address is selected.

❓ The envelope addresses printed in the wrong direction. What's wrong?

If the address prints in the wrong direction on your envelope, the envelope definition is not set up correctly. On most laser printers and many inkjet printers, the short edge of the envelope feeds into the printer first, and the font needs to rotate for the address to print in the correct orientation. In most cases, you'll need to specify Short Edge for the Paper Feed option and Rotated for the Font Orientation option. Here's how you can change the envelope definition:

1. Choose File | Page Setup.

2. Select the envelope definition you are using and then choose Edit.

3. If envelopes feed into your printer with the short edge first, select Short Edge for the Paper Feed option and Rotated for the Font

Orientation option. If envelopes feed into your printer with the long edge first, select Long Edge and Normal for these options.

When I print an envelope, part of my return address is cut off. How can I prevent this?

Here's how to shift the return address farther away from the edge of the envelope:

1. Choose Format | Envelope | Options.

2. Under Return Address Position, increase the Horizontal and/or Vertical measurements. Then click OK.

I want to add a graphic to my envelopes, but I don't see any options in the Envelope dialog box. How do I add a graphic to an envelope?

You can't insert a graphic in the Envelope dialog box. Instead of printing the envelope directly from the dialog box, choose Append to Doc. Once the envelope is inserted in your document, you can edit the text, add graphics, and insert other formatting. Just be careful not to position the addresses too close to the edge of the page or they may not print correctly.

Tip: *Append to Doc also enables you to print more than one copy of the same envelope. After you insert the envelope in your document, choose File | Print and then specify the number of copies you want.*

Answer Topics!

Graphics, Shapes, and Drawings @ a Glance

⇨ WordPerfect 8 has a new feature called the Scrapbook, which stores a collection of images on your hard drive and on a CD. You can drag these images into your WordPerfect documents, Quattro Pro spreadsheets, or Presentations slide shows. This chapter helps you make the most of this new clipart feature.

⇨ After you've inserted an image, text box, equation, or anything else in a graphics box, you can size, position, and add borders to the box, and you can use the tools on the Image Tools palette to crop or rotate the image or change the image's colors. If you have questions about these procedures, this chapter offers answers.

⇨ When you're creating reports, manuals, and other documents, you can use captions to number your images sequentially (Figure 1, Figure 2, and so on). If you want to create a list of figures at the beginning of the document, you can generate a list based on your captions. This chapter answers your questions about creating and listing captions.

⇨   This chapter helps you use WordPerfect 8's new Draw Layer feature. You can use Draw Layer to insert rectangles, ovals, lines, and other common shapes. If you need to create more complex drawings, you can open a drawing window in WordPerfect and use the Presentations menus and tools.

⇨   After you have inserted data in a spreadsheet or table, you can use that data to create charts. You can also create charts from scratch to present data with the visual effects you prefer. You can even create organization charts in WordPerfect. This chapter offers tips on creating charts with WordPerfect.

⇨   WordPerfect 8 includes a new Equation Editor that enables you to create complex equations in a snap. If you need help using the new editor's templates and slots, turn to this chapter.

⇨   If you need to scan an image, you don't need to leave WordPerfect: you can use the Acquire Image command to scan images directly into your document. This chapter shows you how to use this nifty feature—but if you don't have a scanner, you'll have a whale of a time trying to get this feature to work.

CLIPART AND THE SCRAPBOOK

When I click the CD Clipart tab in the Scrapbook, the folders in one of my partitioned hard drives appears instead of the CD. How do I change the directory in the Scrapbook?

After you choose Graphics | Insert | Clipart, the Scrapbook appears with two tabs: Clipart and CD Clipart. The Clipart tab includes a few images saved to your hard drive. However, the vast majority of clipart is located on the CD, which you should get to when you click the CD Clipart tab. However, if the Scrapbook isn't set up properly, it may look on your hard drive instead of the CD for these additional images. Here's how to change the directory:

1.   Make sure the Corel WordPerfect Suite 8 CD is in the CD-ROM drive.

2.   Click the CD Clipart tab.

3. Right-click a blank area of the CD Clipart screen and choose Set Default Folder.

4. Type **D:\Corel\Suite8\Graphics\Clipart**, where *D* represents your CD-ROM drive.

5. Click OK to display the clipart categories on your CD-ROM drive.

I'm running WordPerfect on a network, but I don't have access to the 10,000+ images. How can I get to these images without using the Corel WordPerfect 8 CD?

A Network installation does not automatically install most of the clipart images on the server; instead, the system administrator must make the images accessible to users by copying the Clipart directory (Corel\Suite8\Graphics\Clipart) from the CD to a location on the server or mounting the CD on the network. If your network administrator has already done this, here's how you specify the location of the clipart images:

1. Choose Tools | Settings.

2. Double-click Files and then click the Graphic tab.

3. In the Supplemental Graphics Folder text box, type the full path to the Clipart folder or browse to find its location. Then click OK.

I tried to insert an image from the CD without using the Scrapbook, but I can't find all the .WPG files that appear in the Scrapbook. Can I open or retrieve an image from the Scrapbook without opening the Scrapbook?

If you use Microsoft Explorer to browse the folders on the Corel WordPerfect 8 CD, you'll discover that the folders under Corel\Suite8\Graphics\Clipart contain .SCB images and a few .WPG. images (sometimes called *loose .WPGs*). The .SCB images contain many .WPG images in compressed format that can be accessed only by opening the Scrapbook (choose Insert | Graphics | Clipart) and dragging the image onto the document, as shown in Figure 9-1. However, after you insert a Scrapbook image in a document, you can save it as a .WPG file by clicking it and choosing Save As.

Some .WPG files are stored on your hard drive and on the CD, and you can insert these in your document without opening the Scrapbook. You can also insert .TIF, .PCX, .BMP, and .WPG images

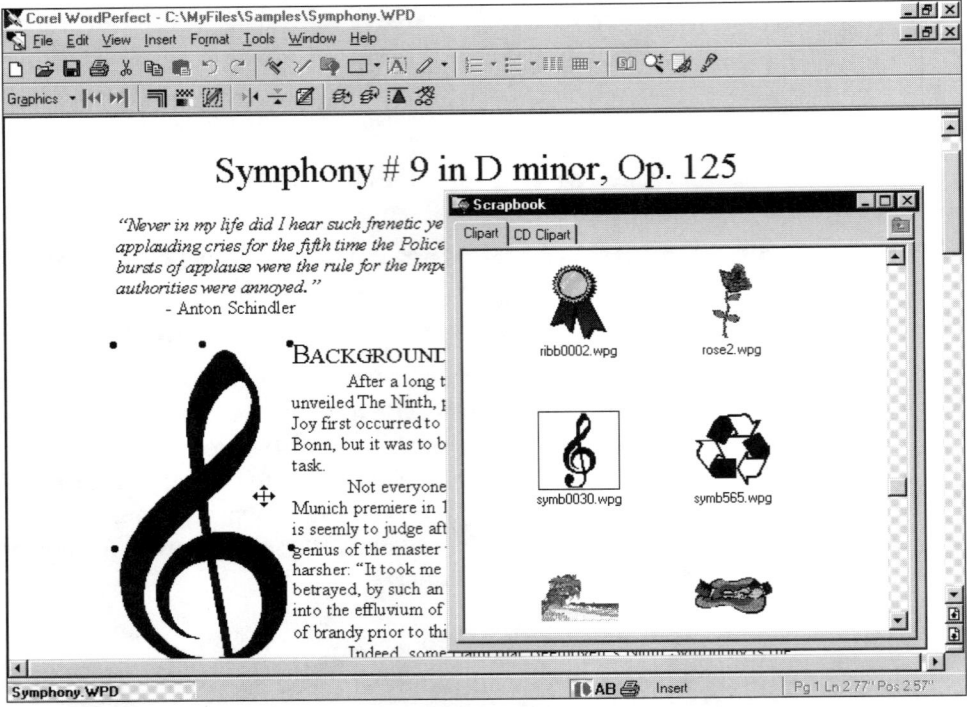

Figure 9-1.   You can place a clipart image in a document by dragging it from the Scrapbook

from previous versions of WordPerfect. To insert loose .WPG graphics and other types of images, choose Insert | Graphics | From File and then select the image. If you want to insert bitmap graphics from the CD, switch to your CD folder. The Corel\Suite8\Graphics\Pictures folder includes several .BMP images that you can insert.

Note: *Clipart filenames on the Corel WordPerfect Suite 8 CD-ROM do not match the clipart filenames used in the Corel Clipart manual. The CD-ROM uses short filenames, and the manual uses long filenames.*

? Is there a way to convert the Standard and Premium QAD libraries in WordPerfect 7 to Scrapbook (SCB) libraries in WordPerfect 8?

No. To use an image included with WordPerfect 7 in WordPerfect 8, you must open the graphic in WordPerfect 7 or Presentations 7 and then save the image as a .WPG file. Corel is working on a version of

Scrapbook that will read .QAD files, but it wasn't available when this book was published.

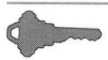 **When I drag to create a graphic and then insert a Scrapbook image, the graphic box disappears. What's wrong?**

Nothing's wrong—the Scrapbook is working as designed. When you drag across a blank area of your document and choose Clipart, the Scrapbook appears, and the box you have drawn disappears for good. The only way to insert images from the Scrapbook is to drag the image into your document; the image is placed where you drag it.

If you want to insert an image into a graphics box you have drawn, you'll need to choose Image From File from the QuickMenu that appears. You can then insert a loose .WPG file or another image from your hard drive or the CD into the box, and the box will remain in your document.

Note: *Dragging the mouse to create a graphic works only if the shadow cursor appears. To display the shadow cursor, you must hold the pointer over a blank area of the document.*

 **The Save Image As dialog box doesn't give me an option for saving an image as a .BMP or .TIF image. How do I convert a .WPG image to another file format for use in other Windows applications?**

WordPerfect doesn't provide many options for saving images in different formats. If you want a wider selection of formats, open your image in Presentations, which lets you save images in a number of formats, such as Windows Bitmap (.BMP) and Encapsulated Postscript (.EPS).

Note: *You cannot use the Presentations drawing window to save these images. You must start the Presentations application, insert the image, and then save the selected image in a different format.*

In addition, a number of commercial programs let you convert graphics files into just about any format without having to insert the images first. You can also copy and paste your image to the Paint program that comes with Windows 95 and save it as a .BMP image.

? Why doesn't my image print in WordPerfect?

First, make sure you don't have the Print Text Only option turned on. Choose File | Print, click the Details tab, and make sure Print Text Only is deselected.

In some cases, graphics that have been pasted into Presentations from another different program, such as Corel Draw 6, do not print when brought into WordPerfect. The graphic will appear in WordPerfect, but it won't print. If this is the case, you can try working around this problem in two different ways. First, try opening the graphic in Presentations and then saving it in a different format, such as .PCX. Second, save the object in the original application and then retrieve the image into Presentations, where you can edit it. This problem seems to occur only with objects pasted from the clipboard.

? When I try to insert a Corel Flow file into WordPerfect, an error message appears. What's wrong?

When you import a Corel Flow 3.0 file into WordPerfect, this error message may appear: "This image cannot be converted to a WPG2 image." If this occurs, copy the image in Flow 3.0 and then paste it into WordPerfect.

? I tried to insert a Micrografx image, but WordPerfect wouldn't convert it. Why not?

When you installed WordPerfect, not all the conversion drivers were included. You can perform a Custom installation to include additional graphic conversion drivers.

1. Run the Corel WordPerfect Suite 8 Setup program and then select the Custom installation.

2. Follow the prompts until the Custom Installation window appears.

3. Click Selection Options, select Deselect All, and click OK.

4. Click Accessories and then select Components.

 Tip: *When moving through the option levels, click the words, not the check boxes, or you'll select everything under that level.*

5. Click Conversions | Viewers | Tools and then select Components.

6. Click Conversion Filters and then select Components.

7. Click Graphics Conversions and then select Components.

8. In the Graphics Conversions window, either click the check boxes next to the Bitmap and Vector options to select them, or select Components and specify the drivers you want to install.

9. Follow the prompts to finish the installation.

? I created labels with the Merge feature and included a graphic to create business cards. However, the file size is almost 3MB. The file won't fit on a floppy disk, and it takes five minutes to open and close. How can I make this file smaller?

Use the Image on Disk option, which creates a link between the image file and the document instead of the adding the image to the document. For example, instead of including 300 copies of an image in your document, you can make 300 references to one copy of the image. Here's what you do:

1. Open the form file containing the labels definition and graphic.

2. Right-click the image used in your business cards and then choose Content.

3. In the Content Type list box, select Image on Disk. Then click OK.

4. If you inserted a Scrapbook image, you'll be prompted to save a copy of the image on your hard drive. Type a name for the file, specify a folder, and then click Save.

5. Click OK and then merge the documents again. The file size will be dramatically smaller.

 *Note:* *When you copy the file to a floppy disk to give to someone else, make sure you include the image file. Tell the person to copy the .WPG file to the default graphics folder, which is usually C:\Corel\Suite8\Graphics\Clipart.*

EDITING GRAPHICS AND TEXT BOXES

? **After I drag a graphic to a particular location on a page, it sometimes moves. How can I make graphics stay where I place them when I edit text?**

WordPerfect lets you anchor graphics to a page, to a paragraph, or to a character. When you edit text, the graphic may move if it is anchored to a paragraph or character. However, if the image is anchored to a page, it won't move, unless it's bumped to the next page. Here's how to anchor a graphic to a page and prevent it from being bumped:

1. Right-click the image and then choose Position.

2. Select Page from the Attach Box To drop-down list.

3. Specify where you want the graphic on the page.

4. Select the Box Stays on Page check box to prevent the graphic from being bumped.

? **When I drag a graphic to size it, the image is distorted. How do I size an image proportionally?**

If you drag one of the corner sizing handles instead of the side sizing handles, the image will be sized proportionally. If you want to make sure the image never gets distorted, even if you drag the side handles, here's what to do:

1. Right-click the image and choose Content.

2. Select the Preserve Image Width/Height Ratio check box and then click OK.

Tip: To size the image proportionally, you can also right-click the image, choose Size, specify a set width, and select Maintain Proportions for Height (or specify a set height and select Maintain Proportions for Width).

? **When I overlay a graphic with a text box, the text sometimes separates from the graphic. How do I keep the text box and graphic together?**

You can do this in two ways. One way is to edit the graphic in the Presentations drawing window. Double-click the image to select it, choose Insert | Text Box, then drag across the area of the image where the text box should appear, as shown in Figure 9-2. After you create the text box, type and format the text and then click anywhere outside the graphic to exit Presentations.

Another way to keep the text box from being separated from the image is to group the text and image boxes together. After you position the image and text boxes as you want them, click the border of the text box to select it and then hold down SHIFT and click the image. Right-click the selected images and choose Group. If you want to ungroup the images, right-click the image and choose Separate.

? I added text to a drawing in Presentations, but the text shifted when I brought it back into WordPerfect. What's wrong?

Text added to a graphic in Presentations shifts about 1/16 of an inch when it is retrieved into WordPerfect. This can cause problems with extremely tight images that need to be exact. If text shifts, try saving

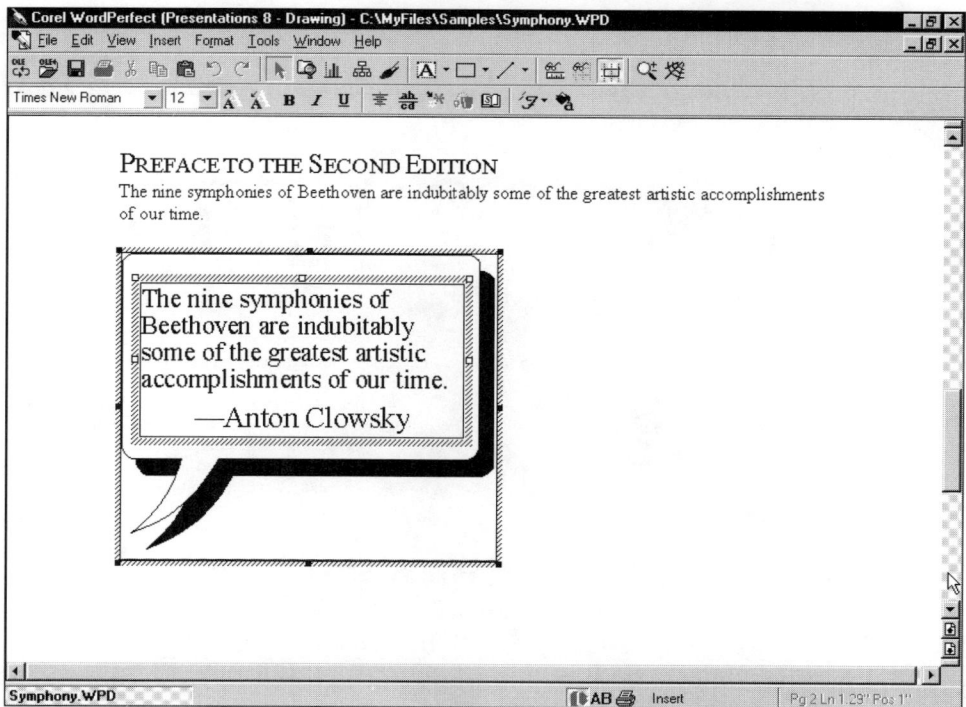

Figure 9-2.   You can add text to an image in the Presentations drawing window

the image in Presentations in a different format, such as WordPerfect Graphics 5. Select the image being edited in Presentations, then Choose File, Save As, then select Selected Image and click OK. Type the name of the image, then select a different format from the File type drop-down list and choose Save.

? There is too much space between the image and the text box. How can I remove it?

You can use the tools on the Image Tools palette to crop the image, as shown in Figure 9-3. You can also use the tools on this palette to rotate and flip images, shift an image with the box, and change the brightness and contrast of an image.

Here's how to crop an image:

1. Right-click the image and then choose Image Tools.

2. Click the Zoom button and then select the Magnifying Glass option.

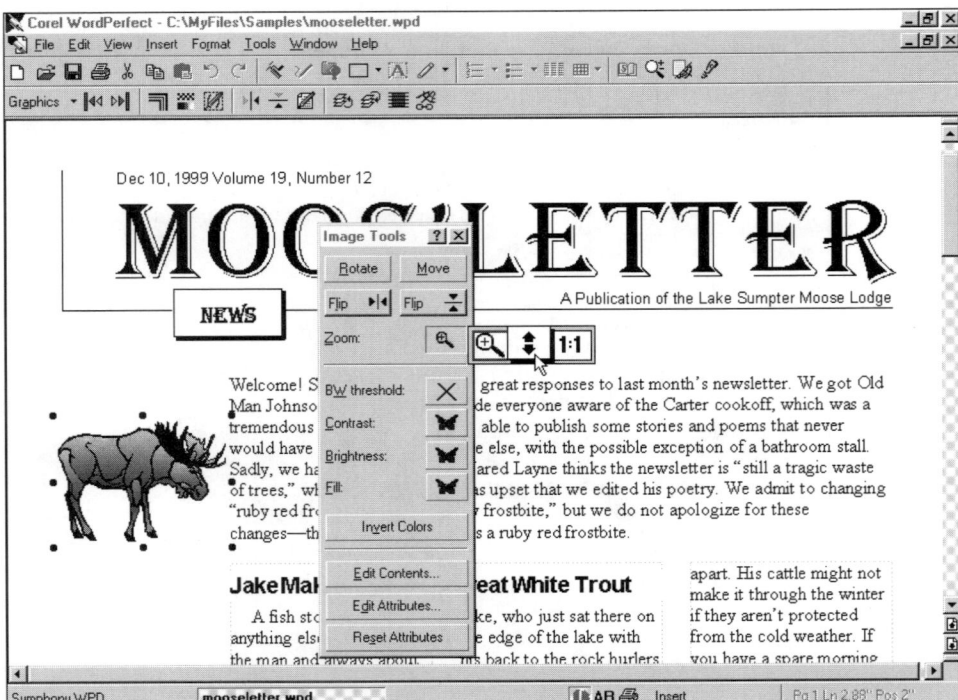

Figure 9-3.   You can use the tools on the Image Tools palette to crop, rotate, and flip images and change other image features

3. Drag across the part of the image that you want to appear in the graphics box. Then close the Image Tools palette.

After I flipped, cropped, and rotated an image, I saved it—but when I reopened the saved image in WordPerfect, all the changes were gone. What's wrong?

When you size, crop, flip, or skew an image in WordPerfect, the image appears and prints that way in your document. However, when you save the image, it is stored as it was originally created, without the changes you made in WordPerfect. To actually make changes to the graphic image, you need to open it in a graphics program such as Presentations, make the changes, and then save it as a graphic file.

I placed a full-page graphics box in the middle of page 1. The box was bumped to page 2 as I expected, but the text below the graphic was moved to page 3 instead of page 1, leaving page 1 blank. What's the problem?

Unlike WordPerfect for DOS, WordPerfect for Windows formats documents from the bottom up. When WordPerfect reads a full-page graphic, it forces the graphic and anything below it to the next page. The graphics box takes up the full second page, forcing the text to the third page.

You can work around this problem by formatting the full-page graphics box with Delay Codes. Here's how:

1. Place the insertion point at the top of the document or after a hard page break.

2. Choose Format | Page | Delay Codes, specify the number of pages you want to skip, and click OK.

3. Insert the image in the Delay Codes window. Then right-click the image and choose Size. Select Full for both the Horizontal and Vertical options and then click OK.

4. Close the Delay Codes window.

Tip: *To edit the image in the Delay Codes window, turn on Reveal Codes, move the insertion point to the location of the Delay Codes, and double-click the Delay code.*

? **While creating business cards, I left enough space for a graphic, but when I inserted the graphic, the text shifted. How can I fix this problem?**

The spacing around the graphics box may push the text over more than you expect. However, instead of meddling with the spacing, simply turn off the Wrap option and make sure the graphic is small enough not to overlap the text. Here's how to turn off wrapping:

1. Right-click the image and then choose Wrap.

2. Select Behind Text (or In Front of Text) and then click OK.

? **I set the Wrap option to Square on Both Sides, but the text wraps through the graphics box. What's wrong?**

If you anchored your graphics box to a character and deselected the Box Changes Text Line Height option, the text above or below the image will flow through the image instead of wrapping around it. To fix this problem, right-click the image, choose Position, and select Box Changes Text Line Height.

? **When I place a graphics box against the bottom and right margins of a page and use an outline, the text that wraps to the next page is not indented properly. How can I fix this?**

This problem occurs when the Wrap option is set to Square on Both Sides. To correct it, right-click the graphics box and choose Wrap. Change the Wrap Text Around option to Largest Side or Left Side, and the text on the next page will be indented properly.

Tip: *If you want text to wrap around the image itself rather than the graphics box, select the Contour Wrap option. If you want the graphics image to overlay the text, select the In Front of Text Wrap option. These two wrap effects are shown here.*

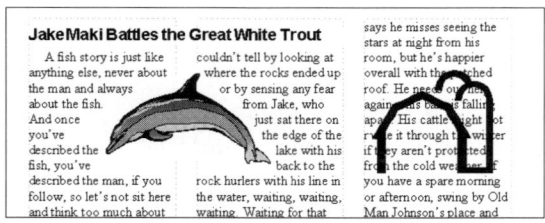

Types of Graphics Boxes

You can create many kinds of graphics boxes in your documents. You can choose Insert | Graphics | Custom Box and then specify the type of image you want to place in your document. You can also change the type graphics box by right-clicking your graphics object, choosing Style, and then double-clicking the type of box you want. Consult this list to determine which type of graphics box to use.

⇨ Image and figure boxes are used to display images. Whenever you insert an image from the Scrapbook or from a disk, the graphic appears in an image box, which doesn't have borders. You can also insert images in figure boxes, which have a single-line border.

⇨ Inline text boxes work well when you want to insert a text box that acts like a character, moving when you insert text before it and changing the line height.

⇨ Table boxes are used to insert tables inside a graphics box. Table boxes are useful when you want to do such things as adding captions (Table 1, Table 2, and so on), rotating the table in your document, and placing text or another table side by side.

⇨ User boxes are commonly used as general purpose boxes that store images, text, and just about anything else. The advantage in using a user box is that your captions are numbered consecutively. For example, when you want to use the same caption numbering for different items, such as tables, figures, equations, and so on, you can place these items inside user boxes. Otherwise, your image boxes will be numbered Figure 1, Figure 2, and so on while your tables are numbered Table 1, Table 2, and so on.

⇨ The Sticky Note text box has a yellow background and covers everything beneath it like, well, a sticky note. The Sticky Note text box is especially useful when you review documents and you want your author to be sure to read your comment.

Warning: *If you want to create captions and lists of figures in your document, be aware that selecting different box styles may cause items to be included in separate lists. For example, numbering in table box captions (Table 1, Table 2, and so on) is different from numbering in image box captions (Figure 1, Figure 2, and so on). For more information, see "Captions and Lists of Figures" later in this chapter.*

When I create rounded corners to turn a graphics box into a circle, the image overlaps the border and is distorted, and the box never becomes a circle. What's wrong?

Instead of creating a square border, you should create a circular border, like this:

If you follow these steps, you shouldn't have any problems:

1. Right-click the image and choose Content. Then select Preserve Image Width/Height Ratio and click OK.

2. Right-click the image and choose Border/Fill. Then select the border you want and select Rounded Corners.

3. Click the Advanced tab in the Box Border/Fill dialog box. Then change the inside spacing to **0.1"** and the corner radius to **10"**. Click OK.

4. Right-click the image and choose Size. Specify the same size (such as **3"**) for the Width and Height Set options. Then click OK.

Note: *When you select Contour wrapping for a graphics box with rounded corners, the text wraps around the box, not around the image.*

 ***Tip:*** *If the image still overlaps the border even after you change the inside spacing, right-click the image and choose Image Tools. From the Zoom pop-up list, select the up and down arrow and then drag the scroll bar up to shrink the image within the box.*

I want to place an image at the bottom of my newsletter across columns 2 and 3, but the Across Columns option in the Box Position dialog box is dimmed. What's wrong?

For the Across Columns option to work successfully, the graphics box must be anchored to the page, and you must select a column option from the Horizontal From drop-down list, as shown in Figure 9-4. First, though, make sure the graphic is placed within the columns, or you may get odd results.

1. Turn on Reveal Codes and locate the Box code. If it's outside the columns where you want the graphic to appear, cut and paste the code anywhere within the columns.

2. Right-click the image and choose Position.

3. Select Centered in Columns from the Horizontal drop-down list.

4. Specify the columns you want to span in the Across Columns text boxes.

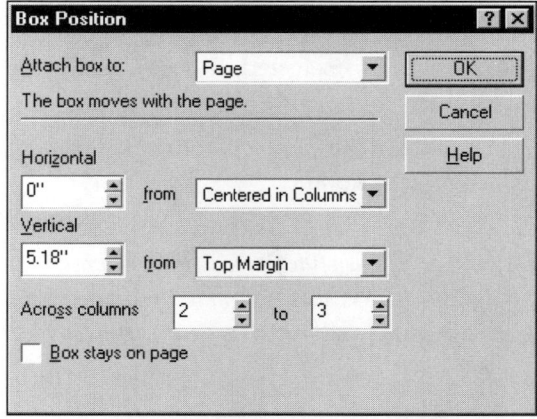

Figure 9-4.   You can use the Box Position dialog box to place an image across columns

Tip: *When you span an image across columns, the image may not entirely fill the columns. Right-click the image and choose Size. Then select Full from the Width options and click OK.*

? In WordPerfect 7, I used the Edit Box palette to quickly save the current box style. In WordPerfect 8, how do I save graphics styles?

You still use the Edit Box palette—but it's not as easy to find. In WordPerfect 7, you clicked the QuickSpot to display the Edit Box palette, which includes the Save Style As option. In WordPerfect 8, the property bars include all the options found in the WordPerfect 7 Edit Box palette—except for the Save Style As option. It's kind of nutty, but the only way to display the Edit Box palette is to turn off the property bar (right-click it and choose Hide Property Bar). Then right-click the image and choose Edit Box to display the Edit Box palette. To save the settings of the selected graphics box, click Save Style As, type a name for the style, and click OK.

Tip: *To display the property bar again, choose View | Toolbars, select Property Bar, and click OK.*

Here is the standard way to create graphics styles in WordPerfect 8:

1. Make sure a graphics box is not selected. Then choose Format | Graphics Styles.

2. With Box selected, choose Create.

3. Type the name of the style and then use the buttons on the left side of the dialog box to customize your settings. Click OK when you're done.

Note: *The style name you type appears in the list with other box styles such as Image, Text Box, and Figure. To apply the style to an existing text box, right-click the image, choose Style, and then double-click the new style you created.*

 *Tip:*   *You can also use QuickFormat to copy graphics box settings. Select a graphics box with the settings you want and then click the QuickFormat button on the toolbar. Click any other graphics boxes to apply the same borders, fills, and wrap options as used in the graphics box you copied. Click the QuickFormat button again when you're done.*

? When I placed the image in a table, it became compressed and distorted. What's wrong?

If an image is inserted in a table row that has a fixed row height, the image will be squeezed into that fixed row height. To fix this problem, you can do one of the following:

⇨ Increase the row height in the table to accommodate the graphic or set the row height to Automatic: Right-click the row, choose Format, and click the Row tab. Specify a taller row height or select Automatic. Then click OK.

⇨ Right-click the image and choose Content. Select Preserve Image Width/Height Ratio and click OK. The image will shrink to fit in the table cell.

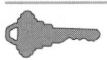 *Note:*   *When a graphics box is inserted into a table with a fixed row height, wrapping is automatically set to Neither Side. To change this, right-click the image, choose Wrap, and select a different Wrap option.*

? When I click a text box to try to move it, instead I select the text inside the box. How do I move a text box?

In WordPerfect 8, the programmers wanted to make it easier to edit text inside a text box, so when you click inside a text box now, the insertion point moves to that location, and you're ready to type or edit text. To select the text box itself, you click its border; then you can move it or size it (you may have to double-click the edge of the text box in some cases). This same procedure applies to table boxes as well.

Note, too, that to display the graphics box QuickMenu instead of the normal text window, you must right-click the border of the text box instead of right-clicking inside the text box.

 *Tip:*   *If you have a large amount of text to insert in a text box, you may want to type and format the text in a separate document and then save the document and use the Filename option in the Box Content dialog box. To do this, create a blank text box and right-click its border. Then choose Content and type the filename.*

When I use a large font in a text box, there is too much space between the text and the top border. How do I remove this extra space?

You can change the inside spacing of the text box. To do so, right-click the border of the text box and then choose Border/Fill. Click the Advanced tab and then select a smaller spacing value from the Inside pop-up palette.

When I rotate text in a text box, the superscript text appears in the wrong position. What's wrong?

This may actually be a problem in the software. If you use a subscript or superscript after a tab or indent in a rotated text box, the superscript may shift slightly. To work around the problem, Corel recommends that you violate one of the golden rules of word processing—use spaces rather than tabs to indent the text.

When I rotate text in a text box, some of the text shifts to the next line. How can I keep the text from moving?

Rotating the text in the text box sometimes causes text to wrap to the next line. After you rotate text, you can click the text box's border and drag one of the sizing handles to resize the text box until the text fits as you want.

CAPTIONS AND LISTS OF FIGURES

I've added captions to all my images, but the captions use two separate numbering sequences. What's wrong?

Graphics boxes are numbered according to the type of graphics box style. There are five graphics box styles, each with its own separate counter: figure boxes, user boxes, text boxes, table boxes, and equation boxes. If you have inserted some images in an image box and others in a user box, you'll end up with two distinct sets of caption numbers. In some instances, you'll want to use more than one set of numbers. For example, you may want captions for table boxes (Table 1, Table 2, and so on) to be numbered separately from those for image boxes (Figure 1, Figure 2, and so on).

If you want all your captions to be numbered sequentially, you need to change the box styles of your images so that all the graphics boxes are image or figure boxes. To change a graphics box style, right-click the graphics box and choose Style. Select the box style you want to use and then click OK. You may then have to move and size some of your graphics and change the border style.

You can also edit the graphics style so that figure boxes and user boxes use the same counter type. Here's how to edit the user box style so that user boxes use the same captions as figure boxes:

1. Click outside a graphics box and then choose Format | Graphics Styles.

2. If you want this change to apply to the current document only, choose Current Document from the List Styles From drop-down list.

3. Select User in the Styles list box and then choose Edit.

4. Choose Caption and then click the Change button next to Counter Type.

5. Click Figure Box and then choose Select.

6. Click the Change button next to Number Style, select FigureNum, and choose Apply.

When you close the dialog boxes, the captions should all be part of the same list.

? **I want caption numbers to be italicized instead of bold, but I don't want to change each caption number. Can I italicize all the caption formatting at once?**

You need to edit the graphics style to change all the caption numbers at once. Here's how you can remove the bold and add italics to your caption numbers:

1. Click outside a graphics box and then choose Format | Graphics Styles.

2. If you want this change to apply to the current document only, choose Current Document from the List Styles From drop-down list.

3. Select the style (such as Image) you want to change and then choose Edit.

4. Choose Caption and then click the Change button next to Number Style.

5. Make sure FigureNum is selected and then choose Edit.

6. Delete the Bold code. Then press SHIFT-END to select the caption and press CTRL-I to turn on italics.

Note: *If you do not select the text before you press* CTRL-I, *the entire caption will be italicized, including any explanatory text that follows the caption number (such as Figure 1. Pine Hollow). You may or may not want to italicize the entire caption.*

7. Click OK and then click Apply.

8. Click OK twice and then close your document.

❓ The table caption appears above a table. I want the caption below the table, but I can't cut and paste it. How do I position a caption?

You can place the caption on any side of the table box on either the inside or outside of the border, and you can rotate the caption. To move the caption to the bottom of the table, right-click the box surrounding the table and then choose Caption (not Edit Caption). Select Bottom from the Side of Box drop-down list and then click OK.

❓ I want to use the sequential numbering feature for captions, but I want to use letters instead of numbers, such as *Figure A*. How do I edit the caption style?

You have to add a counter code and edit the caption style to make these changes. Here's how:

1. Choose Insert | Other | Counter.

2. Choose Create and then type a counter name such as **letters**.

3. Select A,B,C,... from the Single Level Method drop-down list and then click OK. Click Close.

4. Choose Format | Graphics Styles.

5. If you want this change to apply to the current document only, choose Current Document from the List Styles From drop-down list.

6. Select the style (such as Image) you want to change and then choose Edit.

7. Choose Caption and then click the Change button next to Counter Type.

8. Select the counter style you just created and then click Select.

9. Click OK twice and click Close until you return to your document.

Tip: *You can also use counters to create multilevel caption numbering, such as Figure 1.1, Figure 1.2, Figure 2.1, and so on. The steps are rather involved, but WordPerfect Help explains them well. Choose Help | Help Topics, click the Index tab, type* **caption: multilevel numbering**, *and press* ENTER.

When I choose Mark Target to reference a caption, an error message appears, even though the caption is selected. How do I cross-reference captions in graphics boxes?

You need to type text in the Target box on the Cross-Reference property bar before you click Mark Target. Figure 9-5 shows an example of a cross-reference.

Here's how to reference captions in your document:

1. Choose Tools | Reference | Cross-Reference to display the Cross-Reference property bar.

2. To mark a caption, right-click the image and then choose Edit Caption. With the insertion point anywhere in the caption, type a description of the image in the Target text box on the Cross-Reference property bar. Then click Mark Target.

3. Mark any other caption in your document that you may want to cross-reference. Remember to type the description *before* you click Mark Target.

4. Place the insertion point where you want to insert the cross-reference.

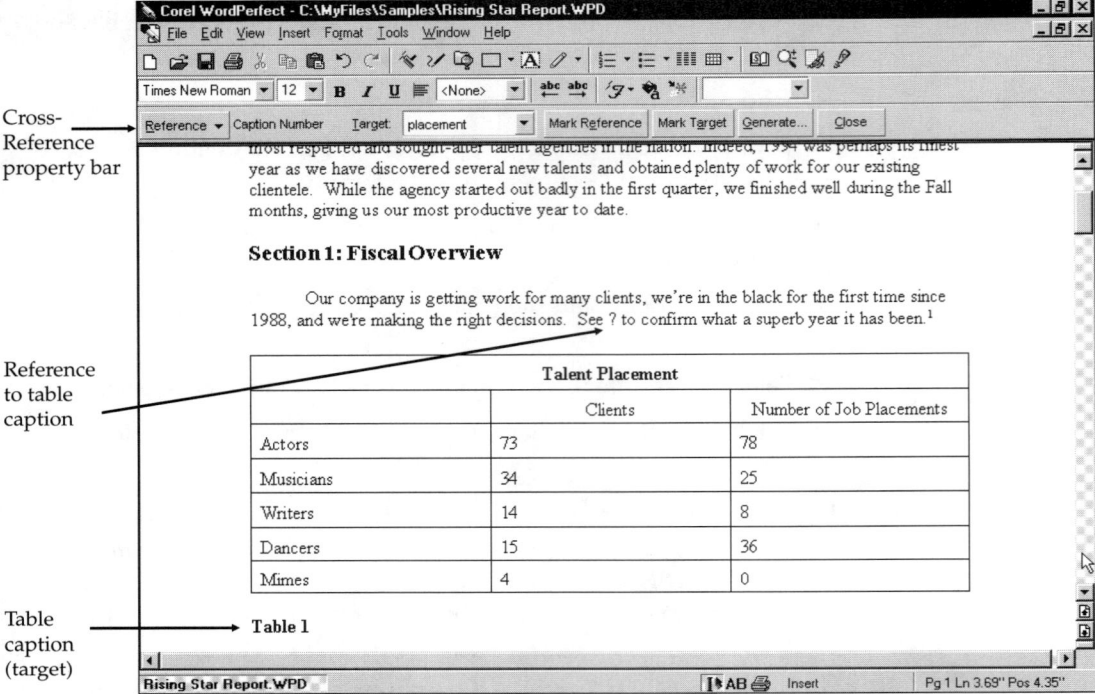

Cross-Reference property bar

Reference to table caption

Table caption (target)

Figure 9-5.   Use the Cross-Reference property bar to reference captions

5. Select the figure you want to reference from the Target drop-down list. Then select Caption Number from the Reference drop-down list on the Cross-Reference property bar and click Mark Reference to temporarily insert a question mark.

6. If you want to include the page number of the caption, type the lead-in text (such as a comma followed by the word "page"). Then select Page from the Reference drop-down list and click Mark Reference.

7. Click Generate and then click OK to generate the references.

? To generate a list of figures, do I need to mark each caption?

No. You can list your captions automatically. Here's how to generate a list of figures, as shown in Figure 9-6.

1. Create the page where your list of figures will appear (usually right after the table of contents).

2. Place the insertion point on a blank line and then choose Tools | Reference | List.

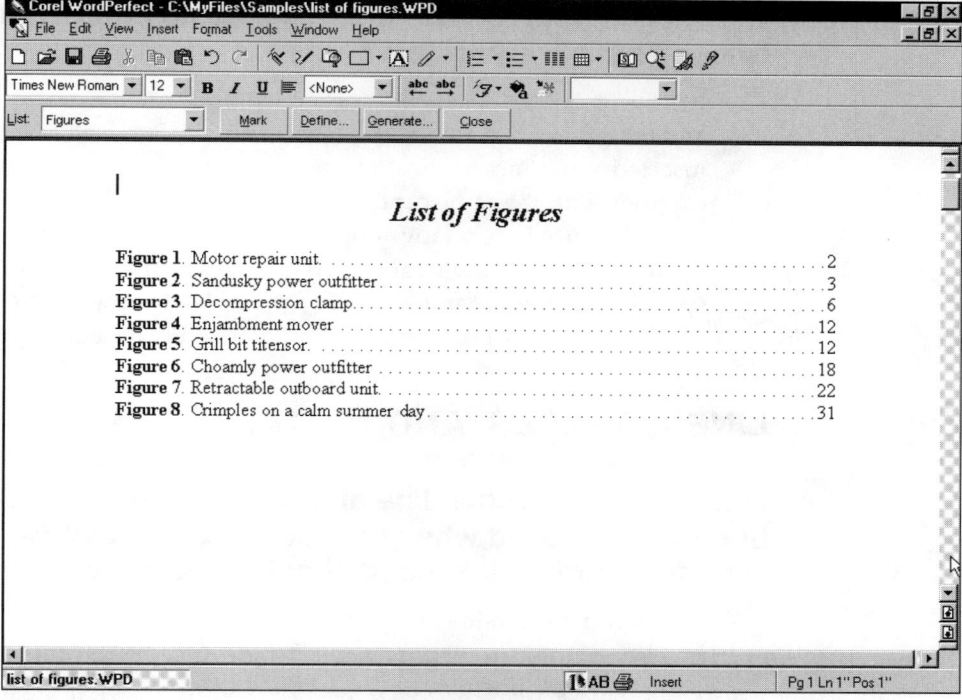

Figure 9-6.   You can generate a list of figures from your captions

3. Choose Define | Create.

4. Type the name of the list definition and select the position and numbering options you want.

5. From the List Box Captions Automatically drop-down list, select .Figure Box (or the box caption you want to use). Then click OK.

6. Choose Insert and click Generate. Then click OK to generate the list of figures.

 *Note:*   *When you generate a list of figures, only the captions of the selected box type appear in the list. If you want captions from other types of boxes (such as user or table boxes) to appear in the same list as your figure box captions, you can either change the box styles so that all the graphics boxes are image or figure boxes, or you can edit the graphics styles of these other box styles (such as table or user) to replace their caption styles with the figure box caption style. For more information, see the first Q&A in this section, "Captions and Lists of Figures."*

? **When I generate a list of graphics, some figures are listed twice. What's the problem?**

It is likely that the boxes being generated twice contain nested graphics, and these nested graphics also have captions. For example, if you inserted a graphics box inside a text box, and both boxes contain captions with the same caption style, this figure will be listed twice. To solve this problem, remove one of the captions for the nested boxes or make sure the box style for nested graphics is different from that specified for the generated list. For example, if you want to list the captions of image boxes, change the style of the nested boxes to user.

LINES, SHAPES, AND TEXTART

? **I inserted a horizontal line at a particular spot on a page, but the line moved when I edited the document text. How can I fix a horizontal line so that it stays where I place it?**

When you insert a line, the default vertical placement is set to the baseline of the current paragraph. When you edit text above the paragraph, the line moves, just like any other paragraph. Here's how you can create a horizontal line and fix it to a spot on a page:

1. Place the insertion point where you want the line to appear.
2. Choose Insert | Shape | Custom Line.
3. Specify the line type, length, thickness, and other attributes.
4. Select Set from the Vertical drop-down list. If necessary, specify the distance from the top of the page. Then click OK.

Note: *To edit a line you've already inserted, right-click it and choose Edit Horizontal Line.*

Tip: *To quickly create a single horizontal line, press the hyphen key (-) four times on the left side of a blank line and press* ENTER. *To create a double horizontal line, press the equal sign (=) four times and press* ENTER. *(This procedure works only if the QuickLines option of the QuickCorrect feature is turned on.)*

? I inserted several shapes to create a drawing, but one of the shapes is completely covered by other shapes. How can I select the buried shape?

Click one of the shapes to select it and then click the Previous Box button. Each time you click the Previous Box or Next Box button, a different shape is selected. Continue to cycle through the shapes until the one you want to edit appears.

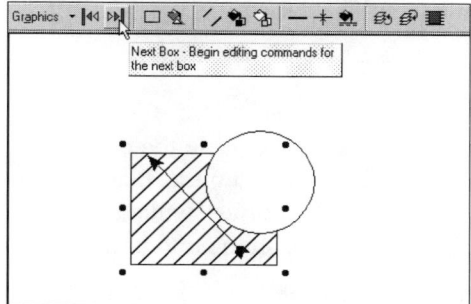

Here are some points to consider when working with groups of shapes:

⇨ You can change the order of the shapes. If one of the shapes is buried, you can bring it toward the front by clicking the Graphics drop-down list on the property bar and then selecting To Front (or In Front of Text if you want to move it to the top of the pile).

⇨ Once a cluster of shapes appears the way you want, and the shapes are in the correct order, you can group the cluster so the shapes don't become separated as you edit the document. Hold down the SHIFT key and click each shape object. Then right-click one of the objects and choose Group. To ungroup the shapes, right-click the group and choose Separate.

? When I right-click a rectangle I created in WordPerfect, the Image Tools palette doesn't appear. How do I rotate a shape that I've drawn?

You can't use the Image Tools palette with shapes you draw in WordPerfect. The Draw Layer feature is designed to produce only simple objects; it does not offer the full drawing capabilities of Presentations. However, here are some ways you can work around this limitation:

⇨ You can cut the object and then paste it as a WPG20 file so that it will rotate. This approach works best with polylines, arrowheads, and irregularly shaped polygons. To use this procedure, cut the object and then choose Edit | Paste Special. Select WPG20 and then click OK. You can then right-click the shape and choose Image Tools.

Tip: *If you know you're going to want to use more sophisticated tools before you draw a shape, choose Insert | Graphics | Draw Picture. You can then use the Presentations tools.*

⇨ If you've inserted a shape using Draw Line, you can rotate the image by editing the points. To do this, right-click the image and choose Edit Points. Place the mouse over one of the edit points, and the pointer will change to cross-hairs. You can then click and drag the shape into a new position.

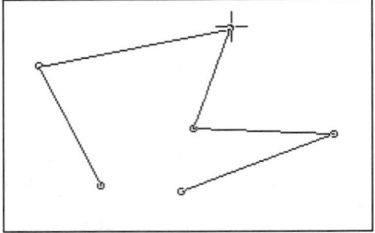

? I've inserted a line, but I can't put an arrowhead on it. Why?

You can add arrowheads and arrow tails only to lines created with the Draw Line or Polyline feature. To turn a line into an arrow, select the line and then select options from the Arrow Start and Arrow End buttons on the property bar.

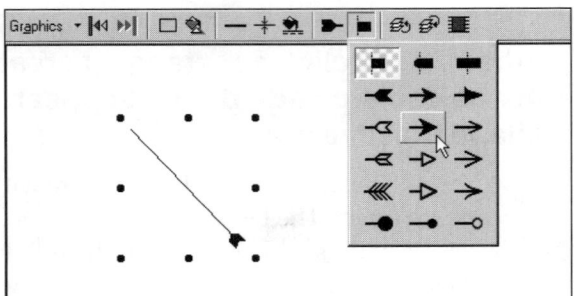

Note that if you inserted a standard horizontal or vertical line, you won't be able to embellish the line with an arrowhead.

? When I displayed the TextArt screen, TextArt 7 appeared instead of TextArt 8. Where is the new Corel TextArt 8?

If you're using WordPerfect 8, the Corel TextArt 8.0 dialog box should appear when you choose Insert | Graphics | TextArt, as shown in Figure 9-7. If the TextArt 7 application appears, you probably reinstalled WordPerfect 7 after you installed WordPerfect 8, in which case TextArt will be one of several features that don't quite work correctly in WordPerfect 8. To fix this problem, reinstall the Corel WordPerfect 8 Suite. You'll now be able to use all of WordPerfect 8's TextArt features.

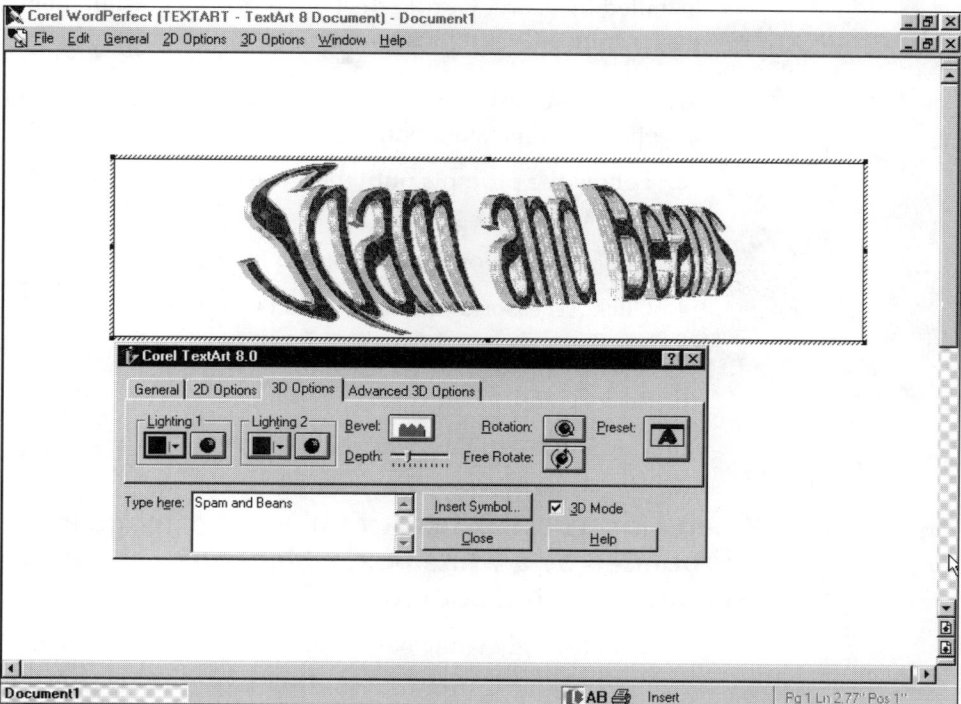

Figure 9-7.   The Corel TextArt 8.0 dialog box lets you insert 3-D images as well as 2-D graphics

When I edit an old TextArt file in WordPerfect 8, the colors change. What's wrong?

If you insert a TextArt design from WordPerfect 6.1 into a WordPerfect 8 document, the colors will be reversed. To fix this, double-click the image and then edit it in TextArt.

Note: *If double-clicking the image opens the design in Presentations, you can no longer edit the image in TextArt. You'll have to re-create the image in WordPerfect.*

I want to use the 3D Options and Advanced 3D Options tabs in the Corel TextArt 8.0 dialog box, but the options are dimmed. What's wrong?

First, make sure the 3D Mode check box is selected. If this option is selected, the 3D effects may not have been included when you installed the Corel WordPerfect Suite. You can install them by performing a Custom installation.

1. Run the Corel WordPerfect Suite 8 Setup program and then select the Custom installation.

2. Follow the prompts until the Custom Installation window appears.

3. Choose Selection Options, select Deselect All, and click OK.

4. Click Accessories and then select Components.

5. Click Corel TextArt and then select Components.

6. Select Corel 3-D TextArt Components and then click OK.

7. Continue with the installation.

When I insert a 3-D TextArt object, the image is surrounded by a white box, which looks bad in Web documents. What should I do?

To avoid the ugly white background, use 2-D TextArt images in your Web documents instead of 3-D images. However, if you really want to use a 3-D image and you know how to edit bitmaps in drawing programs, you can edit the image in Presentations. First, however, you need to import the TextArt image as a metafile picture. Select the

TextArt image and then cut it and choose Edit | Paste Special. Select Picture and click OK. You can then double-click the TextArt image to edit it in Presentations.

? When I try to type text in TextArt, an error message appears telling me that the object is too complex. What can I do?

When 3D Mode is selected and you try to type text in the Type Here text box, the following error message may appear: "3D operation was unsuccessful due to the complexity of the object." If this message appears, close the message, exit TextArt, and delete the box you created. Then create the TextArt image again. If you still can't type text, exit and restart WordPerfect. Then try again.

? I created a TextArt image for my company logo, but I can't figure out how to insert it in the Scrapbook. How do I save a TextArt image?

You can't insert the TextArt image in the Scrapbook, but you can save it as a .WPG image on your hard drive. Here's how:

1. Click the TextArt image in your document to select it.
2. Choose File | Save As, select Selected Image, and click OK.
3. Select the folder where you want to store the image.
4. Type the name of the graphic and then choose Save.

? My TextArt image looks grainy. How can I make it smoother?

You can improve the clarity of a TextArt graphic by adjusting its smoothness. Click the General tab and then select High or Very High from the Smoothness drop-down list. If you're creating a 3-D image, you can also improve the resolution. Click the Advanced 3D Options tab and then select a higher quality from the Quality drop-down list.

Note: *Higher smoothness levels slow down on-screen display, and higher resolution settings increase the size of the file.*

CHARTS

? **In the chart I created, the labels on the x-axis overlap. How can I fix this?**

Right-click one of the x-axis labels and choose Stagger Labels. How's that for a short answer! In fact, you can change just about anything in your chart by right-clicking it and choosing the Properties option at the bottom of the QuickMenu. For example, to change the chart title, right-click it and choose Title Properties. You can then change the text, font, and other characteristics of the title. You can also add legends, labels, and subtitles to your charts.

Tip: *To change the type of chart, choose Chart | Gallery.*

? **I want to create a bar chart that also displays one data series as a line. How do I create a mixed chart?**

You can create a mixed chart to emphasize a set of data, such as Delaney's sales data shown in Figure 9-8. You do this by first creating one type of chart and then editing it to display selected data in another chart format.

Here's how to create a mixed chart:

1. Double-click the chart to edit it.

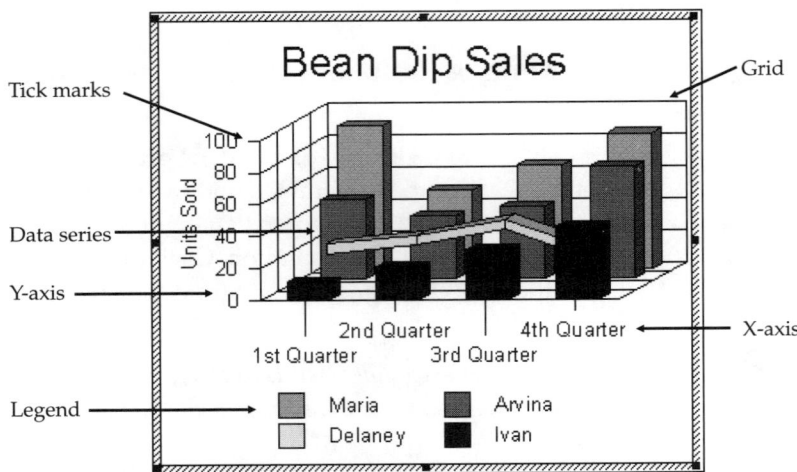

Figure 9-8.   You can edit a chart to create a mixed chart

2. Choose Chart | Layout/Type, select the kind of chart (such as Bar) you want for most of your data series, and then click OK.

3. Right-click the series that you want to change and then choose Series Properties.

4. Select a different Series type (such as Line) and then click OK.

 *Tip:*   *For full-screen editing, hold down the* ALT *key while double-clicking the chart.*

? I created a chart based on table data. How do I update the chart when the table changes?

When you create a chart based on table data by clicking the table (or selecting part of the table) and then choosing Insert | Graphics | Chart, the data in the chart is automatically linked to the data in the table. To edit the data in the chart, you follow these simple steps:

1. Edit the data in the table.

2. Right-click the chart and choose Update Chart from Table.

? I want to create a chart based on spreadsheet data. How do I do this?

To import spreadsheet data to create a chart, do the following:

1. Choose Insert | Graphics | Chart (or double-click an existing chart).

2. Choose Data | Import.

3. Select Spreadsheet from the Data Type drop-down list.

4. Specify the path and filename of the file that contains the data you want to import.

5. Specify the data range or range name you want to import and then click OK.

? I can't find an Organization Chart command anywhere on the WordPerfect menus. How do I create an organization chart?

WordPerfect does not have an Organization Chart command, but Presentations does. You can use Presentations to create an

organization chart, like the one in Figure 9-9, without leaving
WordPerfect. Here's how:

1. Choose Insert | Graphics | Draw Picture to open a Presentations
   drawing window.

2. Choose Insert | Organization Chart and then click inside the
   graphics box to create a chart that will fill the window.

3. Select a predefined chart style and then click OK.

4. Choose Edit | Select | All. Then choose Format | Box Fields. Add,
   delete, move, and rename the assigned fields for each position, as
   necessary.

5. Double-click each placeholder label in the boxes and then type
   your own information.

6. When you finish filling out and editing the chart, click outside the
   chart to return to the document.

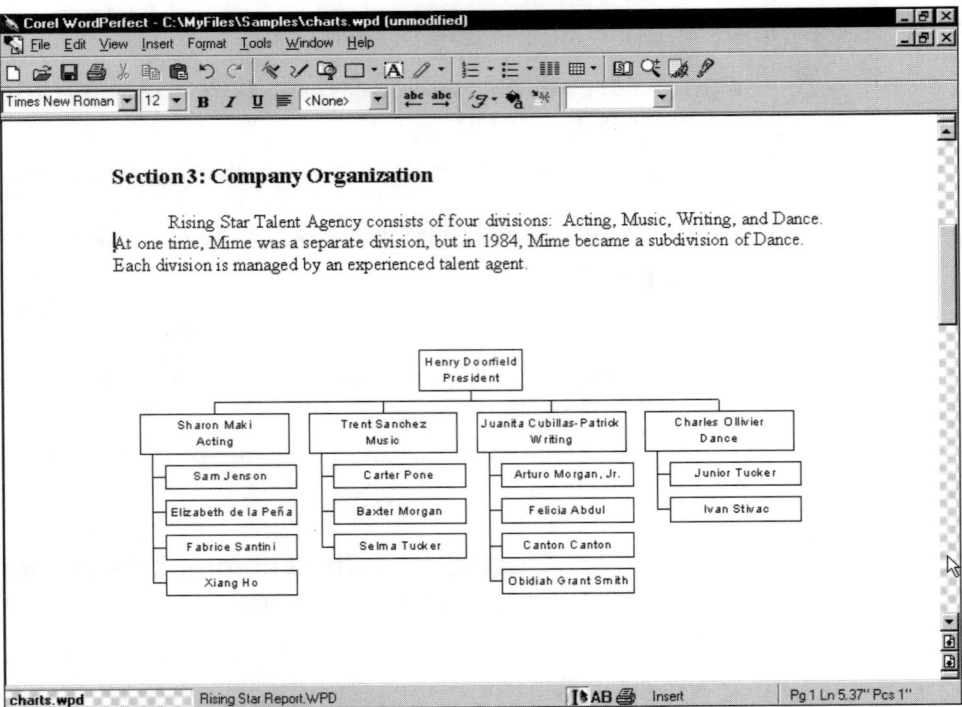

Figure 9-9.   You can create an organization chart in WordPerfect via Presentations

Tip: *You can save time by pressing* TAB *or* DOWN ARROW *to move from one field to another and from box to box while you are editing information inside a box. As you fill in the organization chart, you can right-click it to use editing options from the QuickMenu.*

Note: *If you've typed your organization structure in a WordPerfect outline, you can use that outline to create your organization chart. First, save the outline as a separate document. Follow steps 1 through 3 listed here. Then choose Chart | Import Outline and double-click the outline you saved.*

EQUATIONS

I created an equation in WordPerfect 8 and gave it to a colleague who uses WordPerfect 6.1—but my colleague can't edit the equation. What's wrong?

WordPerfect 8 includes two Equation Editors: the new WordPerfect 8 Equation Editor, and the old Equation Editor used in versions 5.1 through 7. When you create an equation, the new Equation Editor is used by default. However, if you want to edit equations using previous WordPerfect versions, you should use the old Equation Editor.

Here's how to select the Equation Editor for WordPerfect 5.1 to 7:

1. Choose Tools | Settings and then double-click Environment.

2. Click the Graphics tab, select WordPerfect 5.1 to 7 Equation Editor, and click OK. Then click Close.

Note: *If you choose Insert | Graphics | Custom Box and choose either Equation or Inline Equation, the old Equation Editor will be launched even though the new one is selected by default.*

None of the functions I used in the old Equation Editor work in the new Equation Editor. How do I use the new Equation Editor?

If you type any of the old functions such as SUPR or FUNC in the new Equation Editor, the characters will be inserted, and that's all. The WordPerfect 8 Equation Editor lets you create equations by inserting templates and filling in their slots. It provides about 120 templates, including templates for fractions, radicals, sums integrals, products, matrices, and various types of brackets and braces. You can also insert templates into the slots of other templates to build complex hierarchical formulas.

When you open the new Equation Editor, the symbol and template palettes appear just under the menu bar, as shown in Figure 9-10.

To use the Equation Editor, follow these steps:

1. Choose Insert | Equation.

2. Type text or insert symbols and templates to build your equation.

3. When you're done, choose File | Exit and Return to *Document*.

Tip: *For information on inserting symbols and templates, choose Help | Help Contents and find the About Inserting Symbols and Templates topic. You can then click each symbol on the palette to read a description.*

? When I type text in the new Equation Editor, some text is italicized and some text isn't. Why?

The Equation Editor automatically sizes, spaces, and positions symbols, although you can perform manual adjustments if desired.

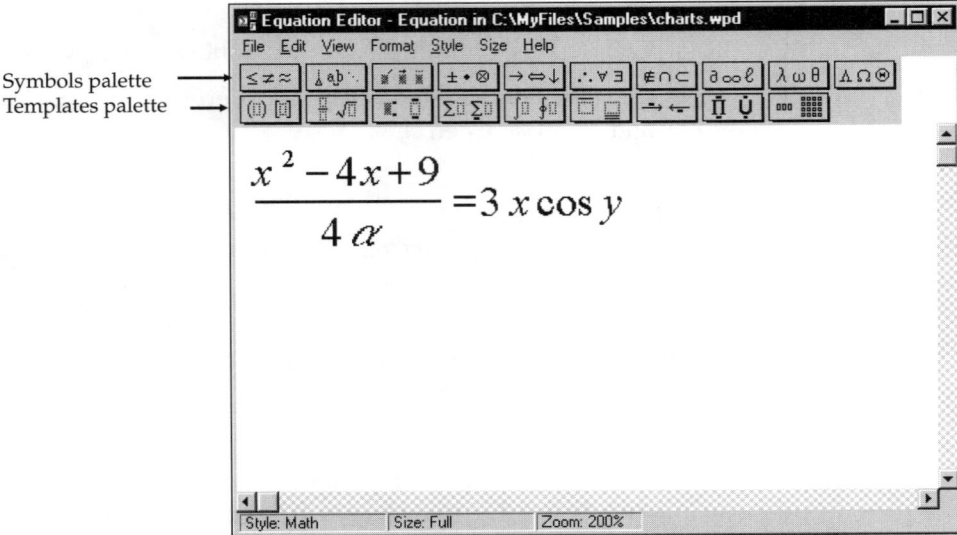

Figure 9-10. The new Equation Editor provides templates for creating equations

For example, radicals and parentheses automatically expand or contract to fit their contents, subscripts and superscripts appear in reduced size, and appropriately sized spaces are inserted around mathematical operators and relational symbols.

The Equation Editor also recognizes standard mathematical abbreviations such as log, cos, and sin, and sets them in the appropriate typeface. For example, if you type **xcosy**, the Equation Editor italicizes x and y, but not cos (*xcosy*), and it inserts thick spaces before and after the cosine function.

Tips on Using the New Equation Editor

Here are some tips that will help you build equations in the new Equation Editor:

⇨   You can use CTRL key shortcuts for inserting some templates. For example, pressing CTRL-F inserts a fraction template. See the "Keyboard" section of the Equation Editor Help for more information.

⇨   You can use the CTRL key to nudge a part of the equation that you want to reposition. Select the character or symbol, hold down CTRL, and then press an arrow key to nudge the item any direction.

⇨   If you want to add or remove italics or make other font changes, select the text and then click Style | Other.

⇨   If you press the SHIFT key as you move the cursor using the LEFT ARROW and RIGHT ARROW keys, the insertion point selects whatever items it passes through as it moves. If the item to the left of the insertion point is a template, you can select it by pressing BACKSPACE. Press BACKSPACE again to delete it.

⇨   Immediately after typing, you can choose Edit | Undo Typing to erase everything that you typed since the last nontyping operation.

⇨   You can select the style of formula you want from the Style menu. For example, if you want to insert Greek characters, choose Style | Greek. After you do so, typing the letter "a" inserts the alpha character (α), typing the letter "b" inserts the beta character (β), and so on.

⇨   Choose View | Redraw to clean up the display of the equation.

? When I press the spacebar in the new Equation Editor, my computer beeps. How do I insert a space?

You cannot press the spacebar to insert a space. Instead, select an option from the second symbol palette from the left.

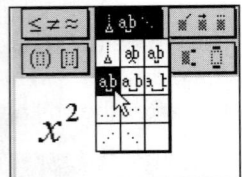

? When I try to start the new Equation Editor, the message "Mathtype is not installed" appears. What's wrong?

Sometimes the Equation Editor is not properly registered in the Windows registry. Corel suggests that you try the following, which may or may not work:

1. Click Start on the taskbar and then choose Find | Files or Folders.

2. Search for the file named EqnEdt32.exe.

3. When the file appears, double-click it.

An hourglass should briefly appear. Then the new Equation Editor should start from within WordPerfect.

? When I copy an equation from WordPerfect to another application, the equation is jumbled. How can I correct this problem?

If you used the old Equation Editor to create the equation, you may not be able to copy the equation to other applications because of the way WordPerfect places information on the Windows clipboard. If you want to share equations among other applications, you should use the new Equation Editor.

SCANNING IMAGES

Using a Scanner

When you *scan* an image, you run a printed document through your printer and end up with either a graphic file, which you can save in .WPG or .BMP format, or a text file. You can scan text only if you have optical character recognition (OCR) software, which scans a hard-copy page of text and creates a text file. OCR software is usually bundled with your scanner—WordPerfect does not include OCR software.

Twain is an industry standard supported on Windows and Macintosh platforms. It provides consistent, easy integration of image data between raster input devices (such as scanners and digital cameras) and software applications. WordPerfect is Twain-compatible, which means that you can access the scanning software directly from WordPerfect—by choosing Insert | Graphics | Acquire Image.

Just as each printer has its own printer driver, each scanner has its own scanning software. Scanning software is developed by the manufacturer of the scanner itself. The nice thing about this for us writers is that when there are problems, we can wash our hands and say, "For more information, consult your scanner documentation"—but I'll try to help as much as I can.

? I scanned my logo to create a graphic file, but the message "Invalid file format" appears when I try to insert it into a document. What's wrong?

Check the file format. Most TIF formats work in WordPerfect, but not all. Scan the image again or resave it in .PCX or .BMP format.

? The Acquire Image command does not appear on the Graphics menu. Why not?

First, make sure you have a scanner with scanner software. If you don't have a scanner, the Acquire Image command will not appear when you click Insert | Graphics. If you have installed scanner software on your hard drive, your drivers may not be up to date. If the current Twain code is an older version, WordPerfect will not be able to interface with the scanning device.

WordPerfect will update these files only if you run a Custom installation—a Typical installation won't let you update the Twain files. If you don't have Twain drivers already installed, no action will be taken by the Setup program. If you run a Custom installation and the Acquire Image command still does not appear, make sure your hard drive contains the right Twain files in the right folders. Here's what to look for:

⇨ When the proprietary scanning software is installed, the Win.ini file will include a [TWAIN] section with a path statement for the source files. Check this path statement and verify that the directory exists and contains the scanning files:

```
Default Source=c:\windows\twain\*.ds and other files
```

⇨ Twain Version 1.6.0.1 must be installed in the Windows directory. The following supplemental files must be present on your hard drive:

Twain.dll	86 kb	9/15/95 10:56 AM
Twain_32.dll	76 kb	9/15/95 10:56 AM
Twunk_16.exe	48 kb	9/15/95 10:51 AM
Twunk_32.exe	68 kb	9/15/95 10:51 AM

If you have the wrong versions of these files, copy the correct files from the Corel\AppMan\Wkswpi8 folder on your Corel WordPerfect Suite 8 CD.

⇨ There must be a data source (*.ds) file located in the Twain (or Twain_32) folder, which is in your Windows folder. The scanning software that was originally installed will build a Twain subfolder and install the (*.ds) file.

⇨ MSVCRT20.dll 248K 7/11/95 9:50 AM should be located in the Windows system folder. This file should have been installed by Windows 95. A copy of the file is located in the Corel\AppMan\Wkswpi8 folder on your Corel WordPerfect Suite 8 CD.

⇨ *VSHAR should be active in the Windows environment. To make sure, click Start on the taskbar, choose Run, type **sysedit,** and press ENTER. Click the System.ini window and then scroll down until you find the 386 Enhanced section. In this section, you should find a line for *VSHAR that looks like the following:

```
[386ENH]
Dev=*VSHAR
```

If these files are present and you still can't use Acquire Image, you may not be able to scan from WordPerfect unless your scanning software is 32-bit software. Contact the manufacturer of your scanning software and upgrade to the 32-bit version of the software. Here are some Web sites of companies that create scanners:

www.brother.com (Brother)
www.canon.com (Canon)
www.epson.com/northamerica.html (Epson)
www.hp.com (Hewlett Packard)
www.logitech.com (Logitech)
www.mustek.com (Mustek)
www.caere.com (OmniPage)
www.visioneer.com (PaperPort)
www.xerox.com/xis/tbpro96win (Textbridge)
www.tamarack.net (Tamarack Technologies)
www.twain.org (Twain Software)
www.umax.com (Umax)

? The message "Scanning Software .exe not found" appeared when I tried to scan. What should I do?

If this message appears, reinstall your scanning software. Replace the Twain and Twunk files as described in the preceding Q&A.

? I installed a Tamarack Technologies 6000c scanner, but the Acquire Image command is not available. Why not?

When you use the Tamarack Technologies 6000c scanner, Acquire Image is not available. According to Tamarack customer support, to use Tamarack's Twain drivers, the application must reside directly below the root directory. This would require WordPerfect to be listed just below the root directory instead of where the installation program places it. You'll have to scan using your scanning software and then retrieve the scanned image into WordPerfect.

? When I try to scan, the message "Out of Memory" appears. What's wrong?

This message may appear when you click the Final button while trying to scan an image. You're probably using DeskScan version 2.3.1, which works fine with applications other than WordPerfect. This error also occurs with several other types of scanners and scanning software. If this error message appears, try some of these options:

⇨ Scan the image from Presentations and then save the image and insert it in WordPerfect.

⇨ Instead of choosing Insert | Graphics | Acquire Image, choose Insert | Graphics | Draw Picture. From the Presentations drawing program, choose Insert | Graphics | Acquire Image.

⇨ Reduce the scanning resolution to 150 dpi.

? I'm using a Visioneer PaperPort scanner. Why can't I use Acquire Image in WordPerfect to scan text?

The type of scanning software you are using determines whether you can scan text from within WordPerfect. Software such as Visioneer PaperPort with either OmniPage Lite or Textbridge Lite will not allow you to scan text from within WordPerfect. The reason is that neither PaperPort nor the OCR software registers any information in the Windows registry, nor is there a way to register WordPerfect with the OCR software.

As a result, you must scan through PaperPort and then drag the scanned text and drop it on the WordPerfect icon. At this point, the OCR software will convert the scanned information to text and place the text in your WordPerfect document.

? I'm using Visioneer PaperPort, but I don't see a link for WordPerfect 8 for Windows. What's wrong?

PaperPort does not support WordPerfect 8 at this time, though the company says it is planning to add a link in the future. If there is an icon (such as WordPad or ABC) that you don't need, you can edit it and set a link for WordPerfect 8. You must also specify the OCR software that will be used. To do this, right-click the unused icon and choose Preferences. In the Word Processor section, choose Browse and select WPWIN8.exe as the program.

? When I scan an image into WordPerfect 8 with DeskScan, the message "File appears to be corrupted" appears. What's wrong?

According to Corel, the graphic image just scanned is not corrupted. The problem may be the DeskScan software settings. A common misconception is that if an image is to be printed on a 600-dpi printer, it needs to be scanned at that same setting. However, this is not the case. Normally, scanning at 100 to 150 dpi is all that is necessary. Scanning at a higher resolution may produce a better-looking image, but the cost of the better-looking image is usually an enormously large graphic file, which must be stored in memory. This large graphic file is what is causing the error message.

Here are two ways to avoid this error message:

⇨ In the DeskScan software, choose Custom | Print Path and then change the setting to a lower number.

⇨ From WordPerfect, choose Insert | Graphics | Draw Picture. Then choose Insert | Graphics | Acquire Image. Because it is a graphics package, Presentations handles scanning differently from WordPerfect.

? My scanned document includes unwanted text boxes and paragraph styles. How can I fix this?

The scanning software is responsible for formatting the text and choosing a font. If your scanned document contains text boxes or paragraph styles, consult the manufacturer of the scanning software.

? I scanned my signature to place it in form letters, but it doesn't look real. How can I keep the signature from looking grainy?

Besides the obvious solution of selecting the highest resolution possible, you can write your signature very large on a sheet of paper and then scan it. A large scanned signature provides better resolution when it's sized down. Here are some other tips for scanning your signature:

⇨ Scan the signature in one color (black on white).

⇨ Save the scanned image using a common graphics type, such as .WPG or a .BMP.

⇨   When you insert the image in WordPerfect, attach it as a character by right-clicking the image and choosing Position. Select Character from the Attach Box To drop-down list and click OK. This ensures that the graphic will stay in the letter closing instead of moving to somewhere else on the page.

⇨   If you plan on using the signature repeatedly, you may want to insert it in a style.

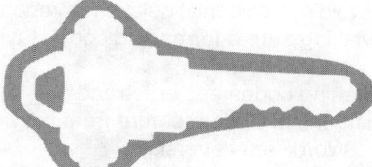

chapter

10 Answers!

Special Features

Answer Topics!

Special Features @ a Glance

⇨ WordPerfect can access several thousand characters, such as typographic symbols and letters in foreign alphabets. Consult this chapter when you want to insert a character in your document that you can't find among the few dozen keys on your keyboard.

⇨ You can insert the date in your document and then have WordPerfect automatically update it whenever the document is opened or printed. You can choose among several date formats—and if you can't find the right date format, you can create your own. Turn to this chapter if you have questions about the procedures for inserting the date.

⇨ Reveal Codes is one of the most powerful troubleshooting features in WordPerfect. When the formatting in your document doesn't look right, you can turn on Reveal Codes to see exactly how the document is formatted. You can then easily delete, move, and edit formatting. For tips on making the most of this feature, read this chapter.

⇨ You may have noticed that certain changes are made while you type. The QuickCorrect feature automatically corrects common typing mistakes and cleans up formatting. For example, QuickCorrect changes "teh" to "the" and deletes extra spaces after a period, fixes capitalization errors (such as "CAlifornia"), and replaces certain key combinations with symbols (such as © and ®) while you type. QuickCorrect also replaces straight quotation marks with curly opening and closing quotation marks. If you have problems using QuickCorrect, turn to this chapter.

⇨ When you need to alphabetize a list of names or arrange rows in a table, the Sort feature helps you do the job. You can sort lines, paragraphs, table rows, parallel columns, and merge data files. This chapter helps you use the Sort feature effectively.

SYMBOLS AND SPECIAL CHARACTERS

? **The Symbols dialog box displays only empty boxes. How can I fix this problem?**

When you choose Insert | Symbol, special characters should appear in the Symbols dialog box, as shown in Figure 10-1. If the characters appear as empty boxes, either the WP Character TrueType fonts are not installed, or Windows 95 is not allowing the use of these fonts. To resolve the problem, you may need to remove and reinstall the WordPerfect fonts.

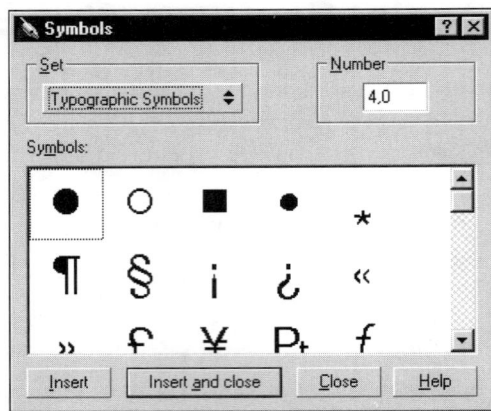

Figure 10-1.   The Symbols dialog box displays special characters you can insert in your documents

To reinstall the fonts, try any of the following procedures:

➪   Reinstall WordPerfect. The Typical installation will install the fonts automatically. If you select a Custom installation, make sure the TrueType fonts option has a gray check mark next to it, indicating that 43 of 1,055 fonts will be installed. If reinstalling the fonts doesn't work, remove the fonts and then run Setup again.

   *Tip: To remove fonts, click Start on the taskbar, choose Settings | Control Panel, and double-click Fonts. Select any fonts you don't need and then press* DELETE.

➪   Delete the WordPerfect fonts from the Fonts folder and then restore them from the Recycle Bin (double-click Recycle Bin, select all the WP fonts, and choose File | Restore). After you restart your computer, your fonts should work. If this doesn't correct the problem, you'll need to remove and then reinstall the fonts.

➪   Remove the fonts and then install them directly from the CD. Here's how:

   1. Make sure the Corel WordPerfect Suite 8 CD is in the CD-ROM drive.

   2. Click Start on the taskbar, choose Settings | Control Panel, and then double-click Fonts.

   3. Delete any font that starts with WP by clicking it and pressing DELETE.

4. Choose File | Install New Font.

5. Select your CD-ROM drive from the Drives drop-down list. Then switch to the Fonts folder (Corel\Appman\Wkswpi8\Fonts\Corelreq in WordPerfect 8 or Corel\Office7\Appman\Wksfiles\Fonts in WordPerfect 7).

6. Choose Select All or CTRL-click the fonts you want to install. Make sure the Copy Fonts to Fonts Folder option is selected and then click OK.

⇨ The Adobe Type Manager and the Adobe Type Manager Deluxe do not display TrueType fonts by default. The WordPerfect Character fonts are TrueType fonts. If you select the Display TrueType fonts option in Adobe Type Manager and restart Windows, you may fix the problem.

⇨ Windows 95 can store approximately 1,000 TrueType Fonts. The exact number of fonts varies depending on the font name and filenames. If the font names average 20 characters in length, Windows 95 will be able to install between 1,000 and 1,500 TrueType fonts. If you have too many fonts on your system, you may need to remove some to get the WordPerfect fonts to work.

? I'm using a French language module, but some of the language characters I insert show up as little boxes. What's wrong?

The selected character map doesn't include the characters you are using. To select a new character map, install a new language module for the language you want to use and then choose Tools | Language | Character Mapping. Character maps show which characters are mapped to a specific font. Select the character map for the language you are currently using and then click Apply. Character maps are listed only for the non-English language modules you have purchased.

 Note: *The character map is supplied by Windows. The characters vary depending on the font selected.*

? My other word processor lets me insert bullet characters from the Zapf Dingbats font. Can I do this in WordPerfect?

To insert special characters from another font in your document, you don't need to use the Symbols dialog box. You just select the font and type the character you need. If you plan on using this character often, you can insert it in a style. Here's how:

1. Choose Format | Styles and then choose Create.

2. Type a name for the style.

3. If you want to place the bullet within paragraphs, select Character (Paired) from the Type drop-down list and then select <None> from the Enter Key Will Chain To drop-down list.

4. Type the character representing the bullet in the font you selected and then select that character.

5. On the Styles menu bar, choose Format | Font, select the font (such as Zapf Dingbats) you want to use, and click OK.

? I need to distinguish the number zero (0) from the capital letter O, but I can't find a Ø character in the Symbols dialog box. How do I create a zero with a slash through it?

You can use the overstrike feature to create a zero with a slash or a number seven with a hyphen through it. Here's how:

1. Place the insertion point where you want the overstrike character to appear.

2. Choose Format | Typesetting | Overstrike.

3. Type the two characters (such as **0** and **/**) in any order and then click OK.

 *Tip:*   *If you plan on using one of these characters repeatedly, you may want to create a macro, a style, or a QuickWord abbreviation.*

? It takes me a long time to find the character I want in the Symbols dialog box. Is there a quick way to print the character sets?

Scrolling through the characters in the Symbols dialog box can be time consuming. You can open the CharMap.wpd file located in the C:\Corel\Suite8\Programs folder to see all the characters that will print on your printer. Then you can print a copy of the file for reference.

I need to type some documents in Spanish. Is there a quick way to insert the ñ and ¿ characters?

Some keystrokes have shortcuts assigned to them. For example, pressing CTRL-W and typing — inserts an em dash (—). To insert the ñ, you can press CTRL-W and type **n** followed by ~. However, even these shortcuts can be time consuming. You'll probably want to create macros for these keys and assign the macros to keystrokes in a Spanish keyboard you create. For example, you can create a keyboard that lets you press ALT-N to insert ñ, ALT-SHIFT-N to insert Ñ, and ALT-/ to insert ¿.

For information on assigning keystrokes to macros, see "Customizing the Keyboard" in Chapter 11.

Tip: *You can compose some characters by pressing* CTRL-W *and then typing two characters that make up a single international character. For instance, to insert the letter "u" with an umlaut (ü), press* CTRL-W, *type u", and press* ENTER. *To create an accented e (é), press* CTRL-W, *type e', and press* ENTER. *You can also create other characters in a similar fashion, such as ñ (n~), ç (c,), å(ao), and æ (ae).*

DATE/TIME

 I inserted a date in my document, but the date isn't updated when I open the document. What's wrong?

You probably inserted date text instead of a date code. Date text never changes. However, a date code displays and prints the current date each time you open or print the document. Here's how to insert a date code instead of date text:

1. Choose Insert | Date/Time.

2. Select the Automatic Update option.

3. Select the format you want and click OK.

Tip: *You can press* CTRL-D *to insert the date as text or* CTRL-SHIFT-D *to insert the date as a code that is updated.*

 **I want to insert the date in all caps, such as "FRIDAY, MAY 09, 1998," but this format isn't listed. Can I insert a date in this format without having to type it manually?**

You can to create a custom Date/Time format, as shown in Figure 10-2. Here's how:

1. Choose Insert | Date/Time and then choose New Format.

2. Delete the dates in the Edit Date/Time Format text box and then insert the Year, Month, Day, and Time codes with the appropriate punctuation and spacing in between.

Note: *The new formats appear at the top of the list. You can delete only custom formats.*

 **How can I change the Date/Time default setting so that pressing CTRL-D inserts my custom format?**

In WordPerfect 8, you can apply your custom Date/Time format to the Current Document Style. After you do so, pressing CTRL-D or

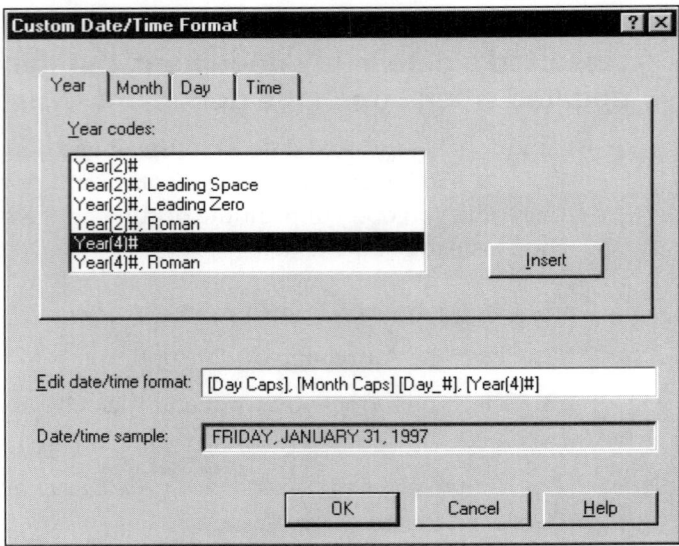

Figure 10-2.   You can create a custom Date/Time format

CTRL-SHIFT-D will insert the date in the format you specify. Here's what you do:

1. Choose File | Document | Current Document Style.

2. If you want this format to apply to all new documents you create, select the Use as Default check box.

3. From the dialog box menu bar, choose Insert | Date/Time.

4. Select the date format you want and then choose Apply Format.

5. Click OK and choose Yes to apply this format to new documents you create.

Note: *You can display the Date icon on the Applications bar by right-clicking the Applications bar and choosing Settings. Select Date and click OK. You can then insert the date by clicking this icon. The date will be inserted in the currently selected date format.*

❓ In a form letter I often use, I want to include a due date that is 10 days from the current date. How can I set this up so the due date is calculated and inserted automatically?

If you want the due date to appear in a paragraph, you can use a floating cell to achieve this effect. Here's how:

1. Place the insertion point where you want the due date to appear.

2. Choose Insert | Table, select Floating Cell, and choose Create.

3. Click the Edit Formula text box to the right of the check mark and type the following:

```
DateText(DateValue(Date())+10)
```

4. Click the check mark next to the Edit Formula text box to insert the formula and then choose Close.

Tip: *To use a different number type, choose Table from the property bar. Then choose Numeric Format and select Date/Time. Choose Custom and select a format from the Date/Time Formats drop-down list.*

REVEAL CODES

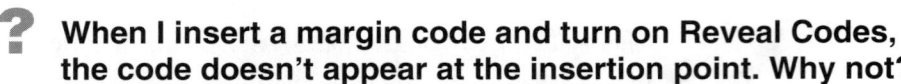

When I insert a margin code and turn on Reveal Codes, the code doesn't appear at the insertion point. Why not?

WordPerfect places certain codes at the top of a paragraph or page that contains the insertion point, depending on the feature. For example, when you change margins, line spacing, or tab settings, the codes are placed at the beginning of the paragraph that contains the insertion point.

When you use some features, existing codes change or are replaced by other codes. For example, if you change the left margin, click somewhere else in the same paragraph, and then change the margin again, only one margin code will appear: the second one. Changing the margin code back to 1 inch (the default) will remove the margin code.

Note: *In previous versions of WordPerfect, you could turn off Auto Code Placement. However, you cannot turn off this feature in WordPerfect 7 and 8.*

I know my document contains a code, but I can't see it in Reveal Codes. Where did it go?

Some codes are embedded within other codes. For example, if you turn on the Heading 2 style and then want to delete the Bold On code, you won't be able to see the code because it's part of the Heading 2 style code. Style and Delay Code codes are the most common types of codes that embed other codes.

You can expand a code to view the codes embedded in it. To do this, choose View | Reveal Codes and then click the code. If you see the code you're looking for, double-click it to edit it. If you can't find the code you're looking for but you can find a Delay Code, double-click the Delay Code, and you'll probably find what you're looking for.

Tip: *To delete a code, choose View | Reveal Codes. Place the insertion point on the immediate left or right of the code you want to delete. Press* DELETE *to delete the code to the right of the insertion point, or press* BACKSPACE *to delete the code to the left of the insertion point. You can also delete a code by dragging it out of the Reveal Codes window using your mouse.*

 **On more than one occasion, I accidentally deleted important codes. How can I prevent this from occurring?**

Choose Edit | Undo immediately after you delete the code. If you want to be prompted whenever you try to delete a code, follow these steps:

1. Choose Tools | Settings and then double-click Environment.

2. Click the Prompts tab. Then select Confirm Deletion of Codes and Stop Insertion Point at Hidden Codes.

Tip: *To move codes, turn on Reveal Codes and then place the insertion point before the codes you want to move. Hold down* SHIFT *and press the* RIGHT ARROW *key until all the codes you want to move are selected. Press* CTRL-X, *move the insertion point where you want the codes to appear, and press* CTRL-V.

 I want a new page size to start on page 2, and I want to make sure that if I later edit the text, the page size code remains on page 2. How can I make sure a formatting code always stays on a certain page?

Use the Delay Codes feature to make sure a formatting code occurs on the page where you want it. This feature works great when you want graphics, watermarks, and headers and footers to appear on a specific page. Here's how to use Delay Codes:

1. Place the insertion point at the top of the document or after a hard page break.

2. Choose Format | Page | Delay Codes.

3. Type the number of pages you want to skip—for example, to always start the new page size on page 2, enter **1**—and then click OK.

4. Change the page size and any other formatting and then choose Close on the property bar.

Tip: *To edit the formatting changes, turn on Reveal Codes and double-click the Delay Codes code.*

I find the Reveal Codes difficult to read. How can I make the codes easier to read?

Follow these steps to edit the appearance of the codes in the Reveal Codes window:

1. Turn on Reveal Codes.

2. Right-click the Reveal Codes window and then choose Settings (choose Preferences in WordPerfect 7).

3. Select a different font face and size.

4. To change the colors, deselect the Use System Colors check box and then select different colors from the Text and Background pop-up palettes.

 I can't find the Initial Codes feature in WordPerfect 8. Where is it?

The Document Initial Codes and Preferences Initial Codes features in previous versions of WordPerfect are now combined into one feature: Current Document Style. You can add codes to the Current Document Style by choosing File | Document | Current Document Style. If you want your changes to appear in the current document only, make sure Use as Default is not selected. If you want your changes to affect new documents you create (similar to Preferences Initial Codes), select the Use as Default option.

QUICKCORRECT AND FORMAT-AS-YOU-GO

A Quick QuickCorrect Example

You may have noticed while you work in WordPerfect that some words appear to change magically while you type. If you haven't noticed this, type the following sentence in WordPerfect:

"i have used teh STarbinger(c program at work."

While you type, the QuickCorrect and QuickFormat-As-You-Go features change the sentence to "I have used the Starbinger© program at work." Straight quotation marks are converted to curly quotation marks, and all-too-common spelling errors are corrected on the fly.

QuickCorrect automatically changes 1/2 to the fraction character. How do I tell QuickCorrect to make the same changes for other fractions such as 1/4 and 1/8?

You can easily set QuickCorrect to create fractions or other characters, as shown in Figure 10-3.

Here's how to add words to the QuickCorrect list:

1. Choose Tools | QuickCorrect.

2. In the Replace text box, type the text you want to replace, such as **1/4**.

3. In the With text box, press CTRL-W and then select the character you want to substitute (fractions are found in the Typographic Symbols set). When you're done, choose Insert and Close.

4. Click Add Entry.

5. Repeat these steps to create QuickCorrect entries for any other fractions or symbols you use often and then click OK.

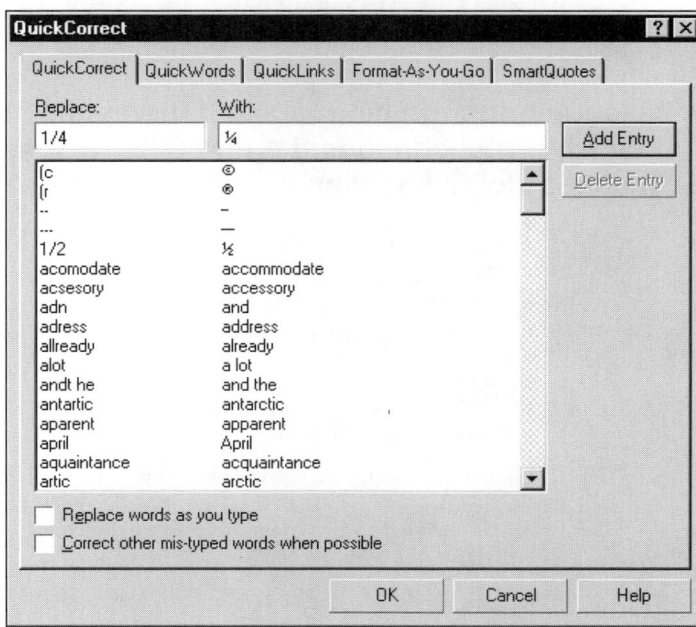

Figure 10-3.   You can use the QuickCorrect dialog box to tell WordPerfect to replace one word or character with another

? **Sometimes I want to use straight quotation marks instead of curly quotation marks. How do I do this without turning off SmartQuotes?**

When you type, the QuickCorrect feature uses SmartQuotes to add curly opening and closing quotation marks around text. When you type a number, however, instead of a closing quotation mark (such as 8"), QuickCorrect uses straight quotation marks, or primes (such as 8"), which are more appropriate for indicating inches, for example. When QuickCorrect makes a changes to your document that you don't like, you can "trick" it into doing the right thing. For instance, if you want to end up with ("), you can type **(3")** and then go back and delete the 3. This is easier than hunting for the " character in the Symbols dialog box. Remember, though, that if you press the spacebar again after you delete the dummy number, the curly quotation mark will reappear.

? **I want to use different quotation marks than the ones inserted by QuickCorrect. How do I change them?**

This is much easier than it was in previous versions of WordPerfect. Simply choose Tools | QuickCorrect, select the SmartQuotes tab and then select the types of quotation marks you want to use from the drop-down lists, as shown in Figure 10-4.

? **I write in foreign languages. It drives me nuts when WordPerfect changes the first letter in a sentence to a capital. How can I disable this feature?**

The Format-As-You-Go feature, shown in Figure 10-5, capitalizes the first word of a document and the first word after a period, question mark, or exclamation point.

Here's how to turn off the Format-As-You-Go capitalization feature:

1. Choose Tools | QuickCorrect and then click the Format-As-You-Go tab.

2. Deselect Capitalize Next Letter after End-of-Sentence Punctuation.

Tip: *After you type an abbreviated word such as "appt." or "dept." in the middle of the sentence, the next word will be capitalized automatically, unless the word is in the Exception List. To add abbreviated words to this list, click the Exceptions button on the Format-As-You-Go page of the QuickCorrect dialog box.*

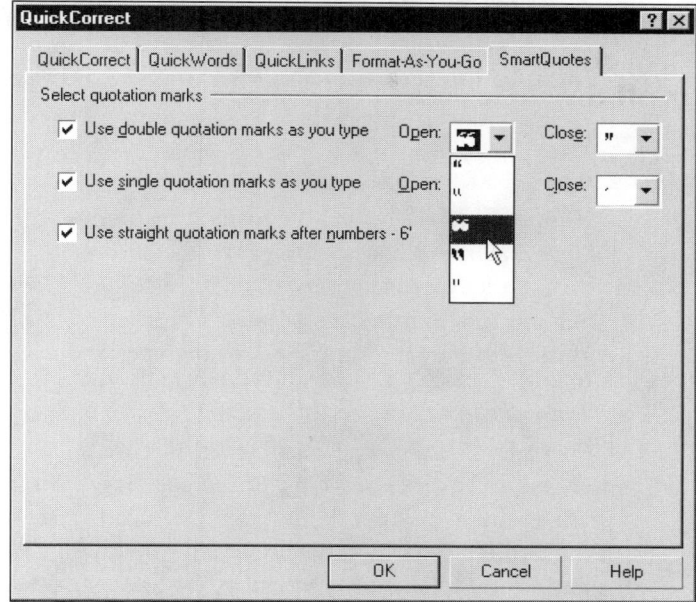

Figure 10-4.   Select the type of SmartQuote you want to use

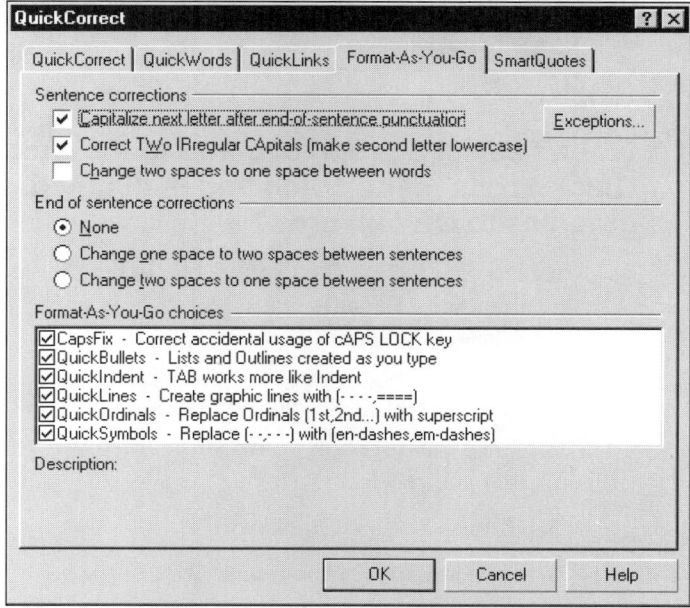

Figure 10-5.   You can select or turn off the Format-As-You-Go options

QuickCorrect versus QuickWords

Just for fun, let's suppose you're writing a paper on hydroxyl reactions, and you have to type the name "penta-*O*-acetyl-℈-D-glucopoyranose" repeatedly. You could use copy and paste, but each time you copy anything else, you'll have to copy the name again. A better approach is to use the QuickWords feature.

QuickWords is a slightly misleading term, because you can store more than words—you can store paragraphs, formatting, tables, and even graphics. All you have to do is select the item you want to repeat in your documents and then choose Tools | QuickWords. Type a name for the item (Corel recommends you precede it with a backslash, such as **\penta**, just in case you ever need to type **penta** by itself) and click Add Entry. The selection is turned into a QuickWord, which you can insert any time in your document.

You can also use QuickCorrect to expand abbreviations. However, QuickCorrect is primarily used to fix simple typing errors, such as changing "teh" to "the" or converting symbols, such as expanding (c) to ©. Unlike QuickWord abbreviations, QuickCorrect abbreviations cannot include formatting, tables, or graphics.

? When I select a graphic to add to the QuickWords list, the QuickWords menu command is dimmed. How do I add graphics to QuickWords?

Instead of selecting the graphic by clicking it, you need to select the graphic in the Reveal Codes. Here's how to add a graphic to the QuickWords list:

1. Choose View | Reveal Codes.

2. Place the insertion point before the graphics box code, hold down SHIFT, and select the text.

3. Choose Tools | QuickWords.

4. Type a name for the QuickWord entry, such as **\lettrhd**, and then click Add Entry.

? When I incorrectly type a contraction with CAPSLOCK turned on, QuickCorrect does not change some of my contractions properly. What's wrong?

You've found a little bug in the software. The CapsFix option in QuickCorrect works correctly only on contractions that do not involve the word "is." For example, if CAPSLOCK is turned on and you type "Can't," "I'm," or "We've" using the SHIFT key for the first letter (that is, if you forget that CAPSLOCK is active), these words will first appear on the screen as "cAN'T," "i'M," or "wE'VE." When you insert a space or press ENTER, however, QuickCorrect will correctly change these contractions to "Can't," "I'm," or "We've."

However, if you make the same typing mistake in a contraction involving the word "is," QuickCorrect will not correctly fix the letter after the apostrophe. For example, if you type "He's" as "hE'S" (because the CAPSLOCK is on), QuickCorrect will change the first part of the word correctly, but not the part after the apostrophe. In this case, you will end up with "He'S."

You'll have to fix this error manually, until the next release of WordPerfect.

? I work at home as well as in an office. Can I share the list of QuickCorrect words I use at work with my home computer?

QuickCorrect entries are stored in the file WT61US.uwl in the Windows folder. You can copy this file from you office computer and take it home, where you can copy it to the WT61US.uwl file in the Windows folder on your home computer. However, any words you added to your list at home will be lost.

 **Note:** *If you live outside the United States, your QuickCorrect file may have a slightly different name. For example, if you're from Wales, your QuickCorrect file is probably named WT61UK.uwl.*

? Can I convert my WordPerfect 6.1 QuickCorrect list to WordPerfect 8?

Yes. Here's how to convert your WordPerfect 6.1 QuickCorrect list to WordPerfect 8:

1. For backup purposes, rename the existing WordPerfect QuickCorrect file (WT61*XX*.uwl, where *XX* represents the language you're using). This file is located in the Windows folder.

2. Copy the WordPerfect 6.1 QuickCorrect file (such as WTSPELUS.qcs) to the Windows folder and then rename it with the same name as your previous QuickCorrect file, such as WT61US.uwl.

Warning: *Any changes you made to the QuickCorrect list, Speller dictionary, or Grammatik in WordPerfect 8 will be lost when you copy WT61US.uwl over the WordPerfect 8 file.*

Sometimes when I choose Tools | QuickCorrect, all of the settings are disabled. Why does this happen?

You probably have a macro or a merge document running. Because WordPerfect doesn't recognize the SmartQuotes inserted by QuickCorrect in macro or merge documents, QuickCorrect is automatically disabled when you're working on these documents. That way, you don't have to worry about turning QuickCorrect on and off. However, your QuickCorrect settings are also disabled for any other document you have open at the time. You may want to close your macro and merge documents to work on these other documents.

If you don't have a macro or a merge document open, QuickCorrect may be turned off because an open document is corrupted. In this case, select the contents of the corrupted file, copy and paste it to a new blank document, and then delete the corrupt document. This should solve the problem.

SORTING LISTS

Sort Terms You Should Know

You can sort five types of data: lines, paragraphs, merge data files, parallel columns, and table rows. Each item you sort is called a *record*, and each part of the record is called a *field*. For example, a table row is a record, and a cell within a row is a field.

In line and paragraph sorts, fields are separated by tabs or indents. Words are separated by spaces, forward slashes (/), and hyphen characters. For example, the date 8/24/98 is actually three words.

The regular hyphen is not treated as a word separator. If you want a hyphen to separate words, press CTRL-HYPHEN.

You can sort *alphanumerically* or *numerically*. Alphanumeric sorts are used primarily for text such as names and addresses. Numeric sorts are used to order numbers. To place numbers in the correct order, you must use the Numeric option. Otherwise, numbers will be sorted according to the first digit, such as 123, 2, 34, 446, 5. A numeric sort would place them in the correct order: 2, 5, 34, 123, 446.

The *key* determines the order in which paragraphs are sorted. You may want to use several keys when sorting. For example, if you are sorting a list of names, the first key may be the last name, and the second key may be the first name. The names are first sorted by last names, and if last names are identical, the names are sorted by the first names.

? The Sort dialog box provides options only for merge operations based on the first word. How do I sort a merge data file by zip code?

You need to create a new sort definition. Merge records consist of fields. Each field contains one or more lines, and each line is made up of words. The sort definition you create needs to specify the Zip Code field. Open your data file and determine the field number for the zip code. Here's how to set up the definition:

1. Open the data file and choose Tools | Sort | New.

2. Type a sort description, such as **Merge by Zip Code**.

3. In the Field text box, select Merge Record.

4. Specify the field number (such as 4) of the Zip Code field.

5. If the zip code is included with other data, such as the city and state, type **-1** in the Word list.

6. Click OK and then choose Sort.

Tip: *You can also select records from the data file so that only data records that match a certain criterion are extracted. For example, you can extract from your data file only those records that include people named Smith who live in Tennessee. To extract records, specify the criteria in the Extract Records text box when creating the sort definition.*

? My table contains dates in MM/DD/YY format. I want to sort the dates in descending order, but I can't make the Sort feature work correctly. What am I doing wrong?

WordPerfect's Sort feature recognizes the forward slash as a word separator, so when you sort dates in the MM/DD/YY format, you're actually sorting three words. To sort these dates correctly, you need to set up three sort keys: one for the month, one for the date, and one for the year. To sort dates correctly, the first key needs to sort according to the year, the second key according to the month, and the third key according to the day, as shown in Figure 10-6.

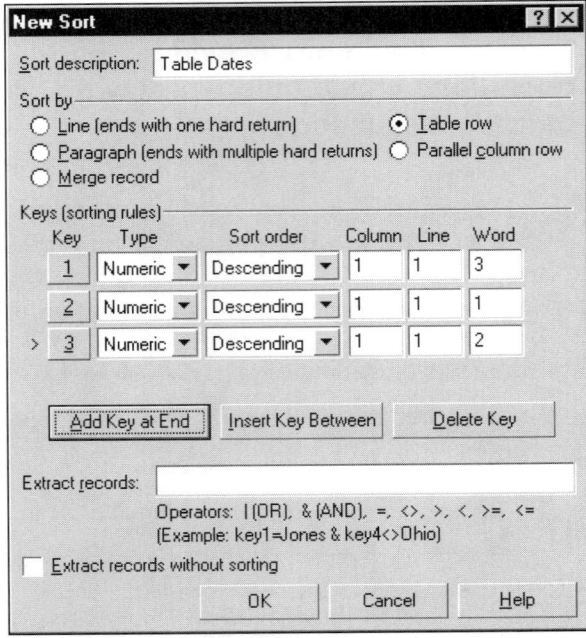

Figure 10-6.   You can set up sort keys to sort dates

Here's how to set up this sort operation:

1. Place the insertion point in the table or select the rows containing dates.

2. Choose Tools | Sort | New.

3. Type a name for the sort definition, such as **Table Dates**.

4. Click Add Key at End twice. Then format the three sort keys as shown in Figure 10-6. Make sure you select Numeric from the Type drop-down list for all three keys.

5. To sort the dates in descending order (newest to oldest) instead of ascending order (oldest to newest), select Descending from the Sort Order pop-up button for all three keys.

6. If your dates are in a table, make sure the Column text boxes contain the appropriate column number. For example, if the dates are in the second column of the table, type **2** in all the Column text boxes.

7. After you've set up the sort keys, click OK and then click Sort.

When I tried to sort a table, the message "Record Exceeds 9K Sort Limit" appeared. How do I get around this 9K limit?

First, make sure the insertion point is in the table when you sort. You may still see this error message if you try to sort too many table rows or tables whose cells contain large formulas or other formatting, such as font changes, text boxes, or graphic images, that may cause the cell size to exceed 9K. To sort, you may have to remove the formatting and formulas.

Tip: To remove formulas, select the table, press DELETE, choose Formulas Only, and click OK.

When I sort labels, some of the text in one label spills over into other labels, and everything gets messed up. How do I sort labels?

When sorting labels, make sure that your labels are separated by hard page breaks instead of several hard returns—hard returns cause the labels to get jumbled in the sort. Then use a paragraph sort to sort labels.

? **My table column contains rows of names (such as Jeremy Carter and Sharon Dee Fowler), but some people have middle names. How do I sort this table by last names?**

If some of your names have middle names while others don't, you can't sort by typing **2** in the Word box, or some names will be sorted by the middle name instead of the last name. For example, Jeremy Carter and Sharon Dee Fowler would be sorted by Carter and Dee. Instead, use negative numbers to count from right to left. Typing **-1** in the Word box sorts by the last word in the line, typing **-2** sorts by the second-to-the-last word, and so on. If you type **-1** in the Word box, Jeremy Carter and Sharon Dee Fowler will be sorted by Carter and Fowler.

? **When I sort names such as Antonio Witherspoon, Jr., they sort by "Jr." instead of "Witherspoon." How do I sort these types of names correctly?**

Those little modifiers such as Jr., M.D., and Ph.D. can really mess up a sort. However, by doing a little touch-up work before the sort, you can solve this problem. Before you sort the list, replace the space between the last name and the description with a hard space, made by pressing CTRL-spacebar. For example, you would delete the space between "Witherspoon," and "Jr." and then press CTRL-spacebar. After you do so, WordPerfect will treat the last name and modifier as if it were one word, and the list will be sorted correctly.

? **I have a list of names, job titles, and starting dates in tabular columns. Why can't I successfully sort the list by job titles or dates?**

Turn on Reveal Codes to see if there is more than one tab code between columns. If you have pressed TAB more than once to line up the data, WordPerfect will read these extra tabs as fields. Go back and set one tab stop for each column, remove the extra tabs, and then try the sort again.

? When I sort paragraphs formatted with hanging indents, the paragraphs sort incorrectly. Is it possible to sort paragraphs with hanging indents?

When you use a hanging indent, WordPerfect inserts an indent code followed by a margin release code. These two codes are considered to be fields in a sort. Thus, you need to sort by field 3 instead of field 1. Here's how to create a sort definition:

1. Select the text you want to sort.

2. Choose Tools | Sort | New.

3. Type a sort description (such as **hanging indent**) and then select Line.

4. Type **3** under Field in Key 1. Click OK and then click Sort.

Customizing WordPerfect

Answer Topics!

Customizing WordPerfect
@ a Glance

⇨ Do you need to use points instead of inches when positioning graphics? Would you like to add the date and time to the application bar? In WordPerfect, you can customize the settings to suit your needs—and if you run into any problems, you can turn to this chapter.

⇨ WordPerfect includes a dozen or so toolbars to help you get your work done. However, if these toolbars don't contain a particular feature that you use often, don't worry. You can add any feature, macro, or application to any toolbar in WordPerfect, and you can even create entire new keyboards with your favorite stuff. This chapter will help you customize the toolbars.

⇨ If you want to run a macro or open a certain dialog box with a quick keystroke, you can edit your keyboard to suit your needs. Consult this chapter if you need help.

CHANGING WORDPERFECT SETTINGS

? I need to use centimeters instead of inches. How do I change the dialog boxes to accept different measurements?

If you just want to use centimeters for a certain document, you can type the number of centimeters followed by "cm." For example, to change the left margin to 3 centimeters, you would type **3cm** in the Left text box. Table 11-1 lists the abbreviations you can type to insert different kinds of measurements.

If you want to change the measurements for the dialog boxes, Reveal Codes, application bar, and ruler, you use the Display Settings dialog box, shown in Figure 11-1, to change the units of measure in WordPerfect.

Here's how to change the default units in WordPerfect:

1. Choose Tools | Settings and then double-click Display.

2. From the Units of Measure drop-down list, select the unit of measure you want to use for dialog boxes and Reveal Codes.

Table 11-1. Units of Measure

Unit of measure	Abbreviation	Description
Inches	" or i	Inserts inch measurements (for example, you can type **8.5"** or **8.5i**)
Centimeters	cm	1/100th of a meter
Millimeters	mm	1/1,000th of a meter
Points	p	In WordPerfect, there are 72 points per inch, not 72.27 points per inch
1,200ths of an inch	w	600w equals 1/2 inch; this unit is useful for very small measurements

3. From the Application Bar/Ruler Display drop-down list, select the unit of measure you want to use for the application bar and ruler. Then click OK.

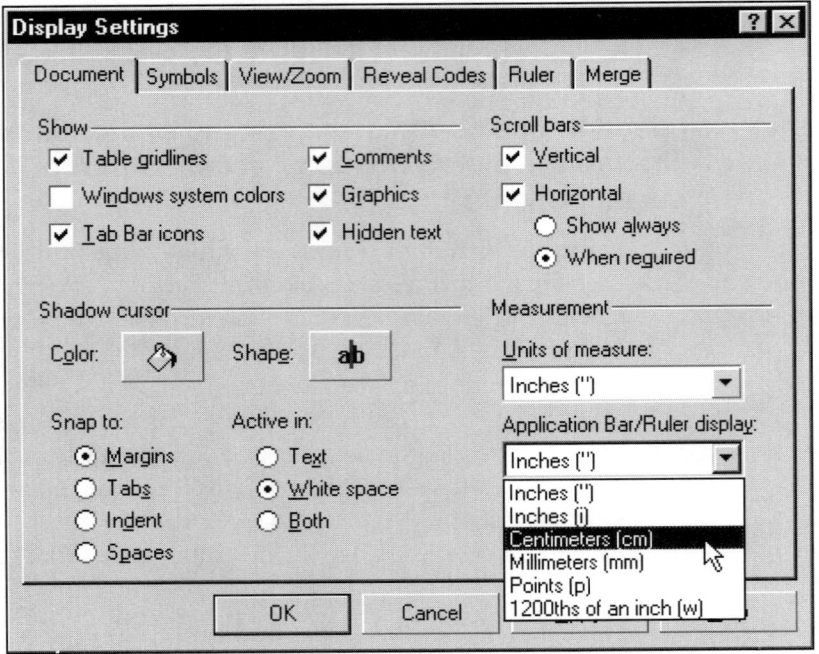

Figure 11-1. You can use the Display Settings dialog box to change the units WordPerfect uses by default

Note: *In case you're wondering, choosing Tools | Settings in WordPerfect 8 is the same as choosing Edit | Preferences in WordPerfect 7.*

The WordPerfect screen has too many bars and lines and cursors. How do I work on a simpler screen?

Some people like displaying the menu bar, a toolbar or two, the property bar, the ruler, vertical and horizontal scroll bars, the application bar, and anything else that will fit on the screen, including margin guidelines. Other people like to display the menu bar and the window to type in—and nothing else. You can customize WordPerfect's settings to suit your needs. Here are some options for changing the appearance of the WordPerfect screen:

⇨ Choose View | Toolbars and then select the items you want to display and deselect the items you want to hide. You can also right-click the toolbar and select any toolbar you want to display or hide.

⇨ To display or hide the scroll bars, choose Tools | Settings and then double-click Display. The Scroll Bars group contains a few options for displaying scroll bars. Select the scroll bars you want to display and then select either Show Always to display the selected scroll bars all the time or When Required to display the scroll bars only when you can scroll.

⇨ To turn off guidelines, choose View | Guidelines and then deselect the guidelines you want to turn off.

⇨ To turn off the shadow cursor, choose View | Shadow Cursor.

⇨ To hide all the bars at once and display a blank screen, choose View | Hide Bars (or press ALT-SHIFT-F5). This option is especially useful when you want to type text without much formatting. Press ESC when you want the bars to reappear.

Clicking the shadow cursor sometimes inserts tabs instead of centering the text. How can I prevent this?

When you hold the mouse pointer over a blank area in your document, the shadow cursor will appear as a bar with one or two arrows, depending on where you hold it. To center text, you click when the pointer appears as a two-headed arrow. If you prefer, you can change the settings so the pointer lets you insert left-aligned, centered, or right-aligned text. Here's how:

1. Choose Tools | Settings and then double-click Display.

2. Under Snap to, select Margins. Then click OK.

 Tip: *You can also change the color and shape of the shadow cursor. Choose Tools | Settings and then double-click Display. Select a color from the Color palette, a shape from the Shape palette, and then click OK.*

Microsoft Word's status bar shows whether I'm using Typeover or Insert mode. Can WordPerfect's application bar do the same thing?

You can add a number of items to your application bar, such as the typing mode and the date and time, as shown in Figure 11-2. If you turn on Insert Mode, you can click its button on the application bar to

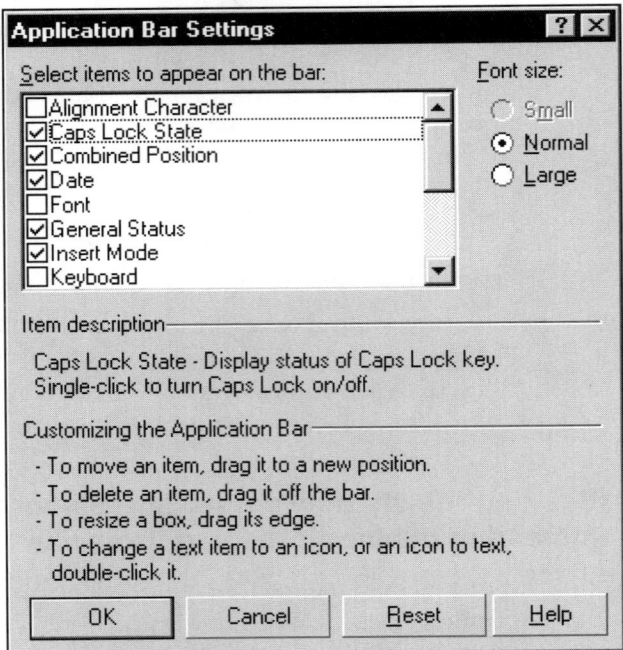

Figure 11-2.   You can add items to the application bar

toggle between Insert and Typeover modes. Here's how to edit your application bar:

1. Right-click the application bar and choose Settings.

2. Select the items you want on your application bar and then click OK.

 I added the Time feature to the application bar, but the time displayed is several minutes behind the time shown on the Windows taskbar. What's the problem?

When you hold the pointer over the Time icon on the application bar, the time displayed is updated only while the document window is being updated by either typing or mouse activity in the window. However, if the program just sits idle, the time will not change. The time will not be updated until you take another action in the application window. The time on the Windows taskbar, on the other hand, is constantly being updated.

Tip: Click the Date or Time item on the application bar to insert the correct date or time into your document.

Note: The Date format on the application bar depends on the format selected in the current document. If the Date format includes a date and time sequence, the time portion of the date will not be updated during that session of WordPerfect when you hold the pointer over the Date icon. However, the time will be updated if you click the Date icon to insert the current date and time in your document.

 **When I hold down BACKSPACE, text is deleted so quickly that I often delete more than I want. How do I slow down the repeat rate of a key?**

The repeat rate is determined by Windows settings. Here's how you can slow down the repeat rate:

1. Click Start on the taskbar and then choose Settings | Control Panel.

2. Double-click Keyboard and then move the Repeat Rate slider toward the slow end and click OK.

Tip: *You can also change Windows settings to control the speed of the mouse. In the Windows Control Panel, double-click Mouse and then look for an option that lets you adjust how fast your pointer moves.*

EDITING TOOLBARS AND MENUS

I want to add the Paste Special button to the toolbar, but I can't find it in the list of features. Where do I find the buttons I can add to the toolbar?

When adding buttons to the toolbar, a common mistake is not selecting the right menu from the Feature Categories drop-down list in the Toolbar Editor, shown in Figure 11-3. In the case of Paste Special, for example, you need to select Edit from the Feature Categories drop-down list; then Paste Simple will appear in the Features list.

Follow these steps to edit the WordPerfect 8 toolbar:

1. Right-click the toolbar and then choose Edit.

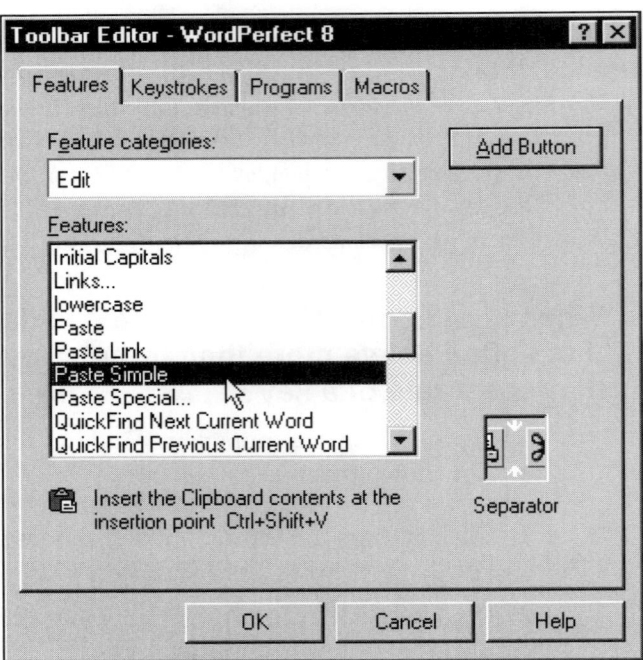

Figure 11-3.   Use the Toolbar Editor to add and remove buttons

2. Select the menu containing the feature you want to add from the Feature Categories drop-down list.

3. Drag the item from the Features list onto the toolbar where you want it to appear.

4. Click OK when you're done.

Tip: *While the Toolbar Editor is displayed, you can remove buttons by dragging them off the toolbar, or you can move them by dragging them to a new location.*

Note: *The number of buttons displayed on a toolbar depends on the size of the screen you are using. If you add more buttons than can be displayed at one time, click the Up or Down button at the right end of the toolbar to display the rest of the toolbar.*

Toolbar and Menu Ideas

The options that appear on the toolbars and menu bar are only the tip of the iceberg; these are only the most common options. You can customize WordPerfect to display many other useful options.

Here are a few examples of buried treasures you can add to your menu bar or toolbars:

⇨ The File feature category includes Close All, Print Page, and Save All.

⇨ The Edit feature category includes Append, Case Toggle, and Find Next, along with options for changing case and pasting in different ways.

⇨ The Format feature category includes Attribute Redline, Attribute Strikeout, Attribute Double Underline, and many other attributes that you may need to use often in certain documents.

Browse through the Toolbar Editor to find the options that will help you.

❓ How can I perform calculations in WordPerfect without using the Tables feature?

In addition to adding features and macros to your toolbars, you can also add other Windows programs, such as Calculator. If you want to add toolbar buttons to launch this or other programs that you use often while working in WordPerfect, here's how:

1. Right-click the toolbar and then choose Edit.

2. Select the Programs tab and then choose Add Program.

3. Browse through the folders to find the application you want and then double-click it. The Calculator program (Calc.exe), for example, is in the Windows folder.

4. Move the program button—in this case, the Calculator button—where you want it to appear and then click OK.

 *Tip:*   *Instead of editing the WordPerfect 8 toolbar, you may want to create another toolbar that you can display in place of—or below—the WordPerfect 8 toolbar. Right-click the WordPerfect toolbar and then choose Settings | Create. Type a name for the toolbar and click OK. You can add features, macros, applications, and anything else to this custom toolbar.*

❓ When I add a macro to the menus, it appears on the menu bar instead of on the Macros submenu. How do I place macros where I want them?

After you insert a macro on the menu bar, you need to drag it to the right location. Here are the steps:

1. Right-click the menu bar and then choose Settings.

2. Choose Edit, click the Macros tab, and choose Add Macro.

3. Double-click the macro you want to use and then click Yes to save the macro with the full path.

4. Click the Menu Editor and then drag the macro that appears on the menu bar to the menu where you want it to appear. Click OK and then click Close.

Tip: *If you want to change the description of the menu or menu item, open the Menu Editor dialog box and then double-click the menu or command. In the Menu Item text box, type the menu name you want to use. Type an ampersand (&) before the character you want to use as a hot key and then click OK.*

I use a letterhead document all the time. To open this file from the toolbar, do I need to create a macro?

No, you don't need to create a macro. Here's how you can place the file on the toolbar:

1. Right-click the toolbar and choose Edit.
2. Select the Programs tab and then choose Add Program.
3. Select WP Documents from the File Type drop-down list.
4. Double-click the file you want to open and then drag the file icon that appears on the toolbar to the location where you want it to appear. Click OK and then click Close.

Note: *If you add a file that does not have a .WPD extension, you will not be able to launch that document in WordPerfect unless the file's extension (such as .LTR or .TXT) has been associated with WordPerfect.*

I placed several macros on the toolbar, but the icons all look identical. How can I make the toolbar buttons I add distinctive?

You can use your drawing skills to edit the button, as shown in Figure 11-4.

Here's how to edit a toolbar button to customize it:

1. Right-click the toolbar and choose Edit.
2. Double-click the icon you want to edit and then choose Edit.
3. Click and right-click colors in the color palette. Then use the left and right mouse buttons to redraw the object.

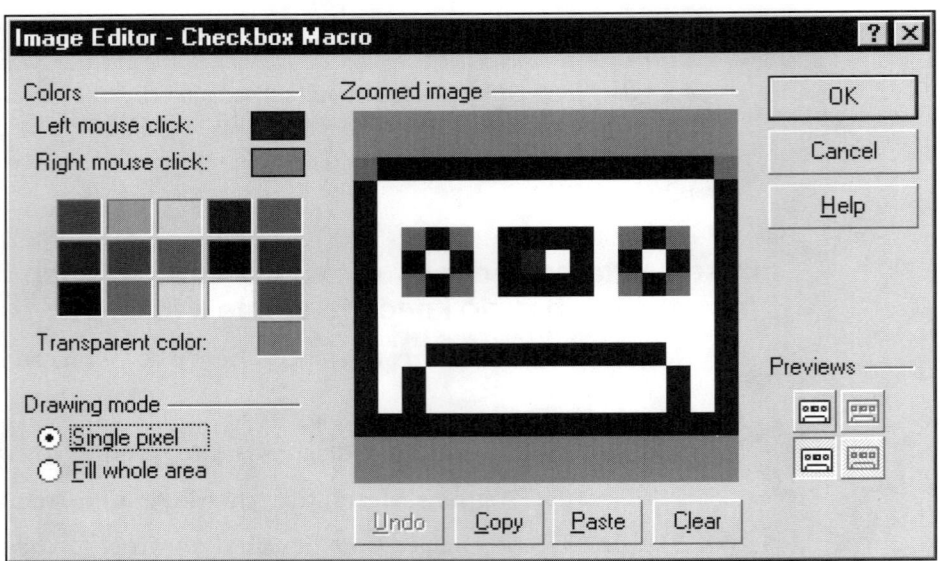

Figure 11-4.   Use the Image Editor to edit toolbar buttons

 *Tip:*   *If there is a bitmap icon you would prefer using, open that object in a program such as Paint, choose Edit | Select All, and copy the image. Open the Image Editor and choose Paste.*

When I hold the pointer over the toolbar, the hand never appears. How do I drag the toolbar to a new location?

Place the mouse pointer on the property bar or toolbar over one of the separator lines or at the end past any of the icons, and the pointer will change to a four-sided arrow. You can then drag the bar onto the document and create a palette out of it. You can also drag the toolbar or property bar to any side of the screen.

CUSTOMIZING THE KEYBOARD

❓ The Font Up and Font Down buttons are useful, but I don't want to click buttons on the toolbar. How do I assign these features to keystrokes?

Just as you can add features to toolbars, you can assign these same features to keystrokes, as keyboard shortcuts, as shown in Figure 11-5. For example, if you frequently use the Redline and Strikeout attributes, you can assign keystrokes to these attributes.

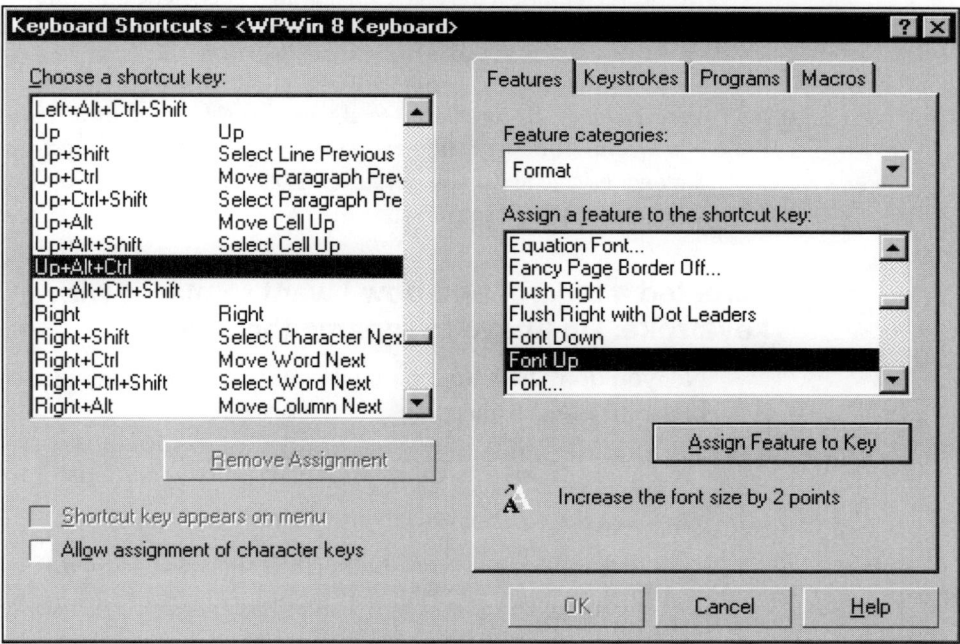

Figure 11-5. You can use the Keyboard Shortcuts dialog box to assign features to keystrokes

Here's how to assign features to keystrokes:

1. Choose Tools | Settings and then double-click Customize.

2. Click the Keyboards tab and then choose Edit.

3. Select an unassigned keystroke (such as UP-ALT-CTRL) in the Choose a Shortcut Key list box.

4. In the Feature Categories drop-down list, select the menu category (such as Format) you want to use.

5. In the list box, select the feature (such as Font Up) you want to assign to the keystroke and then choose Assign Feature to Key.

6. Repeat steps 4 and 5 to add other keystrokes and then click OK. Click Close twice to return to your document.

Warning: *Be careful not to assign keystrokes that are already assigned to other features. Be especially wary of using the ALT key in keystrokes, or you may not be able to display menus with keystrokes. Use the ALT key in combination with CTRL or SHIFT to be safe.*

? I created a macro, and now I want to play it with a keystroke. Do I have to rename the macro?

No, you don't have to rename the macro. Here's how to assign a macro to a keystroke:

1. Choose Tools | Settings and then double-click Customize.

2. Click the Keyboards tab and then choose Edit.

3. Click the Macros tab and then select an unassigned keystroke (such as R-ALT-SHIFT) in the Choose a Shortcut Key list box.

4. Choose Assign Macro to Key, double-click the macro you created, and choose Yes to save the macro with the full path.

5. Click OK. Then click Close twice to return to your document.

How do I create a keystroke that returns me to the insertion point's previous position?

One way to do this is to create a macro that takes you to the insertion point's previous position. While recording the macro, choose Edit | Go To and then double-click Last Position. You can then assign the macro to a keystroke as described in the preceding Q&A.

You can also create a keyboard script that accomplishes the same thing, as shown in Figure 11-6.

To create a keyboard script that returns the insertion point to its previous location, follow these steps:

1. Choose Tools | Settings and then double-click Customize.

2. Click the Keyboards tab and then choose Edit.

3. Select an unassigned keystroke (such as R-ALT-SHIFT) in the Choose a Shortcut Key list box.

4. Select the Keystrokes tab on the right side of the dialog box and then type the following:

   {Ctrl-G}{Alt-P}{Enter}

 **Note:**   *{Ctrl-G} displays the Go To dialog box, {Alt-P} selects Last Position, and {Enter} chooses OK.*

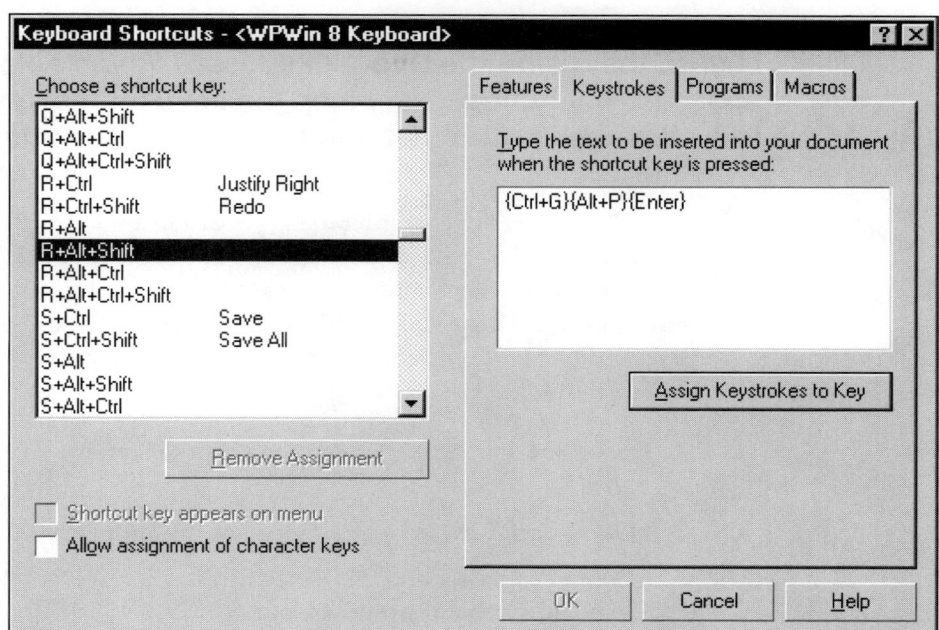

Figure 11-6.   You can create a keyboard script to perform keystrokes

5. Choose Assign Keystrokes to Key, click OK, and then click Close twice to return to your document.

Tip: *You can also create similar keyboard scripts to assign symbols and international characters to keystrokes.*

I selected the WordPerfect for DOS keyboard, but pressing F1 doesn't cancel a dialog box. Instead, a Help screen appears. What's wrong?

Whenever a menu or dialog box is displayed in WordPerfect, WordPerfect always uses the standard Windows keyboard (also called the Windows CUA keyboard), even if you've selected the DOS keyboard. This means that F1 displays a Help screen instead of canceling the dialog box. Even though you can map F1, ESC, and any other key to any function, menus and dialog boxes need to keep the original keystroke settings because they are handled by calls to Windows. You'll just have to press ESC to get out of dialog boxes like the rest of us.

I heard that using the Dvorak keyboard would help me to speed up my typing. Can I map the keys on the keyboard to a character set not defined as a standard keyboard in WordPerfect?

Sure—but instead of changing the keyboard just for WordPerfect, you'll have to change it for all Windows applications. I don't know if using the Dvorak keyboard will speed up your typing, but you can select it to give it a try. You can also select the United States-International keyboard using the same method. Here's how to select the Dvorak keyboard in Windows:

1. Click Start on the taskbar and then choose Settings | Control Panel.

2. Double-click Keyboard and then click the Language tab.

3. Choose Properties and then select United States-Dvorak from the Keyboard Layout drop-down list.

 ***Tip:***   *If you want your Windows applications to sort by the rules of a certain language, you can select that language in a similar fashion. In the Keyboard Properties dialog box, click the Language tab, choose Add, and select the language you want to use.*

Working with Large Documents

Answer Topics!

Working with Large Documents @ a Glance

⇨ Whenever a book or manual involves several writers, or whenever your document becomes so long that it's awkward to work with, you can use the Master Document feature to create individual documents, called *subdocuments*. Then when you need to work with the document as a whole, you can combine the small documents into one large file—a master document. You can edit subdocuments by themselves or as part of the master document. The tips in this chapter help make the Master Document feature easy to use.

⇨ With WordPerfect, footnotes and endnotes are easy to create—and they're also easy to edit, move, and renumber. Footnotes appear at the bottom of the page, and endnotes usually appear at the end of the document, though you can place endnotes elsewhere if you prefer. If you have problems using footnotes and endnotes, this chapter can help you.

⇨ Instead of retyping all your headings at the beginning of your document to create a table of contents, you can generate the table of contents by simply marking the headings in the document. If you used the WordPerfect heading styles, or if you created heading styles with table of contents markings, your headings will automatically be included in the table of contents. Turn to this chapter for help with this useful feature.

⇨ When creating manuals and other long documents, you may need to generate an index. You can mark text for an index in two ways: you can manually mark each occurrence of the index word in the document, or you can list the words and phrases in a concordance file. If these procedures sound tricky, consult this chapter.

MASTER DOCUMENTS

? **Several colleagues and I are writing a manual. We're each working on separate chapters. Is there an easy way to combine the documents without losing the ability to edit the chapters individually?**

If you are writing a manual, dissertation, book, or other long document, you can create a master document that groups all the chapters together. You can then edit the chapters individually or as a whole. Master documents also make it easy to consolidate the table of contents and index. When you print the master document, the page numbering will be sequential from one chapter to the next—you won't have to update the beginning page number of each chapter.

Master documents contain links to other documents, such as your chapter documents, as shown in Figure 12-1. In the context of the master document, the chapter documents are called subdocuments.

Assuming you have already created the chapters for your manual or book, here's how to create a master document:

1. In a new document, type the book title and add any preface material, including the table of contents definition. Press CTRL-ENTER to start a new page.

2. Choose File | Document | Subdocument, select the filename of the first chapter in your book, and choose Include.

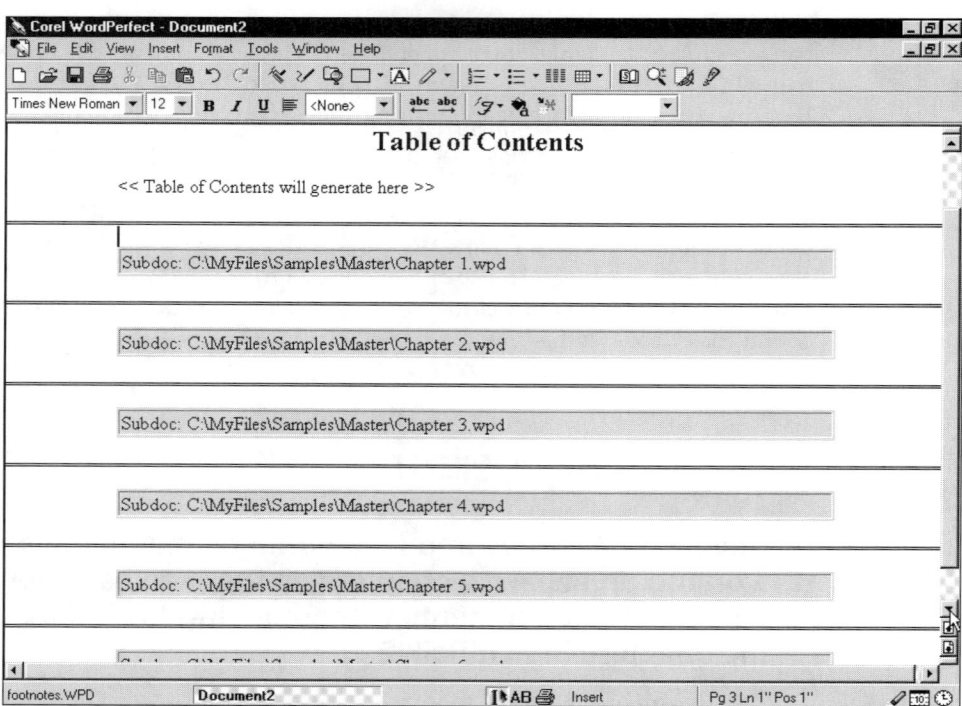

Figure 12-1.   A typical master document shown in Draft view

3. Press CTRL-ENTER to insert a hard page break so that the next chapter starts on a new page.

4. Repeat steps 2 and 3 for each succeeding chapter.

5. If your book will have an index, create an index page and then insert an index definition.

Note: *If any of your subdocuments contains an index definition, you should delete that generated index (and table of contents), including the definition codes. Otherwise, you'll end up with more than one index.*

6. Save the master document.

Note: *If you're using Draft view, your subdocument references will appear as comments. If you're using Page or Two Pages view, your subdocuments will appear as icons in the left margin.*

Tip: *To expand the master document so that all subdocuments are visible, choose File | Document | Expand Master (or double-click a subdocument reference). Then select the subdocuments you want to expand and click OK.*

If I make changes to the subdocument text in an expanded master document, will those changes appear in the subdocument itself?

Absolutely. You can continue to work on subdocuments individually, and these changes (if saved) will appear when you expand the master document. You can also edit the text in the master document. Whenever you try to save the document after you have made changes, you will be prompted to condense the master document. From there, you can select the subdocuments you want to save and condense, as shown in Figure 12-2. Each document is listed twice: once for saving and once for condensing.

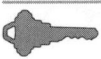

Warning: *If you edit a subdocument within the master document, make sure you condense and save the subdocument before closing the master document. Otherwise, you will have created a second version of the chapter.*

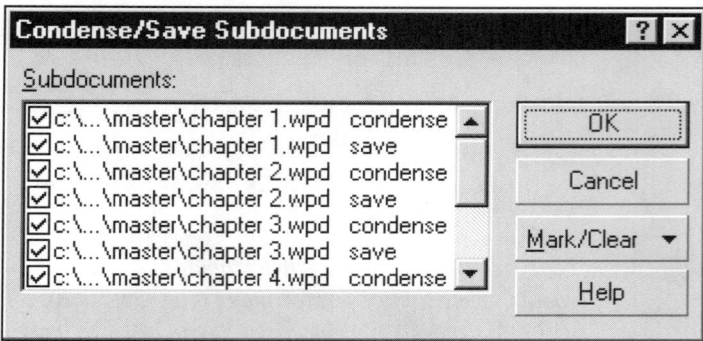

Figure 12-2.   You select the subdocuments to be saved and condensed

Tips on Using Master Documents

Want to make your master document work go more smoothly?
Here are some tips:

⇨ If you plan on creating several master documents, establish
naming conventions for your master documents and
subdocuments. For example, include MD in the master
document name and SUB in each subdocument name.

⇨ When generating master documents with large
subdocuments, you may want to turn off graphics (choose
View | Graphics) to speed things up.

⇨ You may want all your chapters to begin on odd-numbered
pages. To do this, either place a Force Page code in the chapter
heading style for each subdocument, or place a Force Page
code before each Subdocument code in the master document.
To force odd-numbered pages, choose Format | Page | Force
Page, select Current Page Odd, and click OK.

⇨ When deleting or moving subdocuments, condense the
master document first to make sure you include all the codes.
If you insist on moving a subdocument in an expanded
master document, turn on Reveal Codes and make sure you
select both the Subdoc Begin and Subdoc End codes before
you cut and paste.

> ⇨ You can place subdocuments within subdocuments, which can be useful in books that have several parts and chapters within each part. When you expand a master document that contains lower-level master documents, the lower-level master documents automatically expand as well.
>
> ⇨ Before you can print the master document, you need to expand it. Only opened subdocuments are printed. However, subdocuments do not have to be open for you to generate and print the master table of contents and index.

❓ I set the margins and tabs in a subdocument, but this formatting disappeared when I expanded the master document. What did I do wrong?

You probably placed these codes in the Current Document Style. When you expand a master document, WordPerfect ignores the Current Document Style in each subdocument. As a result, each subdocument assumes whatever formatting is in effect at the end of the previous subdocument, including font, alignment, margins, line spacing, tab settings, and so forth. You should place any codes essential to your subdocument's format in the body of the document or in an open style at the beginning of the document, but not in the Current Document Style—unless you want the formatting to disappear when you expand the master document.

 *Tip:* *To ensure consistency in your subdocument formatting, you may want to create an open style containing the margin, tab, alignment, and spacing options you want. You can then insert this open style at the beginning of all your subdocuments so that each subdocument is created with the same formatting in mind. For more information, see "Working with Styles" in Chapter 5.*

❓ The formatting in my heading styles changed when I expanded the master document. Why did this happen?

When a master document contains styles, those styles take precedence over any other styles with the same name in any of the subdocuments.

If you want the headings in your master document to be formatted in the same way as in one of your subdocuments, save the styles in your subdocument and then retrieve them in the master document. See "Working with Styles" in Chapter 5.

If two subdocuments have the same style name but different formatting, the style in the first subdocument takes precedence over any of the following styles. Also, styles with unique names in the subdocument are added to the master document's styles. If all the subdocuments contain different style names, the master document's style list will become large and difficult to manage. When you edit the subdocuments, rename the styles to ensure consistency and delete unnecessary styles.

Tip: Whenever you combine documents prepared by many people, you can expect the formatting to be different, unless you do something about it beforehand. It's a good idea to create a template containing the styles for your project. You can then share that template with your colleagues so that the formatting remains consistent. If you do this, there will be fewer unhappy surprises when you expand your master document.

❓ When I expanded the master document, the message "Subdocument not found" appeared. What's wrong?

WordPerfect stores the complete path- and filename of a subdocument in the subdocument code. If you delete the subdocument or move it to a different folder, you'll see this error message. When the "Subdocument not found" message appears, you need to specify the correct path- and filename. To prevent this message from appearing, move the file back to its original folder or delete and reinsert the subdocument in your master document.

Tip: To make transferring master documents to another location easier, place documents in your default directory, or change your default directory to match the location of your subdocuments before you add the subdocument links (choose Tools | Settings and then double-click Files). If the subdocuments are in your default directory when you add them to the master document, the subdocument links will contain only filenames instead of path- and filenames, making it easier to transfer the master document. However, the recipient of the master document will need to place the subdocuments in his or her default directory as well.

Using Bookmarks and Hyperlinks
in Long Documents

Navigating through long documents can be time-consuming. However, by taking a minute or two to mark key areas of your document, you can jump anywhere in your document without needless scrolling. Select a heading, choose Tools | Bookmark | Create, and click OK. Do this for all the main headings in your document. When you want to jump to a heading, choose Tools | Bookmark and then double-click the bookmark you want to jump to.

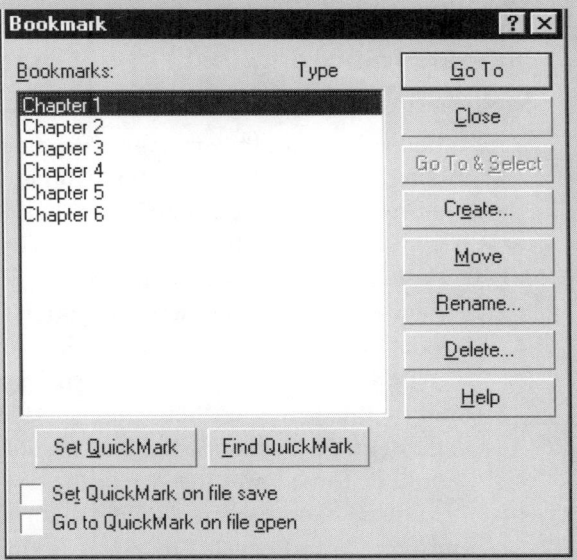

If your document will be viewed online instead of printed, you may want to set up a table of contents that has hyperlink jumps to the bookmarks you set. Readers can then click the topics in a table of contents and jump to those headings. To create hyperlinks, select the title in the table of contents and then choose Tools | Hyperlink. Select the bookmark from the Bookmark drop-down list, select Make Text Appear as a Button, and then click OK. You can also set hyperlink buttons throughout your document so that viewers can return to the table of contents.

When I condensed the master document, the text of one of my subdocuments remained in the master document, and I couldn't condense it. What did I do wrong?

When subdocuments are expanded, each subdocument appears between a Subdoc Begin and a Subdoc End code. If you delete one of these paired codes, WordPerfect will no longer treat it as a subdocument. If you delete a code by mistake, choose Edit | Undo to restore the code.

If you cannot restore the deleted code through using Undo or Multiple Undo, you'll need to select the text and save it as a separate file that can be used as a subdocument again.

When I try to save the master document, a message appears indicating that I'm out of disk space. What's the problem?

When you expand the master document, this document occupies as much disk space as all the subdocuments combined, and WordPerfect requires an equal amount of space to hold temporary files while you work with the expanded document. Thus, unless you have lots of disk space, this error message may appear when you try to save the expanded master document. Although WordPerfect does not impose restrictions on the number of subdocuments you can include in a master document, the amount of disk space does impose a practical limit on the combined size of the subdocuments in your master document. As a rule of thumb, the amount of free space on your drive should be three times the size of the combined subdocuments.

Before you save the changes to the master document, try emptying your Recycle Bin to free up more disk space, delete old .TMP files in your Windows Temp folder, and free up disk space in other ways.

FOOTNOTES AND ENDNOTES

I inserted a footnote at the bottom of the page, but I can't see it. How do I display and edit my footnotes?

In Page view, your footnotes should appear at the bottom of the page, as shown in Figure 12-3.

Footnote reference number   Footnote text

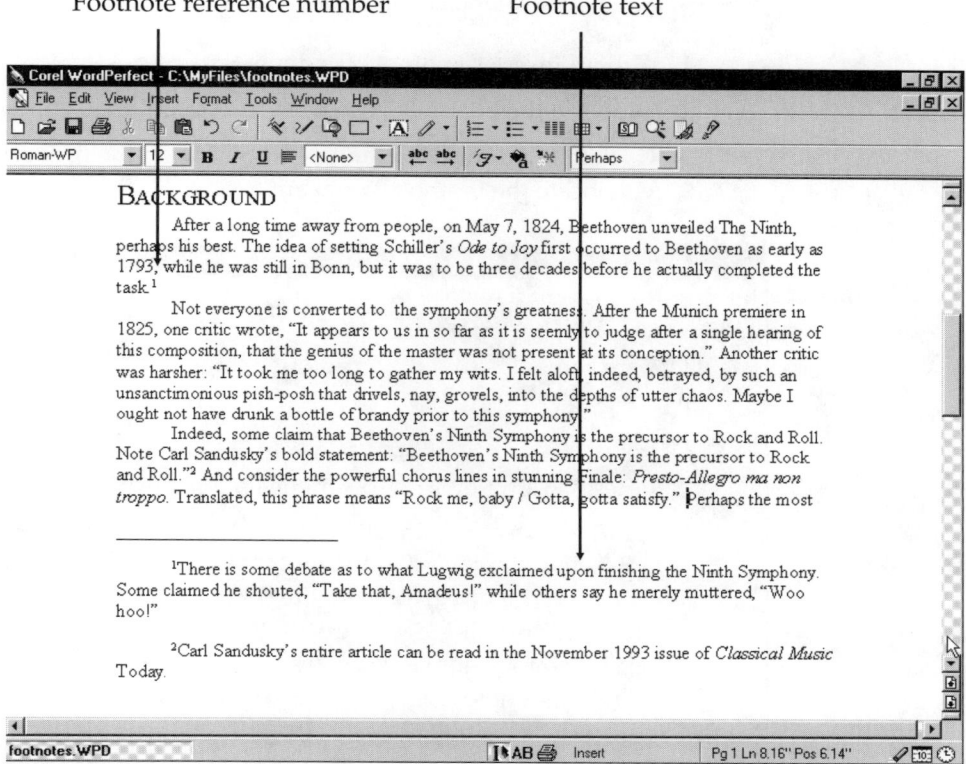

Figure 12-3. Footnotes appear at the bottom of the page

There are several reasons you may not be able to see your footnotes at the bottom of the page. Here are some things to check for:

⇨ Make sure you're not using Draft view. Choose View | Page (or Two Pages) and then check again. If you see the footnote at the bottom of the page, you can click it and edit it.

⇨ Editing may push a footnote to the page before or after where you think it should be. Check the bottom of the next and previous pages to see if your footnote has been moved to a different page.

⇨ If you delete the footnote reference number, the footnote text at the bottom of the page will also be deleted.

Follow these steps to edit your footnote:

1. Choose Insert | Footnote/Endnote.

2. Type **1** in the Footnote Number text box and then choose Edit.

3. Click the Endnote/Footnote Next button on the property bar until you locate the footnote you want to edit.

Tips on Editing Footnotes and Endnotes

Here are some tips for editing and deleting footnotes and endnotes:

⇨ WordPerfect automatically provides spacing between the notes, so don't press ENTER at the end of a note.

⇨ WordPerfect automatically numbers the notes you insert. A note's number is part of the footnote or endnote style, which includes a Footnote (or Endnote) Number Display Code for automatic numbering. If you accidentally delete this number, use Undo to restore it. If you retype the number manually, subsequent notes will be numbered incorrectly.

⇨ When you move document text, accompanying footnotes and endnotes move with it, and their numbers are automatically adjusted. Be sure to include the reference number with the text you are selecting. If you want to cut and paste only a footnote or endnote, the easiest way is to turn on Reveal Codes and select the Footnote or Endnote code.

⇨ Footnotes and endnotes are deleted when you delete the reference number or when you delete all the footnote or endnote text.

⇨ When you use paste to move text from the document area to a footnote, or vice versa, the font size moves with the text. For example, if your document uses 11-point type and your footnotes use the Small font size, when you cut and paste text from the document to a footnote, the pasted text will be in 11-point type, not Small. Instead of pressing CTRL-V to paste, you can press CTRL-SHIFT-V to paste without formatting.

My book has several chapters, and I want to number the footnotes separately in each chapter. How do I restart note numbering?

If you are writing a book with chapters, you can reset your note numbers at the beginning of each chapter. Here's how:

1. Place the insertion point where you want to start renumbering your notes, such as at the beginning of the chapter.

2. Choose Insert | Footnote/Endnote. Then choose Options | Set Number.

3. Type **1** and click OK. Then click Close.

 *Tip:* *If you're using a heading style to format your chapter headings, you can add this set number code to your style. Then you won't have to reset the number for each chapter heading individually.*

I inserted endnotes in my document, but now I want to change them to footnotes. How do I convert endnotes to footnotes?

You can convert endnotes to footnotes or footnotes to endnotes by playing the Footnotes to Endnotes macro. Here's what you do:

1. Make sure the insertion point in your document is not in any footnote or endnote text.

2. Choose Tools | Macro | Play.

3. Double-click Endfoot.wcm to convert endnotes to footnotes, or double-click Footend.wcm to convert footnotes to endnotes.

I want to use a smaller font for footnotes. Can I change the font for all the footnotes at once?

By default, WordPerfect uses the same font settings for footnotes and endnotes as for regular text. However, you can use the Advanced Footnote Options dialog box, shown in Figure 12-4, to change the note font and numbering style, place notes immediately after the referenced text instead of at the bottom of the page, and change other settings.

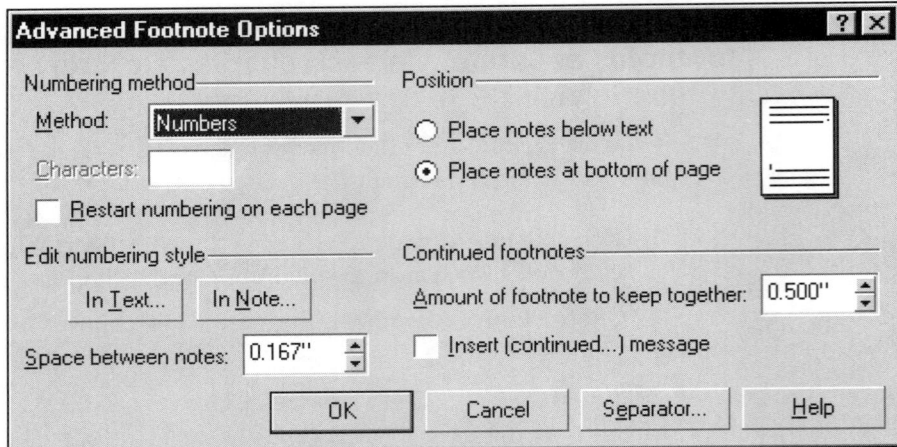

Figure 12-4.   Use the Advanced Footnote Options dialog box to change the
appearance of footnotes

Here's how to change the appearance of footnotes:

1. Place the insertion point where you want the formatting changes
    to begin and then choose Insert | Footnote/Endnote.

2. Select either Footnote Number or Endnote Number and then
    choose Advanced from the Options drop-down list.

3. Make any changes you want to the spacing between notes, note
    position, and other settings.

4. To change the font size to Small, choose In Note, press F9, select
    Small from the Relative Size drop-down list, and click OK.

5. To add a tab at the end of the note so that more space appears
    between the note and text, press END to move past the note
    number codes and then press CTRL-TAB to insert a tab. Click OK
    twice to save the new settings.

Tip: *You can also edit the separator line to suit your needs. Choose Insert*
| Footnote/Endnote, select Footnote Number, and then choose Separator from
the Options drop-down list and make the changes you want.

? After writing a 400-page dissertation, I changed the margins, but the margins in the footnotes didn't change. How can I change the margins in all the footnotes without changing each one manually?

Instead of changing your margins at the top of your document, change your margins in the Current Document Style. When you change formatting such as the font, margins, or tab settings in the Current Document Style, your footnotes and endnotes will reflect those formatting changes. Here's how to edit the Current Document Style:

1. Choose File | Document | Current Document Style.

2. From the Styles Editor menu bar, choose Format | Margins. Then change the margins for your document.

3. If you want these changes to affect only the current document, make sure Use as Default is not selected.

4. Make any other formatting changes and then click OK.

? How do I refer to the same footnote more than once in a document without inserting the footnote itself multiple times?

Sometimes you need to refer to the same footnote in different parts of your document. For example, you may want several items in a list to refer to a note that says "Discount expires July 15." To accomplish this feat, you need to use the Cross-Reference feature. Here's how:

1. Create the footnote or footnotes your want to refer to more than once.

2. Place the insertion point just after the footnote number in the document text.

3. Choose Tools | Reference | Cross-Reference.

4. In the Target text box, type **Footnote1** (or some similar text that identifies the note, such as **Discount Expiration**). Then click Mark Target. Repeat this step for each footnote you want to refer to more than once, using a different target text for each one.

5. Place the insertion point where you want to refer to the existing footnote. From the Reference pop-up button on the property bar, select Footnote. Select the footnote you want to refer to from the Target drop-down list and then choose Mark Reference.

6. Select the question mark that appears and then format it as a superscript by choosing Format | Font and then selecting Superscript from the Position drop-down list.

7. Choose Generate on the property bar and then click OK.

I placed an Index section after the endnotes, but when I added an endnote, it was placed after the Index. Can I change the location of the endnotes?

Yes. Normally, WordPerfect places any endnote you create at the end of the document, after all the codes. However, if your document has an index, you'll want the endnotes to come before it. Here's how to change the location of your endnotes:

1. Place the insertion point where you want your endnotes to appear, such as just above the index page.

2. Choose Insert | Footnote/Endnote, select Endnote Number, and then choose Endnote Placement.

3. If you're using only one set of endnotes in this document, select Insert Endnotes at Insertion Point and click OK. Then click Close.

Tip: *WordPerfect inserts an Endnote Placement code followed by a hard page break to separate the endnotes from the next page of text. If you have already added a hard page break to begin your index, you should delete that code, or you'll end up with a blank page between the endnotes page and the index.*

Note: *Endnotes preceding the placement code are placed at the code. Endnotes that follow the placement code appear at the next placement code or at the end of the document.*

? When I suppress page numbering on the page containing endnotes, two endnotes print over each other. What's the problem?

This problem is rare, but if it does occur, you can work around it by setting the page numbering option to No Page Numbering instead of suppressing page numbering. To do this, place the insertion point on the page where your endnotes appear and then choose Format | Page | Numbering. Select No Page Numbering from the Position drop-down list and then click OK.

? How do I make sure footnotes are restarted at the beginning of each subdocument in a master document?

If you have a master document with each chapter as a subdocument, you may want to reset the footnote numbers to 1 for each chapter. Unfortunately, WordPerfect figures there is no reason to restart your footnote numbers until after you insert a footnote, so it won't let you set the footnote number to 1 at the beginning of each subdocument unless you have already inserted a footnote. To ensure that note numbering starts at 1 in each subdocument of a master document, first expand the master document and then reset the numbering at the beginning of each expanded subdocument. This way, you can change the footnote number to start at 1 in each subdocument, even if you haven't added a footnote to that particular subdocument. To restart footnote numbering, choose Insert | Footnote/Endnote, type **1** in the Footnote Number text box, and click Close.

? I want to place all my endnotes at the end of the master document, but I want them grouped by chapter. How do I do this?

If you want your endnotes to appear at the end of the book rather than at the end of every chapter, insert Endnote Placement codes in the master document, even though all your notes are in the subdocument. After you insert all the endnotes in the master document, you can then insert headings into the endnotes to divide them by chapter. Here's how you can place your endnotes at the end of book, grouped by chapter:

1. Delete any Endnote Placement codes you may have inserted in your chapter subdocuments so that the endnotes will be placed at the end of the document.

2. At the beginning of each chapter, choose Insert | Footnote/Endnote. Then choose Set Number from the Options drop-down list, type **1**, and click OK. Then click Close.

3. Save the chapter documents. Then click the location where you want the endnotes to begin in the master document.

4. Type a heading for the endnotes and then press ENTER twice to move the insertion point to a new line.

5. Type a heading for the endnotes for Chapter 1 and then press ENTER once or twice, depending on how much space you want between your heading and your endnote text.

6. Choose Insert | Footnote/Endnote, select Endnote Number, choose Endnote Placement, and click OK. Then click Close.

7. Click at the end of the last endnote for Chapter 1, and then press ENTER two or more times.

8. Type a heading for the endnotes for Chapter 2.

9. Repeat steps 7 and 8 to insert chapter headings for every chapter in the book.

TABLES OF CONTENTS

? When I generated the table of contents, the headings marked with Heading 2 and Heading 3 styles were not included. How do I include all headings in the table of contents?

When you define the table of contents, you need to specify the number of levels you want for the table of contents. You probably have only one level selected for the table of contents. Follow these steps to define and generate your table of contents properly:

1. Format your headings with heading styles (Heading 1, Heading 2, and so on) that have Mark Table of Contents codes.

 *Note:* *Instead of using heading styles, you can mark your table of contents headings individually. Choose Tools | Reference | Table of Contents. Then individually select each heading and click the appropriate heading level (such as Mark 1 for first-level headings, Mark 2 for second-level headings, and so on).*

2. If the Table of Contents property bar is not displayed, choose Tools | Reference | Table of Contents.

3. Place the insertion point where you want the table of contents to appear and then choose Define.

4. Specify the number of heading levels you want in the table of contents in the Number of Levels (1-5) text box.

5. In the Position drop-down lists, select the numbering method for each level and then click OK.

6. Choose Generate and then click OK to generate the table of contents.

 *Tip:* *If you want to change the format of the table of contents, the best approach is to delete the first table of contents—including all the Def Mark and Gen Txt codes—and start over. If you try to edit the table of contents definition, you'll probably end up with two tables of contents.*

When I generated the table of contents, only the first word in each heading appeared. How do I make sure the table of contents includes every word of every heading?

When you marked the headings for the table of contents, you didn't select the entire heading first. If you merely put the insertion point at the beginning of the heading, WordPerfect assumes that the first word is the only text you want included in the table of contents. Make sure you select the entire heading before marking the table of contents.

 *Tip:* *If you have a detailed table of contents in which some lines take up more than one line, you can remove the hanging indent in the table of contents by selecting the Display Last Level in Wrapped Format option in the Define Table of Contents dialog box.*

? When I generated the table of contents, all the numbers were off by a page. What's the problem?

The most common reason for this problem is that the generated table of contents takes up more than one page, and you did not change the page number value at the beginning of your body text to accommodate the table of contents. If you don't insert a page number code at the beginning of your body text, your table of contents and body text will be part of the same numbering sequence. When you generate the table of contents, if it exceeds one page, it will change the body text page numbers, and the generated references will no longer be correct.

Here's a safe way to set up your table of contents page:

1. Create a separate "Table of Contents" page. To do this, place the insertion point where you want the table of contents to appear and then press CTRL-ENTER to insert a hard page break. Type **Table of Contents** and press ENTER twice. Format and center the table of contents title (but don't use a heading style, or "Table of Contents" will be added to your table of contents).

2. Define the table of contents as described in the preceding Q&A.

3. Move the insertion point to the first page after the table of contents where your document starts (such as the beginning of Chapter 1). Make sure there is a hard page break at the beginning of the chapter.

4. Choose Format | Page | Numbering | Set Value. Type **1** in the Set Page Number text box and then click OK.

5. Generate your table of contents. Your page numbers will now be accurate, even if the table of contents is longer than a page.

 Tip: *In manuals, books, and other long documents, it is a common practice to use lowercase Roman numerals (i, ii, iii) for introductory material. If you want to adopt this style, move the insertion point to the top of the document and then switch to roman numerals in your headers, footers, or page numbers. Just make sure your first chapter begins with the correct numbering style (such as 1, 2, 3) instead of the Roman numerals.*

I don't want my table of contents headings to be formatted like the headings in the document. How can I generate headings as plain text?

If you want the headings in the table of contents generated without formatting, you need to make sure the table of contents code comes after any formatting codes, even in a style. If you're marking your table of contents headings manually, turn on Reveal Codes and then select only the heading without any of the formatting.

Here's how to insert Mark Table of Contents styles properly:

1. Choose Format | Styles, select your first heading style, and choose Edit.

2. In the Styles Editor, delete the existing Mrk Txt ToC codes and make sure Show 'off codes' is selected.

3. Move the insertion point after any formatting codes and just before the Off code. Press SHIFT-END to select the code.

4. Choose Tools | Reference | Table of Contents and then click Mark 1 for the first heading style.

5. Click OK. Then repeat this process for each heading level. Remember to select a different level (such as Mark 2 or Mark 3) for each heading.

I use TextArt for section names, but I can't mark graphics for the table of contents. How can I include TextArt titles in a table of contents?

You can use the Hidden Text feature to create dummy text, and then you can mark this dummy text manually. Here's how:

1. Place the insertion point below your TextArt heading, but don't add any extra blank lines.

2. Type the heading text and then select it and choose Format | Font. Select Hidden and click OK.

3. If the text disappears, choose View | Hidden Text.

4. Select the text and then choose Tools | Reference | Table of Contents. Click Mark 1 or Mark 2 or whatever level you are using.

5. Repeat these steps for each heading in your document.

 *Note:*   *For your table of contents to generate properly, hidden text must be turned on. When you're ready to print your document, turn off hidden text by choosing View | Hidden Text to deselect it.*

? I edited text in the table of contents, but these changes disappeared when I regenerated the table of contents. How can I make my editing changes appear in the regenerated table of contents?

Whenever you regenerate the table of contents, the old table of contents—including any formatting changes—is replaced. If you want to edit the table of contents text, you need to do so after the last time you generate, or you need to make those changes to the marked text within your document.

? I want the first level of headings in the table of contents to be formatted in 14-point Arial and the second level of headings to be italicized. How can I make these changes without having to reformat the headings each time I generate the table of contents?

Each time you generate the table of contents, you'll lose any formatting changes you made to the table of contents. However, you can modify the table of contents heading-level styles (TableofCont1, TableofCont2, and so on) that come with WordPerfect. You can either edit the original styles or take the safer route and create new styles suited to your needs. For example, you can create custom heading-level styles such as TableofCont1a, TableofCont2a, and so on.

Assuming you've already created your table of contents, here's how to edit a table of contents level style:

1. Choose Define on the Table of Contents property bar.

2. Click Styles.

3. Select 1 in the Level list box and then choose Edit.

Warning: *When editing styles, make sure you don't accidentally match the wrong level with the wrong style, such as matching level 1 with the TableofCont2 style. To edit a style, click the number in the Level list box, not the Styles list box.*

4. In the Styles Editor, click Show 'off codes,' select the Off code that appears, and apply the formatting you want (such as 14-pt Arial) to the level-1 style. Then click OK.

5. Select 2 in the Level list box and then follow a procedure similar to the one in step 4 to italicize the headings.

6. Click OK and then click Cancel in the Define Table of Contents dialog box to return to your document—you don't want to insert another Define code in your document.

 ***Tip:*** *These style changes affect only the current document. To use the new style levels in other documents, either you can save the changes in the default template, or you can save these system styles and retrieve them in other documents. See "Working with Styles" in Chapter 5.*

INDEXES

I generated an index, but some references refer to the wrong page, and other references I marked don't appear at all. What's wrong?

When you mark items for your index, it's easy to make mistakes without knowing it. Here are two common mistakes you need to avoid when marking items for an index:

⇨ When marking text for your index, remember to click Mark after you type each heading and subheading. If you forget, no Index code will be placed in your document, and you'll wonder why the index is incomplete.

⇨ When marking items for your index, be sure to click the Heading box before you mark each entry. If you click Mark without entering a new heading, the item will be indexed under the previous entry's heading.

Follow these steps to mark an index properly:

1. Choose Tools | Reference | Index.

2. Select the text you want to index and then click the Heading text box on the Index property bar.

3. If necessary, edit the text in the Heading box and add a subheading that will appear on a new line. Figure 12-5 shows the difference between headings and subheadings.

4. Click Mark.

5. If you want to add synonyms, type a new heading in the Heading text box and then click Mark—you don't need to move the insertion point. For example, you may want to index "Volkswagens" as a heading ("Volkswagens"), as a subheading

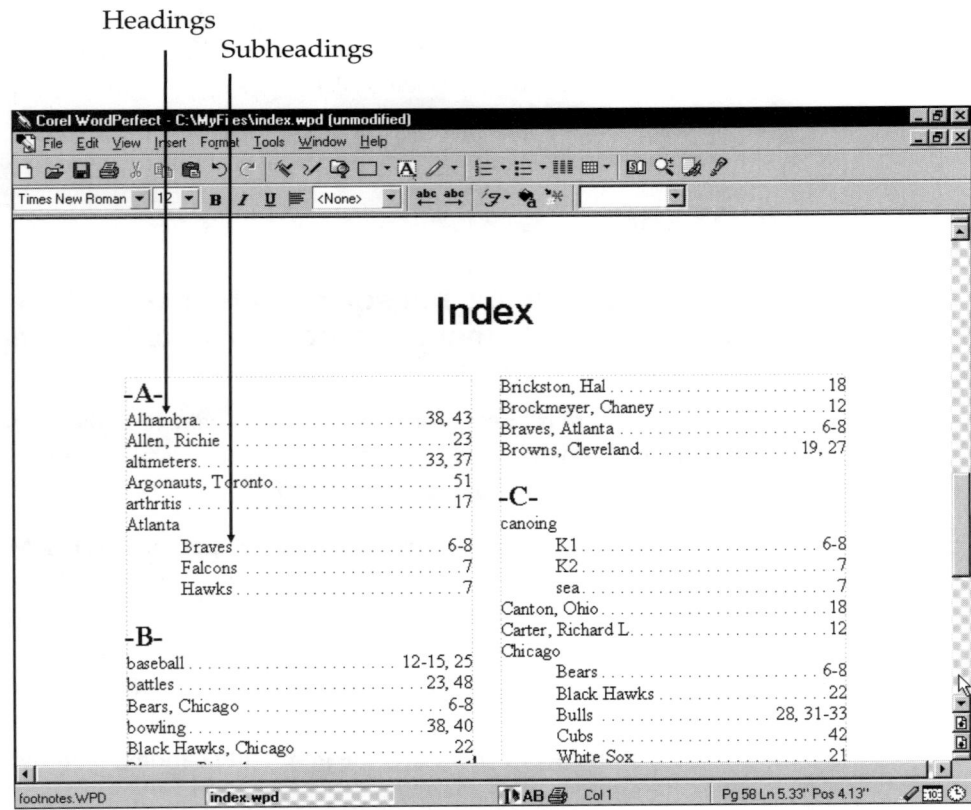

Figure 12-5.   Index with headings and subheadings in the standard format

under "Cars" (such as "Cars, Volkswagens") and as a separate heading in the index called "Beetles."

Tip: *If you know certain Index markings are incorrect, turn on Reveal Codes and delete the incorrect Index codes. When you place the insertion point before an Index code in Reveal Codes, the code expands to display the item's text. After you get rid of the erroneous Index codes, you can add new index markings and generate the index again.*

I am creating a concordance file, and I want "Sharon Baxter," "Ms. Baxter," and "President Baxter" all generated as "Baxter, Sharon" in my index. Can I mark multiple different words so they all generate the same index entry?

You mark the entries in a concordance file just as you mark entries in the document text. For example, if you have typed "Sharon Baxter" throughout the document, but you want this name to appear as "Baxter, Sharon," select and mark the name in that format in the concordance file you create.

A concordance file, shown in Figure 12-6, is a list of words and phrases that you enter in a new document. These words and phrases are used as index items, and the referenced page numbers reflect all occurrences of these items in your document.

Here's how to create a concordance file and mark individual entries:

1. Open a new blank document and save it with whatever name you want.

2. Type an entry and then press ENTER.

Note: *The entry must be an exact match of the text in your document. For example, typing **Sharon Baxter** in the concordance will not cause "Ms. Baxter" or "Shari Baxter" to be included. However, concordance items are not case-sensitive, so "sharon baxter" would be included. You may want to copy and paste text into your concordance to avoid spelling errors.*

3. To customize items in the list, mark the entry just as you would if it were in the document, as described in the preceding Q&A. For example, you can type "Sharon Baxter," "President Baxter," and

"Ms. Baxter" as separate lines in your concordance and then mark each of them as "Baxter, Sharon." Only "Baxter, Sharon" will appear in your index.

4. Save your concordance file. When you define your index, include the name of the concordance file in the Filename text box.

 Tip: *It's a good idea to create a concordance file while you are marking your index. To simplify the process, you can tile your document and the concordance file on your screen. While marking index entries in your document, you can then easily switch documents and add the entry to your concordance.*

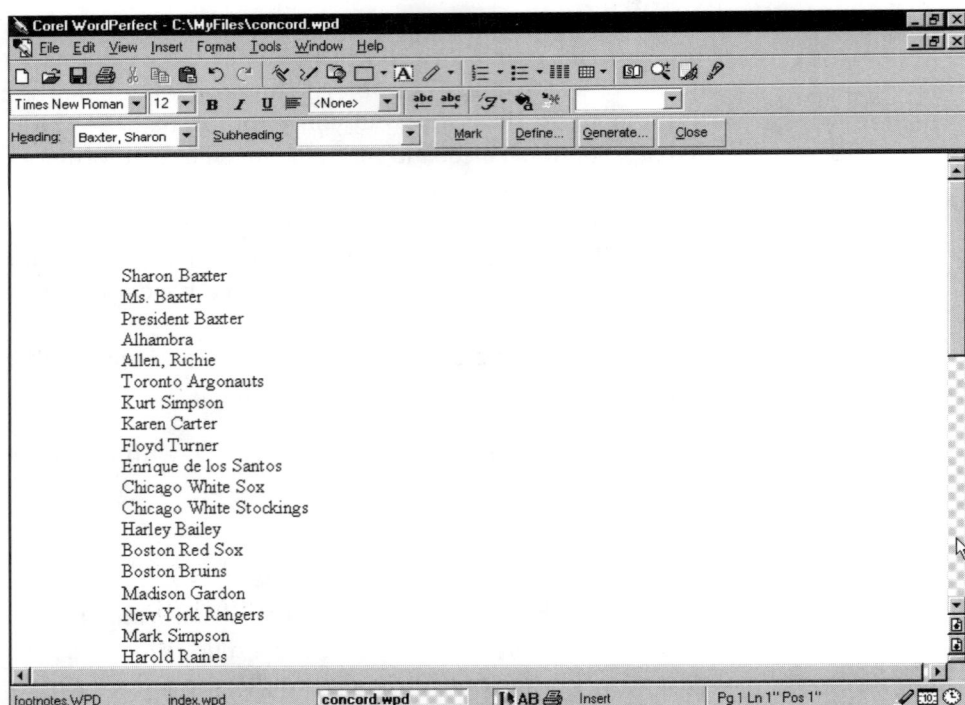

Figure 12-6.   You can use a concordance file to generate your index

? **I want to generate my index in a three-column format, but the index always appears in a one-column format. How do I generate a multicolumn index?**

You need to make sure the Index Definition code is *after* the Column Definition code. This may require you to cut and paste the Index Definition code. Here are the steps for setting up an index in three-column format:

1. At the end of your document, press CTRL-ENTER to start a new page.

2. Type **Index** and then press ENTER twice. Center and format the index title.

3. Move the insertion point to a blank line and then choose Format | Columns. Define the type of columns you want in your index and then click OK.

4. Choose Tools | Reference | Index to display the Index property bar.

5. Choose Define, select the options you want for your index, and click OK.

6. Choose View | Reveal Codes. Then select the Def Mark codes and the Gen Txt codes and press CTRL-X. Make sure you select the beginning and ending Gen Txt codes.

7. Move the insertion point after the Col Def code and press CTRL-V to paste the codes.

8. Click Generate and then click OK to generate your index within the columns.

? **My index includes some headings with only one subheading. When I changed this in the index, the changes were removed the next time I generated the index. How do I edit Index marks?**

Whenever you generate the index, the newly generated index replaces the old one, including any changes you made to the previously generated index. Before you start editing the index, you should make sure the document is in its final format and that all your incorrect index marks are deleted and replaced by new index marks.

How to Create Consistent Indexes

Before you start marking your index, create a small style guide for you and for anyone else who is also indexing. You'll simplify the indexing process if you follow these suggestions:

⇨ Decide on basic style issues, such as whether you generally will use singular or plural nouns (*artichoke* or *artichokes*), gerunds or infinitives (*playing* or *play*), and ending prepositions (*Twain, Mark, writings of,* or *Twain, Mark, writings*). If you create a style guide, you'll prevent a lot of duplicate entries (such as *artichoke* and *artichokes*) that should be one entry.

⇨ Some indexers like to capitalize the main headings and leave subheadings lowercase, while others prefer capitalizing only proper nouns. Decide which format you will use.

⇨ You may want to include cross-references (such as "Spam, 29. *See also* potted meat products") in your index. Keep a list of cross-references in a separate document to include in your final generated index after your final edit. If you have to generate your index again, you'll be able to replace the deleted cross-references more easily.

⇨ Be wary of including too many subheadings under main headings. Too many subheadings can force the reader to thumb through too many pages before finding the information. A rule of thumb is to use at least one subheading if a heading includes more than five page references.

⇨ Consult style guides such as *The Chicago Manual of Style*, which devotes 60 pages to indexing issues. The home page of the American Society of Indexers (http://www.well.com/ user/asi/) lists other publications and indexing services.

It's a good idea to generate your index from time to time as you create it to check for errors, completeness, and consistency. You will probably find things you want to fix—a typo, an inconsistency in wording, a heading that needs subheadings, and subheadings that could be combined. Of course, you can edit the generated index, but if you generate again, you lose your corrections. A better solution is to delete incorrect index codes and then add corrected entries.

? Is it possible to include cross-references (such as "See also Fonts") in the index without having to insert them manually?

Most good indexes contain cross-references to help readers find the information they're looking for. WordPerfect doesn't let you add cross-references to your index except by manually inserting them. One suggestion is to keep cross-references in a separate list and then copy and paste then into your final index.

Another way to insert cross-references is to mark items in your document with a special cross-reference term. For example, if you want to refer readers to the "Fonts" heading from the "Printing" heading, create an index mark with "Printing" as the heading and "zzz. *See also* Fonts" as the subheading. After your index is generated, search for "zzz" and then delete these letters and the page number as well. This solution is somewhat clumsy, but it keeps your cross-references in the document.

Tip: *After your index has been generated for the last time, you may also want to add large capital letters, called* alpha breaks, *to divide each section of the index by letter. Alpha breaks are especially useful in long indexes.*

? Is it possible to index every word in a document?

Yes, you can use a concordance file to create a list of all the words in the document. First, save the document with a different name. Use search and replace to replace all spaces with hard returns to put each word on a new line. Then search for periods and replace them with nothing; do this for all the punctuation in your document. Save this document and then use it as the concordance file when you define your index in the original document.

Macros and Templates

Answer Topics!

Macros and Templates @ a Glance

⇨ The thought of having to create a macro scares some people, but others find macros one of their favorite features. Beginners and experts alike can use macros to get their work done quickly. If you need to repeat a group of keystrokes, you can record a simple macro and play back those keystrokes with a single key press. And don't worry if you run into problems; just turn to this chapter.

⇨ Although WordPerfect macros are often used to record a series of keystrokes, this feature is powerful enough to create small applications. However, almost inevitably when you create macro programs, you will encounter errors while you compile and run them. To help make your macro writing proceed more smoothly, this chapter shows you a few tricks and provides tips for getting out of trouble.

⇨ Although the new projects in WordPerfect 8 have effectively replaced the templates and experts found in previous versions of WordPerfect, you can still create templates of the documents you use most often. For example, if you write the same letter repeatedly, you can create a template and start new documents based on this template. You can set up the template so that when you create a document based on the template, you'll be prompted for information. You can even add your own toolbars and menus to templates. If you have questions about templates, look for the answers in this chapter.

USING MACROS

 While recording a simple keystroke macro, I pressed CTRL-SHIFT-X to try to name the macro, but nothing happened. How do I record a keystroke macro?

If you have used WordPerfect 6.1, you may be in the habit of pressing keystrokes such as CTRL-SHIFT-X in the Record Macro dialog box to create a keystroke macro. However, you cannot press keystrokes in the WordPerfect 7 or 8 Record Macro dialog box. Instead, you can type the keystroke abbreviation, such as **CtrlSftX.wcm**, to create a macro that plays when you press CTRL-SHIFT-X.

Here's how to record a simple keystroke macro:

1. Choose Tools | Macro | Record.

2. Type the name of the macro (such as **CtrlSftX.wcm**) in the File Name text box and then choose Record.

3. Type any text or select any commands and then choose Tools |
Macro | Record again when you're done recording.

Tip: *A better method for creating keystroke macros is to give the macro a
descriptive name and then assign a keystroke to the macro. For more
information, see "Customizing the Keyboard" in Chapter 11.*

I named a macro CtrlSftQ.wcm, but the macro doesn't play when I press CTRL-SHIFT-Q. What's the problem?

Like many other keystrokes, the CTRL-SHIFT-Q keystroke is already
assigned to a different function. Choose Tools | Settings and then
double-click Customize. Select the Keyboards tab and then click
Edit. Look for a keystroke combination that is unassigned (such as
CTRL-SHIFT-X) and then rename the macro. However, you're better off
just giving the macro a regular name and then assigning a keystroke
to that macro.

Tip: *After you record a keystroke macro that you need to use only once or
twice, you may want to delete it so that your Play Macro dialog box doesn't
become cluttered with document-specific macros. Choose Tools | Macro |
Play, right-click the macro, and choose Delete.*

I'm trying to record a macro that creates a text box with a drop shadow. However, after I create the text box, I can't edit it to add the drop shadow. How do I edit a text box while recording a macro?

You can't. While in Macro Record mode, you cannot click anywhere in
the document window, so there is no way to edit the text box without
editing the macro. However, you can create a graphics style that has
the characteristics you want, and then you can select that graphics
style while recording that macro. In fact, if you create a graphics style,
you may not even need to create a macro.

To create a graphics style, choose Format | Graphics Styles |
Create. Then type a name for the style and specify the attributes you
want. When recording the macro, insert the text box by choosing
Insert | Graphics | Custom Box and then select the style you created.
After you insert the text box in your document, you can exit the text

box by choosing File | Close and then continue recording the rest of your macro.

For more information on creating text boxes and working with graphics styles, see Chapter 9.

 I created several macros at home, and I want to use them at work. How do I copy them?

Macros are usually stored in the C:\Corel\Suite8\Macros\WPWin folder (where C represents the drive where WordPerfect is installed). You can copy any macro from this folder to a floppy disk and then copy it to the same folder at work.

Tip: *It's a good idea to make a backup copy of your important macros in case your hard drive crashes or your computer is stolen or some other major problem occurs.*

What is the difference between a macro and a template macro? Which should I use?

Macros that you create by choosing Tools | Macro | Record are stored as WordPerfect documents in a folder on your hard drive. You can play back these macros in any document. When you want to create a set of macros for just a certain type of document, you can create template macros. Template macros are available only when you create a document based on a certain template. For example, if you're writing a series of technical documents, you may want to create a set of template macros that are useful only for those documents. You can create another set of macros used only in brochures and newsletters, and so on. You can also add menus, toolbars, and keyboards to templates. See "Working with Templates" later in this chapter.

Here's how to create a macro that can be used only in a certain template:

1. Open or edit the template you want the macro to appear in (but don't create a document based on the template, or this procedure won't work).

2. Choose Tools | Template Macro | Record and then type the name of the macro.

3. Choose Location, select Current template, and click OK.

4. Choose Record to record the macro.

? When I change the margins while playing the Pleading macro, an error message appears. What's the problem?

This problem occurs in the Pleading macro and any macro using the macro command FormatMarginsDlg(). Corel programmers know about this problem, and they're working on it. Until they fix it, however, you should not choose the Margins button while playing the macro; instead, change the margins after you run the macro.

PROGRAMMING WITH MACROS

? When I was compiling a macro, a syntax error message appeared. How do I fix syntax and other errors in macros?

When you're compiling a macro, you'll see a error message if you spelled a command incorrectly or forgot to include some part of the command, such as a parenthesis or semicolon. When WordPerfect detects an error, it displays an error message similar to the one in Figure 13-1.

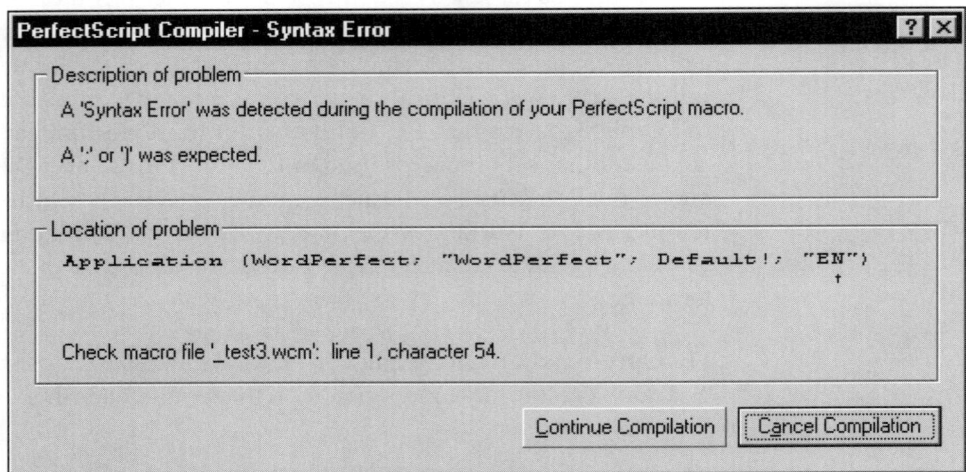

Figure 13-1. Errors are common when compiling macros

It's not always easy to determine the macro's problem just by reading the error message description. In fact, sometimes the error message indicator points to the wrong place in the macro—the real problem may be somewhere else in the line, or even in a previous line.

 ***Tip:*** *If a macro is long and contains many lines, you may want to use the LineNum.wcm macro included with WordPerfect. This macro helps you move to any line and character position.*

If an error message appears when you're compiling a macro, check the following:

⇨ Check for misspelled commands. If you include a "Tpye" command instead of a "Type" command in your macro, WordPerfect will be even harder on you than your fifth-grade teacher.

⇨ Make sure you use straight quotation marks in your macro. When the Macro toolbar is displayed, the SmartQuotes options in QuickCorrect are turned off, but if you turn them back on, or if you edit the macro without the Macro toolbar, the curly quotation marks will cause error messages to appear.

⇨ Check for missing parentheses, quotation marks, braces, semicolons, and exclamation marks and for other punctuation problems. For example, the command Type ("This is a test") will not work if either one of the parentheses or quotation marks is omitted.

⇨ Make sure the variable you're using is not reserved. For example, if you try to use "menu" as a variable, WordPerfect will think you're starting a menu command, and an error message will appear.

⇨ Make sure you haven't split a pair of commands. For example, if you are using the WHILE and ENDWHILE commands within an IF/ENDIF routine, you cannot place the ENDWHILE command after the ENDIF command.

⇨ If you press ENTER in the middle of text enclosed in quotation marks, a boundary line error message will appear. You'll have to remove the hard return before your macro will work. However, you can allow a soft return to break a line in two.

The macro compiled just fine, but when I ran the macro, an error message appeared. What's wrong?

Three kinds of errors can occur in WordPerfect macros: syntax errors, which are found during the compile process (see the preceding Q&A), run-time errors, and logic errors. A run-time error occurs when WordPerfect can't complete a command when you're playing it. A logic error occurs when the macro behaves in a way you don't expect. For example, if you set up a macro to delete all the punctuation in a set of labels and the macro deletes all the text in the label, you must fix the logic error in your macro.

Note: *As a precautionary measure, WordPerfect automatically stops the macro when a run-time error occurs. This prevents the macro from doing more damage. If you want the macro to continue running despite the error, place an Error(Off!) command near the top of the macro. However, use this command with extreme caution!*

If a run-time or logic error occurs, try these solutions:

⇨   Check for references to variables that don't exist. For example, if your macro includes the command Type(NAME), a previous command (such as GETSTRING or ASSIGN) must assign a value to the NAME variable, or an error message will appear.

⇨   Make sure the macro can actually be performed in the particular situation. If the error message "Error processing product command" appears, WordPerfect cannot carry out the specified command. For example, if you have only nine documents and your macro tries to open a tenth, you'll see this message. Similarly, this message will appear if your macro tries to cut text and place it on the clipboard when text is not selected.

⇨   Check the state of WordPerfect when the error occurs. For example, suppose your macro inserts a text box and types some text. Commands such as FileNew, FileSave, and FilePrint that would normally work are not available when the insertion point is in the text box. In your macro, you need to exit the text box (using FileClose) before these other options are available.

⇨   To fix logic errors, you can add a Display(On!) command at the top of the macro so you can see changes as they occur in your document. You can also insert a QUIT command at a different point in your macro each time you play it back to see if you can pinpoint the error.

⇨ To locate errors, you can step through your macro slowly. Insert a Step(On!) command at the top of the macro. As you do so, a dialog box like the one shown in Figure 13-2 will appear that lets you step through your macro. This feature is especially handy if you suspect that one or more of your macro variables contains an incorrect value.

? I wrote a macro that replaces all occurrences of one name in a document and then replaces all occurrences of a phone number. However, when all the names are replaced, the macro stops without replacing the phone number. How do I keep the macro active?

WordPerfect terminates a macro when it encounters a "not found" condition. You can ignore not found conditions by inserting a NotFound(Off!) command at the top of your macro. It is also a

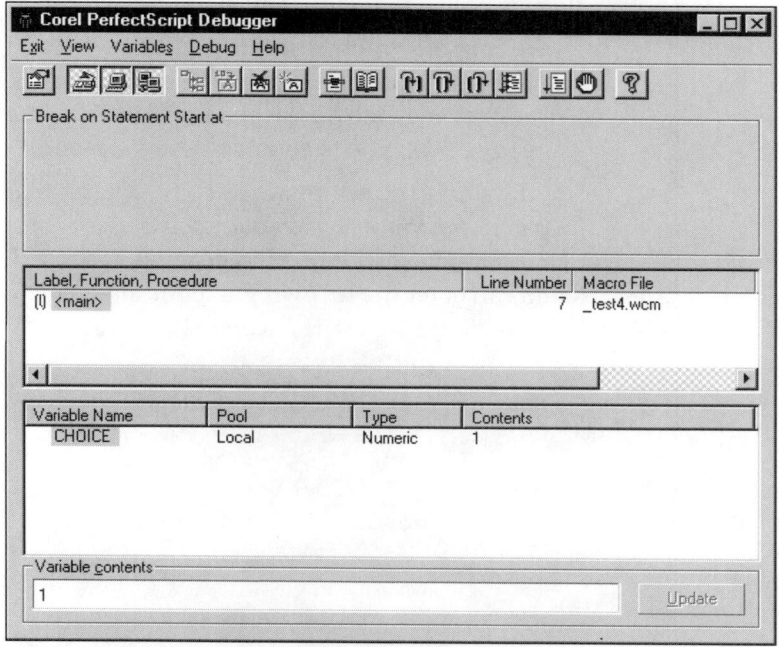

Figure 13-2.   This dialog box lets you step through your macro to locate errors

common practice to use the OnNotFound command to redirect the macro to a different subroutine so that it keeps running. For more information, look up the NotFound and OnNotFound commands in Macros Help.

Tips for Creating Bulletproof Macros

Here are some tips to help you make sure your macros play back correctly:

⇨ Start small and work up. Always test your macro as you create it. Make sure each part works before you create the next part.

⇨ As much as possible, record macro commands instead of entering them manually. Recording macro commands increases the likelihood that the syntax and order will be correct and the command will work in WordPerfect.

⇨ Be sure to take into account the state or context of the macro. If your macro uses a context such as the text box editing window, for instance, note which commands are available to you. For some commands, text must be selected—or not selected—to function properly. Also make sure you're not trying to open one dialog box while another dialog box is already open. Not all commands are accessible in all contexts.

⇨ Make sure a file is present before you have a macro try to open it. A common error is to have a macro try to open a file that doesn't exist or that has been moved to a different folder. You can enter the following in your macro to check for a file before your macro tries to open it:

```
FileExists(report; "c:\mydocs\report.wpd")

IF (report=True)
    FileOpen ("c:\mydocs\report.wpd")
Else
    MessageBox (;; "Report.wpd cannot be
found.")
ENDIF
```

⇨ Never assume anything. For example, if text must be selected before a macro runs, be sure to test for an active selection before the macro does anything else. Instead of just assuming that text will be selected, insert a command that checks to see if text is selected. If text isn't selected, you can pause the macro and flash a message that prompts you to select text. You can then press ENTER to continue the macro. Refer to the next Q&A for more information.

⇨ Keep a library of subroutines that work. After you get a FOREACH loop to work properly, for example, you don't need to reinvent the wheel when you want to use this subroutine in a macro. You may be able to copy and paste the subroutine into the new macro

For my macro to work, text must be selected. How do I make sure text is selected?

For some commands to work in your macro, you need to make sure text is selected. There are several ways to make sure text is selected when you are running a macro. The following example uses this logic: If selected text does not equal nothing (that is, if text is selected), do this. Otherwise do that.

```
IF (?SelectedText<>"")
EditCut()
ELSE
MessageBox (;"Whoa nelly!";"Select text, then replay
the macro.")
QUIT
ENDIF
```

The <> is one of several operators you can use when composing a macro with an IF statement. Table 13-1 shows some others.

Table 13-1.   IF Statement Operators

Operator	What It Means
=	Equals
<>	Not equal to
<=	Less than or equal to
>=	Greater than or equal to

If you want your macro to make sure that text is *not* selected, you can use the following line, which means "if selected text equals nothing":

```
IF (?SelectedText="")
EditPaste()
ELSE
MessageBox (;"Whoa nelly!";"Make sure no text is
selected when you run this macro")
QUIT
ENDIF
```

? I recorded a macro that opens a dialog box and selects options. The macro works fine, but when I look at the macro, the command for opening the dialog box isn't there. Why not?

WordPerfect records complete actions, not the separate steps it takes to perform the action. If you record a macro that includes opening a dialog box, WordPerfect records what you do in the dialog box. If you like, you can have the macro open the dialog box and then pause so you can select options.

? WordPerfect displays an error message when I try to play a macro I created in WordPerfect 6.1 for Windows. Can I play macros I created in earlier versions of WordPerfect in WordPerfect 8?

The macro languages in WordPerfect 6.1, 7, and 8 are nearly identical—but not completely. Most macros created in WordPerfect 6.1 and 7 will run without a hitch in WordPerfect 8. However, a few commands function slightly differently or are obsolete in version 8. If you encounter an error, first try recompiling the macro in WordPerfect 8. Choose Tools | Macro | Edit and then double-click the macro. Resave the macro with a different name. When you click Save and Compile, WordPerfect will let you know where the errors are.

WordPerfect Macros Help displays a list of commands that function slightly differently or that don't work in version 8. Here's how you can view this list:

1. Choose Help | Help Topics and then click the Contents tab.

2. Double-click Macros, double-click Macro Programming, and then click the Contents tab.

3. Double-click Upgrade Help and then double-click About Converting Macros.

 *Note:*   *Online Macros Help is available only if you selected it in a Custom installation. The WordPerfect Macro Help option is found in the WordPerfect category. For more information on performing a Custom installation, see "Adding and Removing Suite Components" in Chapter 2.*

When I compiled my macro, a message appeared telling me that a label was defined but not referenced. However, the macro works just fine. What does this message mean?

You inserted a LABEL command, but you didn't use it. When you use a LABEL command, WordPerfect expects you to reference this command from somewhere else in your macro, usually by using a GO or CALL command. For example, you may place a LABEL(Start@) command at the beginning of your macro so you can later redirect the processing flow back to the start of the macro. If you end up not referring to this command, WordPerfect tells you that there may be something fishy in your macro. If you click Continue Compiling and no other problems occur, your macro will work just fine. However, you may want to delete the unreferenced LABEL command.

I want to create a macro that lets me insert special characters, but the MenuList command doesn't display characters properly. What can I do?

Some people like to use a macro to display their most commonly used symbols so they don't have to hunt for them in the Symbols dialog box. You can create a macro that lets you insert special characters and special codes, as shown in Figure 13-3. In this short example, using the MenuList playing the macro and typing **1** inserts a long dash followed by a hyphenation soft return code, and typing **2** or **3** inserts a superscripted copyright or registered trademark symbol, respectively. You can then assign a keystroke to the macro so that you can play it quickly. However, you cannot display the symbols in the menu that appears. You'll just have to describe them.

? I can't figure out how to use the FOR command. How can I learn more about a command?

First of all, you should probably use the FOREACH command instead of FOR—it's much simpler. Nevertheless, when you want to learn more about a command and to see examples, use Macros Help, shown in Figure 13-4.

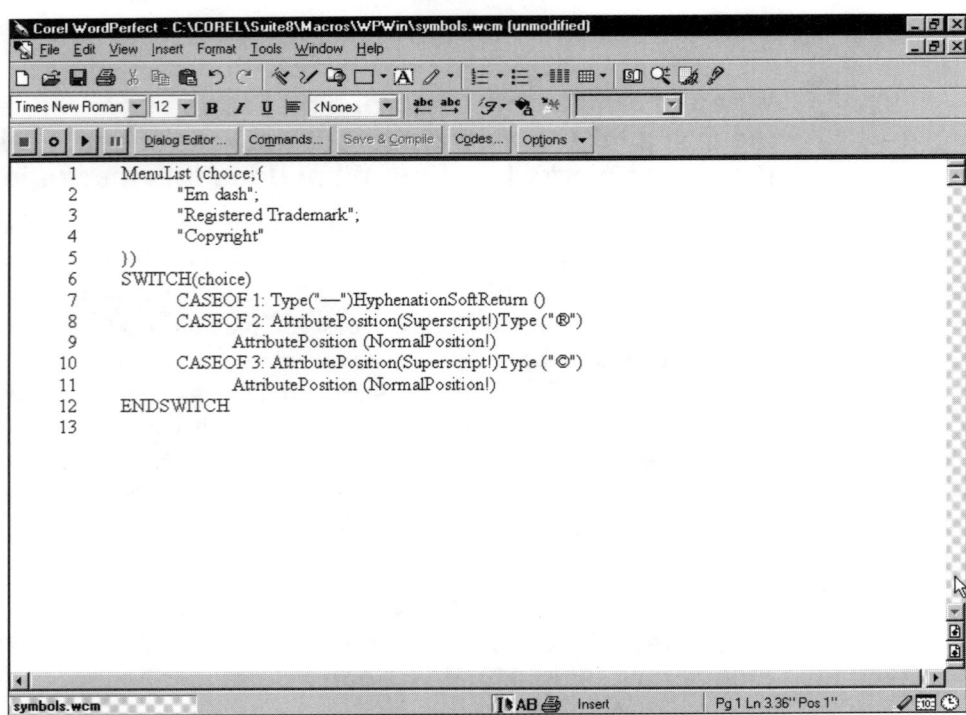

Figure 13-3.   You can create a macro that inserts special characters

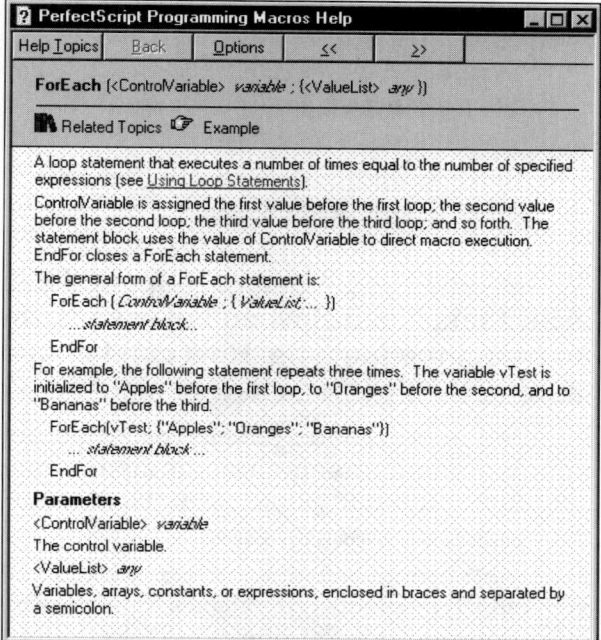

Figure 13-4.   Use Macros Help to learn more about a macro command

---

Note: *Macros Help is available only if you selected it in a Custom installation. The WordPerfect Macro Help option is found in the WordPerfect category. For more information on performing a Custom installation, see "Adding and Removing Suite Components" in Chapter 2.*

? Can I record new keystrokes while editing a macro?

 Yes. You can use the black circle button to record keystrokes.

1. Place the insertion point in your macro where you want to insert the commands.

2. Click the black circle button on the Macro toolbar to open a new window. Then type your commands or select menu options.

 3. When you're finished, click the black box button on the Macro toolbar to return to the macro being edited.

Note: *Sometimes you need to work on a specific file when you record keystrokes. After you click the black circle button, switch to or open the file. When you're done, you'll need to switch back to the new document that opened when you clicked the black circle button. Then click the black square button to return to the macro. Note that you may need to delete the SwitchDoc commands when you return to your macro.*

? While recording a macro, I opened a document as an ASCII text file, but when I play back the macro, I have to select the file type. How can I create a macro that automatically opens a document as a particular file type?

You need to insert a product command that specifies the file type. WordPerfect uses two kinds of macro commands: product commands and programming commands. Product commands control specific features of WordPerfect. For example, if you record a macro in which you change the margins and type text, WordPerfect inserts Margin and Type product commands. You can also add programming commands such as IF and SWITCH to add intelligence and control to your macros.

For example, the FileOpen product command does not include the Format parameter, so if you use this command in your macro and want to display a file with a particular format, you'll need to add this parameter manually. You can use the Corel PerfectScript Commands dialog box (sometimes called the Macro Commands Editor), shown in Figure 13-5, to insert both programming and product commands. You can then edit these commands to add functionality to your macros.

Follow these steps to edit your macro:

1. Choose Tools | Macro | Edit and then double-click the macro you want to edit.

2. Move the insertion point below the FileOpen line where you want to insert the ASCII text file.

3. Choose Commands on the Macro toolbar.

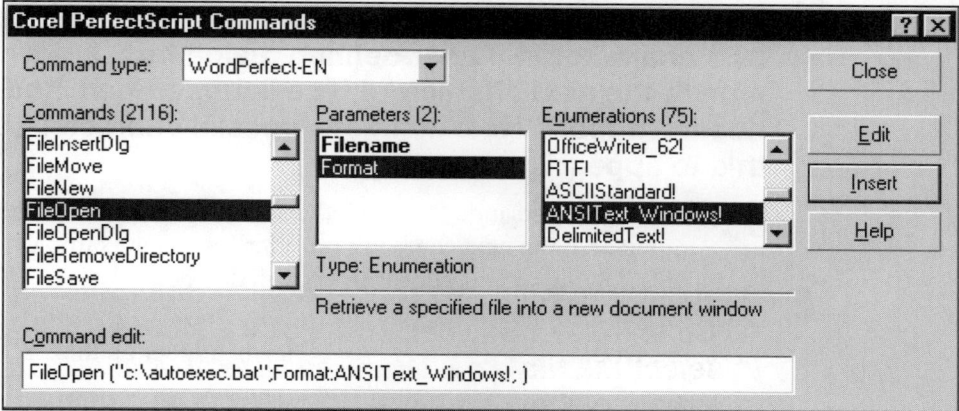

Figure 13-5. You can use the Corel PerfectScript Commands dialog box to insert macro commands

4. To view product commands instead of programming commands, select WordPerfect-EN from the Command Type drop-down list.

5. Select the FileOpen command and then click Edit. Type the path name in quotation marks and select Format. Then select the type of format you want, such as ANSIText...Windows! or ASCIIStandard!, and then click Edit.

6. Click Insert to insert the command in your macro. Then delete the previous FileOpen command.

❓ I can get the FileOpen command to work, but the FileDelete command doesn't work. What's the problem?

When you play a macro with a FileDelete command, the macro may stop and the following error message may appear: "The macro is being canceled because of a 'Not Found' condition processing product command 'WordPerfect.FileDelete.'" If this happens, the filename does not contain a drive and path specification. Although you can use FileOpen to open a file without specifying the filename, you cannot use the FileDelete command without specifying the full pathname.

? **In the macro I'm writing, I want to use an ampersand (&) as a character in a user-defined dialog box, but when I type &, the next character I type is underlined, and the & doesn't appear. How do I get a special character such as this to appear?**

Use two ampersands (&&) together. When you only use one ampersand, the next character is underlined. For example, here's how the following would appear in your dialog box:

If you type:	It will appear as this:
City, state & zip	City, state _zip
City, state && zip	City, state & zip
&City, state && zip	City, state & zip

? **I wrote a macro that finds and replaces a text string, but now I can't stop the macro or exit WordPerfect. What's wrong?**

Your macro is stuck in an endless loop, which causes the Exit command on the File menu to be dimmed because the macro is still playing. You can usually cancel a macro by pressing ESC or CTRL-BREAK.

? **How do I pause a macro so that I can type text in my document?**

Use the PauseKey command. For example, if you type **PauseKey(Enter!)** in your macro, your macro will stop until you press ENTER. If you want to add several lines in your document while the macro is paused, press SHIFT-ENTER.

WORKING WITH TEMPLATES

? **What is the difference between a project and a template?**

A *project* is any document, spreadsheet, template, macro, or application that can be opened when you choose File | New. WordPerfect has created many projects that help you create documents, such as book reports, fax cover sheets, and business cards. A *template* is like a stencil that you can use over and over again to create a certain kind of document.

 Now that projects appear in WordPerfect 8, can I create new projects? Can I still create templates?

You cannot create new projects, but you can still create templates. Corel is working on letting regular people like us create projects, but this feature won't be ready until the Professional version of Corel WordPerfect Suite 8 ships—or later.

Here's how you can create and use templates in WordPerfect 8:

1. Choose File | New and then choose Create WP Template (choose New WP Template in WordPerfect 7) from the Options drop-down list.

2. Type and format the text you want included in the template. If you want to use a document you already created, choose Insert | File and then double-click the file you want to use.

3. When you're done creating the template, choose File | Save.

4. Type a description (which will appear in the New dialog box), type a name for the template, and select the group (such as Custom WP Templates) in which you want the template placed.

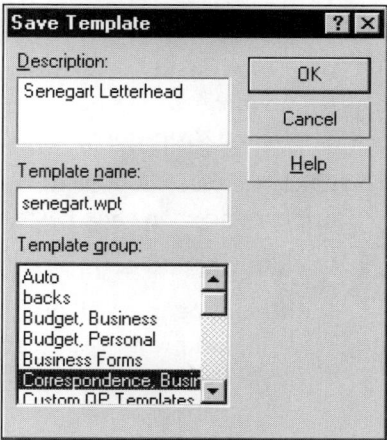

Note: *When you choose File | New, you must select the group in which you saved the template before the template will appear in the list box.*

❓ How do I change the "permanent" information in the Fax Cover Sheet project in WordPerfect 8?

Although you can still create and edit templates in WordPerfect 8, you're better off not messing with the templates and experts associated with projects. Projects in WordPerfect 8 provide a lot of useful information, but their biggest drawback is that they are difficult—if not impossible—to customize. Thus, you'll probably just have to live with the preset information in the projects.

❓ Can I grab addresses from the Address Book and insert them in a template I create?

You can use the Prompt Builder, shown in Figure 13-6, to add variable information to your templates. For example, if you're creating a letter template, you don't want to have to delete the same address and retype a new one every time. Instead, you can add prompts to the template so that when you create a document based on the template, you'll be prompted for variable information. You can link these prompts to Address Book entries.

Here's how you can edit a template to insert prompts:

1. Choose File | New, select the template you want to edit, and choose Edit WP Template from the Options menu.

2. Click Build Prompts to display the Prompt Builder.

3. Click Add and then type of the name of the prompt you want displayed, such as **Address**. If you want to insert information from your Address Book, select the field from the Link to Address Book field drop-down list. Then click OK.

4. Click the place in your document where you want the prompt to appear and then click Paste.

5. Continue to add and paste prompts.

6. If different people will use the template you're creating, you'll want to add prompts that grab the personal information from the Address Book. Choose Personal in the Prompt Builder dialog box

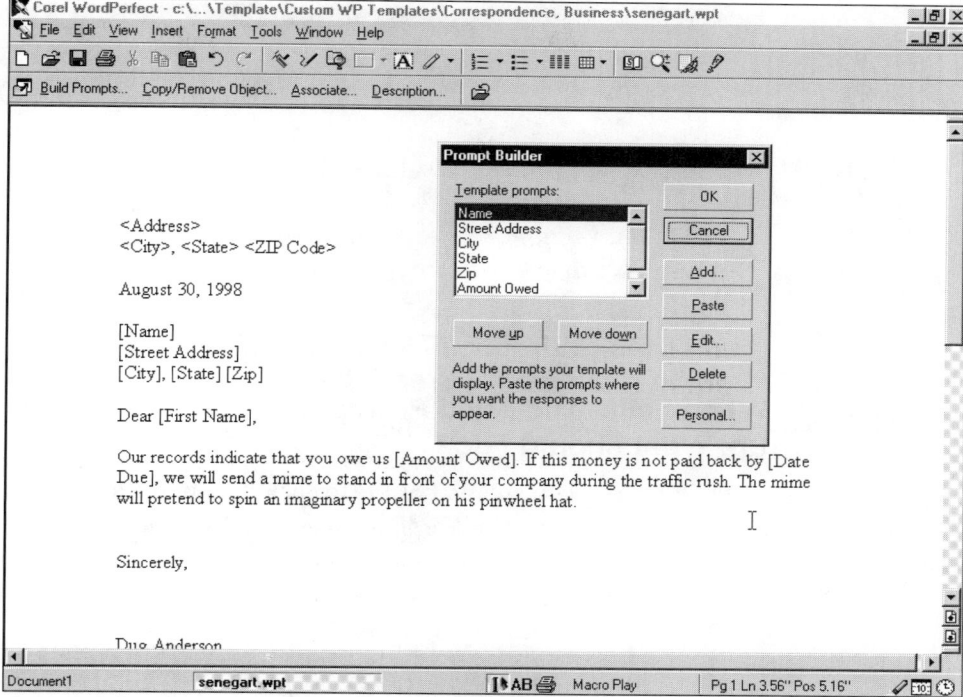

Figure 13-6. Use the Prompt Builder to add prompts to templates

and then paste the appropriate items in your document. In your template, personal information appears between angle brackets (<>) instead of square brackets.

7. Save and exit the template.

Note: *After you choose File | New to create a document based on this new template, the Template Information dialog box lets you type the information for the new document you're creating. If you have linked items to the Address Book, you can click the Address Book button and select an entry.*

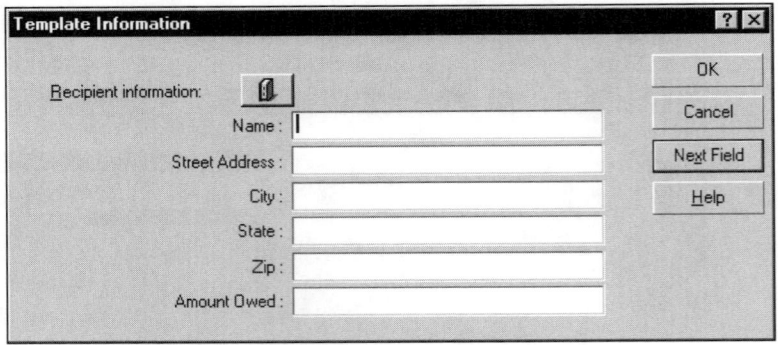

When I click the Build Prompts button, WordPerfect locks up. What should I do?

Of course, you should be able to click the Build Prompts button without locking up WordPerfect—but if this does happen, Corel recommends that you follow these steps after you restart your computer:

1. Choose File | New | Options | Create WP Template (choose New WP Template in WordPerfect 7).

2. Choose File | Close and then click Yes to save changes.

3. Give the template a name, choose File | New, and then select the new template from the list. Then choose Options | Edit Template. You should be able to click Build Prompts without incident.

I want a template I created to appear in the [Corel WordPerfect 8] category. How can I move a template to a different category?

You can copy or move a template to any category you want.

1. Choose File | New and then select the template you want to copy.

2. Choose Options | Copy Project and then select the category (such as [Corel WordPerfect 8]) to which you want to move the project.

? I want to use a particular toolbar when I open a template document, but none of the toolbars appear in the drop-down list. How do I associate a toolbar with a template?

When you create a template, you can add the following *objects* to the document: menus, toolbars, macros, QuickWords, styles, and keyboards. Before you associate a toolbar with a template, you first must copy the object. Here's how:

1. Choose File | New and select your template. Then from the Options pop-up button, choose Edit WP Template.

2. Choose Copy/Remove Object from the Template property bar.

3. Select Toolbars from the Object Type drop-down list. Then select the toolbar (such as Drawing Solid Shape) you want to use from the Toolbars list box and choose Copy. Then click Close.

4. Choose Associate and select the item (such as Graphics) with which you want to associate the item. Then select the toolbar from the Toolbars drop-down list and click OK.

5. Choose File and click Close. Then click Yes to save the changes.

Note: *Associating toolbars in your template with WordPerfect features makes the toolbar appear when you use that feature in a document created based on the template.*

? I want to trigger a custom macro when I open the template, but the <dofiller> macro is already selected. How can I associate my custom macro with the Post New trigger and still retain the template prompts implemented by the <dofiller> macro?

If your template uses automated prompts, the <dofiller> macro is already associated with the Post New trigger. If you replace the <dofiller> macro with your custom macro, the template prompts will no longer work. You can solve this problem by adding the TemplateFill command to your macro. This command serves the same purpose as the <dofiller> macro and causes WordPerfect to display the Template Information dialog box. Here's how to add this command to your macro:

1. Choose Tools | Macro | Edit, type the name of your macro, and click Edit.

2. Place the insertion point in your macro at the point where you want the Template Information dialog box to appear and prompt you for information. For example, if you want to be prompted for the template information before the macro plays, place the insertion point at the beginning of the macro, just after the Application command.

3. Type **TemplateFill ( )**.

4. Click Save and Compile on the Macro property bar and then choose File | Close to close your macro.

5. Choose File | New and select your template. From the Options pop-up button, choose Edit WP Template.

6. Choose Copy/Remove Object from the Template property bar.

7. Choose Macros on Disk from the Object Type pop-up menu.

8. Click the file folder button to the right of the Source text box, select your macro, and click Select. Click Copy and then click Close.

9. To assign your macro to the Post New trigger, click Associate on the Template property bar.

10. Select Triggers and then select Post New in the List list box. Select your custom macro from the Macros drop-down list and click OK.

11. Choose File | Close. Then click Yes to save the changes.

Tip: *Instead of adding the TemplateFill command to a macro, some people prefer to edit the <dofiller> macro to chain to the custom macro. To do this, choose Tools | Template Macro | Edit and then double-click <dofiller>. You can then copy and paste any commands to the <dofiller> macro from your custom macro.*

? I want to insert a date in the template document, but I don't want that date to be updated each time I open a document based on the template. How do I insert the current date without having it updated?

First, you need to create a macro that inserts the current date. Then you need to follow the steps described in the preceding Q&A to associate the macro with the Post New item. Here's what you need to do.

1. Edit the template and insert a bookmark where you want the date to appear. Save the template.

2. Choose Tools | Template Macro | Record. Type a name for the macro and choose Record.

3. While recording your macro, jump to the date bookmark you used in the template. Choose Insert | Date/Time, make sure Automatic Update is *not* selected, and then double-click the date format.

4. Choose Tools | Template Macro | Record to stop recording the macro. Remove the inserted date from your template.

5. Save the template document. Then follow the steps in the preceding Q&A to associate the macro with the Post New item in the template.

Tip: *If you want to run more than one macro, you can use the CHAIN command at the end of the macro to play another macro.*

? When I create a document based on the letterhead template, the insertion point appears at the top of the document. How do I place the insertion point where the letter text should be typed?

Set a QuickMark before you save your template. WordPerfect will automatically jump to the QuickMark you set when you create a document based on your template. Here's how to set a QuickMark:

1. Choose File | New and select your template. From the Options pop-up button, choose Edit WP Template.

2. Place the insertion point where you want it to appear.

3. Choose Insert | Bookmark and then choose Set QuickMark (or press CTRL-SHIFT-Q).

4. Choose File | Close and then click Yes to save the changes.

❓ I edited a template, but when I tried to save it, the error message "Access Denied" appeared. What's wrong?

Here's what probably happened: You created and saved a template and then opened the template to create a new document based on that template. After you edited the document, you tried to save it under the same name as the template upon which it was based, to create a revised version of the template. At that point, the "Access Denied" error message appeared. Solving this problem is easy: make the editing changes to the original template, not to a document based on that template.

❓ I changed the Personal Information for projects to use my boss's name and then tried to create a document, but the old name still appears. How do I change the Personal Information for projects?

If you change the Personal Information just before creating a new project, WordPerfect 8 does not use this new information to create the document, but instead uses the previously selected Personal Information record. The new Personal Information record is not used until you exit and then restart WordPerfect.

Here's how to change the Personal Information:

1. Choose File | New and then choose Personal Information from the Options drop-down list.

2. Click OK. Then select a name from your Address Book and click Select. Then click Close.

3. Exit and restart WordPerfect.

Answer Topics!

Document Sharing and the Internet @ a Glance

⇨   Some documents need to pass through many hands to be edited by committees, staffs, bosses, marketing people, and so on. WordPerfect includes a feature that makes it easy for several people to review a document. Each reviewer can edit the document and send it back to the author, who can then go through the changes one by one and accept or reject them. For help with these document tracking features, consult this chapter.

⇨   If you have a modem and are connected to a network, and if you have the right software installed, you can send e-mail and faxes straight from WordPerfect—and if you need help, you can turn to this chapter.

⇨   WordPerfect includes several features that let you browse the Web. You can insert hyperlinks in your document so that when someone clicks a link in your WordPerfect document, a connection is made to the Internet, and the linked Web page appears. The QuickLinks feature automatically converts Web and e-mail addresses to hyperlinks. If these features seem daunting, look for answers to your questions in this chapter.

⇨   Instead of messing around with arcane HTML tags, you can create and format Web documents in WordPerfect. This chapter provides tips on using the Internet Publisher feature, which helps you create and publish an entire Web site.

⇨   If you want your documents to appear on the Internet with their original formatting intact, you can publish documents to Barista. Barista documents can be viewed on any platform so long as the Web browser supports Java. Consult this chapter if you have any questions about using Barista.

TRACKING DOCUMENT REVISIONS

 My co-workers edited a file, and I want to know what they changed. Is there a way to find out what was changed?

You can use the Add Compare Markings feature (sometimes called Document Compare) to see the differences between the current document and another version of the document saved on disk. When you compare the documents, additions are marked with redlining, and deletions are marked with strikeout lines.

 *Note: The Add Compare Markings feature works only if you've saved the old version of the file as well as the new version of the file. If you replace the old file with the edited version, you won't be able to compare the two versions. It's a good idea to make a backup copy of the file you're having edited. You can also use the Versions feature. See "Working with Files" in Chapter 4.*

Here's how you can compare documents:

1. Open the edited version of the document and then choose File | Document | Add Compare Markings.

2. Specify the name of the older version of file saved on disk.

3. Select the level of detail you want used in the comparison and then click OK.

Tip: To remove markings, choose File | Document | Remove Compare Markings and then click OK.

 Is there a way to easily view and accept or reject changes without having to a create compare file for each revised version?

Instead of relying on the Add Compare Markings feature to see the changes made in a document, you can use the Review Document feature. When you give the original file to your co-workers, then tell them to choose File | Document | Review | Reviewer before they begin editing the document. Then when you get the edited document back, you can open the document, choose File | Document | Review

| Author, and review the changes and use the buttons on the property bar to accept or reject each change, as shown in Figure 14-1.

Tip: *When others edit your document, they may introduce grammatical errors. It's a good idea to check the grammar after you have accepted the changes from your reviewers. Choose Tools | Grammatik and make changes where necessary. You may also want to run Spell Check after accepting the changes.*

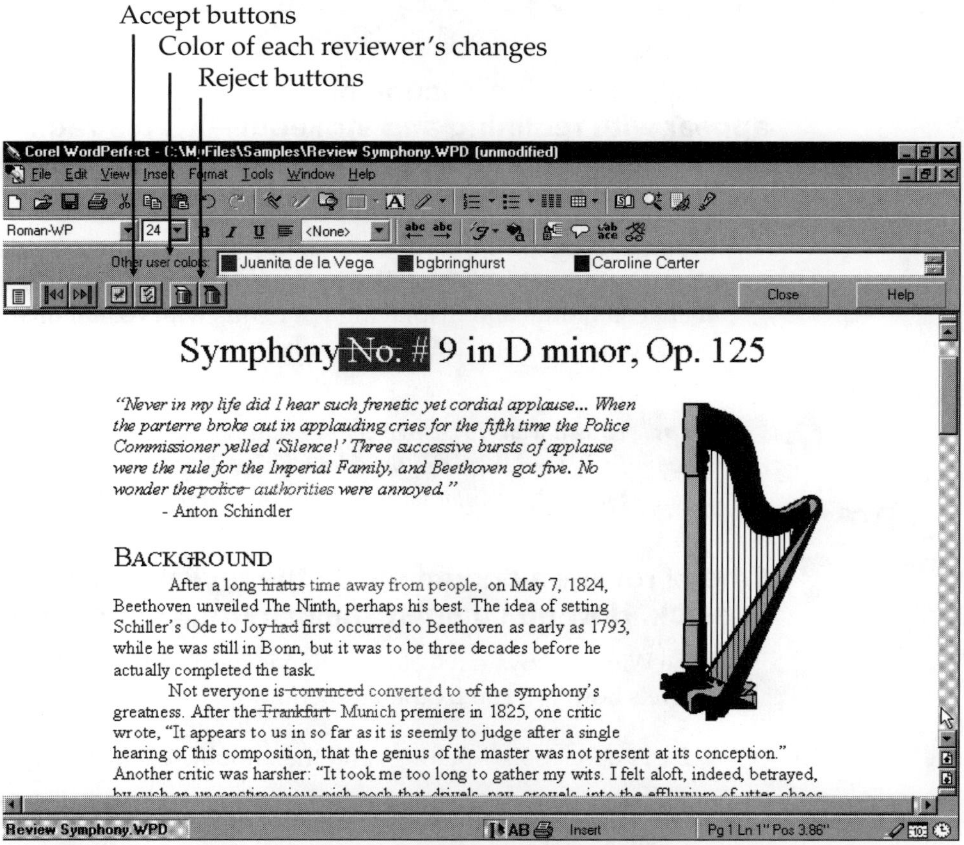

Accept buttons
Color of each reviewer's changes
Reject buttons

Corel WordPerfect - C:\MyFiles\Samples\Review Symphony.WPD (unmodified)

File Edit View Insert Format Tools Window Help

Roman-WP   24   B I U ≡ <None>

Other user colors: ■ Juanita de la Vega   ■ bgbringhurst   ■ Caroline Carter

Close   Help

Symphony No. # 9 in D minor, Op. 125

"Never in my life did I hear such frenetic yet cordial applause... When the parterre broke out in applauding cries for the fifth time the Police Commissioner yelled 'Silence!' Three successive bursts of applause were the rule for the Imperial Family, and Beethoven got five. No wonder the police authorities were annoyed."
   - Anton Schindler

BACKGROUND

After a long hiatus time away from people, on May 7, 1824, Beethoven unveiled The Ninth, perhaps his best. The idea of setting Schiller's Ode to Joy had first occurred to Beethoven as early as 1793, while he was still in Bonn, but it was to be three decades before he actually completed the task.

Not everyone is convinced converted to of the symphony's greatness. After the Frankfurt Munich premiere in 1825, one critic wrote, "It appears to us in so far as it is seemly to judge after a single hearing of this composition, that the genius of the master was not present at its conception." Another critic was harsher: "It took me too long to gather my wits. I felt aloft, indeed, betrayed,

Review Symphony.WPD   AB   Insert   Pg 1 Ln 1" Pos 3.86"

Figure 14-1.   Use Document Review to accept or reject document changes

---

Quick Instructions on Reviewing a Document

Here are some brief instructions you might want to send to your reviewers to ensure that the editing process goes smoothly:

1. Open the document in WordPerfect 7 or 8.

2. Choose File | Document | Review and then choose Reviewer. If prompted, specify your initials.

3. Select a color (except black or white) from the Set Color pop-up palette and then edit the document as usual.

4. Save the document.

? **While I'm editing a document, I don't want my changes to appear with redlining and strikeout—it's distracting—but I still want my changes to be marked for later review. How do I turn off this display while I work?**

You can click the Display Annotations button on the left side of the Document Review feature bar, shown in Figure 14-2, to toggle between hiding and displaying your edits with redlining and strikeout.

 *Tip:*   *If you want to change your default reviewer name, initials, or color, choose Tools | Settings and then double-click Environment. Make the changes in the User Information, click OK, and then click Close.*

? **When I review a document, all the reviewer's changes are in black. How do I display the markings in different colors?**

The Windows System Colors option is selected in the Display settings. Here's how you can fix the problem:

1. Choose Tools | Settings and then double-click Display.

2. Deselect the Windows System Colors option and click OK. Then click Close.

Figure 14-2.   Display Annotations button

? I received a file with redline markings in the right margin. How do I change the way redlining is displayed?

To change the redline display, choose File | Document | Redline Method and then select the way you want the redline markings displayed.

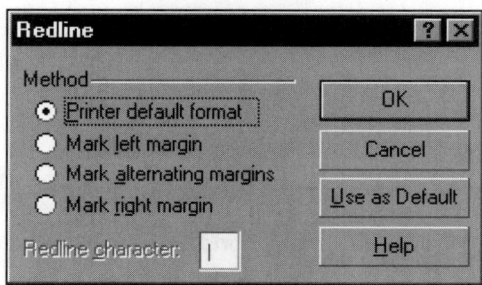

❓ How do I provide instructions in my document without affecting the printed document?

The Comments feature is commonly used to achieve this effect. Choose Insert | Comment | Create and then type the text you want to appear, as shown in Figure 14-3. Click the Close button when you're done.

In Page or Two Pages view, the comment appears as an icon in the left margin. If you want other people to see your comments, this can be a problem, especially if they're using 640 x 480 screen resolution. Reviewers may not be able to see the comment icon in Page view or know that they can click the Comment icon to view it.

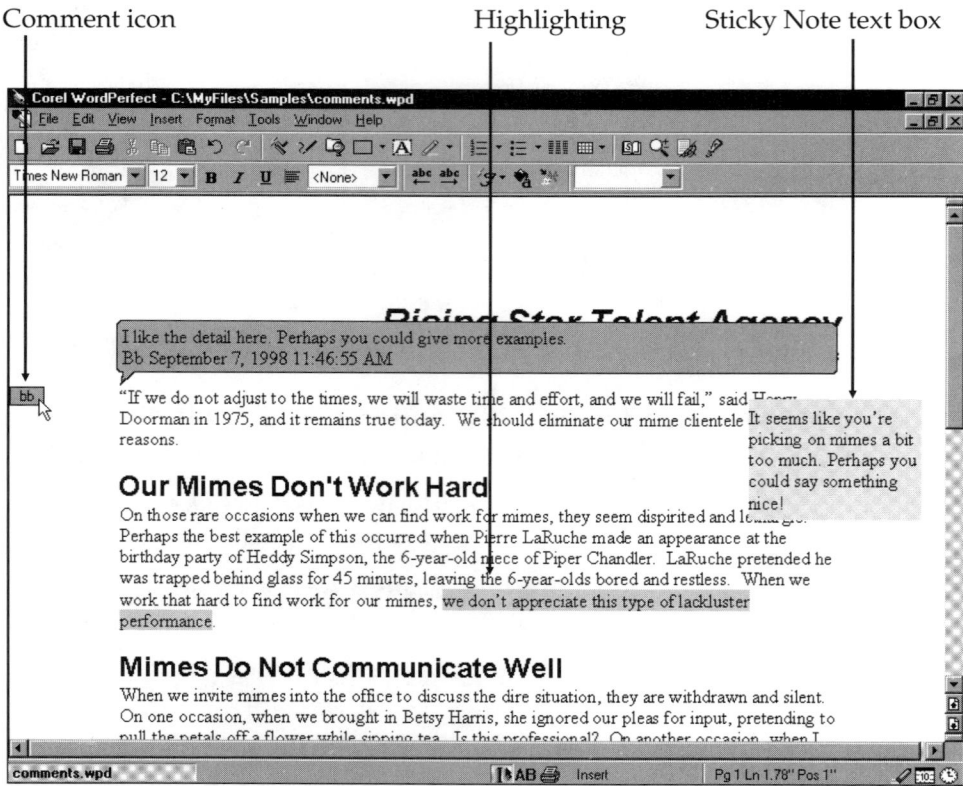

Figure 14-3.　You can add instructions to your documents to provide information to readers

Here are some other suggestions for making your text stand out to reviewers:

⇨ To make sure your readers see a comment, you can insert graphics boxes that act as sticky notes. Choose Insert | Graphics | Custom Box and then double-click Sticky Note Text. You can type your note in the text box that appears and drag its border where you want it to appear.

⇨ You can add highlighting to existing text to call attention to particular parts of your document. You can then, for example, tell reviewers to pay close attention to the highlighted areas. To add highlighting, choose Tools | Highlight | On and then drag across the text you want to highlight. When you're finished marking your document, choose Tools | Highlight | On again (or click the Highlight button on the toolbar).

? I want to print comments, but if I convert them to text, I'll have to delete them later. How do I print comments without converting them to text?

Unless you edit each comment and print the text individually, you must convert comments to text before you can print them. However, here's how you can do this without converting the comments permanently:

1. Save your document.

2. Choose Insert | Comments | Convert to Text.

3. Print the document and then close the document without saving it.

 ***Tip:*** *To create hidden text, select the text you want to hide and then choose Format | Font. Select Hidden and click OK.*

? I deleted a Hidden code, and all the hidden text was deleted as well. How do I remove the hidden text formatting without deleting text?

You must display hidden text before you delete the codes, or else you will delete the text along with the codes. To display hidden text,

---

Comments versus Hidden Text

You may wonder when you should use the Hidden Text feature and when you should use the Comments feature. Although the Comments feature works great for adding notes to yourself and others, the Hidden Text feature is one of those power tools that can be used in many ways.

For example, if you are preparing a test for students, you can format the answers in hidden text. You can then print the same document twice—once with the answers hidden and once with the answers displayed—while working on the same document. Also, if you don't want to spell-check a certain portion of the text (perhaps because it contains numerous foreign or technical terms that will cause the spell checker to pause at every other word), you can format the text as hidden text. Then you can hide this text by choosing Tools | Settings, double-click Display, deselecting Hidden Text, and then clicking OK. When you're ready to print, you can follow the same steps to display the hidden text.

---

choose Tools | Settings, double-click Display, select Hidden Text, and click OK. Then click Close.

E-MAILING AND FAXING DOCUMENTS

? **When I try to e-mail a document from WordPerfect, the wrong e-mail program comes up. How do I open the mail client that my network uses?**

You need to create a Corel Settings Profile that specifies the appropriate e-mail application (called the *mail client*). When you install Corel WordPerfect Suite 8, the setup program creates a Corel Settings Profile for the Address Book, but the only mail client it automatically recognizes is Novell GroupWise 4.1. If you are not using Novell GroupWise 4.1 as a mail client, you must add your mail client to the Corel Settings Profile.

Note: *Corel says it supports WordPerfect Office 4.0, Novell GroupWise 4.1, Digital Teamlinks, and any mail system using the MAPI or CMC standards. Products displaying a "Designed for Windows 95" logo should support CMC mail. Of course, you must be connected to a network to send e-mail.*

Here's how to add a settings profile:

1. Click Start on the taskbar and then choose Settings | Control Panel.

2. Double-click Mail and Fax.

3. Choose Show Profiles, select Corel 8 Settings, and choose Properties.

4. Click Add and then select and configure your mail service. You may need to contact your e-mail provider to learn how to configure your mail service.

Tip: *To e-mail a document from WordPerfect, open and save the document and then choose File | Send To | Mail. Select the profile and send the mail. If you select text, that text will be included in the Message box of your e-mail program.*

❓ When I try to send e-mail from WordPerfect using Lotus Notes, the error message "Novell GroupWise Not Found" appears. How do I get Lotus Notes to work?

You probably previously installed Novell PerfectOffice with GroupWise, but then you removed GroupWise. Unfortunately, the GroupWise entries are still in the registry, and the system is reading them as if GroupWise were the active e-mail program. Thus, when you choose File | Send To | Mail, the error message "Novell GroupWise Not Found" or "Find Files - Find the path to GroupWise 'OFWIN.EXE'" appears.

You need to completely remove Ofwin41 (GroupWise)—including its registry information—from the system. You can either use an uninstaller program to clean up the registry, or you can edit the registry directly by running the Registry Editor (Regedit.exe) and searching for references to GroupWise or Ofwin.exe. After you delete the registry entries for GroupWise, you can select the MS Exchange

Settings profile to activate Lotus Notes e-mail, Microsoft Mail, cc:Mail, or any other mail program.

 ***Warning:***   *Editing the registry incorrectly can damage your system files. Make sure you back up your registry before trying anything. In the Registry Editor, choose Registry and then Export Registry File. Type a filename (such as **regback**) and choose Save. If you make unwanted changes to your registry, you can double-click this backup file you created, or you can choose Registry and then Import Registry File in the Registry Editor.*

When I choose File | Send To | Fax Recipient, my fax software doesn't appear. How do I fax a document from WordPerfect?

To be able to fax your documents from within WordPerfect 7 or 8, you must have a fax modem and a Windows fax program (Quicklink, ProComm, MicroSoft Fax, WinFax, or similar software) installed either on your machine or on a network server. After the fax program is installed, a fax driver should appear on the submenu when you choose File | Send To. If the fax driver does not appear, you can select the fax software driver from the Current Printer drop-down list in the Print dialog box the same way you select a different printer driver in WordPerfect. When you choose Print, the third-party fax software takes control from that point on in the faxing process. If the fax program does not fax the document properly, you're probably having a problem with your fax software.

Here are some suggestions for faxing:

⇨ When you run into a problem faxing from WordPerfect, a good way to determine whether the problem is in WordPerfect or elsewhere is to try faxing from WordPad in Windows 95. If the same problem occurs in WordPad, you're most likely having a problem with the fax driver or software.

⇨ If you select a fax driver in the Print dialog box to fax a document, remember to select a different print driver when you want to print a document.

⇨ If a fax driver does not appear on the list of choices in your Print dialog box, the fax driver has not been correctly installed in Windows. Reinstall the fax software, and make sure the fax driver appears when you click Start on the taskbar and choose Settings | Printers.

⇨ If your fax software is a 16-bit application, start it before you try to fax from WordPerfect, and WordPerfect will be more likely to recognize it.

⇨ Don't be concerned if your fax looks different from your printed document. The fax uses only the fonts available in Windows, whereas your printer has additional built-in fonts.

❓ I installed the Corel WordPerfect Suite 8, and now Microsoft Fax does not work properly. How can I get it to work correctly again?

While running Microsoft Exchange, the Remote Mail and Deliver Now options may be dimmed on the Tools menu, or Windows 95 may lock up when you click the Tools menu. This problem occurs if you're running an older version of Windows 95 (sometimes called Windows 95a) or Microsoft Exchange. To fix this problem, you need to install the Microsoft Exchange Update for Windows 95. The name of this file is Exupdusa.exe (the filename may be different for localized versions of Windows 95).

To obtain the Exchange update, visit Microsoft's Web site for upgrades and support at the following address:

http://www.microsoft.com/exchangesupport

If you want to update Microsoft Exchange to Windows Messaging, you can get Microsoft's Service Pack 2 for Microsoft Exchange. For more information about the service pack, see the following Web site:

http://www.microsoft.com/exchangesupport/content/servicepacks/sp.htm

❓ I fax many letters and documents. How can I create a signature to include in my faxed documents?

If you have a scanner available, you can scan your signature and insert it into a style or QuickWord abbreviation, or you can create a macro that inserts the signature in your letter closing. For more information, see "Scanning Images" in Chapter 9.

CONNECTING TO THE INTERNET

❓ How do I jump to the Internet from WordPerfect?

If you have an Internet service provider, the Netscape browser, and a modem or network connection to the Internet, you can jump to the Internet from WordPerfect. Here are several methods:

⇨ Choose Help | Corel Web Site. This takes you to the Corel Web site. For better technical support information, jump to the following page:

> http://www.corel.com/products/wordperfect/cwp8/ support.htm

⇨ Choose File | Internet Publisher | Browse the Web. From here, you can search anywhere on the Internet.

❓ I'm not using Netscape as my browser, but when I choose Help | Corel Web Site, a message appears saying that WordPerfect cannot find Netscape. How do I use a different Web browser?

WordPerfect Internet Publisher is designed to run with the Netscape browser. Although you can change a setting in the registry to change the default browser, Corel says you will not get the cross-communication you currently get between WordPerfect applications and Netscape. WordPerfect looks at the registry entry at the following location to launch the Netscape browser:

```
HKEY_LOCAL_MACHINE\SOFTWARE\Microsoft\Windows\
CurrentVersion\App Paths\Netscape.exe
```

If you want WordPerfect to run effectively on the Internet, you should use Netscape as your browser. The Corel WordPerfect Suite CD includes a version of Netscape. To install Netscape on your computer, insert the Corel WordPerfect Suite 8 CD and click Netscape Setup. Then follow the rest of the setup instructions.

❓ I tried to create a QuickLink to "Novell," but WordPerfect keeps placing @ before the QuickLink. What's the problem?

There is no problem. Everything is working as designed. WordPerfect places an @ sign before the QuickLinks word, as shown in Figure 14-4, to give you more control over the words that are converted to hyperlinks. If the @ weren't included, each occurrence of the word "Novell" would be converted to a hyperlink, which is probably not what you want in most documents.

Here's how to create a QuickLink:

1. Choose Tools | QuickCorrect and then click the QuickLinks tab.

2. Type the link word (such as **@novell**) in the Link Word text box and then type the URL (such as **http://www.novell.com**) in the Location to Link to text box.

3. Click Add Entry.

4. When you have finished adding QuickLinks entries, click OK.

? Whenever I type e-mail addresses, they are formatted as hyperlinks. How do I turn off this option?

Whenever you type text that WordPerfect recognizes as an Internet URL or an e-mail address, WordPerfect formats the text as a hyperlink so that you or someone else can jump to a site or launch an e-mail

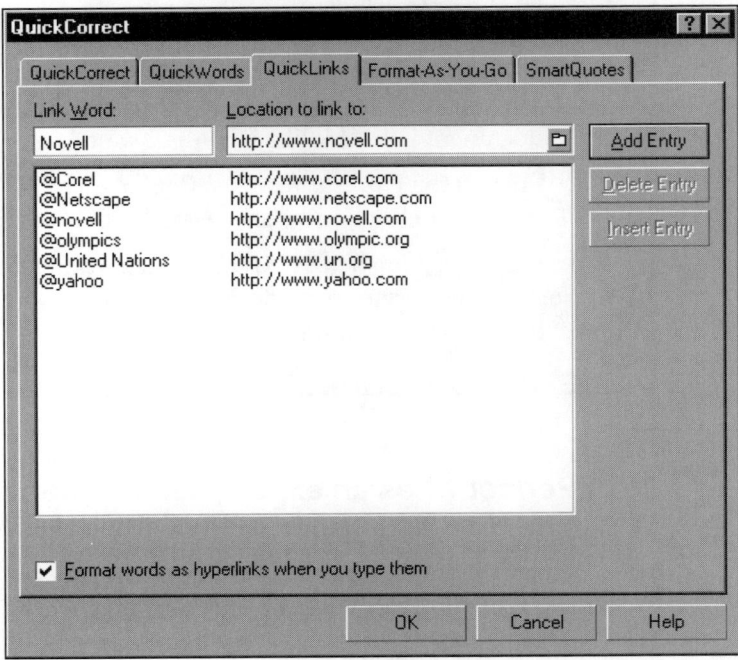

Figure 14-4.   You can use QuickLinks to create hyperlinks

program from within WordPerfect. For example, if you type **www.corel.com** or **bobsmith@zignet.com**, WordPerfect will format these items as hyperlinks.

You may not always want your Web and e-mail addresses to be formatted as hyperlinks. Here's how to turn off this option:

1. Choose Tools | QuickCorrect and then click the QuickLinks tab.

2. Deselect Format Words as Hyperlinks When You Type Them and then click OK.

PUBLISHING WEB DOCUMENTS

Internet Publishing in a Nutshell

Creating a Web site on the Internet requires the following main steps:

1. Plan your Web site carefully. Use the Internet Publisher in WordPerfect to create a home page with a table of contents and any additional Web pages. You can either create the Web pages from scratch or convert existing documents.

2. Edit and test the WordPerfect Web documents as needed. You can choose View | View in Web Browser to see what your document will look like when published.

3. Publish the WordPerfect Web documents to HTML. You can then set up hyperlinks to the resulting .HTM files.

4. Send your finished HTML documents and related files to your Internet service provider (ISP). Then connect to the Web and test the documents again on the Web.

? WordPerfect 7 has an expert that lets me create an entire Web site. How do I create a Web site in WordPerfect 8?

When Corel replaced the experts and templates in WordPerfect 7 with the projects in WordPerfect 8, the Web Page Expert got lost in the shuffle. However, WordPerfect 8 includes a PerfectExpert panel, shown in Figure 14-5, that's great for building single Web pages.

One of the advantages of using the Web Page Expert was that you could create all the documents for your Web site and set up hyperlinks right from the start. However, if you follow these general steps, you'll be able to create a Web site in WordPerfect 8:

1. Create a folder on your hard drive where you want to store your Web pages.

2. Choose File | New.

3. Select Web Publishing from the drop-down list and then double-click [WordPerfect Web Document].

4. Use the PerfectExpert panel to format your Web document.

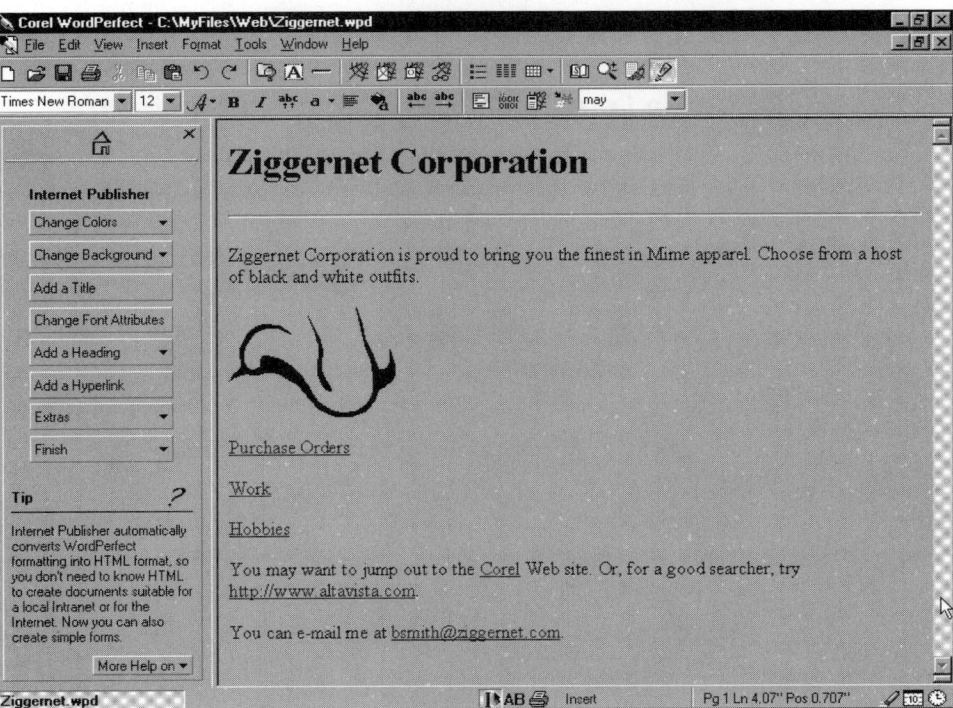

Figure 14-5.   Use the PerfectExpert panel to format a Web document

5. Save the document with a .WPD extension in the folder you created.

6. Choose File | Internet Publisher | Publish to HTML and click OK.

7. Follow steps 2 through 6 to create and save additional Web pages in the same folder.

8. Set up a table of contents on your home page with hyperlinks to the other .HTM pages you created.

 *Tip:*   *It's a good idea to include a link at the bottom of each Web page that takes viewers back to the home page.*

 *Note:*   *When you test your Web pages in your browser, you must include full pathnames for the links to work correctly. However, these pathnames will not work when you upload the files to the Internet. You'll need to place all the Web site files—including graphics—in the same folder and then edit the links to display only the filenames instead of the full pathnames.*

How do I create a hyperlink from a graphic?

You can create a hyperlink by selecting the text or graphic and then specifying the location the link will jump to as shown in Figure 14-6.

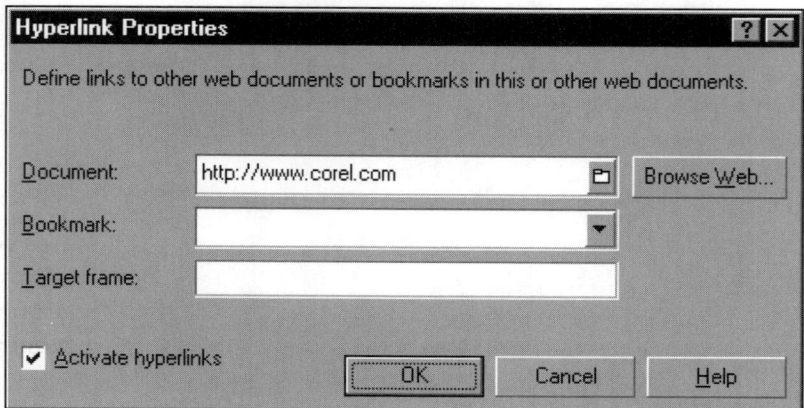

Figure 14-6.   Use the Hyperlink Properties dialog box to create a hyperlink

Internet Terms You Should Know

Web Site: Your collection of pages (the Internet term for documents) on the Web, usually organized so viewers can quickly find the information they need.

Home Page: The first screen viewers see when they come to your Web site. This screen usually acts as a table of contents for the rest of the site.

Link: Text or graphics viewers can click to jump to a different page at your site. Links are highlighted or marked in some other way to tell viewers that they can click them to jump to different locations.

HTML: Hypertext markup language (HTML) is the programming language used to format documents used on the Internet. *Tags*, such as <H2> and </H2>, are the HTML codes used in creating documents. If you want to see what an HTML document looks like, open a Web page in Netscape or another browser and choose View | Document Source.

URL: The uniform resource locator (URL) is the Web site address. A URL consists of the service name, host name, and path to the Web page, such as http://www.corel.com.

Here's how to create a link to enable viewers of your Web page to click a graphic to jump to a different Web page:

1. Insert the graphic in your document.

2. Click the graphic to select it and then choose Tools | Hyperlink.

3. In the Document text box, specify the Web page you want to link to. If you don't know the URL address, click Browse Web, open the Web page, and then close or minimize the browser; the most recent URL address will appear in the Document text box.

4. Click OK to return to your document.

Tip: *It's a good idea to create a text hyperlink in addition to the graphic hyperlink. Some people choose not to view graphics when browsing. You can add a text hyperlink below the graphic, or you can right-click the graphic, choose HTML Properties, and then type the link text in the Alternate Text text box and click OK.*

I want to edit my Web document. Should I edit the .WPD version or the .HTM version?

Although you can directly edit the .HTM file that Internet Publisher creates when you publish the Web document, it's not a good idea. It involves additional prompts and can put your original .WPD file out of sync with the .HTM file that Internet Publisher generates. For best results, edit the .WPD document. When you finish making your changes, choose File | Internet Publisher | Publish to HTML and click OK. Then click Yes each time you are prompted to update all the files associated with the document. When you publish to HTML, WordPerfect converts styles to HTML tags and converts graphics to GIF files.

My home page looks good, but the pages I link to appear as gobbledygook. What's wrong?

You probably linked to the .WPD document instead of the .HTM document. Open the Web pages you link to and choose File | Internet Publisher | Publish to HTML and click OK in each document. Then open your Web home page, right-click the link, and choose Edit Hyperlink. Make sure you're linking to the .HTM file instead of the .WPD file for each document.

Warning: *Whenever you edit a Web document in WordPerfect, remember to use the Publish to HTML option. Just before you close the file, choose File | Internet Publisher | Publish to HTML. Otherwise, your HTML file won't reflect the changes you've made.*

? **When I converted a WordPerfect document to a Web document, my drop caps and paragraph borders disappeared. How can I retain the all formatting in my Web documents?**

When you create or convert Web documents, you'll discover that a number of formatting features disappear or are changed. Some of the most obvious are page numbering, margins, columns, headers and footers, fonts, drop caps, paragraph and page borders and fills, watermarks, and vertical lines. Furthermore, formulas in tables will be converted to plain text, and underlining will not appear in the browser. Don't blame WordPerfect—the arcane HTML language is what causes these problems.

If your document is complex and contains merge commands, columns, or other WordPerfect features that don't convert cleanly to HTML, you may be better off creating the Web document from scratch instead of converting it.

If you don't mind possibly losing some of the WordPerfect formatting features, follow these steps to convert an existing WordPerfect document to HTML:

1. Open the file you want to convert and then choose File | Internet Publisher.

2. Choose Format as Web Document and then click OK.

Tip: *If you really need to keep your formatting intact when you publish to the Web, you may want to use Barista. See "Publishing in Barista" later in this chapter.*

? **I need to create many pages for the same Web site. Is there a way to change the default template so I can use the same background for all the pages I create?**

You can edit the default Web template to change its color and other properties, or you can create your own Web template. Here's how to create a new template based on the default template:

1. Choose File | New and then select Web Publishing from the drop-down list.

Tips on Formatting Web Pages

When formatting Web documents, consider the following:

⇨ WordPerfect is not a Web browser, so the fact that your Web document looks good in WordPerfect doesn't mean it's going to look good to people viewing it on the Internet. You need to check out your document in a Web browser to see how it will really look on the World Wide Web. To preview your document, just click the View in Web Browser button on the Toolbar or choose View | View in Web Browser.

⇨ Web browsers show a document's title in the program's title bar. The first heading you use will be displayed as the title. If the document doesn't use any heading styles, a temporary Windows path- and filename will appear instead. If you want to change the document title, right-click the Web page and choose Properties from the QuickMenu. Click Custom Title and then type the title you want to use.

⇨ Avoid changing the font in your Web pages. If you must change the font, don't use uncommon fonts. Font changes will work on your audience's browsers only if viewers have the same font, so stick to common fonts such as Times New Roman, Arial (or Helvetica), and Courier New. Your best option is to select the default headings from the Font/Size button on the property bar.

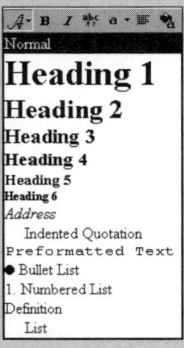

By default, documents on the Web have a light gray background. Although you can create much fancier backgrounds with wavy lines and all sorts of nonsense, you won't do your readers any favors. These types of backgrounds can be difficult to read. In fact, you may want to use a white background, which provides maximum contrast to the text. To change the background and text colors, choose Format | Text/Background Colors.

2. Click [WordPerfect Web Document] and then choose Options | Edit WP Template.

3. To change the background color, choose Format | Text/Background Colors, select the colors you want to use, and click OK.

4. Make any other changes to the template.

5. Choose File | Save As. Then type a description, specify a template name, select the Template group (such as Web or Web Publishing), and click OK.

To create Web documents based on the template you created, choose File | New and then double-click the template you created.

? I want to edit the source code of an HTML document in WordPerfect, but WordPerfect keeps displaying the formatted Web document. How can I open a Web document for editing in WordPerfect?

Here's how to open a Web document in WordPerfect so that you can edit the source code:

1. Choose File | Open.

2. Double-click the Web document you want to open.

3. Select ASCII DOS Text from the drop-down list and then click OK.

4. Make the editing changes you want to the source document.

5. Choose File | Save As. Then select HTML from the File Type drop-down list and click Save.

Tip: *If you need to insert special HTML tags in your document, you don't need to open the document as an ASCII DOS Text file. Instead, open the Web page normally and choose Format | Custom HTML. You can then insert the custom HTML tags, which will be displayed in double-underlined red text. When you're done, choose Format | Custom HTML again.*

When I try to view my document in my Web Browser, the error message "Cannot determine path for Netscape" appears. I'm not using Netscape. How can I view my documents in a browser other than Netscape?

WordPerfect is looking for Netscape, but it can't find it. If you want to use a different browser to view the Web documents you've created, you'll have to open the browser and then open the Web documents in that browser. However, you may want to install Netscape on your computer—even if you don't use it as your usual browser—so you can see how your Web pages look from WordPerfect. To install Netscape, insert the Corel WordPerfect 8 CD into the CD-ROM drive and then choose Netscape Setup.

My Web pages look great on my computer, but how do I get them out on the Internet?

You need to transfer the whole package—including graphics—to the appropriate directory on your Internet service provider's computer. I can't be more precise because the exact steps depend on your Internet service provider. You typically must use the file transfer protocol (FTP) to copy your files to a writeable directory on a Web server computer. Contact your network administrator or Internet service provider for more detailed instructions.

Here's what you need to transfer:

⇨   All HTML files for your Web documents. Do not send the .WPD files.

⇨   All the original GIF and JPEG graphics used in your Web documents.

⇨   Any .HTG folder, which contains graphics the Internet Publisher converted automatically.

 ***Warning:***   *Some Internet service providers require you to use .HTML extensions instead of .HTM extensions, which means you may need to rename your Web documents and edit the hyperlinks accordingly. Check with your Internet service provider to see if this is necessary.*

My links are broken when I publish my document to the Web. What's the problem?

If clicking a hyperlink in your Web page displays an error message, the link is broken. Here are several things that may have gone wrong:

⇨ You may have used full pathnames in your hyperlinks. Remember to edit the hyperlinks to include only the filename, or your readers will not be able to use the links. If the .HTM files are in the same directory, you don't need the full pathname. Also, make sure your hyperlinks jump to .HTM files, not .WPD files.

⇨ You may have typed the name of the Web page incorrectly. Edit the .WPD document in WordPerfect, making sure that the exact filename is used and that the file exists. Remember to republish the document to HTML after you make any changes.

⇨ Uppercase and lowercase letters aren't always treated the same on the Internet, especially when on UNIX systems. A hyperlink to http://mycompany.com/homepage.htm may work just fine, whereas a hyperlink to http://mycompany.com/HOMEPAGE.HTM may fail.

I edited my Web page, but the changes didn't take effect. Why not?

Here are several things that may have gone wrong:

⇨ You changed the .WPD file, but you forgot to publish your file to HTML.

⇨ You changed the .WPD file and published your file to HTML, but you're still looking at the old page in your browser. Click the Reload button or jump to a different page and jump back to the page you want to view.

⇨ You changed the .HTM version of the file instead of the .WPD version. Always edit the .WPD version of the file.

⇨ You changed your files on your hard drive, but you forgot to
upload the new files to the Internet service provider's directory.

? My text boxes are sometimes difficult to read on the Internet. How can I improve their appearance?

Although simple text boxes usually work just fine, text boxes
combined with graphics may not be displayed correctly. For example,
if you have a graphic containing a state map with text boxes that point
out city names, these objects will not be displayed correctly. You can
improve the appearance of text boxes by using the Trace Text option
in Corel Presentations to convert the text characters to graphic images.
Here's how:

1. Create the image in Presentations by retrieving the image (such as
   a map) and adding the desired text boxes (such as the names of
   cities on the map).

2. Save the graphic as a .WPG file.

Warning: *Be sure to save the graphic as a .WPG image before saving it
as a .JPG or .GIF file because once text boxes have been modified using the
Trace Text option, they cannot become text again. Unless you have saved the
original file in .WPG format, if you ever need to edit the text, you won't be
able to do so.*

3. Click a text box to select it and then choose Tools | Trace Text. Do
   this for each text box.

4. Choose Edit | Select | All. Then choose Graphics | Group from
   the property bar.

5. Save this file as a .JPG or .GIF file and then add it to your Web page.

Tip: *Images in .JPG files are usually crisper than .GIF images, but they
are larger and take more time to download on the Web.*

? Why do my Web pages have extra hard returns between paragraphs?

If you enter two hard returns in your document to separate
paragraphs, the paragraphs will be separated by three hard returns

when the document is viewed in a browser. WordPerfect is working as designed. WordPerfect automatically adds space between two paragraphs in Web documents you create, so when you enter two hard returns between paragraphs, an additional hard return appears.

PUBLISHING DOCUMENTS TO BARISTA

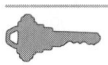 **I uninstalled WordPerfect 7 and installed WordPerfect 8, and now I can't find Envoy. How do I publish documents electronically?**

Instead of including Envoy in Corel WordPerfect Suite 8, Corel included a program called Corel Barista that lets you easily display and view documents published electronically on the Internet. A Barista file is an HTML file that contains a Java applet named Barista.class. Browsers give control to the applet when they encounter the applet type. The Barista applet then reads the rest of the HTML file and uses the additional information to display the document using Java technology.

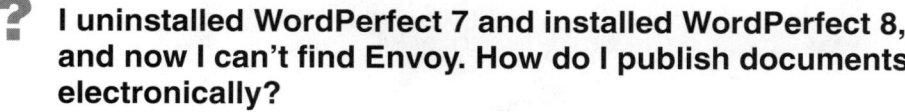 **Note:** *Corel Barista is not installed as part of the Typical installation when you install the Corel WordPerfect 8 Suite. To create a Barista file, you must choose the Custom installation option and install Barista separately. Barista is located under Accessories. For more information, see "Adding and Removing Suite Components" in Chapter 2.*

To publish a document to Barista, follow these steps:

1. Open and save the document.

2. Choose File | Send To | Corel Barista.

3. If you're sending all pages in a single file, specify a location and filename for the Barista file. If you're sending each page as a separate file, create and specify the folder where you want the files stored.

Note: Your work is easier when you post just a single file on your Web server; however, the separate files approach doesn't demand as much time up front from people viewing the document on their browsers since the whole file doesn't need to be downloaded.

4. Choose Send.

5. Upload the resulting file or the contents of the folder you created to the location on the Web server where your Barista Java class files are located.

Note: When you create a Barista file, not all of the information is contained in one file. Like other Web documents, Barista files consist of several files (for example, graphics included in an HTML document are stored in separate files). To display a Web document, the browser must locate all the files associated with that document. You may have noticed that the text in some Web documents appears before the pictures do. This is because the browser is still retrieving those separate graphics files.

Pros and Cons of Using Barista

Before you go nuts and start creating a bunch of Barista files, you should understand the advantages and disadvantages of using Barista. In some situations, Barista is a great program to use for displaying documents on the Web, but in other situations, you may want to consider a different application. Here are some issues to consider:

Pros

⇨ Once you've set up your Web site to use Barista, creating new Barista documents is a snap.

⇨ Barista documents look great. Columns, graphics, and tables all look crisp and clear and properly formatted.

⇨ Barista documents don't require additional formatting.

Cons

⇨ In addition to the documents they view, your readers will need to download the accompanying Java applets. For many people, the wait isn't worth the results.

⇨ Barista documents can't easily be saved or printed from a browser. If you want people to be able to reuse the documents you put on the Web, Barista is not a good choice.

⇨ Barista documents use only Times New Roman, Arial, and Courier, Barista fonts. If your document uses a different font, it will be converted to one of these three fonts.

Barista documents don't show up on all browsers. For example, people using Mosaic or an early version of any browser won't be able to view the files.

? How do I set up my Web site to use Barista?

You need to copy the files and folders in the default Barista folders from your hard drive to your Web site. Of course, this is easier said than done. There are a number of different ways to copy files and folders to a Web site, so I can't be too specific. If you don't know how to copy files and folders to your Web site, talk with your Internet service provider, Webmaster, or intranet manager for information on how this is done and what tools to use. Here are the basic steps for uploading these files:

1. Log in to your Internet service provider, if you use one.

2. Start the tool or application you use to transfer files to your Web site.

Tip: *If you don't have a tool, WS_FTP is an easy-to-use file transfer program that you can download from http://www.ipswitch.com/index.html. It's free to individuals.*

3. Select all the files and folders in the default Barista folder (usually C:\Corel\Suite8\Shared\Barista).

4. Copy these files and folders (some of which contain subfolders of their own) to the directory on your Internet or intranet server in which you want to store your Barista documents.

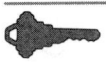

Note: *Remember that Barista documents will work only from the single folder in which the class files are located.*

? I saved the Barista files to the MyFiles folder and now the Barista files I sent will not open in my browser. What's wrong?

The default destination for Barista files is C:\Corel\Suite8\Shared\Barista, where C represents your hard drive. This folder contains the Barista class files needed to open the Barista file in your browser. When you view a Barista file, browsers such as Netscape and Internet Explorer pass control of the viewing process to the Java interpreter that is distributed with the browser. The class files in the default Barista folder enable the Java interpreter to tell the browser how to handle the Barista information. If you save your Barista files to a different folder that does not contain these Barista class files, your files will not open in the browser. You can fix this problem in one of two ways:

⇨ Move the Barista .HTM files you saved to the default Barista folder (C:\Corel\Suite8\Shared\Barista). If you move a Barista document from the location where you created the document, you must also move the image and sound files associated with that Barista document to the same relative path. Otherwise, you will have to edit the Barista document and identify the location of the additional files.

⇨ Copy all the .class and .INF files and subfolders (AnimationLib, Corel, and Spool) from the default Barista folder to the folder where you saved the Barista .HTM files. Perhaps the best way to copy the files is to open the Barista folder and choose Edit | Select All. You can then copy the selected files to the directory where you saved the Barista .HTM file (or files).

Tip: *If you plan on placing your Barista files on the Internet, it's a good idea to save your Barista document in a separate folder and then copy all the class files and Barista subfolders into that folder. That way, you'll know exactly which files need to be included when you copy them to the server.*

Why did Corel ship bitstream TrueDoc fonts with Corel Barista 1.0 but not with Corel Barista 2.0?

Corel Barista 1.0 included bitstream TrueDoc technology, which allowed you to embed fonts that Java 1.0 does not support. Corel eliminated the bitstream TrueDoc fonts for two reasons: to make Barista 100 percent Java-compliant, and because embedding TrueDoc fonts into a Barista document forced all users who wanted to browse the documents to install the TrueDoc font technology on their individual machines. Corel wants to promote the idea that users do not have to install or configure their local machine before they can read Barista documents on the Web.

Corel Barista 2.0 supports the standard fonts that Java 1.0 supports: Courier, Helvetica, and Times Roman.

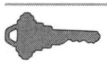

Tip: *Barista documents don't handle curly quotation marks, apostrophes, and other nonstandard characters very well, so you should avoid these in documents you publish to Barista.*

I have Netscape 2.0, but I can't view Barista documents. Doesn't Netscape support Java?

Barista documents are Java applets. Since Java is a relatively new technology, not all browsers support Java yet. Also, earlier versions of browsers, such as Netscape 2.0 and Internet Explorer 2, do not support Java technology. Netscape 2.01 was the first version of Netscape's browser that was Java-enabled. Corel recommends using Netscape 3.0 or Internet Explorer 3.0 or later when viewing Barista documents.

Why doesn't the search key on my browser work when I am viewing a Barista document?

According to Corel, browsers still have some improvements to make in their handling of Java applets. Current browsers pass complete control of the browsing process to the Java interpreter. Unfortunately, the communication between the search buttons of the browser and the Java interpreter is not working.

? When I move my mouse cursor over a hypertext link, why doesn't the cursor change to the pointing hand that indicates that I can jump to a new location?

Once again, you've hit on a communication problem between Java and the browser. The cursor does change to a pointing hand when it is over a hypertext link, but then it immediately changes back to the arrow cursor. Problems like this should be fixed in the next version of your browser, but no one's making any promises.

? When I put my Barista documents on a server for others to view, some people claim they can't view the documents. How do I ensure that all viewers can see my Barista documents?

Corel has a few suggestions that will help you put your Barista documents on a server:

⇨ Make sure that all .BMP, .JPG, .GIF, and other image files are in the same relative directory as the Barista file. You can edit the Barista file in an ASCII editor to change the location of your image and sound files, but check your Barista file afterward to make sure everything works—it's easy to make errors when changing these file paths.

⇨ Make sure that the Barista class files can be located by other browsers. Not all browsers behave the same way when searching for the class files from the Java interpreter. The browser looks for the class files based on the CLASSPATH and CODEBASE variables and the directory location where the Barista classes are stored.

⇨ When Corel released Barista 1.0 technology, the installation added a CLASSPATH setting in the Autoexec.bat file. This feature made Barista less than 100 percent Java-compliant, because Autoexec.bat files do not exist on all operating systems. Corel Barista 2.0 does not add any entries to the Autoexec.bat file, and Corel recommends that if you installed Corel Barista 1.0, you should remove the CLASSPATH setting from your Autoexec.bat file.

⇨ CODEBASE is an optional attribute that can be in the HTML APPLET tag. The CODEBASE attribute tells the browser where to look for the class files the Java interpreter needs. It is important to understand that the path stored in this setting may not be the first place the browser looks for the classes. Here is an example of the HTML document markup:

```
<APPLET code="Barista.class" width=00816
height=01084 codebase="\\US1\Barista20">
```

If you find that many people are having difficulties viewing your Barista documents, first have them delete any CLASSPATH settings in their Autoexec.bat file. Then you should put all Barista documents in the same directory as the class files on your Web server.

If you decide to organize your server so that the Barista documents are distributed in multiple directories, and you want to place the class files in one directory, make sure you add the CODEBASE attribute to all Barista documents in the <APPLET> tag.

Warning: *You can edit the Barista file in an ASCII editor to add the CODEBASE attribute and path, but be careful—it's easy to make errors when editing the document. When posting your class files on a UNIX machine, use care when specifying uppercase and lowercase letters for directory names. Directory names and filenames on UNIX machines are case-sensitive.*

What type of sound file formats do the special effects in Java support?

Java currently supports only .AU sound files. You can find utilities that convert other sound files to .AU format, and you can find products on the Web that will perform the conversions from several sound formats to .AU. You can also embed a sound clip in a WordPerfect document and publish the document to Barista. When WordPerfect publishes the sound to Barista, it converts the sound clip to an .AU file for you.

Will my Corel Barista 1.0 documents work with the new Corel Barista 2.0 class files?

Yes. Simply replace all your Corel Barista 1.0 class files with your Corel Barista 2.0 files.

In a Web browser, can I download a graphic from a page published to Barista?

Any graphics that appear on a Barista page are downloaded when you view the page. They are downloaded to whatever directory the browser uses to save .TMP files. This does not make the files easily accessible. You cannot click a graphic on a Barista page to display a Save dialog box and then save just the graphics image, nor can you view just that graphic as you can with standard HTML documents. If you really want to download a graphic, locate the graphic in the browser's Temp directory while you are viewing the document and then copy the graphic before the .TMP files are deleted.

 *Note:*   *You cannot cut and paste text from a Barista document.*

Graphics are not displayed in my Barista documents when I view them locally with Internet Explorer 3.02. What is wrong?

The problem is that Internet Explorer 3.02 will not let you run applets locally and at the same time open images. Internet Explorer 3.01 returns an error message indicating illegal file access and will not display the files. This problem does not occur with Internet Explorer when the document is viewed from a Web server.

Internet Explorer will display these documents and graphics locally if you set the CLASSPATH in your Autoexec.bat file to point to the latest Barista class files. The path for a Standard installation is C:\Corel\Suite8\Shared\Barista. Because this approach relies on the Autoexec.bat file to find the class files, it is not 100 percent Java-compliant, so Corel does not encourage this practice. You'll need to decide which make more sense for you: viewing the files or being Java-compliant.

15 Answers!

Working with Other Applications

Answer Topics!

Working with Other Applications @ a Glance

⇨ I used to think it was a miracle to be able to copy information from one program to another. Now it's possible to link data so that editing an object in one application updates it in another application. Once you've linked or embedded an object, you can view, play back, or edit the object without having to switch back to the application used to create it—and you can turn to this chapter if you have questions.

⇨ If you have the right hardware and software installed on your computer, you can insert and play back sound and video clips in your document. You can even create sound and video clips for your document. This chapter will help you get started.

⇨ You'll be amazed at how easily you can import or link spreadsheets and database files in WordPerfect. When you import or link a database, select which fields to use, and create queries to isolate exactly the records you want. If you link the data, you can edit the spreadsheet or database in the source application and update it in WordPerfect. For answers to your questions about importing data, consult this chapter.

LINKING AND EMBEDDING

The Lowdown on Linking and Embedding

The actual procedures for linking and embedding data are simple—it's the jargon that's intimidating. Here are some terms you may need to know:

OLE: Object linking and embedding. OLE (pronounced *olé*) is a process that lets Windows applications exchange information with one another. To complicate matters a bit, there are two kinds of OLE—the original OLE and the newer OLE 2, which supports fancy-pants technology such as dragging and dropping objects between applications. There is also an older form of data sharing called dynamic data exchange (DDE). WordPerfect uses DDE if the program with which it's sharing data supports only DDE. This situation doesn't occur very often, and in any case, everything all happens behind the scenes.

Object: Anything—text, graphics, sound clips, video clips, and spreadsheet cells—that can be copied from one application to another.

Source application: The program in which you create the object. Examples include spreadsheet programs, word processors, graphics programs, and sound programs. The source application is sometimes called the *server*.

Client application: The program to which the object is copied. WordPerfect can act as either an OLE source application or an OLE client application.

Linking: The process of maintaining a connection between objects in two applications. If you change the object in the source application, the linked object is updated in the client application. Double-clicking the object in the client application opens the source application and file.

Embedding: The process of copying an object into another application so that when double-clicked, the object can be edited in its source application. The changes you make in one application do not affect the data in the other application.

? I copied a chart from Quattro Pro to WordPerfect. Why isn't the chart updated when I change it in Quattro Pro?

Here are several reasons why your chart may not have been updated:

⇨ You didn't actually link the object. If you simply copied and pasted the chart from Quattro Pro to WordPerfect, or if you chose Paste instead of Paste Link in the Paste Special dialog box, shown in Figure 15-1, your object won't be updated. Paste embeds the object, whereas Paste Link sets up a link between the two applications. Table 15-1 summarizes the differences among linking, embedding, and copying and pasting.

⇨ You haven't updated your links. Choose Edit | Links and then select the link and choose Update Now. If you close the file and open it, you'll be asked if you want to update your links.

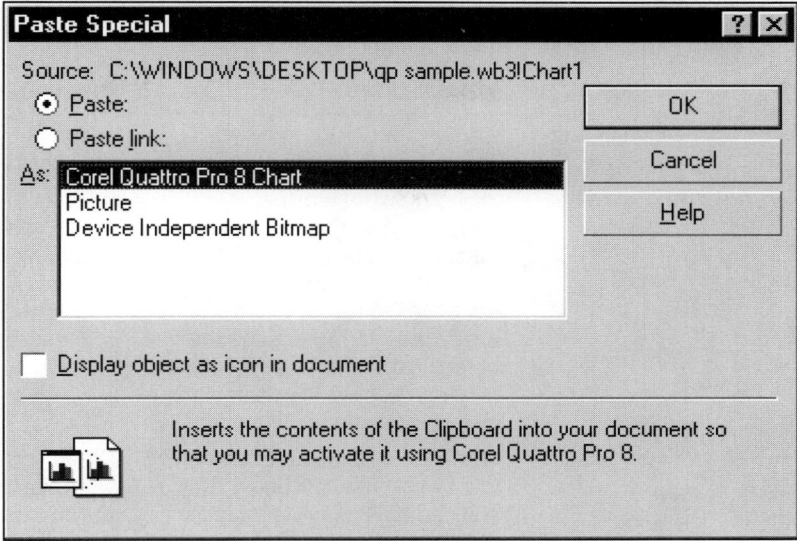

Figure 15-1.   Use the Paste Special dialog box to specify whether an object is linked or embedded

 *Tip: If you don't want to be prompted to update links each time you open a file, you can set the links for manual updating. Choose Edit | Links, select the link, and select Manual. Then click Close.*

⇨ You didn't save the file in the source application. If you don't save the source file in which you made changes, you won't be able to update the link.

Here's how to link an object between two applications so that the data in the object is updated in the client application as the data in the source application (such as a spreadsheet) changes:

1. Save the file in the source application (such as Quattro Pro).

2. Select the object (such as a chart or text) in the source application and choose Edit | Copy.

3. Open the client application (such as WordPerfect) and then choose Edit | Paste Special.

4. Select Paste Link, select the format (such as Quattro Pro 8 Chart) in which you want to save the object, and click OK.

Table 15-1.   Ways of Sharing Data Between Applications

Method	What It Does	When To Use It
Copying and pasting	Copies the object from one application to another with no connections.	When you do not plan on making changes to the object.
Linking	A representation of the copied object appears in the client application, but the object continues to reside in the source application. If you change the object in the source application, the linked object is updated in the client application.	When you want to keep the information updated in both applications, and you know you will have ongoing access to the source document.
Embedding	A snapshot of the object is copied into the client application. Unlike a linked object, an embedded object is not updated in the other application when you make changes. However, you can edit an embedded object—like TextArt—in the source application by double-clicking the object.	When you are not sure you will have ongoing access to the source document, and you do not care about keeping the object updated or minimizing the file size. You do, however, want to be able to edit the object using the source application.

Note: *If you want to embed the object, select Paste instead of Paste Link. Embedded objects increase file size because the object itself is copied into your document. However, a linked document is stored only in the source document.*

I want to link an object that I haven't created yet. Is it possible to link an object while I create it?

Yes. There are several ways you can link data between applications while you work:

⇨   You can use the Windows clipboard to copy and paste information. Choose Edit | Copy in the source application. Then choose Edit | Paste Special in the client application to display the Paste Special dialog box, shown earlier in Figure 15-1.

⇨   You can choose Insert | Object in WordPerfect and then specify the object you want to create or insert, as shown in Figure 15-2.

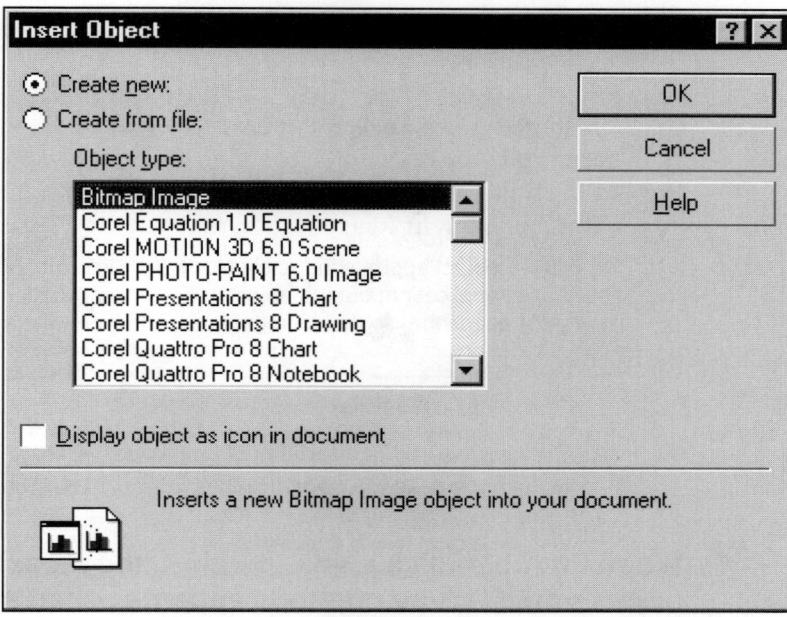

Figure 15-2.   Use the Insert Object dialog box to create or insert an object to be linked

⇨ You can drag and drop the object from one application into another. For this to work, both applications must have OLE 2 capabilities. Fortunately, WordPerfect, Quattro Pro, and Presentations are all OLE 2 compliant, so you're in luck. One approach is to tile the applications. Right-click a blank area of the taskbar and choose Tile Horizontally. Then drag the object from one application to the other (remember to hold down CTRL to copy). Another approach is to drag the object to the other application's icon on the taskbar, wait for a moment for the other application to appear, and then drop the selected object.

Tip: *Pressing* CTRL-SHIFT *while dragging the object into the client application will link the object rather than embed it. You can also right-click the object or file, drag it to WordPerfect, and then choose Link from the pop-up menu.*

Creating Scraps

In many Windows 95 applications, you can select text or an object and then drag the selection to the Windows 95 desktop or to any folder. The dragged object becomes an OLE file with the word "Scrap" in its filename. You can then drag the scrap into open documents, where it becomes an embedded OLE object. After creating a scrap, you can double-click it to edit it using the application in which it was created.

⇨   Choose Insert | Spreadsheet/Database | Create Link. For more information, see "Importing Data" later in this chapter.

❓ When I double-click a link to edit it, the message "OLE object could not be created" appears. What's wrong?

If you renamed the source file or moved it to a different folder, your client application will not be able to find the file containing the object you linked. You may also notice that the message "Unavailable" appears next to the incorrect link in the Links dialog box. Here are two ways to fix this problem:

⇨   Open the client application and choose Edit | Links to display the Links dialog box, shown in Figure 15-3. Select the link and choose Change Source. Locate and select the source file and click OK.

⇨   If you deleted the source file or no longer have access to it, choose Edit | Links, select the link, and choose Break Link. When you break a link, the information remains in your document, but you sever the ties between the client and source applications.

 *Note:*   *You can break a DDE link by deleting the DDE Link codes in Reveal Codes. The information itself will remain in the document.*

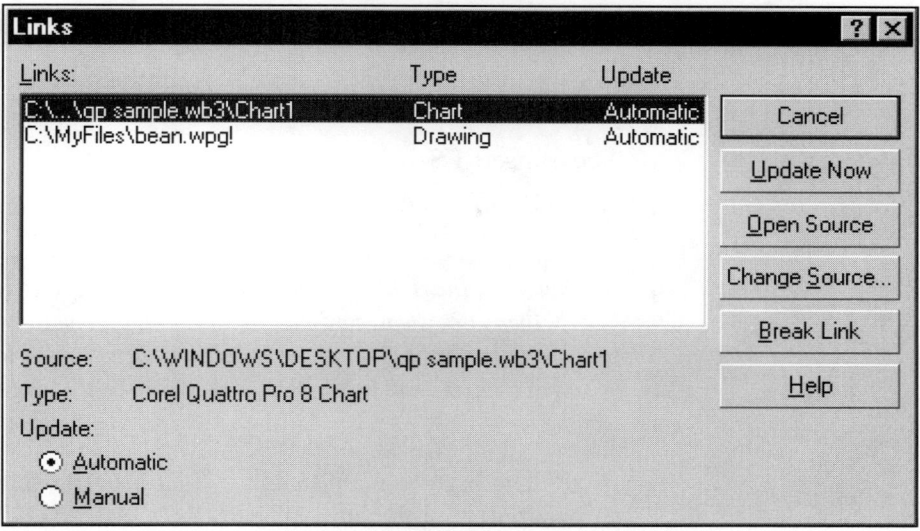

Figure 15-3.   Use the Links dialog box to check and edit links

INSERTING SOUND AND VIDEO CLIPS

? How do I insert and play sound clips in a WordPerfect document?

If you have a sound card and microphone, you can enhance a document by embedding sounds that the user can play. WordPerfect relies on the Windows sound recorder to record sounds. However, in most cases the software shipped with the sound board provides better recording and editing functions, so you may want to use it to record sound clips and then insert them into your document.

 *Note:*   *Keep in mind that sound clips take up a lot of space. The higher the sound quality and the longer the clip runs, the larger the file size.*

Here's how to insert a sound clip into a WordPerfect document:

1. Place the insertion point where you want the sound clip icon to appear.
2. Choose Insert | Sound.
3. Choose Insert and then specify the sound clip filename.

Tip: *If you have the right equipment and you want to record a sound, click Record, then click the Record button and speak into your microphone. Click the Stop button when you're done. You can then choose File | Save to save the sound clip. You can then follow step 3 to insert the sound clip in your document.*

4. Specify whether you want to link to the file or insert the actual sound clip in your document. Then click OK.

Tip: *When you insert a sound clip into a document, WordPerfect places a small speaker icon in the left margin. You can click this icon to play the clip, or you can right-click it to display a QuickMenu. Selecting Transcribe from the QuickMenu displays the Sound bar, which is useful for transcribing the sound clip. Use the Play, Pause, and Replay buttons, and type fast!*

? I recorded a sound clip in WordPerfect, so why can't I hear the sound?

If you recorded a sound clip in WordPerfect but can't hear the sound, here are some things you should check for:

⇨ Make sure your headphones and speakers are turned on and plugged in correctly. Also, try playing the sound at a higher volume.
⇨ Try holding the microphone closer to the sound source when you record the sound.
⇨ Check your sound card setup. WordPerfect uses whatever sound drivers are installed in Windows. You'll need to follow your sound card manufacturer's instructions for installing the sound card.

? **When I click a sound icon to play it, WordPerfect displays the error message "WAVE sound output not available." What's wrong?**

WordPerfect uses the sound capabilities of Windows to play sounds. You must have a suitable sound card properly installed before you can play sounds.

? **When I sent a file to a co-worker, she couldn't play the sound clips. Why not?**

When you inserted the sound clip in your document, you probably selected the Link to File on Disk option, which means the sound clip wasn't actually inserted in your document. Next time you want to send a file, choose Insert | Sound | Insert, specify the sound file, and select the Store in Document option. However, keep in mind that sound files can be quite large; the longer the sound, the larger the file.

? **How do I insert video clips in my document?**

You can insert video clips in your document by inserting video files. Most video files have the extension .AVI, .MOV, or .MPG. To insert video clips, you must have video software. WordPerfect uses the video software that you've installed in Windows.
Here's how to insert a video clip:

1. Place the insertion point where you want your video clip to appear.

2. Choose Insert | Object.

3. Select Create from File, specify the filename, and click OK.

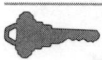 *Tip:*   *If you have QuickTime for Windows installed on your computer, you can double-click QuickTime Movie in the Object Type list box and then specify the movie file.*

IMPORTING DATA

 How do I import a spreadsheet so that changes in the spreadsheet show up automatically in WordPerfect?

If you import a data file, subsequent changes made to the file in the source application program will not be reflected in your WordPerfect document unless you import the data again. However, if you use the Create Data Link dialog box to bring in the data file, as shown in Figure 15-4, subsequent changes made to the source file will be reflected in the WordPerfect document.

Here's how to import a spreadsheet so that any changes you make to the data are reflected in the other application:

1. Place the insertion point where you want the imported data to appear.

2. Choose Insert | Spreadsheet/Database | Create Link.

3. Specify the filename in the Filename text box.

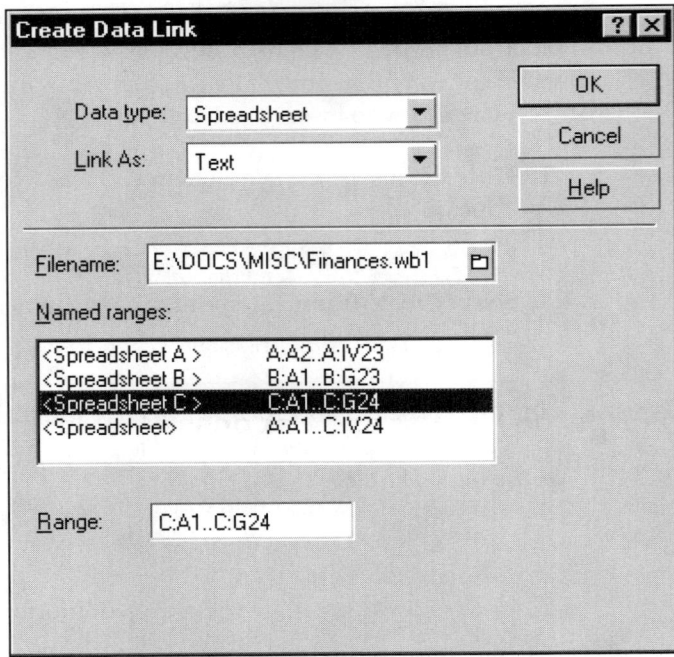

Figure 15-4.   Use the Create Data Link dialog box to link spreadsheet data

4. Select Spreadsheet from the Data Type drop-down list.

5. In the Link As drop-down list, specify whether you want to import the spreadsheet information as a table, as text, or as a merge data file.

6. Click the Named Ranges list box to select a range, or type the specific range (such as **A:A1:C8**) in the Range text box. Then click OK.

Tip: *If you want to import only a few cells into your spreadsheet, you may want to use your spreadsheet program to name the cells. Then you can select the name from the Named Ranges list box instead of typing the cell addresses.*

Note: *WordPerfect imports only the results of spreadsheet formulas—not the formulas themselves. If you edit the spreadsheet data in WordPerfect, the formula results will not be recalculated.*

❓ I edited the spreadsheet, but the data remained unchanged in WordPerfect. What's wrong?

First, make sure you made the change in the source application (in this case, a spreadsheet) and saved the spreadsheet file. Then, in WordPerfect, choose Insert | Spreadsheet/Database | Update and click Yes. Note that when you choose Update, any changes you made to the data in WordPerfect will be lost.

Tip: *If you want to update the links when you open the WordPerfect document, choose Insert | Spreadsheet/Database | Options, select the Update When Document Opens option, and click OK.*

❓ How do I import and link only a few records from a database?

You can use the Query option to specify the criteria for the incoming data. For example, Figure 15-5 shows how you would select only the records of people who owe $100 or more.

Here's how you can import selected information from a database:

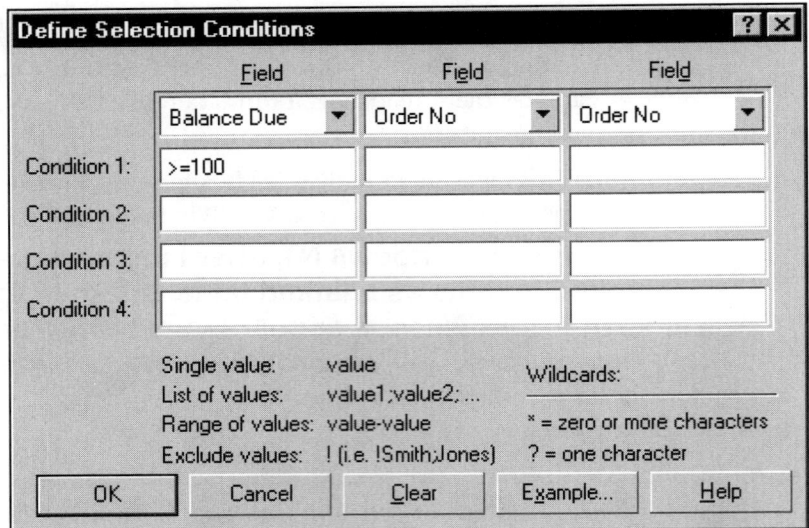

Figure 15-5.   Use the Define Selection Conditions dialog box to specify the criteria for importing database records

1. Place the insertion point where you want the imported data to appear.

2. Choose Insert I Spreadsheet/Database I Create Link.

3. Specify the filename in the Filename text box.

4. Select the name of the database (such as Paradox) from the Data Type drop-down list.

   *Note:*   *For ODBC or ODBC (SQL) to work, you must have correctly set up the appropriate ODBC drivers on your computer.*

5. From the Link As drop-down list, specify whether you want to import the database information as a table, as text, or as a merge data file.

6. Deselect any fields you do not want to import in the Fields list box.

7. Choose Query and then specify the selection conditions. You can choose Example or Help to display information on how to define your selection.

8. Click OK twice to import the data.

? **While running Windows NT, after I import an ASCII delimited text file as a linked table and then update the link, an error message appears, and then WordPerfect shuts down. What's the problem?**

If you're running Windows NT, the following error message may appear when you try to update a link: "Instructions at XXXXXXXXX Referenced Memory at XXXXXXXX. The Memory Could Not Be Written." According to Corel, updating the link corrupts files and closes down the program. Unfortunately, there is no good solution until Corel fixes the problem.

Here's a clumsy way of getting around this problem. Instead of choosing Insert I Spreadsheet/Database I Create Link, choose Insert I Spreadsheet/Database I Import. When you need to update the data, change it in the source file and then import it again.

Index

+, preceding expressions in cells, 229
*, starting a bulleted list, 141
* wildcard, 114, 251
=, preceding expressions in cells, 229
? wildcard, 114
@ sign, before QuickLink words, 420-421
[?(One Char)] code, 80
0 (zero), distinguishing from the capital letter O, 320
"3D operation was unsuccessful due to the complexity of the object" error message, 301
3D options, in TextArt, 300
16-bit CD-ROM drivers, checking for, 21

A

Accept buttons, for Document Review, 411
Acquire Image command, 309
Across Columns option, 287
Add Compare Markings feature, 410
Address Book
  backing up, 8
  Borland database engine error message opening, 25-26
  converting to a merge data file, 242
  creating custom fields in, 237
  creating envelopes using, 268
  customizing the format of, 237
  designating personal information in, 93
  importing Sidekick data into, 238-239
  inserting addresses in templates, 400-402
  inserting special characters in, 240
  maintaining a local, 239
  pages in, 236
  printing, 241
  printing address labels from, 261
  problems starting, 240-241
  selecting records for merges, 251
  sharing on a network, 239-240
  updating in WordPerfect 8, 29
Address labels, changing lines to uppercase, 265
Address to Merge macro, 241
Adobe Type Manager, TrueType fonts and, 319
adrs2mrg.wcm, 241
Advance code, inserting, 168
Advance feature, printing on preprinted forms, 185
Advanced Footnote Options dialog box, 365-366
Alignment, 59-60. *See also* Justification
All justification, 60, 170

COREL MAGAZINE

GET THE WHOLE PICTURE FOR HALF PRICE!
We'll Meet You 1/2 Way

We want you to get a FULL ANNUAL SUBSCRIPTION TO *COREL MAGAZINE* FOR 1/2 PRICE! That's right, a full year's worth of the most exciting and dynamic computer graphics magazine for the design professional and business graphics user today—all for a mere $19.98*U.S.!

This is no half-hearted offer. No indeed. Written by CorelDraw users for CorelDraw users, each colorful issue of *Corel Magazine* helps you get the very most out of your software and hardware.

Read *Corel Magazine*, and if you like it even half as much as we think you will, we'll meet you half-way—take us up on our offer. Just fill out the attached card and fax it back for faster service. We're certain you'll appreciate getting the whole picture at half the price!

(*First time subscribers only!)

Fax To: 512-219-3156 • P.O. Box 202380 • Austin, Tx 78720
WWW.CORELMAG.COM

YES! I WANT THE WHOLE PICTURE FOR 1/2 ICE! Sign me up for my full annual subscription to *Corel azine*. By responding to this special one-time offer, I'll pay $19.98 U.S. and save 50% off the regular sub-scription of $39.95 U.S. (Offer Expires January 31, 1998)

: 512-219-3156

☐ **PLEASE BILL ME $19.98 U.S.**

☐ **PAYMENT ENCLOSED**
(Offer restricted to U.S. only)

E: _____

: _____

PANY _____

RESS _____

_____ STATE

AL CODE/ZIP _____

NTRY _____

NE _____ FAX

L ADDRESS _____

1. Do you use CorelDraw?
01. Yes 02. No

If yes, which version do you use?
40. V7   41. V6   42. V5
43. V4   44. V3
45. Other_____

On which platform?
03. Windows   04. Win 95
05. Mac
06. Other_____

2. Primary use of CorelDraw (circle all that apply:)
30. Multimedia
31. Publishing
32. Technical Documentation
33. Advertising
34. Training
35. Medical Imaging
36. Packaging
37. Artistic Design
38. Signs/Silkscreening/Stenciling
39. Other_____

3. Do you specify, authorize, or purchase computer graphics products or services?
21. Yes   22. No

If yes, circle all that apply:
24. PCs
25. Monitors/boards
26. Input devices/scanners
27. Printers/output devices
28. Hard disks/CD-ROM/tape drives
29. Other_____